THE USES OF SUPERNATURAL POWER

THE USES OF
SUPERNATURAL POWER

The Transformation of Popular Religion in Medieval and Early-Modern Europe

---

GÁBOR KLANICZAY

Translated by Susan Singerman
Edited by Karen Margolis

Princeton University Press
Princeton, New Jersey

© 1990 by Gábor Klaniczay

Published by Princeton University Press,
41 William Street, Princeton, New Jersey, 08540

Library of Congress Cataloging-in-Publication Data

A CIP catalogue record is available from the Library of
Congress

ISBN: 0-691-07377-5

Printed in Great Britain

Contents

vi Contents

Preface

Whenever a book is created out of different essays written with varying purposes over a period of ten years, some sort of explanation seems necessary: what is the principal argument that gives coherence to the assembled whole? This is a moment of illuminating self-examination for the author. Where did the pathways and roads followed during his intellectual wanderings lead him to? Viewing as a group the various subjects that tempted him to investigation, he might wonder whether these topics had found a common ground, and whether they had developed into the possible foundations for a larger edifice. And what had guided him to take these particular routes? Was it accident? Was it the influence of the changing focal points of current historical writing? Or was it some kind of unconscious design, which gradually asserted itself by the logic of the various problems discussed together? In the Introduction I shall share my reflections on these questions with the reader.

Here, in the Preface, I shall concentrate on expressing my appreciation towards the people whose encouragement and help made this book possible. First, I must mention the professors who inspired and guided me to take these directions in research, combining the examination of medieval and early-modern popular religion with theoretical enquiries: Éva H. Balázs, Jacques Le Goff and Jenő Szűcs. While writing these studies, or while presenting them at various conferences and discussions, I have shared my problems with a number of colleagues, and I have benefited from their inspiring remarks, comments, suggestions and criticism. I am especially indebted to János M. Bak, György Bence, Peter Brown, Peter Burke, Carolyne Walker Bynum, Natalie Zemon Davis, Tekla Dömötör, Erik Fügedi, Carlo Ginzburg, Gustav Henningsen, János Kis, Evelyne Patlagean, Éva Pócs, István Rév, Jean-Claude Schmitt, Alfred Soman and André Vauchez.

The publishers who generously gave permission to re-edit and republish here the revised versions of those studies that had already appeared in English are acknowledged separately.

Living in Hungary, but regarding Europe as my wider cultural homeland, I am very happy that the publication of this book makes my studies and reflections accessible to a wider English-speaking public. I am deeply indebted to those who helped make this possible: Peter Burke, whose suggestion that I should unite these studies into an English edition initiated this book; John Thompson, who as editor retained confidence in this unconventional project by an unknown scholar from a remote country. The essays in this book were originally written in English, French or Hungarian. Essays 2, 3, 4 and 7 were translated from French or Hungarian by Susan Singerman. Chapter 2 was written in 1983, chapter 3 between 1979 and 1984, chapter 4 between 1978 and 1987, and chapter 9 in 1988. The versions of all essays that appear here were revised for publication by Karen Margolis from the originals or translations.

Acknowledgements

The author and publishers are grateful to the following for permission to reproduce material which originally appeared elsewhere:

'From sacral kingship to self-representation. Hungarian and European royal saints in the 11th–13th centuries', in *Continuity and Change. Political Institutions and Literary Monuments in the Middle Ages*, ed. Elisabeth Vestergaard, Odense: Odense University Press, 1986, 61–86.
'Le Culte des saints dynastiques en Europe Centrale (Angevins et Luxembourg au XIVe siècle)', in *L'Eglise et le peuple chrétien dans les pays de l'Europe du Centre-Est et du Nord (XIVe–XVe siècles)*, Actes du colloque . . . de Rome (27–29 January 1986), École Française de Rome, pp. 217–43.
'Shamanistic elements in Central European witchcraft', in *Shamanism in Eurasia*, ed. Mihály Hoppál, Göttingen: Herodot, 1984, 404–22.
'Decline of witches and rise of vampires in 18th century Habsburg monarchy', *Ethnologia Europea*, 17 (1987), 165–80.

1

Introduction

Religious conflicts in the Middle Ages

When I began my researches in the 1970s, the problem that initially intrigued me was the set of conflicts within medieval Christianity, particularly in France and Italy, in the eleventh to thirteenth centuries. Examining the controversies that set the heretical movements of the age against the Church and the emerging currents of secular culture (courtly civilization, urban schoolmasters, popular forms of lay spirituality), and reflecting on the recurrent conflict patterns that could be discerned and the varying ways in which the opposed tendencies were interrelated, I was tempted to see this evolution as obeying the inevitable logic and internal rules of a system-like 'symbolic universe' (Berger and Luckmann 1966). Drawing upon the abundant historiography dealing with these questions, and also upon a wide range of sociological and anthropological theories that discuss religion from the point of view of symbols, ceremonies, legitimation processes, and cultural and ideological systems, I formulated three questions for myself.

First: once the various conflicting currents emerged, what means were available for expressing critical, nonconformist attitudes within the Christian culture of the age? And how did the Church try to counter this religious nonconformism, apart from debate, excommunication or the use of force (coercion, persecution)?

Reaching the conclusion that in the long run these conflicts gave rise to a larger pattern of regulating mechanisms, adaptations and controlled symbolic battlefields, my second question followed on: what were the diverging types of religion that were held together by the Church and the culture of the age, and that counterbalanced each other, thus assuring the enduring stability of medieval Christianity?

As a historian, I was less intrigued by the wider theological framework of the debates or by the concrete political settings of the various conflicts, which had already been well elaborated by several historical investigations; my interest centred rather on the symbolic implications of everyday behaviour, the religious life-prescripts, the ascetic performances, the bodily symbols, as opposed to the 'symbolic capital' (Bourdieu 1971) of Church institutions, liturgies and ceremonies. This led me to a third question, which I would now phrase in the following way: could we speak of a kind of 'microphysics' (Foucault 1979) of religious power, where competitive relations and strategic dispositions permeate the entire life-pattern of the actors in the 'religious field'? Individuals, movements and religious institutions become impregnated by the various resources of supernatural prestige available to them in the traditions and metaphors of their symbolic universe, and they articulate this according to the specific 'grammar' of the sacred in their age. They continuously construct and reconstruct their own charisma, while questioning that of their various opponents. Meanwhile, the options at their disposal structure their enterprises into traditional schema such as church–institution, prophetic propaganda or lay spirituality. Do the historical facts available to us confirm this impression?

With the germs of these ideas in mind, I investigated the documents on religious movements in the eleventh to thirteenth centuries, researching their connections with voluntary poverty, the marginal way of life, sexual behaviour, manual work, dress, hairstyles, etc. Chapters 3 and 4 are reworked versions of parts of my two university theses on these subjects in 1974 and 1983.

In search of a 'popular religion'

While working on the history of religious movements, I had to confront problems concerning the differences and the interactions between the various layers of medieval culture. I was led to consider historiographical investigations into 'popular' and 'learned' versions of medieval Christianity. Following the debates on this theme among the French historians grouped around the journal *Annales* (Schmitt 1976; Le Goff 1977), and trying to explain the divergent issues of 'popular' heretical movements and the equally 'popular' magic-oriented religious practices of the medieval peasant culture, I inevitably became involved in the generic enquiries into the concept and the historical transformations of popular culture (Burke 1978). This led me to investigate the work of Mikhail Bakhtin on François Rabelais (1984), a major source of inspiration for historians working in this field (Chapter 2).

Bakhtin's powerful but nevertheless one-sided exposition of the medieval popular 'culture of laughter' made me aware of the possible objections to the label 'popular' (such objections tempt some historians to reject the use of this label altogether). At the same time, when I instead viewed the question from the perspective of anthropological studies (Turner 1974, 1978) or sociological–psychological theoretical writing (Elias 1978), Bakhtin's insights retained their explanatory power and convinced me of the utility of this distinction between 'popular' and 'elite' in the history of culture. I admit that the term 'popular culture' has populistic overtones, which may cause confusion, and I can equally see the ideological conjunctures that contributed to its becoming a vogue subject for study in the early nineteenth century, in the 1930s or in the 1970s (but: are 'system', 'process', 'structure', 'network' or other categories used in historical explanation exempt from similar objections?). Nevertheless, I think the important issue for methodology is to define precisely what one understands by such categories. If we define 'popular culture' (whether shared or rejected by civilized elites) as an orally transmitted, ritually regulated, community-bound culture, opposed to the written, institutionalized, ceremonious 'elite' cultural traditions, it can prove useful as a concept for historical interpretation.

Since the main focus of my interest was the history of medieval Christianity, I began fresh investigations with a view to formulating a more precise idea about the content and the practices of popular religion. The cult of saints and the various magical beliefs associated with witchcraft seemed to provide relevant examples in this respect.

Historical transformations of popular religion

Of course, neither the cult of saints nor the belief in witches was limited to popular spheres. With regard to the former, Peter Brown has even questioned the explanatory value of this 'two-tiered' model (1981). The documentation at my disposal on medieval Hungarian saints (the majority of whom were of royal descent) also points rather to 'elite' motivations in these cults than to manifestations of 'popular religion'. Thus my researches concerning sainthood took me in directions I had not anticipated. Still, the long-term transformations of the medieval cults of holy rulers proved to be instructive in that they also accounted for the historical transformations of popular religion.

This distinct model of sainthood, which first asserted itself on the 'peripheries' of Christian Europe among the newly converted, undoubtedly absorbed important influences from popular religion. Although the sanctification of rulers was devised to counter pagan ideas about 'sacral

kingship', and to coin a new Christian and Church-bound sacral legitimation for rulership, these cults could not avoid being reinterpreted subsequently in the light of the older mythical traditions. When popularized,
their legends tended to incorporate popular ideas about charismatic rulership assuring victory in battle, fertility and well-being in peace (Chapter
5). Searching constantly for actual and convincing representations of the
sainthood of the ruler or his dynasty, these cults expressed the changing
popular preferences for the holiness of the martyr king, the *rex iustus*, the
chivalric *Athleta Patriae*, and ended by seeing in the widowed queens or in
the pious princesses the main representatives of the sainthood of the royal
family (Chapter 6). Finally, when these cults achieved representation by
late-medieval artistic and liturgical splendour (exquisite shrines, funeral
monuments, legendaries, paintings, royal pilgrimages, etc.), their propaganda was intended to permeate popular religion. However, their
unanticipated consequence was that they contributed to the banalization
of this very same charismatic image of the ruler (Chapter 7).

As for the problem of witchcraft, it drove me beyond the boundaries of
the Middle Ages: the major witch-hunts took place in Europe in the
sixteenth and seventeenth centuries. Nevertheless, the manifestations of
early-modern witchcraft are more closely related to the medieval
problems discussed so far than one would at first imagine.

The witchcraft issue is related to the problem of heresies through the
institutional framework and the techniques of persecution. This is what
led many scholars of medieval Inquisition to proceed from the study of
heresies to that of witchcraft, and to explain learned mythologies
associated with witchcraft (such as that of the witches' Sabbath – see
Cohn 1975) by the continuity of the mechanisms of persecution.

Witchcraft is also related in many ways to the cult of saints. As for the
morphological structure describing the operation of (beneficent or
maleficent) magical power, the cult of saints (with the belief in miracle-
working relics) and the popular notions of witchcraft represent two
analogous (though opposed) poles of the wider universe of popular
religious conceptions about magic. This analogy could give rise to
relations of interdependence or complementarity: Peter Brown (1970)
explained the decline of late-Roman witchcraft prosecutions by the
ascendancy of the figure of the saint, who restructured the field of beliefs
in the supernatural; Keith Thomas (1971) related the intensification of
early-modern popular witchcraft panics to the Reformation ban on the
medieval cult of saints and on ecclesiastical 'white magic'.

Bearing these suggestions in mind, and taking a closer look at the
historical evolution of popular and learned witchcraft beliefs, it becomes
obvious that the gradual emergence of witchcraft persecution, and its

sudden decline in the seventeenth–eighteenth centuries, cannot fully be explained as criminal irresponsibility on the part of certain judicial apparatuses (later corrected), or by society's cynical assigning of a scapegoat role to the 'witches' (rendered unnecessary by a later, more balanced situation). Witchcraft beliefs themselves, or rather the inner tensions, the destabilizing transformations of the structures of the popular universe of magic, must have equally had their due share. Popular religion underwent important historical metamorphoses throughout these periods; its situation and evaluation changed radically within the context of late-medieval and early-modern Christianity; it also had its inner dynamics and contradictions, which were capable of generating severe crises, and which thus merit closer scrutiny.

Some of these transformations are analysed in the last three chapters of the book. The historical relations between shamanism and witchcraft (Chapter 8) provide the opportunity to examine how archaic beliefs are assimilated into and transformed within the paradigm of popular witchcraft. In conjunction with Carlo Ginzburg's intriguing findings about the *'benandanti'* (1966), this topic offers the possibility of identifying the changing evaluation of the positive (or at least ambivalent) and the negative figures in popular magic; it also raises the problem of the destabilizing impact of learned (ecclesiastical, jurisdictional) witchcraft notions in the sphere of popular beliefs. The examination of witchcraft conflicts in Hungary (Chapter 9) offers further scope for elaborating on these problems, adding to them some others such as the competitive professional relationship between magical specialists (cunning shepherds, midwives, healers) as a source of mutual accusation.

The decline of witchcraft persecutions (Chapter 10) could also be more fully understood in the light of similar cultural–religious transformations. From the sixteenth century on, each wave of scepticism concerning witches was supported or provoked by the emergence of a different, more attractive belief pattern about the operation of occult, magical powers, at least as much as it was by tolerance or rationalism – first the scholarly, 'hermetic' magic of the late Renaissance, then the French possession scandals of the Jesuitic era, and finally the East European vampire stories of the eighteenth century. I have attempted to relate these typologically different conceptions of magical aggression to the changing contexts of popular and elite culture of the age. Their historical interaction seemed to me relevant to the general history of ideas, understood in the broadest possible sense, and also incorporating the apparently diffuse world of popular religion.

Religion and power

It is impossible to talk about the history of popular religion without considering the power relations that surrounded it, that tried to regulate and repress its various manifestations, or, on the other hand, that were acted upon by its own resources of power. Religious and secular, spiritual and politico-temporal aspects of medieval and early-modern culture underwent just as many divisions or combinations as those aspects that one might label 'elite' and 'popular'. If we wish to give an account of the various manifestations of power in this process, we are brought back to the initial argument of the medieval 'symbolic universe'.

The considerations on carnival-type popular festivities or rebellions could be seen as refining the conclusions of Chapters 3 and 4, showing how the ritual regulations and temporary licences of popular religion contributed to the management of the tensions and the inner contradictions of medieval Christianity. Similar conclusions could be reached if one considers medieval and early-modern campaigns against popular 'superstitions' (Schmitt 1979; Harmening 1979; Burke 1978). Here Michel Foucault's (1979, 1981) vision of power – not simply as repressive force, but rather as one making an investment in social relations, structuring them and creating circumscribed areas legitimating its constant supervision and intervention – seems to me to indicate the starting point of further research. This approach could also find considerable support in the historiography of witchcraft persecution, interpreting it as a kind of 'social strain-gauge' or as an expression of the cultural and religious tensions of the age, and trying to give a more precise description of to how judicial apparatuses, power mechanisms and scholarly treatises were used to manage and contain this tension, rather than allowing it to explode (which actually happened only in rare instances).

The cult of royal saints illuminates the relation of religion and power from yet another angle: that of the religious legitimation bestowed upon the higher instances of secular power. At first sight, one observes here merely the eternal phenomenon of religious cults being put to political use, and political power striving to acquire the halo of 'divine grace'. If we think in terms of the 'symbolic universe' of medieval Christianity, these cults could be included among the wider set of institutions, ideologies and ceremonies that maintained and expressed the precarious balance between ecclesiastical and temporal powers (essential for the stability of the system). Contemplating the long-term evolution of these cults (from the sixth to the fourteenth centuries), one is tempted to ask: which side is using the resources of the other, which one is more successful in dominating the other? Although the first period tends rather to show kings and dynasties expropriating ecclesiastical forms of power (with little attention to religious criteria of sainthood), the sanctification of rulers became, in the long run, a successful means of securing the influence of Christian principles in the exercise of medieval royalty. In the latter centuries of the Middle Ages this form of supernatural prestige could only be obtained with an increasing interiorization of the moral and religious criteria associated with it, and an acceptance of the spiritual tutorship of the actual representatives of the Church (we need only recall the example of Saint Louis of France). On the other hand, the manipulation of this possibility opened up new perspectives of power for female members of the dynasty, or for new ascending dynasties (like the Angevins or the Luxemburgs). As in the previous cases, we have to face a complex system here, rather than the initially envisaged two-sided model combining religious and secular cults – a system that (as I have already hinted, and as I elaborate further in the respective chapters) is embedded in the general transformations and conflicts of medieval Christianity.

Let us now contemplate the range of historical figures discussed in the book: the twelfth-century 'apostolical' religious reformer (whether labelled heretic or not); the ephemeral glory of the foolish carnival figures; the medieval saint, especially the holy ruler; the shamanistic sorcerer, magically protecting his own community; the ambiguous cunning folk or the midwife; the feared and hated witch; the possessed nun with her astonishing performances; and, finally, the haunting image and the terrifying corpse of the returning dead, the vampire. From the point of view of the relation between religion and power, these figures have one thing in common: all of them are real, historical human beings, acceding to religious power mainly through the special charisma attributed to them.

This is, I think, the most important underlying theme of the essays collected in this volume, and the title *Uses of Supernatural Power* alludes to a specific interpretation of charisma, which I would like to refine now in the concluding remarks of this introduction.

Bricolage of charisma

A good starting point is provided by Max Weber's definition of the term 'charisma' as 'applied to a certain quality of an individual personality by virtue of which he is set apart from ordinary men and treated as endowed with supernatural, superhuman, or at least specifically exceptional powers or qualities' (1964: 358). Weber was able to coin an important sociological notion from charisma by extending this property from religious prophets or heroic conquerors to any kind of great innovative personality, and also by including some minor charismatic figures, like the shaman, the berserker or the healer. As might be evident from the list of historical figures enumerated above, I would plead for yet further widening of this sphere of application. Beside the figures that fit the Weberian definition, such as shamans, healers, heretical prophets or holy rulers, I would include the negative, evil personifications of supernatural power, like the ones associated with the witch.

This of course requires some modification in the perspectives of my use of the term: witches, unlike the 'positive' representatives of charismatic power, rarely proclaim their charismatic authority (mainly they deny possession of it altogether), they do not attract 'disciples' or 'followings', they do not institute a charismatic type of authority. Nevertheless, their figure can be made to fit well into more recent analyses of charisma, which concentrate less on the individual or collective experiences of charismatic power, or on the modalities of its appearance, but rather question the cultural and social conditions giving rise to its existence. Edward Shils (1975: 126–34) sees charisma as 'constituted' in definite 'conditions' and 'imputed' to suitable persons by those people, whose 'charismatic propensities are strong enough to respond to such a vision when concretely embodied'. As Clifford Geertz (1983: 122) put it, what occupies Shils is 'just what it is that causes some men to see transcendency in others, and what is it they see'. Without trying to answer this complicated question here, let us note that such a notion of charisma could more easily be extended to negative figures. Legends and cults connected with deceased persons could also be included in this phenomenon – essential with respect to the cult of saints, that special category of charismatic persons within medieval Christianity. This last extension facilitates the inclusion of vampires on our agenda. Thus, by seeing in charisma a capacity to marshal supernatural, suprahuman, transcendental powers, which is ascribed to certain (living or dead) persons by a group of people in a given historical situation, we could obtain a new frame of reference for re-evaluating the effects of charisma in European history. For 'charisma does not appear only in extravagant forms and fleeting moments, but is an abiding, if combustible, aspect of social life that occasionally bursts into open flame' (Geertz 1983: 123).

This neat phraseology leads to my second proposal concerning the historical examination of the various manifestations of charisma. Edward Shils gave an inspiring description of how charismatic power, once manifested, is segregated, disciplined, attenuated and dispersed by various institutional and cultural mechanisms. (A nice example of this is the transformation from early-medieval ideas of sacral kingship to the propagandistic staging of late-medieval royal sainthood, analysed in Chapters 5, 6 and 7.) In the anthropological theory of Victor Turner (1974, 1978), and also in the carnival theory of Mikhail Bakhtin (1984) we find various observations (analysed in Chapters 2 and 3) about the conditions of the social, cultural and ritual construction of the 'extraordinariness' that can add up to the creation of a charismatic person by imputation or by his personal adoption of this role. Similar questions were put by Keith Thomas (1971) and John Putnam Demos (1982) when they tried to understand 'the making of a witch'.

Now, this seems to me to be the heart of the matter: how, by what techniques, in what social and cultural situations, from what typical elements is charisma constituted? I would propose that this constitution is a kind of collective *bricolage* (this term is borrowed from Lévi-Strauss, 1966, and means cobbling together from odds and ends), where various resources of supernatural power, bits and pieces with an embedded significance from a previous existence, are put together, exploited and manipulated by the charismatic person himself and by the group around him, who impute extraordinary qualities to him.

As I stressed in the Preface, in common with most introductions this one was written after the completion of the studies it precedes in this book. It is an outline of the ideas at which I have arrived on the basis of the detailed investigations carried out in the following nine studies. Given the time, I would now like to rewrite them from this unified point of view – but then, that would be a different book.

2

The Carnival Spirit: Bakhtin's Theory on the Culture of Popular Laughter

Bakhtin needs no introduction.[1] It is nevertheless necessary to begin by summing up the main data pertaining to the Rabelais monograph, as a background to weighing up the theoretical lessons contained therein.

Bakhtin started studying Rabelais in the early 1930s in Kustenai, a small town on the Siberian–Kazakhstan border, where he had been exiled for a five-year period. He was nearing 40 by then, and had a decade's creative activity behind him. At the beginning of the 1920s in Vitebsk, Bakhtin had been the central figure in a literary discussion circle made up of philosophers, aesthetes and artists, which was often attended by Marc Chagall who was also working there at that time. Two members of this circle, V. N. Voloshinov and P. N. Medvedev, published three important theoretical discussion documents on Freudianism, on the philosophy of language and on the formalistic tendency in literary analysis. Experts nowadays consider these papers to have been written mainly by Bakhtin.[2]

In 1929, Bakhtin published his first work under his own name – an innovatory analysis of Dostoyevsky's *oeuvre*. After this – apart from two forewords to works by Tolstoy – no published writings by him appeared for thirty-three years. He finished the Rabelais monograph by 1940 and presented it in 1946 as a doctoral dissertation, but he was only awarded the title of 'candidate' (Master's Degree) for it.[3] The manuscript lay in a drawer for decades and it was only after the reprinting of the Dostoyevsky book in 1963 that it was published with some additions, and hence finally reached the public. Bakhtin, who died in 1975, thus lived long enough to enjoy international acclaim.

The Rabelais book presented the public with a number of new discoveries. Over the centuries the creator of French prose literature had been the subject of numerous studies and monographs dealing with his writings, his ideas on religion, his humanist erudition and political activity. Yet all these commentaries omitted the most important aspect of interpretation: they were unable to reveal the guiding principle behind Rabelais' artistic vision. It is this very principle that forms the basis of Bakhtin's book – namely, that Rabelais drew a significant part of his creative inspiration from the culture of popular laughter, which had been banished from elitist culturer ever since the end of the seventeenth century.

The term 'culture of popular laughter' implies far more than a world of comic creativity, i.e. parodies, jokes, farces. Bakhtin regarded this culture of popular laughter as a constantly present, familiar stratum of medieval –Renaissance culture; as the main opponent and worthy rival of the official and dogmatic elitist culture of both the clergy and the laity. A laughter that makes fun of exalted values and gives a twist to everything is at the same time a merciless criticism that permits the recognition and expression of important truths. Challenging the learned culture, which develops and perpetuates its intellectual concepts within the framework of traditions going back a thousand years, the popular culture of laughter can also line up a host of cultural forms and traditions. Its genre, preserved by custom and oral tradition, contains its own aesthetic rules in much the same way as the legitimate arts. Its symbolism reflects not only ancient beliefs and fears but also the basic truths of man's existence and the fundamental laws of society.

In the following pages I shall investigate in three different lines of inquiry how Bakhtin supported his findings concerning the value and historic role of the popular culture of laughter. I attempt to portray his festival theory and his analysis of popular ideas on sensuality–sexuality by comparing them with other related theoretical approximations. Then I shall consider why and with what reservations we can regard as 'popular' the culture of laughter that Rabelais portrayed.

* * *

The popular culture of laughter is so closely interwoven with the riotous and immoderate celebrations at the largest popular festivity of medieval and Renaissance times that Bakhtin frequently calls it the 'carnival culture'. In order to reveal the symbols and general aspects of the culture of popular laughter, he begins by examining carnival customs, which are also a constant feature in Rabelais' writings. In the Middle Ages, the carnival-type festivals – (Feast of the Ass, Feast of Fools, Easter Laughter, etc.) were clearly separated from the group of official – i.e. Church and state – festivities. While the latter provided a ritual framework for the sanctioning of the existing social hierarchy and the powers ruling it, the carnival-type festivity was based on the concept of complete equality. While it lasted, relationships of subordination or superiority were put aside; everyday norms were suspended, and for a brief period it was possible to experience the Utopia of universal freedom and abundance. At such times the powerful were defamed, the guardians of virtue were mocked, taboos were broken and a 'King for the Day' was elected from among the beggars, down-and-outs or youngsters.

Why did the guardians of law and order in most known societies tolerate the regular and ritualistic repetition of such subversive revelry? Anthropologists studying the customs of tribal societies – e.g. Roger Caillois (1938), Mircea Eliade (1957), or Max Gluckmann (1954) – regard these folk festivals as saftey valves. In their opinion, the occasional release of pent-up tension and the temporary suspension of standards made it easier to accept the everyday social restrictions.[4] Bakhtin's book tells us that this view was accepted even in the Middle Ages. He mentions a fifteenth-century Apology, which attempted to defend the Feast of Fools organized by the Church against those who considered it sacrilegious and wanted to have it banned:

> Foolishness, which is our second nature and seems to be inherent in man might freely spend itself at least once a year. Wine barrels burst if from time to time we do not open them and let in some air. All of us men are barrels poorly put together, which would burst from the wine of wisdom, if this wine remains in a state of constant fermentation of piousness and fear of God. We must give it air in order not to let it spoil. This is why we permit folly on certain days so that we may later return with greater zeal to the service of God. (p. 75)[5]

The anthropologists who regard folk festivities as safety valves usually add that the ritual rebellion also reinforces everyday order by firmly impressing on those partaking in it that the very things that are permitted on feast days are forbidden in everyday life. The inverse mirror-image also refers to the status quo.

Bakhtin, however, would not agree with such a purely functional interpretation of festivities. According to him, festivals are designed to achieve a great deal more than guaranteeing everyday order. At such times 'the highest aims of human existence, that is, the world of ideals' can be manifested (p. 9). 'Freedom was not so much an exterior right . . . it was the thousand-year-old language of fearlessness, a language with no reservations and omissions, about the world and about the power' (p. 269). Through his emphasis on the positive ideological content of feasts, Bakhtin's book represents the most important anthropological theory of rituals in the 1960s. It can be regarded in the same category as Turner's 'structure–antistructure' model (see Turner 1974, 1977). The concepts of the two scholars were developed independently: Bakhtin's book did not become known in the West until after Turner's work had been published. It is therefore instructive and interesting to compare their areas of (quite surprising) agreement, as well as their differences.

Victor Turner studied the ritual customs of the Central African Ndembu tribe for several years. He ascribes the same constructive role to rituals expressing the principles of 'anti-structure' and *communitas* as Bakhtin does to carnival-type folk festivities. Turner states that for any group of people to be able to function as a community it is necessary not only that a stable *structure* exists for maintaining social differences, but also that the members of the relevant group should acknowledge their equality among themselves – at least in principle. That is why, in even the most primitive of human societies, the ritual order sees to it that the members of the community are regularly immersed in the values of *communitas* and *anti-structure*. A number of ceremonies serve this purpose. Celebrations of productivity in agriculture and hunting are fitted into the festive cycle of the calendar. Others are held at the main turning-points of life (birth, attainment of adulthood, marriage, death) and at important events in one's social life (electing a superior at work, crises, war) ('rites of passage' – Van Gennep 1909). Some of these rituals turn everyday values inside out: what had been holy becomes profane and a status reversal comes into being for at least part of the feast – the powerful are humbled whilst the weak and the small are granted power. At such times extremes are the rule: complete abstinence may be decreed or wild orgies permitted; a fast imposed or extravagant banquets given. In other words, the participants are made to depart from their usual lifestyle. Consequently, the absolute validity of social differences begins to be doubted and symbolic compensation is given to those who, according to the rules of 'structure', are in a less advantageous position. Through these rituals, future adults, functionaries or chieftains – indeed, entire sections of society – come to understand a conception of *community* that disregards all differences of status and position and is based on complete equality. It is this alternative – which is not necessarily put into words or even thought out – that helps to solve life's problems, to overcome crises and to work out conflicts within the structure.

This definition could well have come from Bakhtin's book. In connection with carnivals, he speaks of the 'temporary abolition of alienation' (p. 10). Whilst analysing the 'inside-out world' of carnivals, he also speaks of 'up' and 'down' changing places, of profanation, of depri-vation of rank and of mocking exaltation. According to Bakhtin, this reversal during festivals 'denies but it revives and renews at the same time' (p. 11), just as the carnival fire revives nature. And, although he does not state it categorically, the implication is clear throughout his book that a higher, almost Utopian, ideal, based on equality, can be observed at folk festivals and in works inspired by popular laughter.

Both Turner's and Bakhtin's community ideal – over and above the structural similarities of the phenomena we have just examined – draw on the same source: the works of one of the most important Utopian philosophers of the twentieth century. Among Bakhtin's favourite reading was Martin Buber's book *I and Thou*, which came into his hands in Odessa in the first decade of the century. Towards the end of his life, talking to his students, he called Buber 'the greatest – if not the only – philosopher in the twentieth century', and acknowledged the latter's 'obvious influence' on his own theoretical development.[6] While in Vitebsk during the 1920s, Bakhtin became extremely interested in the philosophical problem inherent in the communication and mutual recognition of the *self* and *others*. Along with the much-discussed works of the Marburg neo-Kantians (especially Herman Cohen),[7] it was Buber's influence that focused his attention on this problem. Subsequently Bakhtin tried to find an explanation for this problem through the *dialogue principle*, which he defined in his book on Dostoyevsky published in 1929.

Buber's Utopian ideals, the experience of community through a mystic–ecstatic togetherness, are reflected in the descriptions in the Rabelais book, when, in connection with the festive turmoil, Bakhtin remarks: 'The individual feels that he is an indissoluble part of the collectivity, a member of the people's mass body.' (p. 255).

In turn, Victor Turner quotes Buber's above-mentioned book as the most apt description of the principles of *communitas*:

> Community is being no longer side by side (and, one might add, above or below) but *with* one another of a multitude of persons. And this multitude, though it moves towards one goal, yet experiences everywhere a turning to, a dynamic facing of, the others, a flowing from *I* to *Thou*. Community is where community happens. (Buber 1958: 51; Turner 1977: 127)

Neither Bakhtin nor Turner is satisfied with evolving the basic principles of the culture of popular laughter or of the *communitas*–anti-structure, purely by analysing rituals, festivals and symbols. Both seek to find other possible bearers of this set of values. They both emphasize, for instance, the role of fools, court jesters and clowns. According to Bakhtin, such figures had become the regular bearers of the carnival spirit, whilst 'folly is a form of gay festive wisdom, free from all laws and restrictions, as well as from preoccupations and seriousness' (p. 260).

Bakhtin and Turner also reach similar conclusions when considering from which direction the 'higher goals' referred to above can penetrate the social cosmos. Turner's typology distinguishes three possibilities: the

element that swallows up and gives birth at the same time. To degrade is to bury, to sow, to kill simultaneously, in order to bring forth something more and better. To degrade also means to concern oneself with the lower stratum of the body, the life of the belly and the reproductive organs; it therefore relates to acts of defecation and copulation, conception, pregnancy, and birth. Degradation digs a bodily grave for a new birth; it has not only a destructive, negative aspect but also a regenerating one . . . Grotesque realism knows no other lower level; it is the fruitful earth and the womb. It is always conceiving. (p. 21)

Works dealing with the history of civilization and anthropology have produced numerous data to show how, in different ages, the portrayals and manifestations of sexuality and nudity – although the subject of taboos – achieved a ritual function. They turned into a sacred breaking of prohibitions, festive profanity, orgiastic ceremony, fertility rites and exorcism.[9] However, no one besides Bakhtin was able to explain so convincingly and to illustrate so richly the ideological content of this symbolism. Apart from his own personal merits, he must have been helped in this by the particular nature of the material he was studying. Standing in opposition to medieval Christianity, the culture of popular laughter raised the sphere of bodily manifestations to a global principle that surpassed all its predecessors in importance. One cause of this may have been the fact that Christianity condemned earthly pleasures more vigorously than any other religion before it: all concessions to the moral norms of chastity, abstinence, fasting, or mortification of the flesh were considered a sign of human imperfection. Nevertheless, it is important to emphasize that, in other respects, the medieval and Renaissance Church recognized the fact that human nature could not be changed and came to terms with it on countless occasions. The previously quoted Apology for the Feast of Fools makes it clear that the Church tolerated some profanization at carnival times on the periphery of its own festivals. Priests and clerics took part in the medieval and Renaissance banquets of legendary fame; not only were they familiar with the words of obscene satires, coarse anecdotes and jesting rhymes, they wrote quite a few themselves. But all this was only a concession, a tacit acknowledgement that standards alien to human nature could not be maintained in practice. Thus the bodily principles were recognized not within the Christian world-view but through the genre that made fun of it: the culture of popular laughter. Indeed, the latter achieved greater cosmic dimensions in proportion to the glaring contrast between official religious ideology and everyday morality.

This contributed to the crystallization of an ideological synthesis based on bodily principles, the popular Utopia of 'Cockaigne' (Cocagne, Cuccagna, Schlaraffenland), which had a central role in popular descriptions of the hereafter (hell, Paradise) and contributed many components to Rabelais' writings (Cocchiara, 1956). Concentrating the value-judgements of popular laughter into artistic images, the concept of a *grotesque body* was formulated; a concept that also tried to explain the natural environment by means of its ideas – derived from Antique sources – regarding the conformities of the *microcosm* and *macrocosm*.

This concept of a grotesque body reveals the human body in all its changes, its incompleteness, its metamorphoses and its dual polarity. A drama is enacted inside the grotesque body: eating–digestion–excretion, copulation–conception–pregnancy, birth–growth–death. The outlines of the grotesque body are vague; sometimes it is not one body, but two (a couple making love, a mother giving birth, or a complementary twosome, e.g. Don Quixote and Sancho Panza). Representations of the grotesque body show greatly enlarged orifices for the purpose of metabolism and contact with the outside world, allowing us to look through them into the body's inner channels. The protuberances through which the body penetrates its surroundings (nose, ear, genitals) and the matters they discharge assume great importance. Occasionally the whole body opens up (it is being dissected, torn to pieces, or its belly is opened up). At other times – as a miraculous creature – it has abnormal proportions (dwarf, giant), it may be a freak or a creature with the body of more than one species (animalman, birdman).

By relating Rabelais' images to other mediaeval creations representing the grotesque body, Bakhtin acquaints us with a system that gives us a better understanding of an enigmatic dimension in European culture: the series of strange illustrations in mediaeval manuscripts, on column capitals and in the paintings of Bosch and Brueghel.[10]

A consequence of the interrelation between microcosm and macrocosm in the theory of the grotesque body is that the human body contains the Universe through its cosmic particles; by taking food, it eats up the world and conquers it, and after death it is dissolved into the Universe once more. Creations in the culture of popular laughter represent Earth as a huge grotesque body: the sea is salty from the perspiration of earth, hot springs are the result of giants urinating, and openings into the womb of earth – wells, cellars, caves – threaten to swallow us. Hell itself is earth's all-consuming belly. Rabelais' work enables Bakhtin to illustrate now, in this context, certain concepts in learned culture fit into the world-view of popular culture. Rabelais coupled the popular idea of the grotesque body with the Hippocratic system in medicine, in which he was an acknowledged expert. His field of expertise included astrology, another branch of science making use of the concordance between microcosm and macrocosm. Astrology ranked as a respected branch of science until the sixteenth century and sank only gradually to the role of providing prophecies in the pages of popular calendars (Thomas 1971: 283–385; Capp 1979).

It has been clearly shown that, in the culture of popular laughter during the Middle Ages and the Renaissance, the bodily principle had a far greater importance than merely providing the opportunity for obscenity. Bakhtin also shows how this value system was relegated to the background from the middle of the sixteenth century. He contrasts the Renaissance–classicist bodily canon with the popular concept of the grotesque body: the human body is more clearly outlined, those parts that relate to bodily functions are increasingly censored and the orifices are closed. Instead, the emphasis shifts to the front and to individual features (eyes, lips, muscles). The limbs also take up positions appropriate to their function (p. 321). The disappearance of the body's grotesque portrayal is accompanied by the general suppression of the popular culture of laughter. Satires based on a free discussion of sex or gluttony are banned from literature. Farces written for refined court festivals or upper-class drawing rooms could not include any ribaldry, since it was now scorned. The theme of sexuality disappears from public obscene language; it lives on in aristocratic frivolities, in the shape of gossip, betrayed bedroom secrets and obscene libertarian phantasmagorias (p. 105).

Bakhtin's cultural description regarding this subject shows an interesting similarity to a profound sociological study on the process of civilization by Norbert Elias – a book Bakhtin did not know of.[11] Elias depicts the other side of the transformation shown by Bakhtin: he studied everyday behaviour patterns, etiquette and educational advice from the fifteenth to the eighteenth century, and was able to demonstrate how civilization alienated man from his own bodily manifestations. Through the regulation of eating habits, the increasing use of cutlery, the widening prohibition on nudity, finally through the growing sense of shame and disgust regarding bodily functions, a radically new cultural standard came to prevail over people's everyday lives. This eventually played a key role in formulating court etiquette during the age of Absolutism. Looking at the question from Bakhtin's point of view, one may add that this transformation was only possible because the popular culture of laughter suffered a radical breakdown and was pushed into the background.

It is no coincidence that the arguments of Mikhail Bakhtin and Norbert Elias complement each other so well, even though they were using different sources. Elias was Bakhtin's contemporary and both books were written in the second half of the 1930s. There are further close parallels in the later fate of the two books: although Elias' book was published in 1939, it made very little impression, and it was only after it was reprinted and translated in 1968 that success came his way. The close similarity between their cultural–historical concepts can be directly attributed to a common influence: Sigmund Freud's ideas on civilization and on the cultural role of sexuality. Although Norbert Elias briefly acknowledges his indebtedness to Freud, he nevertheless avoids the use of Freudian terminology in his mode of argument. He traces the various aspects of human behaviour back to the formation and transformation of human interrelationships, instead of deducing them from the psychological connections of the 'id', the 'ego' and the 'super-ego'. Elias' socio-historical thesis, which initially appears to be an illustration of Freud's theory on the repression of sexuality and its sublimation into civilized patterns, in fact turns the Freudian connection inside out: he links to one concrete historical pattern of human relationships man's alienation from his biological reality and, on the other hand, the new ideals of civilization that came into being at this particular stage of social evolution.

I have already mentioned in connection with Bakhtin that he was probably co-author of the critique on Freudianism published in 1927 under Voloshinov's name. This work also rejected the Freudian theorems from the 'socio-psychological' point of view, favouring instead the strength of standards and communicative forms within individual social groups.[12] Although Sigmund Freud's name does not appear in Bakhtin's book on Rabelais, the vision of a culture of popular laughter sweeping aside all inhibitions was undoubtedly influenced by Freud's theory of jokes, and the argument is further reinforced by the cultural theory of psychoanalysis. The idea – also mentioned by Freud – that laughter, freed of the 'external and internal censor', helps in the recognition of truth (p. 99) is used by Bakhtin to prove the precise point that true values of civilization do not always come into being through suppression and sublimation; rather, the opposite is true. Secondly, the frank portrayal of bodily realities extinguishes, rather than awakening, fear and ancestral cosmic dread: it dissolves them into laughter (pp. 336–57). In Bakhtin's work, the assessment of sexuality and sensuality depends more on the norms and anti-norms of opposing social classes, more on official or familiar, everyday or festive occasions, than on the structure of personality so emphasized by psychoanalysis, or on sexual experiences in childhood.

A medieval culture of uninhibited laughter, filled with the joys of living, evokes the kind of Golden Age Wilhelm Reich must have had in mind when he developed the theories of Freud, whom he considered his mentor. Reich amalgamated Freud's theories with Marxist ideas and proclaimed the slogan *sexual revolution* – to put an end to the repression of sexuality, be it by civilization or by capitalism.[13] Reich was a passionate critic of the authoritarian middle-class family system and the social order based on sexual repression. His writings did not become popular either until the late 1960s – we do not know whether Bakhtin had any knowledge of them. On the other hand, one may wonder whether Bakhtin's conception does not deserve the same convincing criticism that was recently expressed by Michel Foucault regarding Reich's ideas on sexual liberation (Foucault 1981). Foucault pointed out that the programme of sexual revolution and the one-time Utopian notion of total sexual freedom fulfil functions that are similar to the Freudian theory itself: sexuality is transformed into the source of some kind of primary and universal truth. The energy of the people is directed towards recognizing or liberating this truth, however hopeless a task this may be. Their attention is thereby diverted from other unresolved problems in human relationships or conditions of power. If we think about it, we realize that this criticism is also valid with regard to Bakhtin's conception. He too considers the symbolic forms and general principles in bodily and sexual manifestations as of primary origin and of universal validity. The question, according to Bakhtin, is simply this: when and how far is their public appearance and utterance tolerated? Also: who understands their meaning and, if so, to what extent? He sees very clearly the duality between various norms totally rejecting the bodily and sexual principles and the actual possibility of transgressing these norms. But he does not seem to be aware of the fact that it is exactly the tension originating from this duality that is responsible for making sexuality the central problem and the major source of symbols for certain eras – such as the Middle Ages or the twentieth century. Even so, Bakhtin is still among those who were the most ingenious in giving credit to this concept, so popular in the 1930s and again in the recent decades, by supporting it with an important historical antecedent, the Utopian fancies of the Middle Ages and the Renaissance.

*   *   *

The adjective 'popular', when applied to the medieval and Renaissance culture of laughter, seems at first sight a similarly rhetorical exaggeration, an error of proportion, committed in the name of a similarly characteristic Utopia. Is this not some kind of populism – not at all foreign to Russian culture – that we meet in the pages of Bakhtin's book? For, although it analyses the writings of medieval wandering students, of clerics and of a Renaissance humanist, its hero is nevertheless the 'people', grown into an immortal, almost metaphysical creature. Bakhtin is reproached for portraying a people of such unvarying uniformity that it cannot have existed either in the Middle Ages or in any other era. This point is disputed also by Aron J. Gurevich, the eminent Soviet researcher on the Middle Ages, who could be regarded to a certain extent as Bakhtin's disciple. It is worthwhile to quote briefly from Gurevich's criticism:

> What definition can be given to the term 'people', when it is portrayed as the sole bearer of the culture of laughter? On reading Bakhtin's book, one

cannot help feeling that the author classifies as 'the people' only members of
the lower social classes, peasants and urban artisans, excluding the clergy,
the urban patriciate and, above all, the aristocracy. . . . If it was true (as
Bakhtin emphasized) that for the duration of the carnival all differences
among social classes disappeared and social distances were abolished, this
was only possible if both the lower and upper social classes, the plebeians as
well as the aristocrats, participated in the carnival celebrations. . . . Yet, if
such is the case, what are we to make of the contrast between the two
cultures, as analysed by Bakhtin? Is it justifiable to see in the official culture
of the Middle Ages nothing but a complexity of concepts, which are
permeated through and through by a sense of fear, dread and resignation. . . . and is it possible to free popular culture entirely of the elements of
fear and religious gloom?[14]

Indeed, we can hardly be satisfied by Bakhtin's unrefined definition of
the popular culture of laughter as the archetypal 'expression of folk
consciousness, of folk culture', the forms of which had been 'transferred
to a nonofficial level' with the historical evolution of consolidated state
and class structure, and thus, their 'popular' content increased, 'they
acquired a new meaning, were deepened and rendered more complex'
(p. 6). The mention of people acclaimed as the repository of universal
human values, as the bearer of 'anti-feudal truths', gives rise to memories
of populistic and vulgar Marxist concepts.

However, a second perusal of the book may land the reader on the
horns of a dilemma: is this criticism not too hasty? Regarding Gurevich's
objection: far from excluding aristocrats and clerics from the medieval
culture of laughter, Bakhtin mentions their participation on numerous
occasions. When he talks about the culture of popular laughter, he
emphasizes that it is a culture belonging to *the entire people*; in other
words everybody, without exception, can have a share in it and can
participate in its creative development. When contrasting the culture of
popular laughter with official culture, Bakhtin links the latter not so much
with a social class as with *institutions* (state, Church, civil service,
judiciary, court). Forty years after Bakhtin's description, Peter Burke, in
his study on the history of popular culture from the sixteenth to the
eighteenth century, classifies the social range of the two cultures in a more
precise, but essentially similar manner. According to Burke, it is a false
premise to assume that at the end of the Middle Ages there was an elite
culture for the aristocracy and the clergy and a 'popular' one for the
peasantry and the urban plebeiate. *Everyone* could partake in popular
culture; true, it was the only one for the majority of the people, whilst the
privileged minority had at its disposal a second, elite culture, based on
literacy, on institutions and on erudite traditions. It was only after the
period studied by Bakhtin that this situation was radically altered: when

the ruling minority – the aristocracy, the clergy, the civil service, the well-to-do bourgeoisie – turned its back on popular culture, withdrew from its field of activity and banned its creations from the sphere of elite culture (Burke 1978: 24–8). Indeed, Bakhtin was among the first to draw attention to this historic change.

Let us assume Bakhtin's basic category to mean all the people or, even more broadly, *all mankind*. Let us further take into consideration that the majority of the cultural phenomena he analyses – festive behaviour patterns, ceremonies, man's relationship to his own body and to nature – were universal human occurrences; these occurrences were more affected by different historical periods and their diverse social and institutional systems than by specific differences of class or stratum. If we take all this into account, then Bakhtin could be regarded as a pioneer in another field as well, that of historical anthropology. As I tried to emphasize in connection with the anthropological theory of feasts: the 'people' and the 'culture of popular laughter' are categories that refer to a clearly recognized system of great theoretical significance, to a principle of social organization, to a type of ceremony and cultural form. The interpretation of these categories is one of the most topical anthropological problems of our day. It is true that the twin concepts of 'people' and 'popular' are inseparable from those ideologies, which, instead of explaining anything, rather require to be explained by anthropological theories. Perhaps Bakhtin himself was not exempt from a kind of populism. It is nevertheless noteworthy that the category of the culture of popular laughter contains a clearly outlined, concrete sphere of phenomena and that Bakhtin was able to collate and characterize nearly everything that historically belonged to this category.

It was probably Bakhtin's expertise in philology that enabled him to recognize so unmistakably the characteristic genres of popular culture. In his book, written jointly with Voloshinov in 1929, entitled *Marxism and the Philosophy of Language*, he disputes two different conceptions of language: Saussure's 'abstract objectivism' and Vossler's 'subjectivism', – the latter expounded under the influence of Wilhelm von Humboldt. Bakhtin enters the debate from a standpoint that would nowadays be labelled 'socio-linguistic'. In his study of linguistic signs, the starting point was the communicative position and those 'semiotic communities' that were organized according to social conflicts. Even then, he was more interested in speech, in oral language, in the dialogue of speaker–listener and in the sign language of non-verbal communication, rather than in abstract linguistic standards or written structures.[15] That is the reason why he later felt so much at home with the genres of the culture of popular laughter, where the most important channels were spoken language and non-verbal communication. That is why he recognized with such certainty the diverse genres in the language of the marketplace: the mocking exaltation, the endearing disparagement, the inventory-like enumeration, the barker's shouting, the bragging and the swearing. That is also why he was able to back up all his theoretical statements with illustrations from linguistic history: the grotesque aspect with the medieval version of gibberish, the '*coq-à-l'âne*' (p. 423); the symbolic reversals with linguistic inversions or games based on the breaking of taboos or with prophecies. It was the study of language that led him to portray some characteristic features within popular culture, such as etymology, riddles and proverbs.

Special mention should be made of the method of interpretation that enabled Bakhtin to investigate the meanings of a culture consisting mainly of symbolic and ritual forms and to illustrate them with satirical writings from the Middle Ages and with the works of Rabelais. Peter Burke draws a parallel between Bakhtin's approach and Erwin Panofsky's iconological analysis, which Bakhtin was presumably unaware of. Panofsky's analysis proceeds from three different angles: first, at the level of primary, concrete meanings, then at the level of iconographic meanings, which can be explained in the context of art and literature; he then attempts to unravel the third level of meanings: by interpreting the symbols within them, he illuminates a number of hidden values and ideological features that contemporaries themselves – writers as well as readers – were not necessarily aware of (Panofsky 1939; Burke 1978: 79–80). Bakhtin indeed differentiates these three levels of analysis: first, the factual, biographical and topographical background in Rabelais' writings; secondly, the resonance in Rabelais' writings of the large-scale political connections and the ideological currents of his age; and, thirdly, the carnival level, which is the subject of his own analysis (p. 447). It is at this level, which concerns universal meanings, that it is possible to span the gulf separating our own age from the culture of popular laughter in the Middle Ages, where hardly any primary sources have survived.

In the 1970s, the study of popular culture in the Middle Ages and early modern times became an independent branch of research. Bakhtin's book made a major contribution toward this tendency. His analysis of the inner logic and values residing in the culture of popular laughter put an end to the prejudice that popular culture was nothing but a loose collection of yesterday's vulgarized truths, of 'surviving' ideas, superstitions and biased views. The detailed study of the problems raised by Bakhtin led to the birth of numerous excellent analyses that gave further elaboration to the picture he presented.[16] In this connection, I should like to draw just one general conclusion. Some of these analyses followed in Bakhtin's footsteps by studying the writings belonging to the popular culture of laughter; others concentrated on its religious, magic or everyday manifestations, which Bakhtin seems to have neglected. Both trends, however, emphasized the strong interaction between popular and elite cultures and their cultural and social intermediary mechanisms. After rehabilitating popular culture and acknowledging its characteristics, later studies showed a slight change of focus: the central task became to localize more exactly the ideologies within the process of historical transformation and the series of sociological and cultural variants.

*　　*　　*

This problem takes us back to the basic question in Bakhtin's book: how could François Rabelais – former priest, medical scientist, astrologer, great humanist, protégé of influential politicians, the King's favourite – how could this man be the chief historical representative of popular culture? How can we regard the four volumes of *Pantagruel* and *Gargantua* as the essential synthesis of the culture of popular laughter? These four books contained enormous humanist erudition and displayed the greatest poetic and prose skills of their age; the satires in them were interpreted as dangerous heresies by the theologians of the Sorbonne. No matter how convincingly Bakhtin tries to demonstrate that Rabelais was familiar with the contemporary marketplace and its grotesque manifestations, there is ample evidence to prove that his writings show equally strong cultural influences from other sources. For instance, Jean Larmat documented, with a thoroughness comparable only to Bakhtin's, all the topics and concepts borrowed by Rabelais from medieval literary works that could scarcely be called 'popular'; he also listed the ideas that appear in Rabelais' books as a result of his association with his humanist friends.[17] M. A. Screech, a leading figure in present-day Rabelais research and his most recent monographer, gives an equally thorough account of how topically Rabelais' historical writings fitted into the context of the political, ethical, scientific and religious discussions of his age. He proves with scrupulous analysis that Rabelais' writings include at least as many subtle – and by no means always mocking – references to the Scriptures as coarse swearwords.[18]

In the light of these recent studies, Bakhtin's Rabelais portrayal does seem somewhat one-sided.[19] Even though these studies do not detract from the truth of Bakhtin's interpretation, they draw attention to Rabelais' other values – for instance, to the Erasmian ideal of Christianity, described in *Gargantua*, and to the famous Utopia of the Abbey of Thélème – two concepts Bakhtin found difficult to cope with on account of their serious nature. These recent studies also throw light on those aspects of Rabelais' parody that disclose his undeniable attraction to certain ridiculed branches of science: exegesis, law, cabbalism or astronomy. With regard to this point, all we can say in Bakhtin's defence is that these recent Rabelais interpretations are as equally unable to reconcile the portrait of a humanist Rabelais with his undeniable connections with popular culture, as Bakhtin is able to do the opposite.

It is still Bakhtin who provides the pithiest insights into why and how the two cultures interacted. It is true that the method he employs seems irrational: through his artistic superiority, Rabelais' sense of identity with the culture of popular laughter became the dominant factor; this enabled him to formulate a synthesis regarding the values and symbols of popular traditions going back a thousand years. However, such irrational factors can in no way be excluded from the history and function of art; in fact, we can find explanations for them. Considering the possibilities, we must remember that by the end of the Middle Ages the culture of popular laughter was an 'all people' phenomenon – public property, so to speak. Given that, it is not surprising that it was precisely an outstanding humanist artist who was the one able to formulate its manifestations in the form of an 'encyclopaedia of the new world' (p. 455) and thus express its values in a concrete and authentic way. If we consider the aims of this culture, then Bakhtin's argument sounds convincing, especially as he cites other medieval examples. Bakhtin claims that an artist requires a particular, special viewpoint to be able to illuminate the essence of things. The plague, which completely disrupted everyday life, gave Boccaccio the opportunity to do this. Chaucer built his mosaic from the micro-society of the pilgrims, torn from their home environment and proceeding toward a common sacred destination. Dante condensed a summary of his society's values into the medieval traditions of dreams and visions of the next world. As for Rabelais, it was the pattern of popular festivals that provided him with the artistic tools for 'the most radical, positive and essential inner and outer liberation of speech and thought' (p. 273). Nor is it merely a question of artistic tools: the artist may also strive to employ a range of tools at the disposal of magical–ritualistic ceremonies in their original function – that is to say, he may strive to be a Magus himself. *Pantagruel*, for instance, referred in numerous ways to the great drought which had aroused such eschatological dread just at that time. Moreover, in his own way, Rabelais did everything he could to disperse these cosmic fears by means of his robust vitality and his obscenities, and to reduce them to the role of 'carnival bogeyman'. He mocks even more cruelly the political machinations of the Church, which wished to profit from the situation for its own ends (pp. 336–42). And it is surely hardly necessary to reaffirm that a satire can fulfil such ritualistic functions just as well as a revolutionary manifesto.

It is somewhere here within 'the carnivalization of human consciousness' (p. 273) and its protective and exorcising functions that we must look for the answer to the mystery of Bakhtin's character. Along the way, we might also discover what it is that makes his book such an astonishing piece of reading. How was Bakhtin able to write this sweepingly optimistic panegyric on the culture of popular laughter, on the freedom of carnivals, on cosmic creativity and on such robust sensuality? How was he able to write all this in the atmosphere of the 1930s, in exile, ignored, cut off from the world and in failing health? What applied to Rabelais is even more pertinent for Bakhtin: by studying the culture of popular laughter, he not only achieved 'inner liberation', he also made a stand and a commitment.

3

Religious Movements and Christian Culture: A Pattern of Centripetal and Centrifugal Orientations

In medieval Christianity a number of different religions, cultural traditions and institutions existed side by side. This diversity was in part a heritage of Antiquity, which over the centuries had amalgamated the various components into a system. Because of this, Christianity was able first to become the official religion of the late Roman period, and then to develop into the cultural framework, the 'symbolic universe' (Berger and Luckmann 1966: 92–127), of medieval civilization. This diversity was further enhanced by missionary activity and the resulting vulgarization during the early Middle Ages and by the changing demands of new societies.

Variety and diversity were, however, only two of the major features of the age. It was characterized just as much by unity and universality; it was no coincidence that later the Romantic era considered medieval culture synonymous with the concept of *Christianitas*.[1] On surveying the thousand-year development of medieval Christianity, one can only wonder at the persistence and resilience of the Roman Catholic Church in keeping European civilization united in its Christian aims, even in the face of an increasing number of conflicts and contradictions. Even more remarkable is the fact that for so long the Christian world-view enabled its adherents to find solutions to the basic existential problems within its own framework and by its own methods.

The exclusive authority of the Roman Catholic version within Western Christianity was encouraged by the lack of rivals or alternatives. But, beyond this, unity could only be maintained over such a long period by tolerating variety, by finding new ways to resolve conflicts and then by fitting them into a system that was undergoing a process of continual reform. One might call this an organic evolution, where a tradition and the institution fostering it adjust constantly to changing circumstances; and where, moreover, the institution reinterprets its own functions and draws up new forms and new principles in order to maintain its hegemony in the face of changing circumstances.

It is clear that the neat explanatory patterns are mostly suggested by observers from subsequent periods who always claim to have a better insight into the struggles of past eras caught between confused and undeveloped alternatives; nevertheless, it would be over-hasty to begin accusing functionalism and thereby reject all investigation that tries to recognize more general patterns. If the main determining factors in a culture (in this case Christian religion, the Roman Catholic Church, Latin literacy and Antique inheritance) are laid down for a thousand years, and if in that same culture similar movements and reforms develop independently of each other in space and time (even if based on similar traditions), it follows that systematic study of this culture with its inner contradictions and its mechanisms for creating and resolving conflicts promises valuable explanations.

The symbols, participants and institutions of 'the religious field' fit into a definite structure (Bourdieu 1971). In the case of Western Christianity in the Middle Ages, it is the eleventh to thirteenth centuries that demonstrate the closest correspondence with such a pattern. This period saw the emergence of those spectacular ideological–cultural conflicts that forced the Roman Church to introduce radical reforms. These conflicts arose between the Pope and the Emperor in particular; between the Church and the secular authorities in general; between the various groups of monastic orders and the secular clergy; and among the courtly–chivalric, the urban and the monastic–ascetic value systems. There was also discord regarding the newly formed universities and, above all, because of the emergence of the heretic movements. At the same time, the Papacy could reach the height of its power exactly by successfully controlling these conflicts. Both in the form of the conflicts and in the variety of clerical reactions, we find a regularity that was already effective in Antique Christianity, and that would also prevail in subsequent ages. One might regard this as an obvious outcome, since both the emergence and the solving of problems were conditioned by the central contradictions within the traditions, symbols and institutions of the Christian religion. However, at this point, I prefer to pose this development as a question rather than as a statement, since I intend to explore some aspects of this topic in the following pages.[2]

*   *   *

Anyone wishing to study the contradictions in a religion or in an ideology can approach them from two basic angles. On the one hand, one can explain and harmonize them – by rational or irrational means, by confronting them or by ignoring them. On the other hand, one can try to eliminate the contradictions by distinguishing between the essential aspect to be retained and the distortion to be rejected. Of course, it is difficult to predict in any given case where the dividing line between acceptance and rejection is going to be. Indeed, the numerous attempts at reform can be differentiated by the drawing of these demarcation lines.

In the history of the Christian religion the breakline between contradictions could be drawn, for instance, between the Old and the New Testaments – this was the option of the first significant 'heretic' doctrines,[3], the Gnostics, the Manichees, the Paulicians, the Bogomils and the Catharists after them.[4] As an illustration, let me quote some relevant lines attributed to the Roman Marcion, leader of a sect closely associated with Gnosticism. He uses the contrasts between the two parts of the Bible in support of the dualist doctrines about the existence of a good and an evil God.

> Demiurge, Creator of the world was known to Adam and to the generations following him, but the Father of Christ is not known. Christ himself spoke of Him with the following words; 'No one got to know the Father, only the Son . . .' Joshua conquered the land with violence and cruelty; Christ however, forbids all violence and preaches compassion and peace. Moses intervened in the brothers' quarrel unasked and assailed the evil-doer with these words: 'Why do you beat your fellow-man?' – and the evil-doer rebuffed him, saying: 'Who placed you above us as teacher or judge?' But Christ, when asked to act as referee in an inheritance feud between two brothers, refused to participate in such an affair of justice, because He was the Christ of the compassionate, not of the judging God, and He said: 'Who made me a judge in the quarrel between you?' . . . We can read in the Law: '. . . an eye for an eye, a tooth for a tooth'; but the good Lord speaks thus in the Gospel: '. . . whosoever shall smite thee on thy right cheek, turn to him the other also . . .' The Creator orders the Jewish Christ only to bring back the Jewish people from the Diaspora, but the Good Lord entrusted our Christ with the liberation of all mankind.[5]

One could make a long list of where the various breaklines were drawn up by radical reformers in ancient and in medieval Christianity, and of the ways in which the different contrasts were arranged. However, instead of a catalogue, I should prefer to give – as a starting point of my analysis – a more general classification of the main contradictions within medieval

Christian world-view; this classification has also the merit of being independent of the various historical attempts at religious reform. This classification can be illustrated – even if only in a sketchy and fragmentary fashion – by the judgements on the biological, social and cultural constraints in human life.

It is a striking fact that in most cases we are dealing not simply with contradictory opinions, but with judgements that are diametrically opposed on most basic questions. A significant part of Christian doctrine completely rejects the constraints of life on earth, makes every attempt to overcome them, and opposes them with superior, universal norms, in the name of transcendency. Yet, at the opposite pole, we can find – for the *self-same* constraints – approval, religious sanctification and deduction from divine command.

In Christianity, the doctrine of equality among men was counterbalanced by the espousal of necessary inequality and essential hierarchy. At first, the differentiation among men was made according to religious merit: 'But everyone in his own order; the first-fruits, Christ; then they, that are of Christ, who have believed in His coming' (I. Corinthians 15:23). But the order of merits was used already by Tertullian for the explanation of social hierarchy; the road from here leads through St Augustine and Pope St Gregory the Great to the hierarchic theory of the three orders (Duby 1978: 88–98). The renunciation – as shown by Jesus – of all worldly power and the disinterested air of the phrase 'render unto Caesar the things which are Caesar's' (Matthew 22:1) were somewhat modified by the more loyal tone of the Epistles: 'For there is no power but from God; and those that are, are ordained of God', (Romans 13:1; see also I. Peter 2:13–14). Criticisms of wealth and of luxury by the prophets and in the Gospel, demands for the renunciation of all worldly possessions, became less explicit even during Antiquity. By the first half of the Middle Ages, they were replaced by high regard for wealth: riches are a fortunate endowment, making possible the practice of further religious virtues (charity, donations to the Church), thereby increasing the chances of salvation.[6] Calls in the Gospel for forbearance were suppressed during the Crusades by the echoes of Joshua's trumpets: the killing of man became permissible for a Christian Knight when fighting for a holy purpose – there is a 'just war'.[7] Some Christians abandoned the world they despised in order to torture their bodies in the hope of salvation in the other world; but others admired and praised the perfection and the mystery of divine creation in this world. They studied them and re-created them in an artistic form, hoping to come nearer to God in this way. The anti-intellectual glorification of the idiot and the curses heaped on the literate were a legacy handed down to the Middle Ages by those within the Christian religion who had the monopoly on literacy and culture. Even sexuality, regarded as one of the main sources of sin, acquired a positive religious function. Although Christianity continued to regard virginity and continence as superior virtues, the twelfth century saw marriage raised to the rank of Church sacraments, by virtue of being the institutional framework for procreation.[8]

The above pairs of contrasts are in no way accidental, nor can we consider them unique to Christianity. A similar polarity and contrast can be found in every mythology, religion and ideology that tries to work out a general system for the antinomies in human existence and in the social order (see Berger 1981). Certain aspects of this duality can be described by contrasting the spheres of the sacred and of the profane, as did Émile Durkheim (1926) and Mircea Eliade (1957). All this can also be examined in the form of binary oppositions, according to the procedure used by Claude Lévi-Strauss (1966, 1964–71). I personally find Victor Turner's (1974, 1978) system of anthropological categories the most convenient explanation of this kind of polarity.[9]

*   *   *

According to Victor Turner, this polarity derives from two organizing principles of social existence, having equal rank. One – called 'structure' – is interpreted not as something static, but as a process; it emphasizes the differences between people based on rank, wealth, profession, relations, age or sex. The other – called '*communitas*' – stresses the equality among a group of people, regardless of the above differences, their community being understood in the most abstract sense of the word. Turner also gives the name 'anti-structure' to this second principle when it is expressed in a form that questions some of the basic, everyday truths of life on earth. These truths are challenged by the teeming chaos and absurdity of a 'world turned upside down', accompanied by 'status reversal'. Turner analysed the ritual order of the Central African Ndembu tribe and placed it in a wider, anthropological context. This led to the analysis of the manifestational forms and symbols in these two organizing principles of society. The symbols may have been given different meanings in individual cultures, but were none the less related with regard to basic principles. Using the theory of rites developed by Arnold van Gennep (1909), Turner demonstrated how the majority of (individual or collective) rites of passage make sure that members of the communities are faced regularly with both kinds of value systems on specific occasions such as turning-points in their lives or calendrical rites.

Turner's theory offers an explanation of this polarity in Christianity that is noteworthy from several points of view. He himself made ample use of his own interpretation (1974: 60–96, 166–270; 1977: 106–13, 141–54; Turner and Turner 1978), as did other historians who found his theory applicable (Nelson 1972; Davis 1975; Geary 1978; Brown 1981; Bynum 1984).

One of Turner's observations concerns the characteristic social symbolism of '*communitas*–anti-structure'. The 'superior value system' manifested in rituals of status reversal is expressed, among other ways, by the fact that the small, the weak and the inferior in the structure are given temporary power, whilst the strong, the big and the powerful are forced into humility. Court jesters fulfil the same function as dispensers of justice on a permanent basis, not just on ritual occasions. The Christian world-view transmutes these same ideals into a programme of redemption with a social flavour, aiming to dispense social justice. Hence the charismatic function of the poor, the sick and beggars – a function that recurs over several millennia – and the part that 'voluntary poverty' plays in salvation (Mannteufel 1970; Mollat 1974, 1978). The religious power of the 'weak' position was exploited by medieval Christianity through the Children's Crusade in 1209, as well as through the child prophets in the late Middle Ages.[10] Christianity profited from the power of the weak in a similar way when the religious authority of female mystics was increased in the late Middle Ages,[11] and when the function of the peasant (the *rusticus*) regarding salvation was stressed, a function that did not come to full funition until the Reformation.[12]

The second important aspect of Turner's observations regarding Christianity is that he pinpointed the following: Christianity drafted a life-strategy of the well-known, but not always explicit, principles of *communitas*–anti-structure as a separate system and an example to be followed; this principle was then contrasted with the 'structure'-based organization of life on earth. This is well illustrated by the more radical endeavours of Christianity mentioned above. According to the Bible, Jesus strove to live by the abstract principles of *communitas* and tried to achieve a state of 'permanent liminality'.[13] The same principle was practised, in larger groups, by the Apostles and by the early Christian congregations.

However, the realization of a spontaneous, existential *communitas* is a short-lived attempt that is bound to fail. Nor is structure viable without giving occasional validity to the principles of *communitas*. Those who try to organize their lives exclusively according to the value system of *communitas*–anti-structure can do so only under specially favourable conditions. When these no longer prevail, they can exist only according to the principles of 'normative *communitas*'; here, the rule of the ideals that are not viable in themselves can only be maintained with the help of hierarchies even more rigid than the conventional structures (Turner 1977: 132). And if these principles are to be brought into effect among wider social groups, that can only happen in the form of normative, indeed of 'ideological', *communitas*. Here an even wider set of enforcing mechanisms and artificial structures has to be created, or there has to be some kind of exemption from the compulsory validity of the principles of *communitas*. In addition, those arguments that support the component parts and working logic of 'structure' have to be included in the official system of values. This explains how the other pole in the polarity described above came into being.

It is not difficult to recognize the manifestations of 'normative, ideological *communitas*' in the historical process, whereby a prophetic sect became an organized Church; whereby, as the ideological heir of the early Christians who lived in communities sharing all wealth, it was the immensely rich medieval Papacy, aiming for world domination, that proclaimed the ideals of *communitas*. The model examples of normative *communitas* are the countless historical manifestations of monasticism. From the hermits in the desert of Theba in late Antiquity, through the medieval Benedictines and Cistercians, up to the mendicant orders – everywhere we see proof that those who try to put into practice the ideals of *communitas* cannot maintain and preserve their spontaneous experiment unless they are organized into a system with official rules and financial security. As for the Church organization, the normative *communitas* it had absorbed in numerous ways enabled it to continue acting as the implementer of a perfect lifestyle, while at the same time representing the ideals of 'structure', which had meanwhile been given religious motivation.

Apart from organizational solutions, numerous ideological and symbolic methods are employed to harmonize the contradictory principles of *communitas* and of structure. Within the Christian world-view, the realization of views opposing the structure of life in this world and proclaiming equality is partly relegated to the *past*: it is turned into a nostalgia for a Paradise without work, sexuality, knowledge, suffering, death or the pain of childbirth; it is transformed into the example of Jesus, Son of God, an example one is recommended to follow, however difficult that might be. On the other hand, the Church assigns the full realization of these principles to the *future*: reward in the next world, salvation and the Last Judgement. Contact with examples of past or future perfection gave the Church a number of opportunities to stress and to enlarge its own role of mediator.

The values of *communitas* and of anti-structure also play an important part in Church rituals, in liturgy and in the cult of saints (together with the pilgrimages, legends and miracles related to the latter). This time, however, they are not proposed as ideals to be experienced; instead, like the conventional ritual system, they fit into the interstices of structure, which they only wish to counterbalance on important occasions in the lives of believers, and with a definite regularity.

It is at this point that we can return to our original question. The polarity recognizable in the history of Christianity institutionalized the contrasting principles of *communitas*–anti-structure and of structure in a more contradictory manner than did either the conventional ritual order or the traditional mythologies. The values of *communitas* occupied an eminent position, but were discredited through having acquired normative and ideological functions. By contrast, the principles of structure, no matter how precarious their position in the religion itself, were nevertheless indispensable for the maintenance of ideological *communitas*. Even if the Church did not always sanction them, it was forced to comply with them tactily.

This contradictory situation meant that trends that deviated from the conventions went in opposing directions. They could move towards the ideal of *communitas*, which, in the ideological sense, was the gravitational point of the system; from that ground, they could deliver as sharp a criticism of contemporary society as of the Church, which by then had acquired secular power and was distorting its 'original' ideals. At the same time, they could also rely on those traditional structures that forced the Church into an increasingly ideological reinterpretation of *communitas* with respect to ways of thinking, social life and power conflicts. By referring to former practices in the Church, they could promote a more thoroughgoing acceptance of the views of traditional structures and an increased relegation of false norms. Let us call the views that revived a radical version of the ideals of *communitas* – using an expression borrowed from physics – *centripetal* (tending towards the centre) movement; and let us give the name *centrifugal* movement to those endeavours that obeyed the logic of structure. Let us now examine the prospects and means for reforming the system offered by these to divergent strategies.

> We, the poor of Christ, who have no fixed abode and flee from city to city like sheep amidst wolves, are persecuted as were the apostles and the martyrs, despite the fact that we lead a most strict and holy life, persevering day and night in fasts and abstinence, in prayers, and in labour from which we seek only the necessities of life. We undergo this because we are not of this world. But you, lovers of the world, have peace with it because you are of the world . . . You add house to house, field to field, and seek the things that are of this world . . .[14]

Such were the arguments promulgated by one of the first militant groups of Catharist heresy in 1143 in Cologne. This self-assurance was so shocking to Eberwin, the Prior of the nearby Premonstratensian Abbey, that he addressed his request for help directly to St Bernard of Clairvaux, the most respected religious debater of the time. Bernard castigated with severe proclamations the aberrations of the heretics, who were known to him by hearsay. He could not, however, proffer any effective argument against the credibility of the heretics' apostolic lifestyle and the criticism they voiced from this point of view.[15] It was not the first or the last time that this kind of criticism embarrassed the medieval Church: it concerns the inevitably recurring radical interpretations within Christianity and the centripetal movement described above, which extracted the ideals of *communitas* from the central source of authority, the Bible. We must add that it was not simply arguments and opinions that were brought to bear: the *ethically rationalized* religious lifestyle of the heretics lent weight to their opposition to the religious expertise and the institutional authority of the Church (Bourdieu 1971: 318–20).

From the eleventh century onwards, it was the increasing number of wandering preachers, sects and religious movements that proclaimed the radically interpreted ideals of *communitas*, in opposition to the official version of Christianity and to its representative, the Church.[16] The apostolic lifestyle, as one of the best paths to salvation, is first heard of in the endeavours of the Italian hermit movements, which appeared at the turn of the tenth century.[17] At that point, these ascetics, who rejected society and practised bodily self-torture in solitude, did not represent a serious danger to the Church. Half a century later, their example was used by Peter Damiani, the chief ideologist of the ascetic hermit movement, in an attack on the morals of lay society and the secularized clergy.[18] Yet, at the same time, difficulties arose because laymen were striving to realize the evangelical way of life: the heretics, who appeared in Arras in 1024, although starting out from the ideal of the apostolic lifestyle, arrived at far more radical positions than those of the Italian hermits. They considered it sufficient for salvation to renounce the world, to refrain from all physical desires, to earn their living through manual labour, to harm no one and to help, those who accepted their way of life. What is more, on the same ground, these illiterate laymen pronounced as superfluous all contemporary forms of Church mediation for salvation.[19]

The opportunity for one of the first general formulations of the ideals of radical *communitas* came at the Synod of 1025, which had been convened to condemn the heretics of Arras. Through a characteristic historical coincidence, the same synod enabled Gérard, the Bishop of Cambrai, to draft one of the first versions of the hierarchic social theory of the three orders. This was one of the most extreme Christian syntheses of the principles of structure (Duby 1978: 163–8).

The religious practice rejected by the heretics of Arras was the ritualized liturgical Christianity of the late Carolingian era and of the increasingly popular monks of Cluny.[20] Needless to say, criticism deriving from a religious lifestyle based on the principles of *communitas* rejects all forms of Church mediation – from baptism and communion to the ordaining of the clergy and the Church hierarchy. However, the criticism emphasized mainly problems of a contemporary nature.

The objection to respect for the Cross can be explained by the fact that, in Carolingian liturgy, the Cross had a more important role than any other symbol.[21] The first known heretic in medieval Western Europe, Leutard, who appeared in the year 1000 in the region of Châlons, began his activities by publicly breaking a cross.[22] Peter of Bruis, a wandering preacher who appeared in Provence at the beginning of the twelfth century, gave this rejection a moral justification by claiming that the Cross is the symbol of the suffering and the death of Christ and is therefore not worthy of religious veneration. Moreover, he turned the rejection into a sacrilegious provocation: on Good Friday, he built a bonfire of wooden crosses and roasted meat on it, which he and his followers then proceeded to eat.[23]

'There is nothing that is any more venerable in God's Church than anything you could find in your own bedroom. Why should His Church be holy, since it is built by the labour of man, of mere stones and mortar' – so said the heretics of Arras. These arguments continued to appear regularly among heretics during the next 200 years.[24] The various religious movements used these arguments to object not only to the power symbols of the Church, but also to the differentiation between the holy and the profane spheres. It is noteworthy that these protests were being voiced at the very time when the building of luxurious monastries and cathedrals was gathering momentum. In the second half of the twelfth century, the building of cathedrals was denounced as an unnecessary waste of money, not only by the heretics but also by eminent representatives of the urban intelligentsia. One of these, Peter the Chanter, wrote a special dissertation on this subject, entitled *Contra curiositatem et superfluitatem edificiorum* (on the futility and superfluity of buildings).[25]

The heretics regarded with equal disapproval the veneration of all man-made altars, Christ portraits and icons. Their iconoclastic views (see Ostrogorsky 1929; Bredekamp 1975) are similar to those found in the writings of Agobard, Bishop of Lyons, and of Claudius de Turin (Boshof 1969: 138–58) as early as the beginning of the ninth century. Such views were repeatedly voiced by the various religious movements right up to the Reformation.[26] We can also find the same attitude in the endeavours of the Cistercian reform movement, which could hardly be accused of heresy, although its representatives adopted a great many of the Christian ideals of *communitas*.[27]

It is also no coincidence that the heretics particularly disapproved of the use of incense, the singing of psalms and the ringing of bells. Extremes of this kind in the liturgy were widespread at the turn of the eleventh century; just as widely known was the record-breaking, militant chanting of the Cluny monks (Rosenwein 1971). It is worth mentioning as a matter of interest that, for some reason, singing in Church especially annoyed the heretics in the Middle Ages. In the thirteenth century, a Catharist artisan in Toulouse voiced the opinion that: 'Those who chant incomprehensible words in Church, just want to dupe the simple people.'[28] And according to the Waldenses of the thirteenth century: 'it is the words that have meaning, not the melody, . . . singing in Church is an infernal din',[29] which at the same time 'ridicules God, as if He understood man only when he addressed Him with a song'.[30]

In the eleventh century, the Church tried to keep lay society under its own influence not merely by increasing the splendour of its rituals. It extended its moral and spiritual domination to two important spheres: confession and its accompanying penance (the redemption of sins through varied forms of penitence). Both practices gave the Church greater control over lay society and increased the effectiveness of Christian moral teaching. So after the first upsurge of the 'Carolingian renaissance' the Church began to promote them again in the eleventh century. Then in 1215, after almost two centuries of propaganda, the Church made annual confession compulsory (see McNeill and Gamer 1938; Vogel 1969).

From the tenth century onwards, as a result of its renewed attention to lay society, the Church took an increasingly central part in the sanctification of marriage, which was declared one of the seven sacraments of the Church in the thirteenth century (Hoecke and Welkenhuysen 1981). The moral 'golden mean', specially drawn up for secular society, and the concessions made to structure, naturally met with disapproval from the followers of the ideals of *communitas*. The heretics of Arras – like almost all the religious movements from the eleventh to the thirteenth centuries – rejected the institution of marriage,[31] accepted no middle way between sin and virtue, and considered confession and penitence completely useless.

They felt the same way about another sphere in which, at the time, the Church was trying to increase its intercessionary role: Church rituals connected with the dead. While the Church was collecting from the nobility their biggest donations for prayers said for the dead (Schmid and Wollasch 1967); while the Church was formulating the dogma of Purgatory, which allotted a specific place after death to all sinners, whose further fate depended to a great extent on the intervention of the Church and on the prayers of their living relatives (Le Goff 1981: 294–401); at this same time, the heretics of Arras proclaimed that prayers for the dead were useless and that burial in holy ground was being popularized and by the Church purely for profit.[32]

As we can see, the centripetal movements emerging in the eleventh century within the system of medieval Christianity were quick to question everything that legitimized the views of structure and encased the Biblical ideals of *communitas* within the system of Church intervention. We could complement the criticism of the Arras heretics with the more differentiated arguments, the increasing use of Biblical allusions and the ever harsher criticism of Church luxury voiced by the heretic movements of the twelfth century (such as the Cologne Catharists quoted above). But the two opposing views on religion have been defined sufficiently clearly. Nevertheless, we must mention the methods employed by these movements to infuse vitality into the Christian version of the ideals of *communitas* – ideals that were in danger of being buried for good by the institutional traditions of the Church.

*   *   *

I should like to illustrate with a somewhat remote example one of the typical thought processes of the religious movements. The main characteristic of this way of thinking (the 'first form of Utopian mentality') was found to reside in the so-called *absolute presentness*. It was described by the scholar who established the sociology of knowledge, Karl Mannheim, when he analysed the 'orgiastic chiliasm' of Thomas Münzer and the sixteenth-century Anabaptists.'

> The chiliast expects a union with the immediate present. Hence he is not preoccupied in his daily life with optimistic hopes for the future or romantic reminiscences. His attitude is characterized by a tense expectation. He is always on his toes awaiting the propitious moment, thus there is no inner articulation of time for him. He is not actually concerned with the millenium that is to come: what is important for him that it happened here and now, and that it arose from mundane existence, as a sudden swing over into another kind of existence . . . (Mannheim 1936: 216–17)

The religious movements of the eleventh to thirteenth centuries are still a long way from the radicalism of Münzer, which was the culmination of a historical evolution. Their views still lack the coherence of the set of eschatological ideas which developed under the impact of the doctrines of the Abbot Joachim of Fiore (see Reeves 1969). However, there is early promise of this later development: the religious movements are all characterized by contemporization in the postulates of *communitas*. They showed a stubborn naïveté, or deliberate anachronism, in their opposition to the institutional tradition of the Church, which canonized a large number of compromises into an example to be followed. They condensed into a view of 'here and now' those radical expectations that the Church tried to dissolve into promises of the future, into respect for the past and into religious symbolism of the present. They actualized.

This process of actualization was enhanced by the fact that they rejected all authority within the ideological system of Christianity, with the exception of the Scriptures; even there, they accepted only the parts that are nearest to their own ideals, above all the Gospels.[33] They rejected Church rituals for the simple reason that they are not mentioned in the Scriptures and they tried to discredit preachers by claiming that their sermons were inconsistent with the Bible.[34] All this was greatly assisted by the weapons of oral tradition.[35] The lay, illiterate members of the religious movements startled Churchmen by being able to quote long passages from the Bible, having learned by heart almost the whole of the New Testament.[36] At debates, they made ingenious use of Bible quotations, which they interpreted literally. They rejected the complex techniques used by the Church for the interpretation of texts,[37] as well as the secondary authority of the commentaries. It was this very inconsistency and lack of expertise that enabled medieval heretics to justify their own lifestyle so convincingly, by selecting quotations from the sacred source once compiled by the Church in its own interest. On the other hand, their apostolic lifestyle consistently implemented the ideals of *communitas*: it was enough for the heretics to point to themselves, to have their arguments and their Bible quotations believed by their audience. This fact was of great help to them in their debates against the clergy; it not only made up for their lay technique in quotations and for their inferior erudition, but also quite often tipped the balance in their favour.

In Chapter 4 I return to this point, namely that this kind of apostolic lifestyle bore witness to the literal interpretation of the instructions in the Gospel – right down to the smallest details in appearance: clothes, bare-footedness, long hair and beard. The same literal interpretation was found in the few simple rituals practised by the lay movements following the Biblical pattern: the washing of feet,[38] the kiss of peace[39] and the blessing of bread.[40] The leaders of several heretical sects carried the imitation of Christ to the extreme of going around accompanied by twelve disciples and a woman dubbed the Virgin Mary.[41]

The religious movements also extracted from the Bible those instructions that show the way to the formation of a lifestyle according to the ideals of *communitas* – the modes of liminality. This meant the cutting of family and kinship ties, the rejection of worldly goods, the breaking away from friends and the giving up of permanent residence; it meant starting a new life outside all social and economic classes and earning a living by manual labour or by begging. Using modern terminology, we could say that the Gospels recommend 'dropping out', or at least living on the margin of society, to those who wish to put into practice the ideals of true *communitas* even before its arrival (redemption).

Being on the margin of society is a position that displays different characteristics in every social system; it is a position designated by every age in different place and for different people. Medieval marginality included not merely those living on the edge of society (Schmitt 1978; Le Goff and Vincent 1979). It included those living in towns, which until the eleventh to twelfth centuries had a very uncertain legal standing, then, at a later date, also the lower urban classes, who were excluded from burgher status (Geremek 1976, 1987). It included the society of medieval roads, where one could meet not only penniless wanderers, but also merchants, vagrant students, comedians and highwaymen, escaped serfs heading for the towns and pilgrims; then, from the end of the eleventh century, for about 150 years, there were also the Crusaders on their way to conquer the Holy Land. By voluntarily undertaking marginality, the medieval religious movements entered a variegated social environment, which became the source of a great many innovations during the eleventh to thirteenth centuries. Medieval marginality enabled the religious movements to practise within society the ideals of being an outsider, those of liminality and of *communitas*. As for the changes in the medium of marginality, they explain a great deal about the characteristic features of the various religious movements.[42]

At the beginning of the eleventh century, only the hermitic lifestyle, with its complete rejection of society, was able to satisfy the requirements of the apostolic way of life. By the middle of the century, however, it was urban marginality that produced one of the most important religious movements of the age: the *pataria* in Milan (Violante 1972; Miccoli 1977; Cracco 1977). At the end of the eleventh century, in the wake of the tumult accompanying the first Crusade, the appearance of a large number of wandering preachers turned that Crusade into a mass movement. The most renowned among these preachers was Peter the Hermit, whose prophet-like appearance was of great help to him when enlisting crowds for the conquest of the Holy Land. But he also used the opportunity to popularize the religious ideals of the Gospel (Hagenmeyer 1879; Blake and Morris 1985). Even when enthusiasm for the Crusades abated, wandering, itinerant preachers like Peter remained characteristic figures on the roads of Europe. Layman, defrocked priests and monks proclaimed the ideals of the religious movements outlined above; they all managed to gather followers and attract attention with their harsh criticisms.[43]

In fact, after the first serious conflict, the Church gave some of them the opportunity to form their own reformed monastic order (Norbert von Xanten – Premonstratensians; Robert d'Arbrissel – Fontevrault; Stephen of Muret – Grandmontines; Bernard of Tyron – Tyron, etc.) (Milis 1979). Many, however, were not prepared to enter into such a compromise with the Church; and it was from among their number that the first notable leaders of the heretic movement emerged: Peter of Bruis, Henry of Le Mans, Tanchelm, Arnold of Brescia (Frugoni 1954; Manselli 1975: 59–110). It was these travelling preachers who first united into a spectacular system of symbols the requirements for the lifestyle of the marginal wanderers of the roads: torn, shabby clothes, constant wandering, begging. A description of Henry's character begins: 'his unconventional way of life was on the surface unlike that of ordinary folk – shelter in the houses of burghers, a night's lodging as a transient, a meal, a bed in a garret . . .'[44] Bernard of Clairvaux gives a similar description of Arnold of Brescia: 'he is a wanderer and an exile on this earth; he constantly acts among strangers in a way he would never allow himself to do a among his own people.'[45]

It would perhaps be more apt to call these wandering preachers ideologists of anti-structure and of permanent liminality, rather than of *communitas*. Their extravagant appearance, their resounding criticism pretending to religious expertise, their spectacular symbols, their flamboyant behaviour, which could mobilize the crowds in the streets, in the marketplaces and on the roads – all this presented a hitherto unknown danger for the Church. By now it was no longer a question of fighting the secret organization of a few sects; the Church was now faced by rebellious crowds, led by 'new prophets' who came openly to the fore. Whenever the travelling preachers appeared, 'the whole world is stood upside down'. Peter the Hermit, Robert d'Arbrissel and Henry were surrounded by penitent prostitutes, who vowed to lead decent lives, get married, or even wished to become nuns. The followers of Peter of Bruis not only roasted their meat on the Cross on Good Friday; they also vandalized churches, destroyed holy images and forced captured priests to enter into marriage in ostentatious ceremonies. Around 1112, Tanchelm arranged an engagement party with the Virgin Mary herself – or rather her holy image – and then collected wedding gifts from those present. In 1116, in Le Mans, there were converted clerics sobbing at Henry's feet. In the middle of the century, Arnold of Brescia used his religious arguments and symbols for urban rebellion and the fight against the Papacy.[46]

As I have already mentioned, several of these wandering preachers – after initial scandals and clashes with the local clergy – managed to get themselves and their order accepted during the last wave of Gregorian Church reform. Although this acceptance meant that they had to give up their radical opposition to the Church – if they ever reached such extremes – they nevertheless retained their connection with heresy in their aims, in their symbols and in their preaching techniques. The best example of this use of marginality and anti-structure as a religious argument is provided by St Bernard of Clairvaux. He started out as a reformer, but later became the aggressive, orthodox champion of twelfth-century Christianity. Let us quote him:

> A good sort of playing this . . . by which we become an object of reproach to the rich and of ridicule to the proud. In fact what else do seculars think we are doing by playing when what they desire most on earth, we fly from; and what they fly from, we desire? [We are] like acrobats and jugglers, who with their heads down and feet up, stand or walk on their hands . . . And we too play this game that we may be ridiculed, discomfited, humbled, until he comes who puts down the mighty from their seats and exalts the humble . . .[47]

In the second half of the twelfth century, the picture of marginal society underwent a change. The many-hued diversity began to fade and the ensuing change came so quickly that it was astonishing even for contemporaries. The highways were now thronged with crowds of the poor, who had broken away from their village communities but found no homes in the towns. As the division of labour between village and town developed, the first of the truly devastating famines occurred. It was also at this time that the army of starving beggars became a menacing crowd demanding care, and poverty turned into a social problem (Goglin 1976: 49–80; Mollat 1978: 78–145). All this undoubtedly contributed to the criticisms voiced by the heretic movements in the second half of the twelfth century. In their attacks they now concentrated wealth – mainly on the wealth of the Church – whilst in their ideals they focused on voluntary poverty (Mannteufel 1970).

It is no coincidence that even the Catharist sect, which revived in its dualist interpretation of Christianity the doctrine of Manichaeism,[48] did not try to attract followers with its secret doctrine or counter-dogma; instead, its members practised the apostolic lifestyle in a more radical fashion than ever before – living, like the Cologne group of 1143, 'as the poor of Christ'.[49] Voluntary poverty formed the central ideal of another large heretic movement in the twelfth century: the Waldenses (Selge 1967; Manselli 1975: 111–26). Peter Valdes, a rich merchant from Lyon, who first appeared around 1170, proclaimed the necessity of carrying out the commands of the Gospel, word for word: 'If thou wilt be perfect, go sell what thou hast and give to the poor; and thou shalt have treasure in Heaven; and come and follow me' (Matthew 19:21). The Waldenses were the first to declare that the lifestyle of the true have-nots, namely the beggars, was the only one that could lead to an apostolic way of life. Their example attracted numerous followers in the next centuries: St Francis of

Assisi organized his lay community according to similar ideas,[50] as did the Apostolic Brethren at the end of the thirteenth century (Spätling 1947), and the movements of the Saccati and Fraticelli at the beginning of the fourteenth century.

Marginality provided the favourable medium necessary for the spontaneous attempts to make 'community' a reality. This is indirectly endorsed by the fact that, when these movements broke with marginality, sooner or later they turned into a normative, ideological *communitas*, similar to the early Christian movement. Some of these groups organized themselves into a counter-church, like the Catharist and Waldensian movements; others applied to the Church for permission to live in the towns, among them the Humiliati (Zanoni 1921; Grundmann 1935: 72–90; Bolton 1971), some groups of Waldenses, such as the Poor Catholics, led by Durand de Huesca (Thouzellier 1966: 215–425), and the Franciscans, who were organizing themselves into a mendicant order. Becoming a *communitas* was no problem for an order that was able to enlarge the sphere of its activity within the bosom of the Church – even if the recurring inner crises of the Franciscans and the appearance of the Spiritual Franciscans demonstrated that this change was by no means smooth. For the heretic movements, however, it meant the loss of their earlier credence. It is no coincidence that both the Catharist and the Waldensian heresies survived longest in environments where they had to preserve their marginality, namely among the nomadic shepherd societies in the Pyrenees and in the Piedmontese Alps (Le Roy Ladurie 1978; Gonnet and Molnár 1974: 138–210).

I shall return to this topic later. Here, I will limit myself to describing how the medieval religious movements, modelled on a spontaneous form of *communitas*, exploited the opportunities afforded by marginality. This is also something Victor Turner regards as one of the characteristic manifestations of *communitas* and of liminality. Society during the eleventh to fourteenth centuries provided no possibility of forming Utopian communities within the heart of society according to these ideals. The first time this occurred was at the beginning of the fifteenth century, in Tabor, within the Hussite movement; then again, at the time of the Reformation in Münster, and later still among the radical sects of the English revolution (Seibt 1972: 145–55, 182–94; Hill 1972). However, a discussion of these later developments would exceed the scope of this study.

So far, we have surveyed the centripetal movements developing within medieval Christianity: their critical assertions, their thought processes and their social environment. We have explained the similarities in medieval religious movements by the logical separation and opposition that occurred between *communitas* and 'structure' within the framework of Christianity. We have also found an explanation in the fact that these movements drew on the same holy sources and more or less on the same institutional traditions for the conceptual framework and operational model necessary for their opposition.

Finally, we must mention that the heresies themselves established an *apocryphal* tradition; they bequeathed to each other their techniques of criticism and their models of behaviour. Moreover, certain medieval heretic movements, such as the Bogomils and the Catharists, inherited apocryphal traditions from the Manichees of Antiquity.[51] In spite of this, it would be a mistake to talk of a connection leading from the first medieval heretic movements to the Reformation: the possibilities for inheriting apocryphal traditions are very limited. There was no truth in the supposed close link between heresies in Antiquity and in the Middle Ages and the heretic conspiracies, which had been compared to 'Samson's foxes, with many heads, but with their tails tied together' (Judges 15:4) – these surmises existed only in the imagination of the inquisitors. The basic correspondence in the aims and methods of propaganda among these movements derived from the limited prospects for legitimate opposition within Christianity; it originated also from the attractions of the ideals of *communitas*–anti-structure, which could be called the focal point in the symbolic universe of Christianity.

*   *   *

If I were to attempt a brief description of the manifestations of *centrifugal* movement, I would have to emphasize first of all that they are more varied than the centripetal strivings: they attempted to widen, in every possible direction, the sphere of acceptable manifestations in the Christian culture of the age. Within medieval Christianity, there were diverse social, organizational and power interests, promoting further conciliation with the principles of 'structure'. Churchmen as well as laymen were among its supporters. It was thanks to these centrifugal endeavours that Christian culture in the Middle Ages was able to satisfy increasingly varied expectations of a social, political and cultural nature.

It would be sheer audacity even to attempt a systematic characterization of the diverse centrifugal endeavours similar to the one I gave of the religious movements tending towards a centripetal orientation. Such a portrayal would have to provide a picture of the whole of Christianity.[52] Centrifugal manifestations include the whole of medieval secular culture (both the courtly and the urban variety); liturgic art, which was becoming secularized in many respects; the development of the medieval legal system and legal thinking; the changing, increasingly flexible regulation of economic life; the religious–ethical judgement on sexuality and carnality; and the relationship to nature – to mention just a few relevant fields.

Nevertheless it is necessary to give one or two examples purely for illustration. I shall demonstrate how 'centrifugality' prevailed in the symbolic system of medieval Christianity by a brief discussion of two subjects: the problems of popular religion and of medieval university erudition.

During the past few decades, popular religion in the Middle Ages has been newly discovered as a popular subject for research; so I can perhaps dispense with a more precise definition of it.[53] If I approach it from the angle of popular culture, which is equally often discussed (see Burke 1978), it suffices to remark that by 'popular' manifestations I mean the religious views held not only by peasants or by lay people generally but also by a great many Church people. There is no doubt that the term 'popular' and those terms associated with it, such as 'superstition', 'magic', or 'vulgarization', contain a value judgement that goes back a long way and is by no means objective (see Harmening 1979; Schmitt 1979: 27–42). At the same time, it is obvious that the ritual forms, the folkloric elements and the mythological bases of popular religion which caused frequent problems for reform-oriented medieval clerics, constituted a singular variant of Christianity; its systematic analysis and careful interpretation could eliminate the false value-judgement of a pejorative classification.

As a starting point we can say that, with respect to the formation of the popular variants of medieval Christianity, the religious interest of lay people influenced the changes that ensued. Religious interest, according to Bourdieu (and to Weber before him), explains the claim that religion justifies the legitimacy of the position of given social groups and endows their characteristic features with religious values (Bourdieu 1971: 311–13). But religious interest can have a much bigger effect: it includes the expectation by laymen that religious practice should be able to regulate, by sacral–ritual means, the rhythm of the life of the individual, of the family and of society as a whole, and provide a solution for the conflicts that occur in those spheres. The Church could only preserve its exclusive authority over lay society throughout the Middle Ages if it fulfilled these expectations completely. This view is indirectly supported by subsequent historical evolution. After the success of the various reform movements (Lutheranism, Calvinism, Puritanism) representing the centripetal endeavours portrayed above, and campaigning against the magical elements that had penetrated Christianity, the reaction of popular religion was that the belief in witches and other 'superstitions' became much stronger among the ordinary people during the fifteenth and sixteenth centuries (Thomas 1971).

Let me illustrate, with a few examples, that popular religion conformed in diverse ways to the religious interest of laymen. It regulated the times of work and rest and the periods of fertility in the year; the festive cycle and the liturgy of the Church calendar provided a Christian version of the pagan fertility rituals (Le Goff 1960; Gurevich 1985). In times of war and before battles, each side tried, by means of Church blessings, to secure divine assistance for itself (Gaier 1966; Graus 1977). The strange ritual of barbarian jurisdiction – the ordeal – was reinterpreted and used in Christian terms (Radding 1979). The cult of relics satisfied the demand for 'objects that are near at hand and can be influenced magically'. The Church stressed the ability of saints to bring about cures and to perform miracles; by encouraging their veneration and by associating them with local interests, the Church forestalled a demand for diverse magic services.[54] The fundamental turning-points in the lives of individuals were given a religious framework through a series of 'rites of passage' (baptism, marriage, extreme unction, burial).

Under the pressure of the religious interest of laymen, popular religion brought about a deliberate integration of pagan and antique elements, a shift of emphasis within Christianity and a rehabilitation of the views of 'structure'. Thus popular religion created a system of ritual and of belief that fulfilled the expectations that could not be met by evangelical religiosity based on the principles of *communitas* or by the 'elite culture' of Church Christianity.[55]

As a second example, let me refer to the counterpoint to the popular Christianity of the Middle Ages: the *philosophical–scientific* endeavours of the university intellectuals, which also owed their increasing autonomy to centrifugal aspirations.[56] In the twelfth century, schoolmasters paved the way for philosophical and scientific investigation within Christian culture with two innovative demands. Spurred on by the incentive of a rational explanation of faith – which can be associated with St Anselm and with Abelard – they intended to learn more about the truth of the Revelation by means of *logic* and the *observation of nature*. It is no coincidence that these two undertakings met such fierce opposition in the twelfth century – the linking of the notion of truth with rational or empirical criteria stands in opposition to every religious authority. The work conducted in the field of the natural sciences at the School of Chartres was frequently met by disapproval. It is a well-known fact that Abelard, the most eminent scholar of dialectics, was subjected to gross vilification.[57]

Rather than direct confrontation, the majority of intellectuals sought support in the increasing prestige of Antiquity – in the wisdom of the 'Ancients'. They made pragmatic suggestions for the integration of ancient philosophical material, which was being translated and disseminated on an increasing scale. For example, the Englishman Daniel Morley wrote in the twelfth century:

Let no one be shocked, if, when discussing the creation of the world, I mention not the Fathers of the Church, but pagan philosophers; it is true that they were not believers, but we must include in our teaching some of their assertions, because they seem most convincing. 'Rob the Egyptians of their treasures and enrich the Hebrew people with them' – thus ordered the Lord, when He delivered us from Egypt so miraculously. So, according to the command of the Lord, and with His help, let us rob these pagan philosophers of their wisdom and of their eloquence; let us rob these unbelievers in such a way, that the loot will reinforce our faith.[58]

In the thirteenth century, there was no longer any need for this kind of naive reasoning. The modern approaches were given a legitimate place at the universities; the new endeavours in philosophy and in the natural sciences accepted and studied nature and progressed according to the rule of reason, in the footsteps of Aristotle. It now seemed that these trends could be reconciled with the principal aims of Christian theology. At the same time, other tendencies in centrifugal thought were trying to liberate philosophy and the sciences from the role of being a mere verificatory system of faith. The Averroistic doctrine of *veritas duplex* – branded as heretic – was no longer willing to reconcile the possibly differing religious and philosophical–rational conclusions, but wished to maintain them side by side, giving them equal value. In the fourteenth century, the Franciscan Nominalists opened up new possibilities for scientific investigation by renouncing the rational or empirical verifiability of faith: they aimed to separate what the previous centuries tried to join.

*   *   *

After this brief description of some centrifugal endeavours, it is possible to discuss more precisely the logic of the system within which the centripetal endeavours of religious movements presented themselves. Perhaps it will also become clearer why the inner contradictions of medieval Christian culture became more pronounced in a centuries-long process whereby, under pressure from new centripetal and centrifugal enterprises, the principles of *communitas* and of structure gained the upper hand in ever-renewed forms. What I wish to mention in conclusion follows clearly from the above: the two types of religious aspiration balanced each other, and could be played off one against the other. Their permanent tension contributed to the survival, occasionally to the reform, of a Christian culture united, framed and governed by the Church.

Let us give a few examples. It was no coincidence that, during the eleventh-century Church reforms, Pope Gregory VII supported the lay religious movement of the Patarines and other similar centripetal movements. On the one hand, they seemed to be appropriate political allies against supporters of the Emperor and the power of the Bishops who opposed the domination of the Papacy. On the other hand, at a time when the Church was trying to free itself from the influence of secular power, its authority was re-established through the stricter application of some of the ideals of *communitas*: celibacy was made compulsory and there was a campaign against simony (the selling of Church offices).[59] These same considerations enabled several religious reform movements to be integrated into the organization of the Church as reformed monastic orders. The past radicalism of their founders described in their legends, and the new rules, which made concessions to the realities of structure but preserved parts of their original ideas, enabled these reformed monastic orders to enrich and modernize the institutional structure of the Church.

The logical opposition of centrifugal and centripetal endeavours is illustrated by the attitude of Peter Abelard, an oft-persecuted, leading figure in the ranks of the twelfth-century urban intelligentsia, and a reformer of dialectics and of ethics. He spoke with sarcastic contempt of two contemporary wandering preachers, both accused of heresy: Peter of Bruis from the South of France and Tanchelm from the Low Countries.[60] Nor did the Emperors defying the Holy See display more tolerance than the Church itself towards religious movements that proclaimed the ideals of *communitas*. It was in vain that Arnold of Brescia counted on the alliance of Frederick Barbarossa: the Emperor had him burned at the stake without a second thought (Frugoni 1954: 41–79). As for popular religion, it often showed even less tolerance than the Church towards many itinerant preachers or religious movements: for instance, in Soisson in 1114, whilst the Bishop was in Beauvais seeking instructions from a higher authority, the *populus* burned at the stake some imprisoned heretics to make sure they did not get off with a milder sentence.[61] A similar fate was meted out by his audience to Peter of Bruis in 1113 in Saint-Gilles. Indeed, until the middle of the thirteenth century, popular intolerance remained the greatest danger for many heretic groups.[62]

The ideologies of *communitas* and of structure also clashed in the dispute between urban clerics and schoolmasters, who supported a rational explanation of faith, and the twelfth-century representatives of new ideological *communitas*, the Cistercians and the Premonstratensians. The founder of the Premonstratensian order, Norbert, and two leading figures among the Cistercians, Bernard of Clairvaux and Guillaume de Saint-Thierry, conducted what almost amounted to a crusade against Abelard; indeed, they succeeded in having his views declared heretic.[63] The campaign against the urban intelligentsia and the value of schools found support in some anti-intellectualistic passages of the Bible and in a mysticism of Eastern origin. The most important mystical propaganda document of the twelfth century, a eulogy for the Carthusians (who take a vow of silence), was written by Guillaume de Saint-Thierry in the course of the debate with Abelard.[64] Norbert was dissuaded by his companions from going to study in Laon, since he had already learned everything that mattered in 'the school of the Holy Ghost'.[65] The often-quoted letters written by Bernard of Clairvaux gave similar advice: 'Believe him who has already tried it out: there is far more to be gained from forests than from books. The trees and the stones will teach you things that you will never hear from school-masters'; 'in the shade of the trees you will become aware of what you could never learn at school.'[66]

The alternatives that existed within medieval Christian culture could be played off against one another. The best illustration of this is the ecclesiastical policy of Pope Innocent III (1198–1216), which amounted to a second reform of the Church. The Papacy lent its support to the universities, at that time struggling for existence against the local secular and Church powers, and at the beginning of the thirteenth century placed them under its own direct jurisdiction. The Papacy also realised that budding scholasticism, that theoretical armament of the twelfth-century intelligentsia, could also be used to give dogmatic support to a Catholicism under threat from various heresies.[67] It was in view of such considerations that the Papacy gave certain twelfth-century religious movements official Church permission to proclaim and to practise the *communitas* ideals of the Gospel. Popular heretical symbols were put to the service of the Church by the Humiliati of Milan, by the Poor Catholics (seceded from the Waldenses) and by the Franciscans of Umbria. In fact, they became the main champions in the struggle against heresy.[68] The same applied, to an even greater extent, to the Dominican mendicant order, which was initially formed by deliberately appropriating the propaganda methods of the heretics and then turning these against them.[69] However, the mendicant orders, which determined religiosity in the thirteenth century, achieved more than simply stopping the upsurge of centripetal endeavours. They fully exploited, on several fronts, their own particular variant of the *communitas* ideals. After entering the universities, they quickly gained leading positions and prevented the excessive secularization of secular masters.[70] At the same time, they used the ideals of voluntary poverty and of asceticism to exercise greater control over secular culture and popular religion; they attacked fashion, luxury and the values of courtly–chivalric culture, and they initiated a new campaign against popular 'superstitions'.[71]

4

Fashionable Beards and
Heretic Rags

---

*Life is content with an even tongueless philosophy, my very attire is
eloquent. A philosopher, in fact, is heard so long as he is seen. My very sight
puts vices to blush.*

Tertullian, On the Pallium

In a *fabliau* dating from the twelfth century entitled *The Ill-fitting Coat*, a
wandering knight who turns up at the court of King Arthur offers a
fantastic garment as a gift:

> He adroitly produces a cloak the like of which had never been seen. Indeed!
> The work of fairies! Dazzlingly beautiful, made of a lovely, unknown
> material. I do not know myself what it is made of. But I will tell you
> something else quite unheard of about it: the fairy who made it put the
> power to discover false ladies in the cloth. If the woman who puts it on has
> betrayed her husband in any way, it will never fit correctly. And the same is
> true for maidens who have wronged their lovers; the coat will never fit but
> will be either too long or too short.[1]

One by one, the ladies in waiting try on the cloak, at first eagerly, then
reluctantly, finally only by order of the King; but it fits none of them: the
foot, the knee or the bottom sticks out. At last however, one lady is found
whom it fits perfectly because of her unblemished fidelity.

On further reflection, the fable concerns not only the fidelity of women,
but also the symbolism of costumes. The magic cloak – like all
garments – tells us important things about the identity of its wearer. At
the same time, being *magic*, it also discloses what its wearer wishes to
hide: it reveals his – or her – true nature. Clothes can be a disguise: one
can constantly change one's identity by means of external appearances.

The magic cloak will not permit any possible divergence between the proclaimed message and the truth: the outside shows what the inside is like – it fits only those who merit it. A strange, not necessarily desirable, Utopia, which at the same time expresses some of the medieval dissatisfaction regarding the ambiguous and uncertain symbolism of clothes.

In the Middle Ages, the norms regarding clothes were based on the nearly timeless precept that differentiations in social structure should be recognized by means of dress, hair and beard.[2] However, at the same time – thanks to Christianity – clothes were endowed with a number of moral–symbolic interpretations. The hidden anomalies in this system were brought to the surface by a gradual change in attitude between the eleventh and thirteenth centuries. This resulted in fierce arguments with regard to dress and beards. The controversy was caused on the one hand by the fashions prevalent at royal and aristocratic courts, and on the other by the symbolic attire of the ascetic religious movements, which opposed in equal measure the opulence of the Church *and* of the laity. However, before giving an account of this strange 'semiotic warfare', let us survey two aspects briefly: the views Christianity inherited from Antiquity and the authorities supporting it in the symbolic interpretation of man's outward appearance.

*   *   *

Beginning with a quotation, let us pay attention to Isaiah's prophetic address to the ancients of his people and its princes:

> You have ravaged the vineyard, and the spoils of the poor are in your houses. Is it nothing to you that you crush my people and grind the faces of the poor? . . . Then the Lord said: Because the women of Zion hold themselves high and walk with necks outstretched and wanton glances, moving with mincing gait and jingling feet, the Lord will give the women of Zion bald heads, the Lord will strip their foreheads. In that day the Lord will take away all finery: anklets, necklaces, lockets, charms, signets, nose-rings, fine dresses, mantles, cloaks, flounced skirts, scarves of gauze, kerchiefs of linen, turbans, and flowing veils. So instead of perfume you shall have the stench of decay, and a rope in place of a girdle, baldness instead of hair elegantly coiled, a loin-cloth of sacking instead of a mantle, and branding instead of beauty . . . (Isaiah 3: 14–24)

The invective of the Prophet Isaiah makes us realize that dressing luxuriously is not just stealing the 'spoils of the poor'; it promotes sinful temptation and the futile pleasures of this world. Therefore it is to be abolished and replaced by the sackcloth of penitence. But the shabby clothes of the ascetic represented more than mere penitence: apart from eschewing worldy vanities, they proclaimed sympathy with the underdogs of society; they opposed the prominence of affluence and beauty; and – in the terminology of Victor Turner – they expressed the principles of 'anti-structure' and of *communitas*.³ It is no coincidence that this humble attire became a kind of uniform, first for the Prophets, then for the proselytizing Apostles: Isaiah himself 'walked naked and barefoot for three years' (Isaiah 20: 3). Elijah was 'a hairy man with a leather apron around his waist' (II Kings 1: 8) and John the Baptist's clothing 'was a rough coat of camel's hair with a leather belt round his waist' (Matthew 3:4). Jesus instructed his disciples to take 'no pack for the road, no second coat, no shoes, no sticks' on their journeys (Matthew 10:10). He knew that their humble attire would lend credence to their preaching.

The moral principles proclaimed through the external signs of voluntary poverty were spectacular and self-explanatory – thus protest movements have always been only too keen to use them as weapons. Humble attire was first formed into an ideology in the fourth century BC by Cynic philosophers. They followed the example of a barefooted, roughly clad Socrates, who proclaimed the richness of the have-nots. Diogenes 'the dog' wrote: 'I walk in a double coat, with a beggar's sack on my shoulder, a walking stick in my hand . . . I live not by human prejudice, but according to nature, directly under Zeus . . .' He allegedly defended his attire before 'Plato the Sage' with the following words:

> You despise my coat and begging sack, these heavy, uncomfortable articles of clothing, but you are wrong. They may be heavy and uncomfortable for you, because you are accustomed to tickling your palate at the banquets of tyrants; you adorn yourself with the wool of sheep, not with the virtues of your soul . . . but in my opinion, I benefit mankind more than most people, not only with my possessions, but because everyone sees me exactly as I am. . . . my soul is free of wicked desires and vainglory, it is truthful and contemptuous of all lies.⁴

It is important to mention the symbolism of Cynic attire when describing Christian ascetic dress, because the Cynic movement was vigorously revived during the spread of Christianity in the decadent imperial civilization of the second century. Indeed, more than once, contemporaries linked the two movements and their similar appearance. For example, Peregrine, who 'grew his hair long, wrapped himself in a rough cloak, put a sack over his shoulder and carried a stick', was a Christian missionary before he began preaching Cynic philosophy.⁵ In Rome, in the middle of the second century, Justin, the famous apologian, wears a 'philosopher's dress', the so-called *pallium*. At the end of the second century, in missionary vein, Tertullian recommends the same attire to the men of Carthage, saying: 'A better philosophy has now designed to honour thee, ever since thou hast begun to be a Christian's vesture!'[6]

Let us recall some of the justifications for Cynic dressing in the late Antique period, as interpreted by Lucian:

> You there – he asks the Cynic – why in heaven's name have you the beard and the long hair, but no shirt? Why do you expose your body to view, and go barefooted, adopting by choice this nomadic antisocial and bestial life? Why unlike all others do you abuse your body by ever inflicting on it what it likes least, wandering around and prepared to sleep anywhere at all on hard ground, so that your old cloak carries about a plentiful supply of filth, though it was never fine or soft or gay?

The Cynic, after denouncing the wastefulness of civilization and praising the wholesomeness of nature, the example of the gods, of the heroes and of the ancient manly virtues, finally summarizes his philosophy in the following words:

> . . . never may I reach out for more than my share, but be able to put up with less than my share. Such, you see, are our wishes, wishes assuredly far different from those of most men. Nor is it any wonder that we differ from them in dress when we differ so much from them in principles too . . . If good men need one particular dress of their own, what would be more suitable than this dress which seems quite shameless to the debauched men and which they would most deprecate for themsevles? . . . this worn cloak which you mock, and my long hair and my dress are so effective that they enable me to live a quiet life doing what I want to do and keeping the company of my choice.[7]

Although the ascetic–symbolic attire tended by its very nature to be men's wear, both among the Cynics and the Christians, it nevertheless aimed for a symbolic abolition of differences between the sexes, as well as between social classes. This was prevalent in both the prophetic and early Christian tradition. For instance, we read the following in the apocryphal gospel of Thomas: 'Jesus said to them: "When you make the two one, and make the inside like the outside, and the outside like the inside, and the upper side like the under side, and [in such a way] that you make the man [with] the woman a single one, in order that the man is not a man and the woman is not a woman . . . then you will go into [the Kingdom]." '[8] In contrast with these extreme manifestations of anti-structure, both the Old and the New Testaments adhere rigidly to the basic tenets of structure: differentiation between the sexes. As Mosaic law prescribes: 'A woman shall not be clothed with man's apparel: neither shall a man use woman's apparel. For he that doeth these things is abominable before God' (5 Moses 22:5). St Paul also has a few remarks to make about hairstyle: 'Doth not even nature itself teach you that a man indeed, if he nourish his hair, it is a shame unto him? But, if a woman nourish her hair, it is a glory to her; for her hair is given to her as a covering' (I Corinthians 11: 14–15).

Regarding man's appearance, the Bible gives us two different views, thus reflecting the inconsistency characteristic of early Christianity, which I have already discussed in greater detail.[9] On the one hand, we have the poverty–ascetism symbolism in anti-structure–*communitas*; on the other, the strict separation of male–female indicators, in order to strengthen symbolically the social differences within Christian communities.

The same ambivalence is to be seen in the writings of the Church Fathers about the first centuries of the Christian Church. In the third and fourth centuries, Egyptian hermits and monks attempted to return to the apostolic way of life, in a manner comparable to medieval religious movements: they imitated the dress of the Prophets and Apostles and tried to outdo them in ascetic fervour.[10] According to chronicles, some hermits had only their bodily hair to protect them from the cold of the winter and the heat of the summer, once their clothes disintegrated completely.[11] Others declared that a clean body and clothes were the signs of an unclean soul.[12] At any rate, the rejection of worldly attire in favour of beggarly clothes became a minimum requirement for hermits and monks. For instance, we are told of the Abbot Arsenius who lived in the fourth century: 'While he lived in a palace, he dressed better than anyone else, but after joining the monks, he wore more humble clothes than anybody else.'[13]

As Antique monasticism was becoming firmly established, humble attire contributed significantly to the survival of a normative *communitas*: it gave a formal framework to a way of life according to the Gospel. From the time of St Pachomius, the ritual start to a new life of religion was marked by discarding worldly attire and adopting a monk's habit.[14] Cassianus wrote in the fifth century that this ritual means 'not only that he has been despoiled of his former things but also that he has put aside all worldly pomp and descended into the poverty and necessity of Christ and that he should now . . . receive the stipend of his service from the holy and pious grants of the monastery and, knowing that he will henceforth be clothed and fed therefrom, he will have nothing, and yet will not be solicitous for the morrow'.[15] So, apart from the moral message, monastic attire became a uniform for monks, who – though equal among themselves – were dependent on a monastery;[16] at the same time, the attire served as a distinguishing sign for different communities.[17] Naturally its symbolic meaning remained and, indeed, it became an effective weapon of propaganda for the Christian way of life – especially from the fourth century onward, when the number of monastic comunities increased, not only in the desert, but also in towns. It is in this sense that the monastic example is referred to in the fourth century by St John Chrysostom (347–407), who was Archbishop of Constantinople and a fanatical ascetic:

> Those who desire public esteem, wealth and luxury, ought to be taken to the communities of these holy men – there would be no need for my words after that. . . . No wonder that the poor complain among themselves, saying: 'executioners, the riff-raff, the children of slaves, whores and pimps have a more respectable appearance than us, who were born free and earn our living with honest work. We couldn't dream of the wealth they possess. . . . ' . . . But on seeing the monks, they are reminded of the very opposite. They see the sons of rich and distinguished people in clothes that even the poorest among them would scorn. And they also see that these people are happy in these humble clothes. Think of the solace this gives to the poor and needy. While the rich, if they visit such places, may well feel ashamed and return home in a more modest, reformed frame of mind.[18]

Here we can speak of a deliberate ideological exploitation of the symbols of ascetic dressing: for the poor and for the critics of social differences, a solace; for the rich, a moral improvement.

A similar ideological and normative change occurred during the third and fourth centuries when criticism of affluence and of luxury was replaced by a campaign against 'female finery' (a divergence also made use of by the Prophet Isaiah). This point of view considered the symbolic meaning of dress in relation to sexuality and carnality rather than to social structure. This was in keeping with the development that, at that same period, accorded increasing religious and symbolic content to sexuality – or rather to its restriction through marriage or chastity.[19] Thus carnality headed the list of secular values to be rejected with the help of external signs.

Tertullian recommended to Christian virgins the model of 'Arabia's heathen females . . . who cover not only the head but the faces also', arguing for the compulsory wearing of veils.[20] He also defined the manner and amount of physical grooming permissible for women seeking to please their husband:

> Do go forth [to meet them] already arrayed in the cosmetics and ornaments of prophets and apostles; drawing your whiteness from simplicity, your ruddy hue from modesty; painting your eyes with bashfulness, and your

mouth with silence; implanting in your ears the words of God; fitting on
your necks the yoke of Christ. Submit your head to your husbands and you
will be enough adorned . . . Clothe yourselves with the silk of uprightness,
the fine linen of holiness, the purple of modesty.[21]

The apostolic 'constitution' in the *Didascalia* gave a similar warning to
husbands in the middle of the third century: 'You also shall not grow the
hair of your head but cut it off; and you shall not comb and adorn it nor
perfume it, so that you do not bring upon you those women who are out to
capture or are captured by lust. You also shall not clothe yourself in
beautiful garment and also not be shod on your feet with shoes whose
workmanship is of the lust of foolishness.' It also admonished women:
'You therefore, woman, shall not adorn yourself that you may please
other men. And you shall not be plaited with the dresses of harlotry, nor
clothe yourself in the garment of harlotry nor be shod with shoes so that
you resemble those who are in this way.'[22] Thus came into being the most
effective analogy for restraining women's fashion: the adornment of
the body equals 'harlotry'. In the same spirit, Clement of Alexandria (d.
circa 215), St Cyprian (200–258), St Jerome (*circa* 342–420) and St
Chrysostom all pursued their zealous activity to achieve the regulation of
female dress styles.[23]

So we can see that the original symbolic interpretation of dress styles
formulated by ancient Christianity underwent considerable change over
the centuries. It was moderated into a monastic uniform with a ritual
function, a propaganda weapon for the Church and a regulator of
women's embellishment. Even the Church was forced to dissociate itself
from its original meaning, which was being revived by movements now
deemed heretic, such as the Gnostics and the Messalians. St Jerome
cautioned one of his followers, saying: 'Avoid men, also, when you see
them loaded with chains and wearing their hair long like women, contrary
to the apostle's precept, not to speak of beards like those of goats, black
coats, and bare feet braving the cold. All these things are tokens of the
devil.'[24]

It is no wonder that the symbols of dress were discredited through this
manifold and contradictory usage. Lucian condemned as trickery the
appearance of the Cynics and claimed that they had gold in their
haversacks instead of black bread.[25] In the fifth century, Salvianus, a
presbyter from Marseilles, argued with representatives of the ascetic view,
saying: 'Do not think that you can practise the lie of a monastic life by
wearing a habit, the lie of loyalty with a chain belt, or the lie of sanctity
with your cloak (*pallium*) . . .'[26] Let this warning stand as the final point
in the presentation of the 'Antique heritage'.

With the fall of the Roman Empire, both the topic of luxury and the arguments regarding the moral value of humble attire were thrust into the background for a lengthy period. This is understandable, since humble dressing can acquire a symbolic religious function only when affluence and luxury pose a problem. It is no coincidence that in AD 816 the Synod of Aachen, laying down regulations for the dress of the Benedictine monks, stressed that monks should *not* wear the humblest (*vilis*) of clothes, or the most expensive, but something in between.[27] Criticism of luxury in dressing and pronouncements about the normative views of man's appearance and humble, ascetic attire, for the sake either of propaganda or of ideology, do not recur until the eleventh century; it was only then that medieval society emerged from subsistence economy, and certain sections of it, mainly the aristocracy, were in a position to indulge once again in luxury.

*   *   *

We do not know very much about the mode of dress in the early Middle Ages. Fragmentary data show dress to be an ethno-political sign, like the beard of the Longobards, or Theoderic's long hair, worn as a royal emblem;[28] and, later, the similarly charismatic role of long hair in the Merovingian dynasty (Schramm 1954–56, I: 119, 229; Hoyoux 1948). Charlemagne's decree on dressing issued in 808, which regulated the attire of social categories, certainly indicated that even then clothes were an expression of social differences.[29] The importance and conscious consideration of ethnic differences in dress become evident from Charlemagne's biographies, which all emphasize that

> he wore the national dress of the Franks. Next to his skin he had a linen shirt and linen drawers; and then long hose and a tunic edged with silk. He wore shoes on his feet and bands of cloth wound round his legs. In winter he protected his chest and shoulders with a jerkin made of otter skins or ermine. He wrapped himself in a blue cloak and always had a sword strapped to his side, with a hilt and belt of gold or silver. . . . He hated the clothes of other countries, no matter how becoming they might be, and he would never consent to wear them. The only exception to this was one day in Rome when Pope Hadrian entreated him to put on a long tunic and a Greek mantle, and to wear shoes made in the Roman fashion; and then a second time, when Leo, Hadrian's successor, persuaded him to do the same thing.[30]

We learn from the chronicle of Notker that Charlemagne compelled his subjects to respect and to continue to wear Frankish attire when they tried to replace their 'old ways', first by the 'short striped tunic' of their 'Gallic enemies', then by the short tunic of the Friesians, instead of wearing their own style of long clothes.[31]

The problem of luxury with regard to clothes first reappeared in the tenth century as a phenomenon characteristic of the other half of Christianity – Byzantium. Liutprand of Cremona, returning from Byzantium in 968 filled with the poor neighbour's jealousy, contrasted the 'effeminate', long-haired, fox-like appearance of the Byzantine Emperor with the bearded, manly image of the Frankish King. However, luxury, this long-forgotten problem of fashion, was soon causing trouble also in the Occidental sphere of Christianity. The first alarming manifestations were noted around the middle of the tenth century by Ratherius, the Bishop of Verona. Then Bruno, the Bishop of Cologne, brother of Emperor Otto I, also dissociated himself from the luxury seekers: 'He frequently declined to wear the kinds of soft and fine clothing in which he had grown up and come to manhood, even when he visited the courts of kings. Amidst purple garbed courtiers and knights radiant in gold, he wore simple robes and rustic sheepskins.'[32]

By the beginning of the eleventh century, a veritable wave of fashion is reported by Raoul Glaber, a chronicler at the turn of the millennium. The courtiers of Queen Constance, third wife of the French King Robert the Pious, caused a scandal in 1002. Among them the men were the worst offenders.

> Men puffed up with every sort of levity, corrupt in manners and in dress, dissolute in their use of arms and the embellishments on their horses, cutting their hair as far back as the middle of the head, shaving their beards like actors, utterly obscene in their style of hose and leggings. . . . They show no respect for faith or peaceful harmony, and – oh, what shame! – the Franks and the Burgundians, who were once counted among the noblest of nations, have begun to imitate them eagerly, competing with them in perversity. . . . [33]

The new style continued to spread in accordance with the rules and caprice of fashion: the French blamed the southerners for these scandalous customs, while the Germans held the French responsible. Siegfried, the Abbot of Gorze, complained in 1043:

> The honour of the kingdom, which in the reigns of previous emperors flourished most decently, not only in respect to clothes and custom but also feats of arms and chivalry, in our days is brushed aside, and the scandalous rule of French frivolities displaces it. Men cut their beards, for instance, and – shameful to behold! – they shorten and deform their garments in a manner most vile and execrable. . . . They seek out the ways of dress of foreigners, and their perversities cannot be far behind. They are striving in

all ways to be like their enemies, men plotting against them, and, more lamentable still, such men not only avoid correction, but are taken into the close favour of the king and of certain other princes. . . . Others, putting aside all shame, then strive to do likewise, seeing their fellows rewarded and unpunished; they even strive to think up mad novelties on a still greater scale.[34]

The arguments are worthy of attention. The main anxiety of eleventh-century clergy was that the scandalous new fashions would overturn society's moral order, which increasingly came to mean a strict differentiation of social categories. For instance, the fashion for shaving appropriated the distinguishing feature of the clergy, for they were the only ones to shave in the early Middle Ages. In the middle of the eleventh century, a Bavarian monk reported that a young nobleman, although innocent, was found guilty in a blasphemy trial just because he was clean shaven.[35] The anecdote about William the Conqueror is in the same vein: his army is supposed to have caused panic among the English at the Battle of Hastings in 1066 because they assumed that the smooth-faced enemy soldiers were clergymen.[36]

In the 1030s, the confusion in dress-signs – Cluniac monks, for instance, indulged in knightly splendour – was one of the factors that provoked Adalbéron, Bishop of Laon, to formulate clearly his celebrated theory on the three orders of medieval society.[37]

However, before going into clerical reaction to the medieval emergence of fashion, let us examine a second wave of fashion, handed down to us in the shocked descriptions of contemporaries at the end of the eleventh century. By then, the once outrageous novelties had become the custom, and the new 'hooligans' – young courtiers and urbanites in northern France and England – drew attention to themselves with their long beards, long curly hair, wide, full-length robes and that peculiar novelty, 'pulley shoes' – all in complete contrast to earlier fashions.

The first detailed description of the new fashion is from 1094, from the Court of William (Rufus) II, King of England. St Anselm, who had recently arrived from France to take up office as Archbishop of Canterbury, was extremely shocked by the conditions he found. 'Now at this time it was the fashion for nearly all the young men of the Court to grow their hair long like girls; then, with locks well combed, glancing about them and winking in ungodly fashion, they would daily walk abroad with delicate steps and mincing gait. . . .'[38] Two well-known chroniclers from the first half of the twelfth century, William Malmesbury[39] and Orderic Vital, drawing on Eadmer's descriptions from the beginning of the century, gave a vivid account of the English court, accused of immorality and sodomy. Let us quote Vital's passionate words:

> After the death of Pope Gregory and William the Bastard and other pious leaders, the healthy customs of our fathers almost wholly disappeared in the regions of the west. Our ancestors used to wear decent clothes, well-adapted to the shape of their bodies; they were skilled horsemen and swift runners, ready for all seemly undertakings. But in these days the old customs have almost wholly given way to new fads. Our wanton youth is sunk in effeminacy, and courtiers, fawning, seek the favours of women with every kind of lewdness. They add excrescences like serpents' tails to the tips of their toes where the body ends, and gaze with admiration on these scorpion-like shapes. They sweep the dusty ground with the unnecessary trains of their robes and mantles; their long, wide sleeves cover their hands whatever they do; impeded by these frivolities they are almost incapable of walking quickly or doing any kind of useful work. They shave the front part of their head, like thieves, and let their hair grow very long at the back, like harlots. Up to now penitents and prisoners and pilgrims have normally been unshaven, with long beards, and in this way have publicly proclaimed their condition of penance or captivity or pilgrimage. But now almost all our fellow countrymen are crazy and wear little beards, openly proclaiming by such a token that they revel in filthy lusts like stinking goats. They curl their hair with hot irons and cover their heads with a fillet or a cap. Scarcely any knight appears in public with his head uncovered and decently shorn according to the apostle's precept. So in their outward dress and bearing they reveal their character and show in what fashion they follow the narrow path of God.[40]

It is difficult to form an exact picture of how the new fashion spread. It seems to have appeared first in northern France and extended from there to the British Isles. According to Orderic Vital, the pulley shoes were an innovation of Fulco, Prince of Anjou, who wanted to hide 'his ugly bunions'.[41]

The first clerical condemnation of long hair and long dress came from the Walloon Tournai. There, the ravages of an epidemic of ulcerous dermatitis called the 'fire of St Anthony' were blamed by Bishop Ratbode on 'disorderly clothes and hair'. 'He summoned the members of the entire parish to the Church of the Holy Virgin . . . and cut short the long hair and floor-length clothing of more than a thousand young men, because their purpose was dissipation and there was no need for them.'[42]

This odd ritual of cutting men's hair and clothes was regularly repeated during these decades. St Anselm also resorted to this measure in the court of William Rufus II in 1904, on Ash Wednesday, when he blessed only those 'whose hair was cut in a manly fashion'.[43] In the court of the English King, Henry I, it was Bishop Serlo who shortened the curls of the courtiers.

> When he had finished speaking the king consented in a mood of elation, as did all his magnates, and the bishop, ready for action, immediately drew scissors from his cloak-bag and proceeded to cut the hair, first of the king, and then of the count [of Meulan] and most of the magnates with his own hands. The king's whole household and all who flocked to follow their example were close-shorn; dreading a royal decree they anticipated it by cutting off the tresses they had hitherto treasured, and trod their once-cherished locks under foot as contemptible refuse.[44]

The Church backed up these actions with further decrees. In 1096 the Synod of Rouen barred from churches any man whose hair was not cut 'in a manner not befitting a Christian'.[45] In 1102 the Synod of London introduced a similar interdict.[46] But all this did not prevent a change in public taste and opinion. By around 1130 in Flanders it was the man who did *not* wear a long beard who was considered 'ridiculous and effeminate'.[47]

Despite the sparse data and the moralists' biased exaggerations, nevertheless a clear picture emerges: in eleventh-century Western Europe, we are dealing not simply with scandals brought about by extravagant dress, but with the cultural appearance of the modern operation of fashion. Here, too, fashion was responsible for periodic changes in human appearance, sometimes going from one extreme to the other, with regard to dress, accessories, hairstyle and beard. When studying the fluctuations in modern fashions, A. L. Kroeber discovered surprisingly systematic cycles. During the past 300 years, the dimensions of women's evening dress (length, width, decolletage, etc.) changed every 50–60 years from one extreme to the other (from minimum to maximum). Although the validity of this finding is unlikely to go back as far as medieval cycles of fashion, it is gratifying to ascertain a similar rhythm in the eleventh-century fashions discussed above; short, tight-fitting styles were followed by long, loose, baggy ones (Kroeber and Richardson 1940; see Young 1937).

What is even more striking is that another connection demonstrated in modern fashions is equally applicable: the fluctuation in the fashion of the male beard and hairstyles follows the changes in female dress: when women wear short dresses, men shave, whilst men wear beards when long dresses are the fashion for women (Robinson 1976). Apart from the cyclical aspect, another important feature of modern fashions is to be found in the fluctuation of medieval fashions: the way in which they spread within society. Styles usually enter a cultural community from the outside; inside they spread vertically downwards, following the steps of cultural vulgarization. Orderic Vital makes special mention of the fact that the extreme fashions among knights 'were soon imitated by the burghers, then by the peasants and finally by all the common people'.[48] The dissemination of fashion is infectious, unstoppable; at the same time, once it has spread it stops being a fashion – it turns into mere habit.

The appearance of fashion in the eleventh century was the result of cultural exchanges within medieval civilization. Simultaneously, fashion itself stimulated the absorption of culture and the more intensive exchange and traffic of cultural products. However, whilst the traditional mode of dressing – i.e. according to social categories, the sexes and ethnic groups – fitted easily into the institutional rules of a closed ideological system, fashion immediately conflicted with the differentiations of 'structure' and the Christian view regarding the symbolic functions of dressing. Let us survey, from these two points of view, two popular fashions in the eleventh century.

The attacks on the new ways of dressing and their 'morality' – no matter how much they remind us of the perennial arguments against fashion – corresponded to the aspirations of the Church in the eleventh and twelfth centuries. They attest to the attention paid to lay society by the Catholic Church, just then in the process of the Gregorian reform. The priests and the monks of the period tried to promote the 'Christianization' of lay society and its submission to increased Church control by working out moral doctrines that satisfied the basic requirements of lay society – the principles of 'structure' – whilst reconciling them with Christian values. These purposes were served by the sanctification of marriage, by the movement called the 'Truce of God', and by the Crusades, which directed the aggressive energies of the militant nobility outside the Christian world.[49] The criticism of fashion fits into this conception. But it also demonstrates how deeply the Church moralists of the eleventh and twelfth centuries were rooted in the warrior values of the early feudal era: the criticisms did not include complaints about the immorality of women (it was not until the arrival of chivalric poetry in the twelfth century that women's fashion was mentioned in detail) – the main fear was that aggressive male virtues would become extinct in society.

In connection with the fashion of shaving, Siegfried, the Abbot of Gorze, grieved for the bygone German courtly virtues at the beginning of the eleventh century. Yet this same fashion was considered by Orderic Vital as the embodiment of ancestral manly virtues, and it was the new fashion of long curly hair that became the symbol of femininity, causing young men to be likened to girls, even to whores. St Anselm cut youngsters' ringlets into 'a manly shape', and another bishop would not allow Knights to join the Christmas procession until they shortened their hair with their own swords.[50] 'All of you wear your hair in woman's fashion, which is not seemly for you who are made in the image of God and ought to use your strength like men. . . . By growing their hair long they make themselves seem like imitators of women, and by womanly softness they lose their manly strength and are led to sin, and often fall wretchedly into hateful apostasy.' Thus ran the sermon given by Bishop Serlo to the household of Henry I. And when he finished, he pulled out a pair of scissors from his sleeve. According to him, even the wearing of beards made the young stray from the path of manly virtues. Although one could hardly regard beards as feminine, nevertheless they promoted fornication: 'They refrain from shaving their beards for fear that the short bristles should prick their mistresses when they kiss them, and in their hairiness make themselves more like Saracens than Christians.'[51]

The civilization based on courtly–chivalric ideals came into being at this period. The Church opposed to this lifestyle the ideal of *miles Christi*, setting the Crusades as an aim, and the chivalric orders that were being formed in the wake of the first Crusade as an example. The Knight beseeching his Lady's favours and the Knight going into battle to defend Christianity present two different courtly ideals. They were contrasted by Bernard of Clairvaux in his proclamation glorifying the Templars (1136). Appearance and clothes play a central part here too – the worldly vanities of fashion prevent a Christian Knight from fulfilling his function, which is fighting:

> As you probably all know from experience, a brave fighter needs three basic qualities. Circumspection, agility and quickness in duelling and moving, and bravery to wound and kill the enemy. Why then do you let your hair grow like women; the locks hanging into your eyes hinder your capacity to see. Your arms are weighed down with puffy sleeves, you have difficulty in reaching out from them with your hands. . . .

The ascetic fighter serving religious aims is the exact opposite of all this:

> his hair is cut very short, for the Apostle himself said that it was shameful for a man to wear long hair; he never combs his hair and seldom washes; he goes around with a stubble and covered in dust, his body is chastised with an iron shirt and worn out by the heat . . . he is disgusted with the plays of jesters, storytellers or singers, and he despises frivolous love songs. . . .[52]

It was no accident that Bernard of Clairvaux linked the criticism of fashion with a general rejection of the courtly–knightly culture, of *l'amour courtois* and the poetry of the troubadours, which all began to flourish just at that time. He realized that they stemmed from the same source: the centrifugal endeavour that tried to make room for the values of a secular culture within medieval Christianity.

But neither St Bernard, nor his contemporaries, found satisfactory arguments to counteract the attraction of fashion. It was in vain that priests and monks pronounced the fashionable apparel unmanly, immoral and unsuitable for knightly functions: they were not the ones to prescribe the norms of manliness, the manner of knightly fighting or courtly etiquette. And it was utterly useless to advance the argument that fashions confused the distinguishing signs that were meant to separate the individual categories of social structure; that the followers of these fashions looked like clowns or priests with their shaven faces; that they resembled condemned prisoners with their shaven foreheads; or little girls, whores or even penitents with their long hair; or the Saracens with their silk garments.[53] The followers of fashion have sufficiently sharp eyes to realize when a dress sign does not distinguish them to their satisfaction. Fashion aims to refine distinctions, not to blur them. It is only outsiders who are confused by dress signs – which rather amuses secular fashion experts and certainly does not worry or disturb them.

One of the reasons why the objections to fashion were so feeble was that the representatives of the Church – having ignored this problem for centuries – were no longer sure how to interpret the symbolism of dressing, and applied the relevant Christian views inconsistently. Although they mentioned again and again that dress signs also mirrored man's faith, in reality a good Christian was to them someone who followed the rules obediently. They did not understand the symbolic value of certain signs and there was no logic in their impressionistic interpretations. All this is well illustrated by the judgements on the most shocking fashions in the eleventh century: men's beards and hairstyles.

*   *   *

Let us first take another look at the heritage of Antiquity. In the judgement of beards and hairstyles within late-Antique Christianity, the influence of tradition is the same as in the judgement of dress: the manly naturalistic ideals of the Cynics, the use of symbols by the Jews (as recorded in the Old Testament) and the ideals of civilization in late-Antique Rome. As far as the Cynics were concerned, they considered hirsuteness, long hair and a beard, as much 'an ornament of man, as a mane is for a horse or for a lion'. These features were also a symbolic opposition to the civilization of the unmanly 'debauched' wastrels who 'smooth and depilate every part of their bodies, not even allowing any of their private parts to remain in its natural condition'.[54]

The beard was a symbol not only of manliness, but also of wisdom, and the Cynics capitalized on their sense of symbolism by adopting the prestigious 'philosopher's beard'. It is possible that the tradition of portraying St Paul with a conventional long beard also has its origins here, namely through the influence of Plotinos' bearded statues.[55] Long hair and a beard are also symbols of male strength among the Jews. Mosaic law and the story of Samson prove that the cutting of hair or beard was not favoured (3 Moses 19:27, 21:5; Judges 16:17). It was through the same belief that the Prophets who rejected society, the Apostles and later the Egyptian monks let their hair, beard and bodily hair grow long. At the same time, like the Cynics, they rejected the Roman custom of shaving and depilation. There is a long list of bearded Prophets, Apostles and monks, the best-known being St Bartholomew, whose special distinguishing features were 'his black curly hair, hanging down over his ears, his pale face, large eyes and his long beard, touched with white'.[56] The *Didascalia* also recommended this naturalistic view to Christian men of the third century:

> Do not adorn the beauty of your nature which is given you from God . . . it is not lawful to grow the hair of your head and to comb it and wipe it, for this is a pleasure of lust . . . You shall not destroy the hairs of your beard and you shall not alter the form of the nature of your face and change it beyond God's creation because you wish to please men.[57]

Respect for the natural state also explains the indignation of Churchmen at women's use of cosmetics, hair dyes and wigs:

> For they who rub their skin with medicaments, stain their cheeks with rouge, make their eyes prominent with antimony, sin against Him. To them, I suppose, the plastic skill of God is displeasing! In their own persons, I suppose, they convict, they censure, the Artificer of all things . . . Whatever is born is the work of God. Whatever, then, is plastered on [that], is the devil's work. To super-induce on a divine work Satan's ingenuities, how criminal is it!

– writes Tertullian.[58]

The naturalistic view of beards and hairstyles and the symbolism attached to it implied vigour, wisdom, energy, ocassionally even sexual potency (Leach 1958). This view is not contradicted by the fact that in exceptional cases (on the occasions of disasters or at times of mourning) both Jewish and Christian ritual prescribed the tearing, or even complete shaving, of hair and beard. The Prophets might even call upon the whole nation to do this: the breaking of taboos has a ritual function in all religions; it helps to distinguish between everyday and exceptional situations.

During Antiquity, when it came to official stipulations on attire for Christian priests, monks and penitents of a special religious category, the Church was faced with the following dilemma: should they prescribe for the clergy the naturalistic view and the ascetic norms of hermits; or should they pronounce the shaving under extraordinary conditions as a symbol indicating the rejection of worldly values? After a debate lasting several centuries, the decisions were contradictory. Canon 25 of the *Statuta ecclesiae antiqua* at the end of the fifth century, usually attributed to the fourth Synod of Carthage in 436, decreed that 'a cleric should neither grow his hair, nor cut his beard'. The Greek Orthodox Church still adheres to this decree. Nevertheless, it was the Romans' custom of shaving that was handed down to the Middle Ages by the Roman Church. Through incorrect copying, they altered the meaning of the above canon to its opposite (either by leaving out the word 'cut', or by inserting the word 'but' in front of it).[59] This was supplemented, from the seventh century onwards, by the requirement of a further haircut, the tonsure. The beard and hairstyle of monks seemed to follow more closely the ascetic norms: both St Augustine and St Jerome – though not with complete approval – mentioned the long-haired bearded monks (*criniti fratres*). Later however, just as in the case of non-monastic priests, the Western and Eastern Churches went their separate ways: while the latter remained bearded, the former continued to shave and wear a tonsure – as we find out from the *Regula* of Columban.[60] As for penitents, from the time of St Jerome they were sometimes ordered to grow their hair and beard for the duration of their penitence, while at other times they were to shave completely.[61]

When medieval clerics began to reinterpret their inherited symbols, the already confused system of meanings became even more complicated. St Gregory the Great, commenting on Job's cutting his hair, compared hair to 'superfluous thoughts born of the soul'; hence he advised that it should be cut.[62] Isidore of Seville compared the tonsure-cut of clerics to 'the cleansing of the body from sin'.[63] According to the twelfth-century Honorius of Autun, the tonsure gave clerics a 'childlike' purity, as well as being a 'sacrifice to God'.[64] 'He rejected the secular way of life [*saeculum*], cut his hair and beard': we can read this about a number of ninth–eleventh-century saints with regard to the beginning of their monastic life.[65] The Benedictine order, which turned the cutting of hair and beard into a ritual event to be accompanied by benedictions, also shared the view that those who cut their hair 'rid the body and soul of sin, when removing the curls growing on their heads'. We read this in the writings of the Abbot Smaragdus at the beginning of the ninth century.[66]

So hair and beard, as symbols of virility, acquired in the Middle Ages a more 'sexualized' meaning than at any previous period. This is the dominant interpretation in the critiques of fashion by Orderic Vital, which we have already discussed. Let us quote here the most relevant passage, attributed to Bishop Serlo. The latter endeavoured to deter men at the English royal court from letting their hair and beard grow long by giving the following interpretation to the appearance of penitents:

> It is not for beauty or pleasure that penitents are instructed not to shave or cut their hair, but so that those who, in the sight of God, are bristling with sins and unkempt within, may walk outwardly bristling and unshorn before men, and proclaim by their outward disgrace the baseness of the inner man. Long beards give them the look of he-goats, whose filthy viciousness is shamefully imitated by the degradations of fornicators and sodomites, and they are rightly abominated by decent men for the foulness of their vile lusts. . . . This punishment is just, for their nature is also stained by fornication. With their long locks, these penitents resemble women, and this proves that they have sinfully abandoned male steadfastness for the sake of female softness. . . .[67]

We may add to these descriptions the text of Hugh of St Victor, writing in the middle of the twelfth century, who compared the tonsure to circumcision and the shorn 'superfluous' hair to the foreskin.[68] Bearing all this in mind, we have to take into account the psychoanalytically based anthropological theory that considers the cutting of hair and beard as a symbolic castration. It would certainly have explanatory value with regard to clerics in the tenth–twelfth centuries (Leach 1958; Hallpike 1969).

The accumulation of status symbols, religious symbolism, sexual connotations and all kinds of obscure interpretations (for instance, according to the twelfth-century Paris theologian, Jean Beleth, beards were formed from secretions in the stomach[69]) makes twelfth-century debates about beards and hairstyles rather confused. It is no coincidence that the only comprehensive treatise on beards in the Middle Ages, Burchard of Bellevaux's *Apologia de Barbis*, was written at this time.[70] The Cistercian Abbot wrote his work for Cistercian lay brethren, called *barbati*, to explain the importance and meaning of their custom:

> We [monks] wear a crown on our heads by cutting a tonsure in our hair; we also cut our beards, thereby baring our souls, because we strive for perfection in spirit and soul, cropping every unnecessary worldly sentiment

and desire. You [lay brethren] do not have a tonsure and do not cut your beards, because you lead humble lives, working the soil. . . . We, beardless and tonsured, sow in your souls and harvest in your bodies, since – bearded and long-haired – you work for us and you are protected and comforted by your long hair and your beard outdoors, in the cold winter weather. . . .[71]

This entertaining work summarizes the above-mentioned points: Biblical allusions and a series of 'exterior' and symbolic meanings. Burchard gives a detailed list of fashionable beards, secular as well as religious: he makes fun of 'the bird-tail beard', the 'forked beard', the 'curly beard': and the 'military beard' (which is shaved round the ears).[72] There is no comprehensive solution to these contradictory interpretations, because, as Burchard astutely points out: 'since there is a time for everything, and since different people like and are suited to different things, there is a right time for growing hair and beards, just as [there is a right time] for cutting them, depending on how people interpret their hidden religious meaning [*sacramentum*], or good manners and decency in their customs.'[73]

*   *   *

In the twelfth century, the external signs of both the Church and secular society were becoming increasingly diverse and the value judgements on them more and more contradictory. This led to the recognition and acceptance of an increasing diversity in the meaning of symbols. Yet, at the same time, there was an attempt to bring back less ambiguous valuations. The eleventh and twelfth centuries brought not only the renaissance of secular culture and fashion, but also the emergence of the religious movements that tried to revive a radical interpretation of Christianity. Together with the values of anti-structure and *communitas*, there was a reappearance of the symbols that used to represent them among the early Christians and the Egyptian monks.

In the Church of the early Middle Ages, the required appearance for penitents was humble, unkempt attire, bare feet, and long hair and beard. In accordance with the then commonly known symbolism of Christian dress, the early Fathers of the Church prescribed the attire that seemed to them most suitable for those desiring purification. As I demonstrated above, all this was regarded by medieval clerics and even laymen as the mark of shame, the instrument of expiation and the special distinguishing sign of members of a certain religious category. The return to the original religious meaning of these symbols was advanced by two new phenomena in the eleventh century: the spread of the hermit movements and of pilgrimages.

We have already spoken of hermits, who were the first in the Middle Ages to proclaim the religious purpose of the apostolic way of life. Their attire expressed the complete rejection of civilized life and they sought means to mortify the body, which they considered the seat of sinful desires. At the beginning of the twelfth century, the following was written about Stephen Muret, founder of the order of Grandmont: 'He tried to submit his body to strict self-restraint and to make it follow his spiritual endeavours. He took up the fight against the deceitful body and the fickle soul by wearing a hairshirt which cut into his flesh, and by completely wearing out his body he succeeded in triumphing over himself'[74] By this time, the hermit garb (*melota*) made of rough cloth, the barefootedness and slovenly appearance had a definite religious value for hermits. We cannot speak of symbolism yet: the attire is here more the means to achieve religious perfection, just one in a whole list of ascetic techniques (self-flagellation, chains, ropes and belts worn under the habit, sleeping on a stone bed and all kinds of other self-torturing inventions).[75] Nevertheless, to the outside observer, these methods must have been criteria of sanctity – providing anyone was able to witness with their own eyes these solitary champions of asceticism.

On the other hand, they could see, in ever-increasing numbers, the groups of pilgrims who were now appearing in the wake of the brisk commerce of the eleventh century and the Crusades, aimed at conquering the Holy Land. A pilgrimage was often a means of penitence, so pilgrims in general wore the attire prescribed for penitents. But a pilgrimage could also be a voluntary undertaking, in a spirit of adventure, in the hope of a miraculous cure, or through true religious incentive. At any rate, the clothing worn by pilgrims differed in one essential aspect from that worn by penitents: pilgrims did not wish to humiliate themselves before their family or close community, and their appearance reflected the way of life and ideals of a religious community advancing towards a sacred goal and hoping for purification through the universal values and relics of Christianity (Labande 1958: 168–9). As Victor Turner showed in his fine analysis, a pilgrimage provided the conditions appropriate to preparing the participants for absorbing the religious ideals of *communitas*. This happened automatically, since pilgrims were removed from their families, their homes, their work, their entire ordinary lives (Turner 1974: 166–230; 1978). It is no coincidence therefore that pilgrims, and those observing them, could have easy access to the symbolic interpretation of humble attire and the evangelical doctrine of voluntary poverty. This is illustrated by one of the most popular legends of the Middle Ages, the legend of St Alexis, which appeared in the eleventh century, not only in Latin, but in a splendid French version written in verse.[76] Alexis flees from his home and lovely young wife in Rome, because 'he loved God more than his family'. The last scenes of the story paint a moving picture of Alexis as a pilgrim. His shabby rags and long, dishevelled hair lend his appearance a misleading aspect, but also provide it with a strange religious value. After long years of wandering, he returns to his home, but his parents do not recognize him until he is on his deathbed and, too late, they reproach themselves for their blindness.[77] Presumably, after hearing the story, the audience was expected to look differently on pilgrims in rags.

At the beginning of the twelfth century, wandering preachers and their followers could gain prestige from their attire, which proclaimed voluntary poverty and a marginal way of life. Descriptions of them repeatedly give details of their startling appearance. Peter the Hermit, who preached in support of the Crusaders, 'walked in his bare feet, over his naked body he wore a rough woollen tunic, which he covered with an ankle-length cloak and a hood made of frieze.'[78] Robert d'Arbrissel, who preached in the Loire region, 'covers his naked body with a habit made of hair-cloth and with torn bits of frieze. His bare legs show from under his rags, he has a thick beard, but cuts his hair short above his forehead and goes among the people in his bare feet.'[79] A monk compares the heretic Henry of Le Mans to a leper, on account of his 'torn and filthy clothes'.[80] Henry's appearance in Le Mans in 1116 was chronicled thus: 'Hair cropped, beard untrimmed, tall of stature, quick of pace, he glided along the ground barefoot as winter raged; easy of address, awe-inspiring in voice, young in years, scornful of ornate dress.'[81] Arnold of Brescia 'tortured his body by fasting and by wearing clothes made of rough material' and 'his disciples who imitated his austere customs won the trust of the people with their modest appearance and way of life.'[82]

Representatives of the Church had nothing but half-hearted, clumsy arguments to advance against the powerful dress symbols of the heretic wandering preachers, with their apostolic lifestyles and prophet-like appearance. As Otto of Freysing wrote about Arnold of Brescia: 'His clothes proclaim religion, but his doctrines do not serve it in any way.'[83] Marbod, the Bishop of Rennes, while reprimanding Robert d'Arbrissel, tried to argue for some kind of 'golden mean':

> Even when wearing humble clothes, let common sense and the authority of custom guide you. . . . True, it is immoral to long for precious possessions, but it is folly to avoid conventional yet cheap clothes. Your dress does not need to glitter, but it does not have to be filthy either. It is more praiseworthy to show humility in silk clothes than to parade arrogantly in rags.[84]

Such counter-arguments did not in the least detract from the religious credit of the lifestyle of these new apostles, or from the popularity of the evangelical *communitas* ideals they proclaimed. There was the rare occasion when the unusual-looking preachers were received with distrust: for instance, the inhabitants of the Loire region took Bernard of Tyron's community for Saracens, because of their long beards and 'slovenly clothes, quite unlike those of monks'.[85] Most often, however, the hostile feelings were dispelled when 'God's new prophets' supported their lifestyle with convincing arguments and criticisms of luxury in the Church. In Le Mans, there were 'sobbing clerics, sitting at the feet of the preaching Henry' and 'the crowd threw mud and dirt at the priests who tried to argue with him'.[86]

Henry of Le Mans expressed his ideology of dress not only through his own appearance, but also by his methods of conversion. When he decided to persuade prostitutes in Le Mans to lead a better life, 'he called on all women who up to then had been leading an immoral life, to take off all their clothes and burn their dresses and hairlocks in front of everyone.' After that, 'all the street-girls were given a piece of material costing four solidi, hardly enough to cover their nakedness, then, on Henry's demand, the young men of the town married them all.'[87] The basic idea behind this sensational ceremony was that 'the naked should wed the naked', without dowry or Church blessing, simply by agreement. It is noteworthy that Henry associated the cutting of hairlocks and the burning of ornate dresses with the renunciation of immoral lifestyles. And he linked the beginning of a new life with the donning of humble attire – which was also the custom among monks.

Dress had an important part to play in the attitude of even those wandering preachers who did not criticize the ruling Church from the viewpoint of poverty. Tanchelm of Flanders and the Breton Eon de Stella – if we are to believe descriptions of them – infringed the dress norms set by the Church from the opposite extreme: they wore provocatively ornate, extravagant clothes. Tanchelm, who led such a pure life that his disciples venerated him with an almost God-like respect and even drank his bathwater, 'wore glittering, gilded clothes and tied gold-embroidered ribbons in his three long plaits.'[88]

But all this simply lends colour to an otherwise bleak picture: religious movements in the twelfth century found their way back to a strict interpretation of the dress symbols of voluntary poverty. This gave them a useful weapon against the wealthy Church and its splendidly attired prelates. The orthodox wing of these same religious movements, acknowledged as reformed monastic orders (the Cistercians, Premonstratensians and Gilbertines), did make an attempt to reform clerical and monastic dress. (This for instance, was the main subject of the criticism brought by Bernard of Clairvaux against Cluny.)[89] However, their puritan appearance could not compete with the prophetic look of the wandering preachers and heretics, who presented the more varied symbols of the marginal lifestyle. Nor could they be a match for the boost that the rapid growth in the poor marginal population in the second half of the twelfth century gave the heretics in their criticism of luxury.

Members of the Catharist sect calling themselves 'the Poor of Christ', and their *perfects* who vowed to lead an ideal life, (Borst 1953: 203–8) arranged their appearance according to the well-known formula: 'they go about in their bare feet, are thin and pale through fasting',[90] they grow their beard[91] and often their hair is also long, 'like a woman's'.[92] They differed, however, from their predecessors the wandering preachers, in being able to make a more conscious use of dress symbols in their debates against the Church. For instance, in 1165, in Lombers in the South of France, they reproached the Bishops for 'wearing white, sparkling clothes and jewelled gold rings on their fingers'.[93] At the beginning of the thirteenth century, during a debate with the papal legates, who were preaching against the Albigensians, the Catharists referred to their own way of dressing: 'How can you believe these people who preach to you the word of our poor and humble Lord so arrogantly, from horseback, fitted out with such luxurious things? We, on the other hand, preach the word of Christ while living in poverty, humility and self-restraint. Everything we tell you is supported by our own actions and way of life.'[94]

However, with the gradual development of the Catharist counter-church, the apostolic way of life and voluntary poverty were increasingly overshadowed. In the course of the thirteenth century, the Catharists tried to recruit new followers, not so much through the moral values of their lifestyle, but rather with the efficacy of the rites and sacraments in their own church, along with their dualist myths (Borst 1953: 120–8). On the other hand, the Waldensian movement, which appeared around 1170, based all its endeavours on the idea of voluntary poverty. Peter Valdes' first followers set off on their missionary tours in pairs, barefoot, wearing coarse woollen clothes, living on alms. In other words, they modelled themselves on the Apostles.[95] Like the Catharists, they opposed the established Church and believed that dress fulfilled an ideological function: 'The masters of the Roman Church are conceited both in their mode of dress and in their morals', were the opening words of a statement by a Waldensian preacher at the beginning of the thirteenth century.[96]

The Waldenses came to be commonly known as the *Insabbatati* or *Sandaliati* (sandal-wearers) because they introduced the wearing of sandals after the apostolic model.[97] However, the sandal rapidly became the privilege of chosen elite functionaries within the Waldensian sect – similar to the Catharist *perfects*. The sandals signified that their wearers – by dint of their lifestyle – were entitled to administer the sacrament to followers of the sect.[98] A similar change in the use of dress symbols was even more pronounced within the Catharist sect. In the

thirteenth century, the dress of the Catharist *perfects* – a long brown or
black cloak – became a virtual uniform whose role was more sacramental
than ideological.[99] In the South of France there were female Catharist
communities with a lifestyle similar to that of nuns. Among them the
donning of a 'heretic's dress' fulfilled the same function as in the monastic
orders: this act signified the beginning of a 'pure lifestyle', when they
received the appellation, 'dressed-up' heretic woman (*heretica vestita*).[100]
But the heretic counter-churches were also subject to the habitual transformations which affect religious movements when they became institutionalized: they too, could only pass on the spontaneous ideals of
communitas by means of normative *communitas* – through changing
their original symbols into ideological–ritual functions.

*   *   *

By the beginning of the thirteenth century, the largest religious
movements of the twelfth century were on the threshhold of becoming a
church. Meanwhile, the established Church had learned from them how
to make ideological use of dress symbols and was now turning this
knowledge against them. I have already mentioned the anti-heretical
attitude of the more moderate religious movements sanctioned by the
Papacy. Here I would like to discuss in more detail the function of dress
symbols in this connection.

The first religious movement to be restored to favour, the sect of the
Humiliati, continued to stipulate as one of its most important requirements that its members 'should not put on bright clothes but be satisfied
with the most simple kind'.[101] Some renegade Waldenses returned to the
bosom of the Church with the new name of Poor Catholics, under the
leadership of Durandus de Osca and Bernard Prim. But they remained so
attached to their former appearance – long hair like laymen and Waldensian sandals – that people continued to regard them as heretics, no matter
how much they preached against the Catharists. Pope Innocent III had to
issue a number of strong warnings to persuade them to wear a tonsure and
conventional footwear.[102] The last off-shoot of twelfth-century religious
endeavours, the Franciscan movement, initially combined the Waldensian
lifestyle of voluntary poverty and begging with the earlier models of
hermitic asceticism. Some of its followers wore chains under their habits
until St Francis forbade this practice, deeming it senseless.[103]

The new orders, which brought the symbols of the apostolic lifestyle
into line with those of the Church, signified a double gain for the Church.
In the eyes of laymen they helped to restore the shaken religious authority
of the Church. They also succeeded in invalidating the heretics' justifications for their dress and religious lifestyle. What is more, by making
better use of the same ideological symbols, they turned the tables: by the

beginning of the thirteenth century, the mendicant orders were accusing the Catharists of being in league with usurers and the rich (Borst 1953: 188–9).

The consciously Machiavellian character of papal ecclesiastical policy can be seen in the foundation of the other mendicant order, the Dominicans. From 1206, the Spanish Bishop Diego of Osma and Dominic preached as papal legates in the Albigensian region. They soon realized that they could only compete successfully with the popularity of the heretic *perfects* if they and their companions also wore apostolic dress at debates. From then on, they too appeared in towns in humble clothes, walking barefoot, begging and preaching against the heretics.[104] Innocent III immediately lent his support to their reform, and that same year recommended this example to others as the most effective approach to countering the heretics.[105] and, while the Franciscans continued for centuries to wear the mark of their origins as a religious movement, the Dominicans were organized as a Church order from the very beginning. For the latter the system of values of the religious movements and the idea of voluntary poverty were only aspects of the many ways to fight the heretics. They were not as important as theological erudition, the preparation of scholastic polemics, or keen inquisitorial activity. Yet, in spite of their differences, the Franciscans and Dominicans made use of Christian dress symbols in similar ways in order to stabilize the Christian symbolic universe. This proved not only to be an excellent tactic in the struggle against the heretics, but also brought about a new approach to the criticism of lay fashions and made possible their more efficient control.

The moral preaching by the mendicant orders of the thirteenth century rediscovered the most effective argument used by the Prophets and the Apostles: populist demagogy. In their criticism of fashions, they coupled the moral objections of their twelfth-century predecessors with the evangelical rejection of wealth and luxury: 'we do not see the wives of peasants and burghers wearing dresses with long trains; only those women who count themselves among the nobility drag these behind them. But the trains of the noble ladies are superfluous, and many a poor woman could have a whole dress from this surplus. . . .' ran the preaching of Etienne de Bourbon against the fashion of long trains on women's dresses at the beginning of the tirteenth century.[106] But the mendicant orders were not content with proclaiming their persuasive new arguments in varied forms and in different places; they also found institutional ways of regulating society. They organized lay religious corporations as third orders. The members of these, whilst not renouncing their families or secular lifestyle, tried to follow the principles of the friars.

The rules for these 'penitent brotherhoods' and third orders began, almost without exception, with prescriptions for dress: 'The members of this brotherhood are to buy clothes made of plain, undyed woollen cloth . . .'[107]

The propaganda of the mendicant orders brought secular dress nearer to the religious–ascetic system of symbols. Parallel to this, the Papacy, which by now relied on the mendicant orders, tried to discipline secular dress after the fourth Synod of Lateran (1215) by making the wearing of distinguishing signs compulsory. This affected mainly the three principal enemies of Christian society: the heretics, the Saracens and the Jews. After 1229 the heretics had to proclaim their religious error by sewing a yellow cross on the front and back of their dress. For the Jews, as a result of pressure by the Synod of Lateran, the wearing of various marks of disgrace became compulsory from the 1220s in Italy, France, Spain, England and Germany. These could be red or yellow circular signs (*rota, rouelle*); Jew's hat (*Judenhut*); or ribbons, veils, or earrings.[108]

Apart from propaganda conducted by means of religious symbols and the branding of enemies of the faith, the mendicant orders could not forgo the third important dimension: theoretical systematization. In the second half of the thirteenth century, Guilielmus Peraldus produced an all-embracing scholastic summary, entitled *Of Virtues and Sins*.[109]

In a somewhat drier style than the Cistercian Abbot writing on beards, but employing the methods of the new theological science, Peraldus produced arguments first about the adornment of the body, then about dress; all this accompanied by warning examples, a list of 'the twelve follies of embellishment', specific criticisms of various adornments (train, sandal straps, beribboned headdress, wigs, etc.) and manifold illustrations of the guilt of women who wore beautiful dresses.

Thus in the first half of the thirteenth century, a hitherto unthought of system of regulations came into being. Its aim was to restrain secular attire, which was becoming increasingly splendid and colourful both at court and among the bourgeoisie. The success of the ideals promoted by the mendicant orders was mainly due to the huge, campaigning lay religious movements, such as the *Alleluia* movement in 1233 and the Italian peace campaign in 1260.[110] Their vast membership reinforced the influence of the mendicant orders with the same evangelical religious principles that had supported the heretic movements in the twelfth century – albeit at the expense of the feudal lords, the urban aristocracy and the Bishops.[111] It is true that certain heretic movements – similar to those of the twelfth century – did emerge in this last wave of the voluntary poverty movement, such as the radical *Saccati*, the *Fraticelli*, who had broken away from the Franciscans, or the Apostolic Brethren, led by Segarelli. However, the propaganda of the mendicant orders was able to combat these movements in the same way as it had countered the earlier heretic criticisms. At the same time, they made good use of the influence they had gained in the towns of Italy and in the South of France in order to crush secular culture: they introduced decrees prohibiting the wearing of luxurious dresses, jewellery, or materials woven with gold thread. And they compelled women to cut their hair or to wear a head covering.[112]

The mendicant orders mounted their most vigorous campaign against the heretics in the South of France. Here, the main victims of the Crusades, the representatives of the chivalric culture of the 'Midi', soon begin to object to the pressure put on them. Guilhem Montanhagol, a Toulouse poet, wrote the following in a satirical poem aimed at the friars: 'If he leads a pure life, no man becomes the enemy of God by putting on beautiful clothes. Just as they [the friars] will not go to Heaven, merely because they wear a white cowl and a black habit. . . .'[113] We have reached here, again, the most pertinent objection to symbolic–ascetic attire: 'a man does not become a hermit on account of what he wears', says Rutebeuf. In the *Dit dou Sourcetain*, we read that clothes (*roubes*) can be lies (*lobes*), and that the barefooted, begging monks are nothing but cheats: in the *Roman de la rose*, Jean de Meun calls them simply the *faux-semblant*.[114] It is no coincidence that these arguments, which had existed before but by this time had acquired the status of proverbs,[115] were voiced with increasing frequency during the thirteenth century. Whilst fashion broke the norms of clothing only tacitly, in practice, the opinion that 'clothes maketh not man' opposed the concept of a symbolic way of dressing itself.

By the end of the Middle Ages, the ideological use of symbols by the mendicant orders, and the reaction to this, detracted from the religious value of the dress symbols described above and discredited the *communitas* ideal derived from the Gospel. This explains a great deal about the religious values adopted in the late Middle Ages, which differed from those current in the twelfth century; above all, it makes it clear why these late medieval religious movements turned towards self-deification and the development of a mystical, individual relationship with God (Lerner 1972). The loss of credibility of dress symbolism also accounts for the fact that among some sections of late-medieval religious movements another symbol came to embody the ideals of Christian *communitas*: the collective nudity of the Adamites (Werner 1959). However, there is no scope here for a deeper analysis of these issues.

On the other hand, it is important to note that the ideological and institutional regulation of dress in the form of increasingly strict decrees on dress styles, functioned not just until the disintegration of the medieval Christian culture. Indeed, certain restrictions have survived to turn up in diverse guises even in our own time. It seems that fashions have to repeat the fight for their existence from one era to the next (Eisenbart 1962). Nor did the symbolism of Christian dress die out: in the late Middle Ages, it was embraced by the Beguines and the Beghards; it also reappears in modern times among several Messianic movements, within sects and among the Utopian practitioners of the ideals of *communitas*. It was even to be found, not that long ago, in the appearance and dress of the hippies.

But what about the magic coat that truly fits only the person who has merited it through his virtues; the magic coat that can reveal the true inner nature of its wearer; the magic coat of the *fabliau* that I mentioned in my introduction? Are we still waiting for that coat – or aren't we?

5

From Sacral Kingship to Self-Representation: Hungarian and European Royal Saints

For the year 1083 the early thirteenth-century *Annales Posonienses* record the following events: King Solomon 'is put into prison, King Stephen, his son Henry and Bishop Gerard are elevated and King Solomon flees.'[1] This brief account conveys the essence of the first canonizations in Hungary, initiated by King Ladislaus I (1077–95). Having defeated, expelled and later (when he tried to regain power) jailed his cousin Solomon, the legitimately crowned king of Hungary (1063–74) Ladislaus had now been ruling for seven years without being crowned. Although his power was firmly established, he seems to have thought it judicious to strengthen his legitimacy (which was based on the rather archaic principle of *idoneitas*) by establishing a cult of sainthood focused on the person of Stephen I (1000–1038), the first Christian king of Hungary and the first personification of the Christian charisma of the Arpadian dynasty. By becoming the patron of this cult (and of that of Stephen's son Henry, who died young before he could succeed his father), Ladislaus could effectively present himself as Stephen's true heir and definitively eliminate his rival Solomon (Györffy 1977a: 393–4; 1977b: 542ff).

It is from this basic perspective that I should like to approach the problem of royal sainthood in medieval Hungary: by describing how these religious cults were employed for political ends. Without denying other aspects of these cults, I will consider them as distinct forms within the vast complex of the sacral legitimation of kingship in the Middle Ages. The cult of holy kings, princes, queens, princesses and the claim of sainthood for entire dynasties have their own long history (see Górski 1969; Nelson

1973; Hoffmann 1975, Folz 1984). The evolution of these cults and their chronological and geographical distribution present an instructive example of continuity and change in the Middle Ages. We can observe here how similar institutions and similar ideas were used and interpreted differently according to different ages and settings.

The history of royal saints in Hungary offers the possibility of shedding light on several different stages of this evolution in Europe from the eleventh to the thirteenth centuries. Before describing this in detail, however, it is necessary to give a brief account of how this model of sainthood evolved up to the eleventh century.

*   *   *

The model of royal sainthood originated in the early Middle Ages, drawing elements from three different traditions: the sacral and divine attributes of Hellenistic rulers and Roman emperors (Taylor 1931; Alföldi 1970; Price 1984), perpetuated in the Middle Ages by Byzantium; the 'charismatic' qualities ascribed to Germanic and other medieval pagan princes or kings (Vries 1956; Sacral 1959); and of course the cult of Christian saints, formed in late Antiquity (Brown 1981). Nevertheless, the concept of royal sainthood cannot be regarded as a Christianized version of the first two traditions, or as a secular and political distortion of the third – the formation of this new model of sacral kingship and royal sainthood took place over several centuries. Karl Hauck's seminal thesis (1950) treated royal sainthood as a Christian variant of the Germanic *Königsheil*, a power inherited by the members of certain dynasties (who claimed it through divine descent), a power that assured victory in battle, fertility and well-being in peace. Hauck's intriguing and widely accepted hypothesis has been justly criticized by František Graus, who found counter-examples among the first holy kings of medieval Europe, those of the Merovingian period (Graus 1965; 313–34, 390–432). Graus pointed out that the saint kings and princes (the Burgundian Sigismond – 523; the Vizigothic Hermenegild – 585; and the Merovingian Clodowald – sixth century) as well as the holy queens of the period (Clothilde, wife of Clovis I; Utrogotha, wife of Childebert I; Radegonde – 518–87 – wife of Clothar I; and Bathilde – 657 – wife of Clovis II) acquired the title of sainthood not as a sacral dimension of their function as rulers, but, on the contrary, rather because they abdicated, retired to a monastery, or suffered martyrdom.

This of course does not mean that in popular belief or even in the self-image of the rulers of Merovingian times there were no traces of the notion of the sacral character of kingship. Legends and supernatural powers were attached to Gunthram (592): it was asserted that, while sleeping, his soul left his body in the form of a lizard and discovered treasure hidden on the other side of the nearby river – a 'soul-journey' demonstrating clear shamanistic traits (Lixfeld 1972). Dagobert II (656–61, 676–79), who became a cult figure long after his death, was believed to have been a promoter of fertility (Folz 1963). These and other legends testify to the persistence throughout this era of sacral ideas connected to kingship. The same could be said about the magical meanings attached to the long hair that was the charismatic attribute of the Merovingian kings (Hoyoux 1948). One could say the Merovingian rulers had less need to display the Christian saintly attributes, because they could preserve in some measure their pre-Christian ones. On the other hand, one can understand why the Merovingian Churchmen resisted an eventual transformation of the image of the Christian saint: in its original form, the figure of holy man was the diametrical counterpart of the representative of the secular power, balancing the latter's authority with that of God, and correcting (often by his own self-sacrifice) the effects of the latter's injustice (see Brown 1981: 100–20).

Nevertheless, the multiplication of royal and princely saints, however insignificant as rulers and humble as persons they were reputed to have been, contributed in the long run to the formation of a model of royal sainthood, in which royal functions themselves could be interpreted as saintly attributes. We can see the first steps toward this in the cult of Saint Bathilde, who earned respect not only by her life as a nun after her retreat, but even before that by her policy as regent, supporting new ecclesiastical foundations, collecting relics, reducing taxes, prohibiting the trade in Christian serfs (Nelson 1978). In the same period – that is, in the seventh century – we can observe the emergence of this new model in Anglo-Saxon Christianity.

Alongside the significant instances in Anglo-Saxon royal sainthood of the 'Merovingian' model of holy kings who abdicated and became monks – Caedwalla (685–8) and Ina (726), kings of Wessex; Sebbi (694), king of East Saxony; Ethelred (774–84), king of Mercia (Hoffmann 1975: 16–17) – the cults of several Anglo-Saxon kings from the seventh to the tenth centuries were able to combine the pagan cult of Woden-descendant kings (Chaney 1970: 7–33) with the new model of Christian saints, uniting martyrdom with the idea of the perfect Christian ruler. Oswald (641) of Northumbria, Oswin (651) of Deira, Ethelbert (794) and Edmund (839) of East Anglia, and the Anglo-Saxon Edward (978) are the most noteworthy representatives of this type. The pagan aspect of these cults is illustrated by the holy trees, springs and animals associated with them in the legends of the following centuries (Chaney 1970: 64, 131–5; Hoffmann 1975: 32–8, 52–3). These concepts are also attested to in Alcuin's letter to Aethelred, king of Northumbria (793): 'We read that the king's goodness equals the welfare of the whole people, victory of the host, mild climate, fertility, male offspring and health.'[2] Note here that this notion of the leader invested with supernatural powers and thus providing magical protection for his own community is based upon the archaic religious model of beneficent sorcery, of shamanism. As for the Christian aspect, royal sainthood incorporated the values of the *rex iustus*, who converted his people to Christianity, supported church institutions, and waged war on paganism to the point of dying a martyr's death. Hagiography assists this assimilation by identifying the betrayed, suffering martyr king with Jesus Christ and his Passion (Hoffmann 1975: 23–31, 38–46).

Anglo-Saxon kingdoms were not only the forgers of the new religious model of holy kings, but were also the first to exploit these cults to achieve political goals. Under their patronage, the new cults became weapons in the struggles between rival dynasties, or against claims by pretenders. They were most frequently invented and used by those who were less favourably placed in the traditional system of inheritance. Oswald's relics were taken into custody by his brother Oswiu, who thus eliminated Oswald's son, the 'traitor' Ethelwald, from the succession (Hoffmann 1975: 28–9). New dynasties often tried to strengthen their roots by supporting cults of the saint kings of the preceding dynasty. Thus the cult of the last king of East Anglia, Saint Edmund (killed in 869 by the Vikings), was spread primarily by the succeeding Wessex rulers, Edward I, Aethelstan and Edmund I in the tenth century. And although Saint Edmund later became the symbol of battles against the Danes and was depicted as taking his revenge personally on Sven Forkbeard (who died shortly after demanding an unjust tribute from Saint Edmund's Abbey), Sven's son and successor, Knut the Great (1014–35), granted special privileges to the abbey and became a prodigious patron of the same cult (Hoffmann 1975: 44–6).

Marc Bloch has observed that new ruling dynasties always try to compensate for their inferior prestige with a new kind of sacral legitimation (1983: 79–85). In this context we observe that, while royal sainthood was more and more frequently utilized for such purposes in Britain, the Carolingians and the Ottonians (following Vizigoth and Byzantine examples) preferred another course: they revived the imperial traditions of sacrality and added to them with the newly invented Christian rites for sanctifying a ruler – unction and coronation (Nelson 1971; Bloch 1983: 64–74). The widening inventory of sacral emblems (Schramm 1954–6) was soon extended to include the ideology of the ruler as *vicarius Dei* and as possessor of 'two bodies': one personal and one sacral–institutional (Kantorowicz 1957; Ullmann 1963). The Ottonians crowned all this by collecting and redistributing holy relics (Leyser 1979: 75–108). When the Capetians come to power in France, we see yet another invention: the healing of the scrofulous by the miraculous 'royal touch', a capacity inherited within the dynasty but exercised only by consecrated kings on ritual occasions. This innovation was soon imported to England by the Plantagenets, who coupled it, characteristically enough, with the promotion of the cult of a new royal saint: Edward the Confessor (Bloch 1983: 27–49; Barlow 1980).

By the eleventh century we can see the cult of holy kings as an established – though by no means unique or even predominant – method of providing religious support for royal power. To identify it more exactly, we could call it the Anglo-Saxon way. However, the eleventh-century evolution and diffusion of the different forms of sacral legitimation of kingship in Europe require a further and different characterization. For the sake of brevity, let me adopt a model of 'core' and 'periphery' in medieval Christian Europe. Apart from the geographical convenience of viewing Europe from its late-Antique, Mediterranean centre, this dichotomy corresponds to the contemporary distinction between those territories Christianized for several centuries, and those only recently converted to the Christian faith. One gets the impression that already by the high Middle Ages core territories were hostile to royal sainthood and preferred a more distinctly institutional and elaborately symbolic formulation of royal sacrality. In this respect, sixth to seventh century Britain, cradle of the new form of royal sainthood, could be considered to be one of the peripheries of Latin Christianity, still in the process of conversion. The subsequent evolution of the sacral legitimation of kingship continued in line with the distinction sketched out above.

As for the 'core', let us select as an example Robert the Pious, second king of the emerging Capetians, and the first, according to the descriptions, to exercise the prestigious new rite of healing the scrofulous. In about 1040, one of the outstanding religious personalities of the age, Helgaud de Fleury, wrote a *Vita* of this king, to be read on every anniversary of his death, just as the saints' legends were (Helgaud 1965). In this document Robert was accorded all the attributes of a saint ruler, yet there is no evidence that the Capetians ever attempted his canonization. If we look at this document more closely, we can discover important new traits in the eleventh-century French conception of the king's sacrality and religious perfection (Carozzi 1981). The *Vita* (itself prepared for liturgical purposes) placed great emphasis on the liturgical sacrality of the king (*ordinatio, benedictio, assumptio in regem, unctio*), and on his liturgical function as *rex et sacerdos* – *sacerdos* is the sense of learning and also because of his personal supervision of the proper execution of liturgy both inside and outside the Church (Robert opposed the sacrilegious use of the Host in ordeals). Here too we can see the parallel between king and Christ. However, they were equated not in their martyr's death but at the level of their everyday perfection in life. Robert was said to be the first ruler who adopted voluntary poverty, he was a caring pastor of his flock, he healed afflictions, appeared frequently in public surrounded by twelve representatives of the poor (recalling the Apostles), and provided alms for many more.

As for the periphery, we can see the emerging popularity and the efficient political exploitation of royal sainthood in the countries newly converted to Christianity. Three examples should be mentioned in this respect: the Bohemian, the Norwegian and the Russian.

Saint Wenceslaus was murdered in 929 on the order of his mother Drahomira and his brother Boleslav. His personality was in many ways similar to that of the Merovingian and Anglo-Saxon royal saints. Wenceslaus was the typical unwilling ruler, characterized by his mother as 'spoilt by the priests to the point of becoming a monk': this is also illustrated by the fact that, instead of showing a firm hand, he ordered the gallows to be destroyed.[3] On the other hand, he suffered the martyr's death just as stoically as some of the Anglo-Saxon kings, and his cult acquired a political function just as quickly as the ones in Britain. Boleslav himself ordered the transfer of Wenceslaus' body to the castle of Prague three years after his death. In the eleventh century he was frequently mentioned as the chief patron of the Premysl dynasty and of the whole Czech people: he performed miracles for them in the battles against their Polish enemies (Graus 1975: 165–70). It is interesting to note that in the eleventh century the cult of his grandmother Ludmilla was annexed to his cult, completing the legendary image not only through the conversion of the Czechs (she was wife of Bořivoj, who is asserted to have initiated the conversion), but at the same time by enhancing the dynastic dimension of this royal sainthood.

The cult of Saint Olaf – adversary of Knut the Great, organizer of the Norwegian Christian Church, and one of the last descendants of the Ynglings to claim divine origin – began almost immediately after he was killed in the battle of Stiklestad (1030). In his cult we can observe a direct Anglo-Saxon influence, represented among others by Bishop Grimkel, invited to Norway by Oswald to organize the Church, and later one of the chief promoters of Olaf's cult. In the eleventh- and twelfth-century legends and sagas of Olaf, the usual themes are abundantly and comprehensively present: he dies like Christ pierced by a lance, his blood has a healing effect, his death is immediately followed by the eclipse of sun, drought and bad harvests, his corpse is revealed by a column of light, like that of Saint Oswald, his nails and his hair keep on growing after his death, as happened to Saint Edmund. The fate of his cult was also typical in that all the rival pretenders sought to profit from it. Sven, son of Knut the Great, tried to make use of it, as his father did with the cult of Saint Edmund: in 1031 he ordered the first laudatory poem about the new saint from Thoranin Loftunge. Olaf's son, Magnus, exiled to the court of the Russian prince Jaroslav the Wise, had his prospects rated higher by a notable Norwegian aristocrat, Einar Bogenschüttler. He was right: with Jaroslav's military support (and aided also by the saintly intervention of his father), Magnus returned victorious in 1035 and occupied the throne. The cult naturally flourished during his reign (1035–47), but was really exploited not by him, but by his uncle, Harald Haardrade, Olaf's half-brother, who succeeded the childless Magnus to the throne (1047–66) and, supported by the growing cult of Olaf, managed to secure the rule of Norway for his children (Hoffmann 1975: 58–89; Blom 1981; Nyberg 1981).

On the Eastern periphery of Christianity, in the Kievan Rus, the new faith and the new type of rulership were also backed by the cult of royal saints. The obvious candidate for assuming this role would have been the first Christian ruler, Vladimir, (1015), whose memory did indeed inspire such effective preparations as the eulogistic sermon pronounced around 1050 by metropolite Hilarion comparing the great ruler to Constantine (Müller 1962). His life and legend was written at the end of the eleventh century by a monk called Jacob, in whose account these analogies proliferated: Vladimir was called the thirteenth Apostle and the second Moses who made a second Jerusalem out of Kiev. Probably due to Bohemian influence, Vladimir's grandmother Olga was accorded a role of saintly conversion similar to that of Ludmilla, and was compared in this function to Helen, mother of Constantine.[4] None the less, despite spectacular scenes of Vladimir destroying the idols of Perun and Chor, it seems that this image of conversion was insufficient for a cult in eleventh century Russia because it lacked the popular theme of martyrdom – Vladimir only became canonized in the thirteenth century, and it was not his cult but rather that of his two martyr children that became the symbols of the Rurik dynasty in the eleventh century.

In 1015, after the death of Vladimir, his sons Boris–Roman and Gleb–David were slain by their elder brother Svyatopolk, who was defeated in his turn by a fourth half-brother, Jaroslav the Wise. Perhaps it was the firmness of Jaroslav's rule that made superfluous the institutionalization of the spontaneous cult of his brothers or that of his father. Instead, the cult of Boris and Gleb was propagated by Vseslav, prince of Polock, who, already in the 1050s had named his four sons Boris, Gleb and (making a separate use of the saints' Christian names) David and Roman. The same can be observed in the case of Jaroslav's two youngest sons, Vjatsheslav and Igor, who gave similar names to their children in 1055 and 1059, while the heir Isyaslav found nothing wrong in naming his son Svyatopolk in 1050. Nevertheless, the elder brethren were soon to realize the importance and the usefulness of the emerging dynastic cult, and they appropriated it by building a new church for the two martyrs in Vyshgorod, and by staging a solemn canonization in 1072. The three brothers Isyaslav, Svyatoslav and Vsevolod significantly chose to carry the relics of Boris and Gleb on their own shoulders at the solemn translation. Svyatoslav was not only blessed by the metropolite with the head of St Boris and with the hand of St Gleb, but he claimed to have one of St Gleb's fingernails lodged in his skull after the blessing, as a special favour of the saint.[5] We could compare this to the attitude of the Norwegian kings who reserved for themselves the privilege of personally cutting Saint Olaf's perpetually growing nails and hair: these kings had realised that they had to cling to these relics, their greatest treasures.

If we examine the Bohemian, Norwegian and Russian cults together, we can detect two common features, which were already present in the Anglo-Saxon cults but were more sharply accentuated here. These cults not only legitimated the claim of a certain branch of the ruling dynasty to retain power with the support of the cults they patronized, but, in fact, also contributed to the institutionalization of the new royal power. They constituted an intermediary phase between rulership bound to the innate virtues of a certain dynasty (constantly giving rise to rivalries between the pretenders) and the more stable hereditary order, where one lineage could assert its supremacy. How far the cult of the holy founding-father could promote institutionalization is demonstrated by the extreme case of Norway, where in the twelfth century, during a new challenge to the throne, the whole country was offered to Saint Olaf, *rex perpetuus Norvegiae*, and was governed by the kings by right as his vassals (Hoffmann 1975: 88–9). On the other hand, we should note another remarkable trait of these cults: they constituted an original type of sainthood. In the Anglo-Saxon and Scandinavian cases they melded the pre-Christian cults and the legendary elements of the sagas together with a special cult of royal martyrdom parallel to that of Christ. In the Bohemian and the Russian cases we find a further accentuation of this martyr aspect, almost to the extent of eclipsing the image of the ruler: Boris and Gleb – supported by the example of Wenceslaus, referred to in their eleventh-century *Passio* – constituted a special category in the family of aspirant Russian saints: the *strastoterptsy*, those who accepted martyrdom with a kind of mystical resignation (Ingham 1984).

*   *   *

Having sketched this 'core–periphery' model of the polarization of ideas and cults in the religious legitimation of rulership, we can situate the two important new cults of the end of the eleventh century – the Hungarian and the Danish – in an intermediary position between these two poles.

The first striking feature about the Hungarian canonizations in 1083 is the fact that this was not the establishment of a single cult or that of a pair of saints, but a series of canonizations lasting several months, providing the Hungarian Church with five native saints in a single campaign. The festivities started on the 16th of July with the elevation of Zoerard-Andrew and Benedict (two hermits who had lived at the beginning of the century) in the North of Hungary, in Nyitra.[6] Shortly after there followed the canonization of Bishop Gerard, who came from Italy to the court of Stephen, then became one of the dominant organizers of the Hungarian Church and was slain during the pagan uprising of 1046 near the mountain in Buda, which has since then borne his name.[7] The canonization took place in the south of Hungary, at his grave in Csanád, in the presence of King Ladislaus. The main event of this round of canonizations was, of course, the *elevatio* of the remains of Stephen, on which occasion a Diet was convoked at his grave in Székesfehérvár, on August the 15th, the anniversary of his death. His grave could be opened only after three days of fasting and the liberation of the imprisoned Solomon. There followed a series of miraculous healings, and on the 20th of August Stephen's corpse, 'spreading a delicious odour of balms', was exhumed and transferred to a new silver sarcophagus (Györffy 1977a: 389–90). Finally, on the 4th of November, again in Székesfehérvár, a new synod declared the canonization of Imre (Henry, Emery), Stephen's son.

If we look at the *Legenda Maior* of Saint Stephen, probably written just before the canonization (the author is unknown),[8] we can see that the aspirations of this deliberate state–Church policy went even further. Alongside the above-mentioned saints, all glorified in this legend and ranged around the person of Stephen as his holy team, we find allusions to the cult of Saint Martin, a major medieval saint popular in Hungary because of his Pannonian origin,[9] who became the patron of the first Benedictine monastery founded by Stephen at Pannonhalma in the year 1000. We hear, too, of Saint Adalbert, major apostle of Central Europe, national patron of the Bohemians and the Polish (probably the model for the canonization of Gerard);[10] and another future saint, the 'pious' Henry II, brother-in-law of Saint Stephen, is also mentioned (Klauser 1957; Pfaff 1963).

The complexity of this canonization programme reveals first that Ladislaus and his followers recognized the importance of the cult of saints tied to the royal dynasty and to the Hungarian Church, which until then had no saints of its own. The emergence of this strategy should be explained on two levels: by the internal need to which it responded and by the external influences from which it derived.

As regards Ladislaus's need for clearer legitimacy, which I have already hinted at, I must stress here that by these canonizations he was able to resolve the problem of the need for sacral legitimation of kingship, which his predecessors had already attempted to tackle. After renouncing the pagan sacral prestige of the Arpadian dynasty and accepting Christianity, Stephen's eleventh-century successors tried to rely upon the new sacral symbols and the actual support of the three major authorities of the age – the Papacy, the Holy Roman Empire and the Byzantine Empire. However, Andrew I (1046–61) supplemented the dynastic principle and foreign support with the title *Dei annuente*, and Géza I (1074–77) named himself *rex consecratus*.[11] Ladislaus seems to have had a highly superior understanding of how to manipulate superhuman powers. His skill is revealed not only by the successful project of the canonizations but also by the several legendary deeds attributed to him by the *Gesta Ungarorum*, written at the end of the eleventh century.[12] He had visions – in one of them his brother Géza was crowned, according to a Byzantine tradition, by an angel;[13] in battle, angels with fiery swords came to his aid;[14] he reinterpreted pagan traditions in Christian terms when a legendary stag carrying candles on his head indicated to him the site of a new church to be founded; 'this was no stag' – he is reported to have said – 'but an angel of God: it was not antlers that you saw but wings . . . and the place indicated by this angel is where we should build a house for the blessed Virgin.'[15]

It is small wonder that a ruler of such religious sensibility should appreciate the benefits of a new cult around the person of Stephen, the first Christian king of Hungary. The addition of Imre, whose historical character was much paler than his father's, can be explained as follows: Stephen (with the help of one of his learned clerks) accomplished the *Admonitions* to his son Imre, a text prepared for the education of his future heir, describing how an ideal Christian ruler should behave.[16] According to the chronicles, Imre indeed acquired all the virtues and capacities required, but was not able to exercise them because of his early death (1031). In the account of the chronicle, Stephen's successors all possessed only some of the required virtues, which explains their short-comings; whereas Ladislaus actually possessed them all, so he could be considered a kind of reincarnation of Imre, the true heir of Saint Stephen, as it were.[17] As for Gerard, it was not only the model and the popularity of Adalbert that accounted for his canonization, but also two further facts. First, paganism was still a menacing problem in Hungary – in 1061 there had been a second pagan uprising, against which the cult of the bishop killed in the first uprising was mainly directed. Second, just a few years before the canonizations, another event reminded Ladislaus that a martyr bishop could be a source of a great power. Boleslav II, the Polish prince, was obliged to flee to the safety of Ladislaus' court after causing the murder of Stanislaus, Bishop of Cracovia (later to be the Polish national saint) in 1079. Finally, the two hermit saints had the merit of already being the focus of a local cult (which the other new saints had not); they even had their legend written by

Bishop Maurus before 1074,[18] so they were able to balance the cult of the other more political saints with some contemporary features of eleventh-century spirituality.[19]

After this overview of the domestic political motivations, let us examine the external influences upon these canonizations. Here we have to take into account above all the role of dynastic connections, since the canonization of holy ancestors was mainly a dynastic affair – a matter of dynastic prestige and a source of rivalry between different dynasties. It is not impossible that the Hungarian kings could have obtained information about the Anglo-Saxon holy kings, for two grandsons of Saint Edward fleeing from Knut the Great, found refuge at the court of Saint Stephen. Some sources even claim that Edward married one of Stephen's daughters. After their return to Britain in 1057, the couple's daughter Margaret became queen of Scotland – yet another prospective saint.[20] A closer influence could have been the Bohemian and Moravian cult of Saint Wenceslaus, with which Ladislaus must have been well acquainted, since Otto I, prince of Moravia, was his brother-in-law and his ally in battle. He must have heard frequently about Saint Wenceslaus, who was depicted on the coinage, to whom miraculous victories were attributed and to whom many churches were dedicated in the second half of the eleventh century.[21] However, the closest model must have been the Russian. The Arpadians had multiple dynastic links with the Ruriks (among others through Ladislaus' grandfather's wife) and this close alliance was renewed by Ladislaus when he travelled in 1073 to the Kievan court to ask for help against Solomon, just at the time of the canonization of Boris and Gleb.[22] It seems fair to say that the idea of Hungarian canonizations was the secret weapon he brought home from Kiev.

When speaking of foreign influences, however, I have to stress that they comprised only the idea and the political function of the cult of holy predecessors, and not the religious content of these cults. If we examine the legends of Saint Stephen, we find a striking contradiction with the models of royal sainthood examined so far. First of all, Stephen was neither a martyr nor a mild-hearted, monkish figure, but a firm-handed ruler, whose just cruelty (about which we also know from other historical records) was emphasized in the *Legenda Minor*, prepared shortly after the canonizations.[23] His cult was in complete contrast to the pagan ideas of sacrality; thus, although such traditions did exist in Hungary and are documented in thirteenth-century chronicles (which describe myths of the Hunnish origin of the Hungarians and the saintly character of the Arpadian dynasty[24]), we find no trace of a fusion of Christian and pagan traditions similar to that in England or Scandinavia. Instead, what we find in the legends are elements that echo the new leading motifs of eleventh-century Occidental spirituality, as expressed in the life of Robert the

Pious. Stephen, called *miles Christi*, strove to assure peace and to defeat the enemies of the faith. As the coordinator of the conversion of Hungarians and of the work of all other saints connected with him, he was an apostle. He was a leading patron of the pilgrimages that had recently flowered, founding hospices for Hungarian pilgrims in Jerusalem. He was a great charity worker, helper of widows and orphans – as the *Legenda Maior* informs us. These traits were further emphasized in his early twelfth-century legend compiled by Bishop Hartvik, who added a (probably fabricated) detail that the canonizations were carried out in the presence of papal legates.[25] Hartvik ended the legend with some ideological speculation about the Hungarian holy crown and about the Virgin Mary as patron of Hungary.

The twelfth-century legend of Stephen's son, Imre, also confirmed to this Occidental orientation: probably drawing on the model of the emerging cult of Henry II (his uncle), this legend emphasized mainly the theme of virginity and continence in marriage – a recurring motif of twelfth-century spirituality, also popularized by the legend of Saint Alexis.[26]

Influenced in form and political function by the models of the 'periphery', but in religious and ideological content coming closer to the models of the 'core' – this characterization is appropriate not just to the Hungarian holy kings but also to the Danish. On the basis of the detailed investigations of Erich Hoffmann (1975: 89–126), Thomas Riis (1977: 195–215) and Tore Nyberg (1981), let me briefly educe a few motifs of the cult of saint Knut (1080–6), which tally with the historical pattern outlined above. Here again we can sense the presence of the Anglo-Saxon and the Norwegian models, reaching a further degree of elaboration in the image of Christian royal martyrdom. The king's charismatic functions are also appropriately emphasized in his role as regulator of fertility – hence the famine that followed the death of Knut.[27] On the other hand, in the Knut legends (in his *Passio* written around 1095 and in the *Gesta* of Aelnoth written in the first decades of the twelfth century[28]), we can find contemporary phraseology similar to that of the legend of Saint Stephen. The *Passio Sancti Canuti regis et martyris* used the labels *civitas Dei* and *civitas diaboli* to describe Knut's conflicts with his subjects and his brethren. He is described as the model Christian lord, the teacher of the people and the great supporter of the Church, exacting harsh tithes. His campaigns in England were explained according to the emerging and sophisticated ideology of the 'just war', liberating the Anglo-Saxons from the Normans and at the same time educating his own people who were living in lascivious idleness (Hoffmann 1975: 106). Aelnoth granted Knut the epithet *athleta Christi*, and the way Knut is likened to Christ in his martyrdom could give rise to the supposition that Aelnoth knew of the political treatise of the Norman Anonymous, which stressed the similarity of King and Christ, thus strengthening the religious prestige of royal power against the views advanced by the Gregorian reform.[29]

Finally, it should be emphasized that Knut was the first holy king whose canonization took place according to the emerging new model: with papal consent and in the presence of papal legates (Kemp 1948: 70). As for the canonization of his martyr nephew Knut Laward (1131), let us note that it coincided with the church coronation of his son Waldemar (1170), supported by this new cult. This also illustrates what I shall not describe in detail now: that the cult of saint kings and princes typically played a similar role in the dynastic conflicts and consolidation of a new order of succession in Denmark as elsewhere.[30]

＊　　＊　　＊

With the establishment of these new cults in Hungary and in Denmark this particular form of sacral legitimation of royal power acquired its most modern lineaments. The sufficiently elaborated model of royal sainthood became now more than an ideological tool of the 'periphery'; it began to have an impact throughout Europe. From the beginning of the eleventh century there had been various attempts in the Holy Roman Empire to procure the canonization of Mathilda (wife of Henry I),[31] and at the end of the eleventh century Adelheid (wife of Otto I) was actually included in the *Catalogus Sanctorum* by Pope Urban II (Klauser 1957: 38). The cults of Edward the Confessor and of Emperor Henry II were also emerging in the first half of the twelfth century (Scholz 1961; Kluaser 1957).

These royal cults acquired a special significance owing to the conflict of spiritual and temporal powers over the supremacy initiated by the reform papacy of Gregory VII. In a famous letter written to Herman, Bishop of Metz, Gregory VII stated that there were scarcely any holy rulers in the history of Christianity, while there were many saintly priests and monks.[32] In a similar spirit, Saint Bernard of Clairvaux wrote to Emperor Conrad III, who was striving to get Henry II canonized, that every elect of God was *rex et sacerdos*.[33] As Renate Klauser put it (1957: 48–52), the royal canonizations of the twelfth century represented the reply of the Hohenstaufen to the provocative thesis of Gregory VII. The first step was taken in 1146 when Henry II was elevated by Pope Eugene III, but the major new political cult was that of Charlemagne, canonized in 1165 by the joint efforts of Frederick I's chancellor, Reginald von Dassel, and the anti-Pope Pascal III (Folz 1964). A year earlier, in 1164, these same people arranged for the relics of the Biblical *drei Könige* to be transported from Milan to Cologne – as further support for the notion of royal sainthood (Hofmann 1975). We could add to these events the activities of the English king Henry II, who was known for his conflicts with the Church.

He not only popularized in England the French-style charismatic healing rites already mentioned, and achieved the canonization of Edward the Confessor in 1163, but in addition probably advised Emperor Frederick I to initiate similar actions (Scholz 1961: 53).

These twelfth-century canonizations were joined by new royal saints from the 'periphery': three more Russian princes – Mstislav Vladimiro-vitsh (1075–1132), Rostislav Mstislavitsh (1125–67) and Mstislav Ros-tislavitsh (1179);[34] Saint Eric of Sweden (1160) (Hoffmann 1975: 197–204); a whole series of saints from the Serbian Nemanja dynasty;[35] and also, in a second Hungarian canonization in 1192, Saint Ladislaus, to whose religious sensibility I have already paid tribute.

How did the cult of Ladislaus fit in with this new phase of royal sainthood? For the sake of brevity I shall mention only two important aspects. One is that the cult (as shown by the political circumstances of its establishment and by late twelfth- or early thirteenth-century legend) perpetuated the Hungarian model of royal sainthood: it offered political benefit and opportune ecclesiastical merits on the one hand, and, on the other, continued the resistance to the incorporation of any folkloric legendary elements. Ladislaus was elevated by Béla III (1176–96), the exceptional ruler at the end of the century, who succeeded in ending a long series of rivalries for the Hungarian throne. Ladislaus – like Saint Stephen – was depicted in the legend as the brave organizer of the country and the Hungarian Church (the 1083 canonizations are listed among his principal achievements). He was described as a pious ruler and a brave fighter against the pagan Cumans. According to his legend, this last quality earned him the title of leader of the First Crusade, a role he was unable to fulfil because he died too early.[36]

It is this 'military', 'chivalric' character of Ladislaus (viz. the epithet *athleta patriae* frequently applied to him) that points to the other, more specific reason why this Hungarian cult was in accord with a newly emergent feature of royal sainthood in the twelfth century. There is no need to stress how much the spirit of the Crusades and the cult and legends of Charlemagne transformed the image of royal saints in this direction. This is reflected by the victorious characterization of Saint Eric as well as the increasingly frequent stories of the military miracles of Saint Wenceslaus (Graus 1977). The chivalric character of Saint Ladislaus is even more evident in a series of frescoes based on an unofficial legend described in Hungarian chronicles (rather than in the usual way in hagio-graphic writings). According to this story, the king saved the life of a bishop's daughter who had been abducted, bravely fighting and defeating the monstrous Cuman, and then had a rather romantic interlude with the rescued woman.[37]

It might be of interest to note that the chivalric ideals that infiltrated the cult of Ladislaus came to Hungary not so much from the West as from

Byzantium. We can detect here the joint influence of the Greek 'military saints' (Andrew, George, Theodor, Demetrios) and the chivalric style of the court of Manuel Comnenos, who happened to be the grandson of Ladislaus. Incidentally, it was here that Béla III, the initiator of Ladislaus' canonization, grew up in exile.[38] It must have been from Byzantium that Béla III imported to Hungary this image of the chivalric military saint, which destined Saint Ladislaus (along with Saint George) to become the patron of late-medieval Hungarian chivalry in the fourteenth century.[39]

*   *   *

Royal sainthood, this triumphalist aspect of twelfth-century European Christianity, was an attempt to provide a counterweight to the papal ascendancy in political theory as refined by Hugh of Saint Victor, Bernard of Clairvaux and John of Salisbury (Ullmann 1963: 609–51). In the thirteenth century, the notion of royal sainthood began to decline somewhat, but it did not fade away; it led rather to the emergence of new forms. To conclude the evolution described here, let me indicate these directions.

One was further religious refinement in the cult of Saint Louis, who not only presented an ideal image of the just ruler, and not only died a martyr's death in the crusade, but also succeeded in incoporating the major religious message of the thirteenth century, that of the mendicant orders, his principal advisers (Vauchez 1981: 414–17). This character-istic is even more strongly expressed in the life of his nephew Saint Louis of Anjou, who did in fact become a Franciscan monk (Vauchez 1981: 265–8).

Another change in royal sainthood in the thirteenth century was feminization. This time it was Central Europe that produced a great number of saintly or blessed royal widows and princesses, the most noteworthy of whom were the Silesian Saint Hedwig, Saint Elisabeth of Hungary an Saint Margaret of Hungary. This feminine version of royal sainthood also absorbed the influences of the mendicant orders, which reformulated the model of royal sainthood according to the contemporary vogue for female sanctity. The holy princesses, living in convents built near the royal palaces and surrounded by aristocratic widows and daughters following their example, constituted a kind of female 'celestial court' as a counter-part to the male, secular one. Their new spiritual prestige additionally gave these princesses unprecedented political influence: they frequently attempted to mediate in political and dynastic conflicts.[40]

A third direction of transformation, which was also assisted by the great numbers of holy princesses, was the systematization of these cults to form a dynastic cult and to extend the claim of sanctity to whole dynasties. Here we can observe the resurgence of the archaic conception of hereditary sanctity, depicted in the case of the Serbian Nemanja dynasty by the representation of the holy kings and bishops of the family within the iconographical scheme of the Tree of Jesse.[41] In Hungary, illustrations of dynastic and national saints tended also to show these figures grouped together. In the diptych prepared by order of King Andrew III in 1290, the saints of Arpadian origin were shown for the first time united in a single iconographic group.[42]

This third line of evolution does not indicate, however, the resurgence of the early-medieval Germanic conception of *Geblütsheiligkeit* (consanguineous sanctity), but points rather to the dynastic and religious propaganda activities of the new fourteenth-century dynasties – the Angevin and Luxemburg rulers. Supporting their claims with long lists of saintly ancestors (compiled with a new quality of genealogical awareness and learning), quantity seems to have been more impressive for them than the precise religious or ideological content of these cults. On the other hand, they knew how to combine the late flowering of Central European dynastic cults with a modern form of self-representation, that of the proto-Renaissance princes. They completed the process of attenuation and dispersion of the charisma of sacral kingship, a tendency underlying the whole historical development described above. One could say that they rounded off a medieval passage from a concept of charismatic authority in the sense of Max Weber to another type, outlined by the analyses of Edward Shils.[43]

6

Legends as Life-Strategies for Aspirant Saints in the Later Middle Ages

In a fit of rage after a quarrel with his son, Philip the Good, Duke of Burgundy, walked out of his residence in Brussels alone. In the night he lost his way in the forest. When he finally arrived back home, still furious, a knight of his court, Philippe Pot, hit upon an ingenious way of calming his lord down: 'Good day my lord,' he said 'good day; could you tell me what is happening? Is your majesty playing the role of King Arthur or that of the brave knight Lancelot?'

The revival of 'historical ideals of life', as Johan Huizinga, the greatest exponent among historians of the 'waning' Middle Ages, has called it,[1] seems to be a ubiquitous feature of fifteenth-century religious, courtly and urban cultures. Kings, generals, even popes took on the roles of Caesar, Alexander, Hannibal, Arthur, Charlemagne; Knights imitated Tristan, Roland, Lancelot; writers, poets, historians tried to emulate Virgil, Livy or Tacitus; those with a religious vocation were occupied with the 'Imitation of Christ', to quote the title of the most famous religious handbook of the age. Apart from historical models of Antiquity or of the mythologized early Middle Ages, by this time some more recent prescripts also ranked among the ideals that inspired emulation; those of Saint Francis, Saint Clare, Saint Louis King of France, Dante or Giotto. These life models were handed down to the next generations in a variety of ways: they were expressed in literary forms (legends, *exempla*, historical works, biographies, chivalric romances, etc.) to be read, sung or preached from the pulpit; they were performed on the occasion of religious and secular feasts (passion plays, Corpus Christi pageants, royal progresses, court festivals); and they were depicted iconographically. If we take the approach that 'life history' and its repeated performance is a cultural construction (Bertaux 1981), the examination of such historical ideals of life can provide rich material for analysis.

To start with, any student of medieval religious and secular biographies must take a sceptical view of the authenticity of these verbal, iconographical representations, which are heavily influenced by stereotypes. The quest for historical accuracy and the search for the individual suggest rather that the apparent impact of historical life prescripts conceals a historical variety of much greater diversity. This suspicion appears especially legitimate in the case of medieval saints or candidates for sainthood, whose legends were written with the manifest aim of proving their conformity to one or other of the historical models of male or female sainthood. How can we analyse the individual's choices from the different scripts available, or the tension between images of a good life and actual deeds, if we are provided only with biased (for or against) representations created in retrospect and based unashamedly on stereotypes?

Viewing the long-term historical evolution of later medieval Christianity – from the twelfth to the fifteenth centuries – the diverse historical documentation clearly indicates a gradual process of development. For the purposes of the present argument I would characterize it by a paradox: on the one hand, a greater awareness of the self and individuality, and, on the other, a greater capacity to conform to historical models of life. The first element of this paradox has been discussed amply by medievalists (Ullmann 1966; Morris 1972; Benton 1982; Bynum 1982; Gurevich 1985), who over the past few decades have demolished the Burckhardtian cliché according to which the concept of the individual in European history made its glorious appearance for the first time during the Renaissance. The second part of the paradox requires some examples. Let me select these from the sphere of religious history, which relates more closely to my present argument.

When we consider medieval imitations of historical life models, the point of departure should be the example set by Christ and the Apostles. The *imitatio Christi* had already been one of the most powerful ideals for those aspiring to holiness in late-Antique Christianity (Brown 1983). After a long interruption by early medieval religiosity, which tried instead to obey the divine precept by means of liturgical splendour and meticulously detailed monastic rules, eleventh- to twelfth-century religious reform movements rediscovered the force of the *imitatio Christi*. They tried scrupulously to realize the so-called *vita apostolica*, to adhere to it in all internal *and* external features of morality. 'If thou wilt be perfect, go and sell what thou hast, and give to the poor' – this evangelical command (Matthew 19:21) was carried out literally in the 1170s by the heretic Peter Valdes, or somewhat later by Saint Francis of Assisi. It exemplified the emerging individual's capacity to break out of their given social status by conversion to a 'classical' religious way of life. By choosing to follow the 'original', apostolic model, a confrontation was forced with both secular and religious contemporary alternatives.[2]

After the intense twelfth- to thirteenth-century discussions about the various models of exemplary Christian life that could lead to salvation or sainthood (see Constable 1985), there were some moments in the thirteenth century when the religious Utopia of an entire lay society adhering strictly to evangelical principles seemed to be approaching.[3] Friars following the *forma beati Francisci*, third orders, Beguines, lay brotherhoods, religious knightly orders, saintly rulers, pious craftsmen – each social stratum was provided with specific religious prescripts for life, and the existence of a large number of 'modern saints' seemed to demonstrate that the capacity to follow these socially diversified precepts had increased.[4] On the other hand, this historical learning process also had its reverse side, illustrated by the knightly example I quoted at the beginning of this chapter. People became more conscious of roles and career scripts, and tried to criticize, to decipher, to unveil them. For example, the major Christ-imitator figure, the friar, was portrayed in the thirteenth-century *Roman de la Rose* as the archetypal cheat: the *faux-semblant*.

It is in the context of this wider evolution that I should like to describe a concrete case, that of Margaret, the thirteenth-century Hungarian saintly princess. Analysed within the comparative framework of royal female sainthood, her life provides an indicative example of how an emerging new model of religious perfection, supported by ancient and recent legends, could become a prescription for a number of Central European princesses to aspire to similar glory.

*　　*　　*

Margaret's life (1242–70) covers the important period of Hungarian history when the country was being rebuilt following the devastating invasion by the troops of the Mongol Empire in 1241–2. Her life and vocation were, in fact, directly related to this event. After the terrible defeat of the Hungarian troops in 1241, King Béla IV fled with his family to Dalmatia on the south-western edge of the country. It was here, in Klis, on 27 January 1242, that his eighth daughter Margaret was born. The parents had made a vow to offer their future child, if a daughter, as a sacrifice to the service of God, 'to bring relief to the country and to themselves'. The country was indeed freed of the occupiers and Margaret did indeed go into a convent. At the age of 4, supervised by Olimpiadis, a widowed lady-in-waiting at the court of Queen Maria Laskaris, she was given to the St Catherine convent of Veszprém, a Cistercian nunnery where about a dozen aristocratic *oblatae* (emulating the royal vow) formed a kind of kindergarten. Later, in 1252, she was moved with seventeen of her sister nuns to the new convent built for her on the Rabbit Island, near Buda, on the site of a mansion owned by her mother. She made her solemn oath in 1254 on the occasion of the General Chapter of the Dominican Order held at the newly constructed S. Nicholas monastery in Buda, and she was consecrated by the new general master of the Dominicans, Humbert of Romans.

Margaret's religious life had two major aspects. One could be characterized as a conscious resistance to her father's recurrent attempts to divert her from her original vocation by marrying her to secure new dynastic allies. In 1249, at the age of 7, Margaret, aided by her Dominican confessor Marcellus, first refused to marry Leon, son of the Prince of Galitsia (her sister Constance married him instead); then, in 1255, she rejected another Polish prince. The major conflict of her life came in 1261, when Béla wanted to marry her to Ottacar II of Bohemia. She refused, and when her father insisted, invoking her duties of obedience as a daughter and raising the possibility of papal absolution, she affirmed her fidelity to her oath and to her holy masters. To render the parental project impossible, she had herself consecrated as a virgin by Friar Marcellus (then Prior Provincial of the Hungarian Dominicans). The rejection of a final marriage proposal (around 1268 to Charles I of Anjou) apparently brought her and, indeed, the whole Dominican Order into disgrace: from that time on King Béla transferred his favour to the Franciscans.

I shall return later to the analysis of the religious significance of her refusal to marry, as well as the details of the second aspect of her religious life, the typical practices of her ascetic Dominican spirituality (mortification of the body by wearing a sackcloth shirt, self-flagellation, nightly cathartic prayers), which appear to have exhausted her vital energies prematurely: she died in 1270 at the age of 27.[5]

The surviving hagiographic documents about her are the most detailed of their kind in medieval Hungary; an early legend quite free of hagiographical elements, written before 1274, very probably by her confessor Marcellus, also contains details of miracles reported at the first investigation of her sanctity,[6] and the depositions of the 110 witnesses testifying at the second Papal investigation from 23rd July to 20th October 1276[7] (the various other legends of the following centuries all base their biographical evidence on these documents[8]). Margaret rapidly became an important cult figure within the Hungarian church, although a variety of factors delayed her actual canonization until 1943.

Before drawing attention to particular features of Margaret's biography that add colour to this brief stereotypical life history and contextualize its significance, I should like to dwell briefly on the extent to which her case embodied a contemporary stereotype. Throughout the earlier periods of the Middle Ages, female religiousity was considered suspect for various reasons. In twelfth-century Europe, it was manifested less in officially recognized, canonized forms than in lay religious communities and heretical movements. In the thirteenth century, however, it became one of the newly recognized religious innovations which held a great fascination for the people of the time.[9] James of Vitry, the enthusiastic biographer of the early Beguines, has characterized this female piety as follows:

> Young maidens gathered together, joined by widows and married women who had received their husbands' permission to exchange carnal for spiritual marriage. Noble and powerful women abandoned their earthly inheritance and numerous possessions, preferring to live humbly in God's house rather than in a den of sinners. Rejecting offers of marrriage, these maidens of illustrious lineage put aside their noble parents along with the allure of their precious garments in order to become the brides of Christ, to live in poverty and humility and to serve the Lord devotedly under difficult conditions, wisely rejecting temporal and deceptive wealth in favour of spiritual possessions.[10]

The emerging female piety won support from a number of new religious foundations, orders and third orders. It took the ascendant cult of the Virgin Mary as its historical model (Warner 1976), and the figure of Saint Clare, the female counterpart of Saint Francis, as its major contemporary reference point (Brooke and Brooke 1978). The new policy of papal canonizations also revealed a change of opinion on the part of the Church on this question. Two saintly queens from the eleventh century, Cunegond (wife of the emperor Henry II) and Margaret (Queen of Scotland) were canonized in 1200 and 1249 respectively (Vauchez 1981: 427). Margaret's model, however, had of necessity to be a contemporary: her aunt, Saint Elisabeth of Hungary. After the death of her husband, (Louis IV, landgrave of Thuringia), Elisabeth spent the rest of her life engaged in charity work in the leper hospital in Marburg, under the strict supervision of her cruel confessor, Conrad von Marburg. She was canonized in 1234, three years after her death.[11]

Elisabeth's life and saintly glory became the major career script not only for Margaret, but also for a dozen other saintly or blessed princesses in the region. The Central European dynasties quickly grasped the usefulness of this new form of prestige. Soon they were all competing to set up pious foundations for their princesses and widows – followers of the example set by Elisabeth. In Silesia, Saint Hedwig and the Blessed Anne; in Little Poland, the Blessed Salomea and the Blessed Cunegond; in Bohemia, the Blessed Agnes – they were all contemporaries and relatives of Saint Margaret (see the genealogical table in Figure 6.1). They became the most

Figure 6.1 Saints in thirteenth-century Central European dynasties

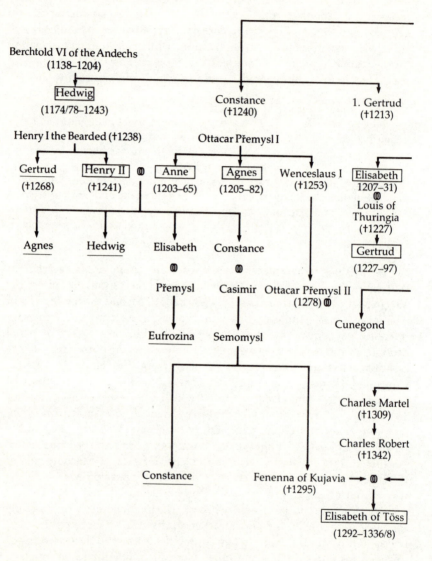

Key:

names in boxes = saint or blessed member of these dynasties

names underlined = nuns

Note:

The figure is not a complete genealogical table; it contains only
the names of those who are relevant in this context.

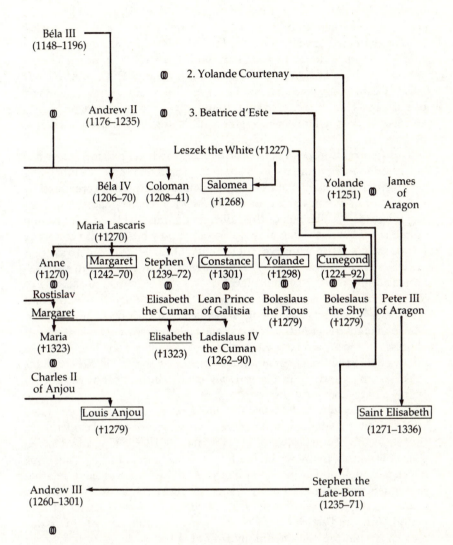

Béla III
(1148–1196)

2. Yolande Courtenay

Andrew II
(1176–1235)

3. Beatrice d'Este

Leszek the White (†1227)

Béla IV   Coloman   Salomea   Yolande   James
(1206–70)   (1208–41)   (†1268)   (†1251)   of
                                                                              Aragon

Maria Lascaris
(†1270)

Anne   Margaret   Stephen V   Constance   Yolande   Cunegond
(†1270)   (1242–70)   (1239–72)   (†1301)   (†1298)   (1224–92)

Rostislav   Elisabeth   Lean Prince   Boleslaus   Boleslaus   Peter III
                             the Cuman   of Galitsia   the Pious   the Shy   of Aragon
Margaret   (†1279)   (†1279)

Maria   Elisabeth   Ladislaus IV
(†1323)   (†1323)   the Cuman
                                            (1262–90)
Charles II
of Anjou

              Louis Anjou   Saint Elisabeth
              (†1279)   (1271–1336)

Andrew III   Stephen the
(1260–1301)   Late-Born
                                                            (1235–71)

Agnes Habsburg (†1364)

honoured followers of Saint Elisabeth. Finally, several generations later, the Blessed Elisabeth of Töss, the last Arpadian princess, completed this group.[12] If we consider that all these princesses gathered around themselves in their nunneries dozens of other royal and aristocratic daughters (these convents were kinds of female 'celestial' courts situated near to the male-dominated secular courts), we can almost speak of a veritable fashion taken up by these emerging Central European royal or princely courts. To give an example, of the thirty-seven known members of Margaret's monastery on Rabbit Island, three had been royal princesses and sixteen were widows or daughters of the higher aristocracy (counts, palatines, etc.).[13]

This Central European vogue for female sanctity combined with royal or princely sanctity is remarkable in many respects. It gives an intriguing new form to the sacral claims of those dynasties formerly represented by the cults of holy kings and princes like Stephen, Henry, Ladislaus of the Arpadians or Wenceslaus of the Bohemian Premysl.[14] Instead of paying religious tribute to the chivalric *rex iustus*, it now became the task of the female members to ensure dynastic sanctity. One might venture to say that the claimed inherent sainthood of these dynasties seemed now to be transmitted through a type of matrilineality – as, for example, in the case of Saint Elisabeth through her daughter the Blessed Gertrud, or with Saint Hedwig, whose martyr son Henry was killed by the Mongols in 1241, and whose daughter, grand-daughters and further descendants were all abbesses of the Cistercian nunnery of Trebnits, which she founded. It is not by chance that we encounter in her legend the Biblical image (Romans 11:16) of the saintly branches growing from saintly roots or the goodly fruits coming from goodly trees.[15]

The extent to which these female candidates for sainthood were linked with dynastic prestige can be illustrated by a variety of factual evidence. In the fourteenth-century account of Saint Hedwig's life, a long and detailed genealogical treatise (never before found in hagiographical writings) was appended, describing the 'magnificence of her lineage' and relating subsequent generations of descendants to her saintly person.[16] There are similar examples from the lives of all the other female saints of that period. But the best illustration of the prestige function of this pious movement and the cults stemming from it is the way that the establishment of the new cults was chronologically interrelated. Hedwig was canonized in 1267 (and this canonization was supported by the Bohemian king, Ottacar II, who hoped thus to strengthen his claim to Silesia).[17] Soon afterwards, in 1269–70, Cracow was the scene of the growing cult of Salomea, and this was witnessed by King Stephen V of Hungary, Margaret's brother, who happened to visit his Polish relatives exactly during this period.[18] In July 1271 the Hungarian clergy began their investigations to establish Margaret's sanctity, following the favourable reception of Stephen V's request by Pope Gregory X.[19]

The most interesting aspect from the point of view of my present argument, however, is how all these saintly princesses strove to follow the example of Saint Elisabeth, whose legends must have provided them with their life strategy – how to become a saint within a royal or princely court of the age. How influential this model must have been is most clearly demonstrated in the second half of the century by the famous mystic nun of Helfta, Mechtild of Magdeburg, who had a vision about Elisabeth explaining that her mission was to set an example to 'the impious women sitting in the castles'.[20] In Margaret's case, her parents' vow that she would be an *oblata* was very probably in emulation of a similar offer by Elisabeth and her husband Louis in 1227 to commit their future child, if a daughter, to a religious career. Significantly enough, Margaret was consecrated as a virgin before a Saint Elisabeth altar in her cloister. One of the witnesses who testified to Margaret's miracles had a vision of an angel, recommending him to 'trust Margaret exactly as she trusted Saint Elisabeth'.[21] Margaret's first legend states quite explicitly: 'she frequently meditated upon her aunt, the Blessed Elisabeth, whose glorious merits are celebrated joyfully by the mother Church . . .' In caring for sick sisters, 'washing their heads, feet . . . cleaning their beds, laundry . . . she followed with eager piety the footsteps of her aunt Saint Elisabeth'.[22] That this emulation must have been inspired by acquaintance with one of Elisabeth's legends can be verified by the fact that, according to the nuns testifying at Margaret's canonization investigations, when she refused to be married she made use of the same threat as Elisabeth had used when relatives wanted to force her to remarry: that if it were done against her will she would cut off her nose and lips to make herself ugly.[23]

Similarly, in 1234 Elisabeth's cousin, Agnes of Bohemia, pledged her hospital foundation 'to the example of the Blessed Elisabeth';[24] Anne, her sister, sent gifts to Elisabeth's grave in Marburg and established a new altar for her; Cunegond and Elisabeth of Töss saw Saint Elisabeth in dreams and visions.[25]

*   *   *

What was the significance of this new-style female piety? What made Elisabeth's career so attractive to the aristocratic ladies of Central Europe? I have designated their nunneries as 'celestial' female courts; I shall now elaborate this metaphor.[26] I am not so much concerned with the fact that these nunneries were actually provided by the royal and aristocratic families with all the wealth needed for an aristocratic way of life (e.g. Margaret's convent became within a few decades one of the richest ecclesiastical institutions in Hungary). What interests me rather is the fact that, instead of ostentatiously displaying these riches, the saintly princesses designed their 'celestial courts' to become the symbolic counterpoint of the male-dominated secular courts.

Their ascetic behaviour not only involved regular mortification of the flesh in order to experience personally the suffering of Christ, it constituted a conscious counteraction to the hedonism of contemporary courtly ideals. Poverty in dress, as all the legends emphasize, was practised with the express aim of humiliating wearers of costly courtly garments: Margaret made a point of doing the filthiest jobs in the new dresses she received from her parents, until the exquisite materials became dirty and ragged.[27] The story of Hedwig's life emphasizes constantly that she did not wear fine purple or wool garments, gold-adorned veils, pearls, precious diamond rings or fashionable shoes 'like the others' at court. She always went barefoot until she had to be ordered by her confessor to put on sandals so as not to hurt herself too much.[28] (On the subject of shoes: Margaret had a special self-torturing shoe prepared for herself from the skin of a hedgehog.[29]) The ceremonial entry of Agnes of Bohemia and 'seven of the noblest aristocratic maidens' to the Clarissan convent that she founded was followed by her 'putting down the hated royal garments, and having her hair cut'.[30]

In matters of food, Saint Elisabeth set the example by refusing to consume any kind of food at court meals that could be suspected of coming from unjust exploitation of the poor. In general, all these female saints are reported to have refused to participate at lavish court meals; on the other hand, they were renowned for their excessive fasting habits.[31] The refusal to eat secular food was at the same time – as Caroline Bynum (1987) has recently underlined – a special form of religious devotion: the saintly princesses reserved themselves for the spiritual food, the Host. Margaret worshipped the Host with tears in her eyes, and at certain periods of the year she was reported to have taken the Host as her only nourishment.[32] Hedwig was famous for going to communion as many times as she could ('in sola missa non est contenta ducissa/ Quot sunt presbiteri, missas tot oportet haberi'[33]). Eating the Host symbolized simultaneously a mystical and bodily union with the flesh of Christ. The devotion to Christ, whose brides they claimed to be, also accounted for the obstinate refusal of these women to marry, or in the case of widows to remarry, or, as in the case of Salomea and Cunegond, to consummate their marriages, thereby preserving their virginity.

At this point one might ask whether we are dealing here with true reversal, or with just a rephrasing of the womanly role, in this case directed towards the person of Jesus Christ, which thus provided a spiritual context for the eternal female functions even in their most bodily aspects.[34] However, if one views the careers of these women as a whole, one realizes the profundity of this distinction. What would normally signify success and achievement for princesses (beauty, high marriage, abundant dowry), represented the greatest danger for our heroines; whereas renunciation, suffering and tribulation became the milestones of their religious achievement, the final aim of which was the irrevocable departure from earthly, courtly surroundings: death.

These princesses demonstrated their opposition to the secular court by inverting their status and embracing humility: Elisabeth forbade others to call her *Domina*.[35] Margaret 'worked together with the servants of the convent. She shared their tasks beyond her strength and her dignity. The more she surpassed everybody with her nobility, the more she strove to show herself as the most humble'.[36] As one of the nuns reported at the canonization investigations, Elisabeth frequently said: 'My God, I'd rather be a poor handmaid than the daughter of the King, so that I could serve God much better'.[37] The nuns who testified reported frequently that among Margaret's most miraculous deeds was her acceptance of the vilest, most humiliating tasks, such as cleaning or emptying the latrine and washing slaughtered animals' intestines.[38] Of course this humiliation became the source of a special kind of symbolic power. As the legend of the Blessed Agnes explains: 'the humility of this glorious virgin radiated like the diamond in a golden setting, making her beloved by God and worthy of imitation by others . . .'[39]

The princesses' symbolic power was partly expressed by their supernatural capacities of prophecy, ecstasy, levitation, and miracle working. (It is interesting to note that some of Margaret's miracles – making the rain come, the sun appear or the river flood at will – reflected traditional, perhaps shamanistic, mastery of the forces of nature.[40]) But the more interesting aspect of the princesses' power was not at all symbolic: from their nunneries, their celestial courts, these princesses began to exercise a very real influence in secular matters. We have already seen, in relation to their rejection of marriage, how successful they were in gaining the right to decide their own fates. In fact, this meant nothing less than breaking out of the traditional female role, that of being an object of exchange, a mere link in the dynastic chain. As for charity, it was a type of religious redistribution of wealth, an example of the 'righteous' exercise of power. Elisabeth distributed grain from her husband's stocks during famine and turned his palace into a hospital. Agnes and Margaret distributed the royal gifts endowed on their monasteries to the poor, to lepers and to widows.[41] Most of the princesses were successful mediators in family conflicts: after several years of devastating war between King Béla IV and his son Stephen V, the 'Younger King', the mediation of Cunegond and Margaret helped to bring about a peace treaty concluded in 1265 in Margaret's convent, probably in her presence.[42] Saint Hedwig even interfered in the judgements of secular courts and in matters of legislation; the Blessed Agnes carried on a correspondence with the Pope.[43] The celestial courts became real centres of power, paving the way for a kind of female emancipation in the surrounding regions and starting an evolutionary process that led within a century to the extraordinary political prestige of Saint Catherine of Siena, or, a century after that, to the charismatic actions of Joan of Arc.

However, two more centuries had to pass before this career pattern could be emulated by a simple peasant girl. In thirteenth-century Central Europe, only princesses could be elevated to sainthood. And not even they could stand alone: everywhere around them were powerful allies, their Cistercian or mendicant confessors, who guided them in carrying out the precepts of their new lifestyle. Was it not rather these men who staged these 'celestial courts', directing their actresses to influence and reshape the neighbouring secular courts according to their own objectives?

There were many precedents in the history of Christianity for such an alliance between religious reformers and pious aristocratic ladies; let me refer only to the most famous cases, those of Saint Jerome advising Eustochium, Paula and several other pious women, or Saint John Chrysostom drawing strength from the passionate support of Olympias.[44] In the twelfth century, with the medieval re-evaluation of women's religious roles, this cooperation took shape again, with two new-style, mixed religious foundations: Robert d'Arbrissel's Fontevrault (see Dalarun 1985) and Abelard's initiatives and designs for 'Paraclet', Héloise's monastery at Nogent-sur-Seine. When Abelard was defining the tasks of the male spiritual supervisor of a female monastery, he drew, characteristically enough, upon secular courtly imagery rather than upon the existing models of nunneries:

> He should be like a steward in a king's palace who does not oppress the queen by his powers but treats her wisely, so that he obeys her at once in necessary matters but pays no heed to what might be harmful, and performs all his services outside the bedchamber without ever penetrating its privacy unbidden. In this way, then, we want the servant of Christ to provide for the brides of Christ, to take charge of them faithfully for Christ . . . he . . . will faithfully keep their bodies from carnal contamination . . . guarantee their bodily purity as far as he is able . . .[45]

A few decades later, when this ideal had been attained by Cistercians, Franciscans and Dominicans, these spiritual guardians obviously became a major influence in the lives of the saintly women. It was they who worked out the rules of the women's behaviour, and who urged them to keep to their chosen path. In Saint Elisabeth's case this sometimes meant truly violent constraint: Conrad of Marburg demanded complete obedience to his commands, kept her in complete isolation towards the end of her life, and had her beaten ruthlessly when he found her disobedient. 'If I fear so much a mortal man,' she is reported to have said, 'how much more frightened should one be of the Lord Almighty, who is lord and judge of everything.[46] The influence of confessors was not as brutal in the other cases discussed, but it must have been equally strong: we need only refer here to the above-mentioned collaboration between Saint Margaret and Marcellus, which effectively countered all attempts to marry her for dynastic purposes.

The alliance of princesses and confessors did not end even at the grave: like new kinds of toubadours, it was these very same spiritual leaders who wrote the first legends revealing the secrets and singing the glory of the noble maidens, queens or princeses.[47] Following the genre revived by Abelard[48] of the religious praise of virtuous women, they competed in the poetical elaboration of the new theme: womanly perfection as seen by the men of religion.[49]

Needless to say, all this sublimation must have been burdened with rich ambiguities concerning heavenly and earthly love. This was the reason why, from the twelfth century on, many contemporaries, Saint Bernard among them, were warning of the dangers of a closer cohabitation of nuns and monks, or even of any regular spiritual links between them.[50] Although after serious hesitations the new tendency prevailed, the intimate contact of the brides of Christ with their spiritual guardians did generate some malicious accusations. Such was the case with Cunegond and her Franciscan confessor, Bogufalus, who had striven previously to promote the cult of the Blessed Salomea. He contributed to the foundation of Cunegond's saintly fame after she became a Clarissan nun by proclaiming that she had preserved her virginity throughout her marriage, and thus merited, like her sister Margaret, the *consecratio virginum*. The empirical basis of this testimony must have given grounds for rumour, for we learn from her legend that Bogufalus later had to be removed from the convent of Sandecz to Gniezno, after being accused of fornication. Cunegond was able to clear herself from the humiliating charges only by means of a miraculous levitation and the apparition of a celestial light which poured down upon her.[51]

Leaving aside profane details, one could say that, in becoming the religious educators of saintly princesses in Central Europe, the mendicant orders were merely following their pragmatic instincts. Where the reform of secular society could be achieved by the reform of urban statutes, as in Italy, they became urban functionaries; where the battle against heresies was the most pressing problem, they became inquisitors; where theological ideas had to be put in order, they became university masters; where the royal court had to be reformed, they tried as court confessors to educate the 'Christian prince' – as in the case of Saint Louis or even of Béla IV.[52] In thirteenth-century Central Europe their influence upon pious princesses proved to be one of the best ways of achieving change. These princesses became kinds of media; they represented, voiced and incarnated the new mendicant ideas about court and rulership.

*   *   *

At this point I can return to my initial problem: what exactly was the role of the legends in this evolution? In Margaret's case several witnesses testified to the fact that she regularly heard about and mediated on various legends, such as that of Saint Thomas à Becket, which inspired her to wear sackcloth and to long for martyrdom.[53] Her legend also tells us that

> she frequently thought and spoke about the lives of her predecessors. About the sainthood of Stephen, first king and apostle of the Hungarians, about his faith and Catholic preaching, which diverted his people from idolatry, and is still echoed by the mother church. She thought about the holy virginity of the son of Stephen, Imre, who, after being betrothed to the daughter of the Roman emperor, saw a divine vision, and subsequently with his bride preserved intact his virgin purity every day of his life. After Henry's death this was even testified to by his bride. She has also thought about the life of King Saint Ladislaus, who, as the chronicles tell, governed the country with glory and protected it from attack, especially from the devastations of the pagans from the east. Saint Ladislaus was involved frequently in ecclesiastical matters, royal legislation, speeches and other saintly matters: he even forgot his bodily rest and passed the nights without sleeping.

This description is concluded with the previously quoted example of Saint Elisabeth.[54] It is obviously Marcellus who speaks here, and it can hardly be doubted that the pedagogical instruction compiled from the legends of Hungarian saints was recommended to the royal court as a form of current morality, just as strictly as it was presented to Margaret as a model of spirituality. What we witness here is no less than the recycling of *post hoc* idealizations of the heroes of past legends into a current praxis of education, of career formation and of a religion-based politics. It is not by chance that these were the very decades when, after so many kings and emperors had been celebrated posthumously as saintly persons for dynastic purposes, and described in unrealistic, stereotypical legends, the first really holy king of the Middle Ages, Saint Louis of France, tried his best to attain these very ideals.[55]

Two further facts must be mentioned here that rendered the legends increasingly effectual as a means of pedagogy in the second half of the thirteenth century. The friars not only popularized them by a more efficient manner of preaching than their predecessors, but made out of them successful and popular anthologies like the *Legenda Aurea* of James of Voragine (composed around 1264 and probably quite soon known to Hungarian Dominicans).[56] These collections provided the religious reader with a variety of prescripts for each status – for female saints the models of, for example, Saint Agnes, Saint Agathe or Saint Catherine were surely highly influential. There was also another development which made legends more important for aspirant saints from the beginning of the thirteenth century. As André Vauchez (1981) has demonstrated, papal canonization policy clearly preferred sainthood to be attained within the lifetime rather than rest on posthumous accounts of miraculous deeds, which had until then represented the most overwhelming argument for the sanctity of a candidate. From then on, to be a candidate for sainthood became a more rational and less apparently suprahuman enterprise. Of course, conformity to a prescript that could be followed, if not by everybody, then at least by a large number of people, was not enough: very soon it had to be coupled with mysteriously prophetic, cathartic, mystical skills, clairvoyance and other ecstatic religious capacities. But even these could be mastered by ambitious individuals with the support of their communities.

One final question remains. The impression of an increasing uniformity and of a more and more perfect realization of model behaviour is based on images derived mainly from hagiographical documents. Can we accept this? Or were these 'celestial courts' perhaps no more than the literary representations of a mendicant dream of female royal sainthood? By comparing Marcellus' version of the Margaret legend with the testimonies of the thirty-eight nuns and several friars (including Marcellus) who were eye-witnesses of Margaret's life, it is possible to check the information given by the legends, and at the same time to develop a fascinating enquiry into history and folklore.

On the basis of an impressionistic contrast between the various accounts, we can identify significant differences. The nuns (especially those of lover social origin) tended to underestimate or to misinterpret the modernity of Margaret's spirituality. It was they, above all, who described Margaret's self-humiliation in the coarse scatological terms appropriate to this world turned upside down. It was also they who attributed to her the shamanistic-type miracles. Their recollections show no awareness of any clear line of religious career or 'life history', although they were asked to speak *de vita et conversatione Margaritae*. Whereas the legend described a neat evolution (Margaret's childhood sensibility accomplishment of her spiritual perfection / acquisition of the central role in her community / tribulations and conflicts resulting in a kind of martyrdom/finally the supreme glory at death), the nuns' testimonies consisted of a patchwork of anecdotes, embedded in the continous flow of daily convent life routine.

However, on one point the nuns' testimonies provide an interesting corrective to the legendary image, revealing better than Marcellus the modernity of Margaret's new-type female spirituality: the diligent and meticulous observation of minor details of religious cult (prayers, genuflections, etc.), the emotional weeping over the human passion of Christ, the tender motherly or sisterly care for the members of the community. The nuns also testified more accurately about the excesses of this new type of female spirituality (probably disapproved of by the confessor): the frequent cathartic praying and the repeated torture of self-flagellation. And they seemed to be very genuinely fascinated by the major miracle: a royal princess sharing their humble life.

The alliance of friars and princesses did have its effect. Despite some violent counter-reactions, like the anti-Christian way of life of Margaret's nephew, King Ladislaus IV (the Cuman), by the fourteenth century the Central European courts had become almost anachronistically religious: Charles IV was designated *rex clericorum*. The Polish Elisabeth, wife of the Hungarian Angevin king Charles Robert, directed religious representation at the Hungarian court for five decades, and ended her life as Regent of Poland. The two thrones of her son Louis (the Polish and the Hungarian) were inherited by his two daughters, Mary and Hedwig.[57]

However idealized an image we get from the legends, the life strategies for women developed in the celestial courts of thirteenth-century Central Europe must have had some real impact upon the fate of women in the secular courts of the period immediately following. And – as our initial example of Philip the Good illustrates – they might have contributed to the fact that by the end of the Middle Ages the capacity for role-playing had reached such a high degree of perfection.

7

The Cult of Dynastic Saints in Central Europe: Fourteenth-Century Angevins and Luxemburgs

In a letter written in 1269, Charles I of Anjou described the young King Stephen V as 'a valiant, strong prince, descended from a line of saints and great kings'. With the aim of uniting the House of Anjou with the House of Arpad, Charles was proposing, using Bernard, Abbot of Montecassino, as intermediary, a double alliance between his son, the future Charles II, and Maria of Hungary on the one hand, and between Ladislaus IV (the Cuman) and Isabelle of Anjou on the other.[1] Indeed, the description used by Charles in this letter is more than an empty compliment. The founder of the new royal House of Anjou was only too aware of the importance of initiating kinship ties with the royal saints of the Arpad dynasty.[2] This is evident also from his testimony given in 1282 at the canonization proceedings for his elder brother, Louis IX. As far as Charles was concerned, it went without saying that 'sacred roots' – i.e. the Capetian dynasty – 'produced sacred branches'.[3] It is understandable, therefore, that he was seeking to augment the prestige of his new royal line and to spread his 'sacred roots' through well-chosen alliances with other dynasties.[4]

The fruits of this idea of a hereditary sanctity can best be seen at the canonization of a truly new 'sacred branch' of the Naples House of the Angevins: the canonization in 1317 of Charles's grandson, Louis of Anjou, Bishop of Toulouse, who died in 1297. In the oration, delivered by François de Meyronnes, the main claim for Louis' sanctity was the fact that he was 'born into a line of saintly personages'. On the paternal side he was related to Saint Louis, whilst his mother was 'Maria of Hungary, who comes from the family of Hungarian kings: Saint Stephen, Saint Henry and Saint Ladislaus'. The Franciscan preacher added that 'only one woman of royal blood has recently been canonized, namely St Elisabeth, who belonged to the same family as the mother of our Blessed Louis'.[5] It is obvious that the growing renown of the Angevins' sanctity served to increase the prestige of the new dynasty. However, it is not the fact that these cults served a political purpose, but rather their exceptional success, that makes these endeavours on the part of the Angevins worthy of interest.

The canonization of Louis of Anjou was a truly great family enterprise: the case was petitioned first by the father, Charles II, and then by the younger brother, Robert, then Duke of Provence, whose exertions were crowned with success. (Toynbee 1927; Laurent 1954; Vauchez 1981: 266–7). After acceding to the throne of Naples, Robert continued to exploit the cult of the family's new saint: he attended his exhumation in 1319 in Marseilles and had Louis' main shrine and his right hand brought to his own capital. His queen, Sancie of Aragon was to donate one of her gold crowns for Louis' sumptuous shrine. This was followed in Naples by other foundations, statues and paintings attesting to the reputation of Robert's pious brother. (Bertaux 1990; Kleinschmidt 1909).

Iconographic remains reveal the close integration of saintly ancestors into the image of the royal family. It is significant that in the first painting commissioned by Robert – probably in 1317 – from Simone Martini, Saint Louis of Anjou is shown placing the crown on his brother's head. At a later date, at the request of King Robert, it was deemed necessary to insert the legend of Saint Louis of Anjou into the Angevin calendar prepared before 1317 (at present in the Staatsbibliothek in Vienna), which already included detailed portraits of King Saint Louis and of Saint Elisabeth of Hungary.[6] Likewise, on the tombstones of Maria of Hungary, of King Robert and of Charles of Calabria, all sculpted by Tino de Camaino, the enthroned figures of Saint Louis of Anjou and of King Saint Louis are to be seen. On the monument to Catherine of Austria, who was Robert's first queen, the dominant figure is Saint Elisabeth. On the frescoes in the church of Donnaregina d'Ungheria, the holy lineage is completed by a host of saints from the House of Arpad: Saint Stephen, Saint Ladislaus, Saint Elisabeth and even the Blessed Margaret, aunt of Maria of Hungary. Robert and his queen, with their son Charles and granddaughter Jeanne, are depicted kneeling on either side of Christ and Saint Louis of Anjou on the murals in the monastery of Santa Chiara; whilst the frescoes in the church of Santa Maria Incoronata show the Seven Sacraments as a family chronicle: naturally, the ordination is depicted as the anointing of Saint Louis of Anjou, while the seventh sacrament – marriage – is symbolized by the union of Queen Jeanne with Louis of Taranto (Bertaux 1900: 639; Kleinschmidt 1909: 200).

Thanks to Robert's efforts, the cult of saints in the Angevin dynasty spread not just through his own domains, but also wherever his political influence was felt: in Florence, in Siena, in Assisi and through the works of no lesser painters than Giotto, Ambrogio Lorenzetti and Simone Martini. Profound piety – or skilled propaganda? These two concepts are not necessarily contradictory in the cases under discussion here. Robert was buried in the habit of a Franciscan friar; after his death, his Queen Sancie entered the convent of Santa Croce in Naples, taking the name of Claire (Bertaux 1900: 627). At the same time, it is a fact that the Angevins of Naples made use of the cult of their saintly ancestors to enhance their own dynasty – and exploited these cults to an extent that has never since been equalled.

*   *   *

This picture corresponds to the historical and artistic evidence from Angevin times in Hungary. One might even say that the accession of Charles Robert (Carobert) to the vacant throne of the Arpad dynasty – which had become extinct in 1301 – was the first (and most spectacular) result of the dynastic policy initiated by Charles I and strengthened by the cult of the family saints. Charles Robert gained the Hungarian crown not just as a descendant of the Arpad line (through the above-mentioned dynastic alliance), but far more as heir to Hungary's 'royal saints' and as the pretender most able to reaffirm and continue this sanctity inherent in the Arpad dynasty.[7] In fact, there was a rivalry among the candidates in this field: the first pretender, Wenceslaus Premysl, son of the Bohemian king Wenceslaus II, hastily changed his name to Ladislaus after his crowning in 1301.[8] It was not accidental, therefore, that during the vicissitudes of the Interregnum one of the most important aspects of Charles Robert's diplomatic activities consisted in emphasizing his links with the saintly kings of Hungary.

In 1307 the Bishop of Zagreb, Augustine of Gazot, wrote an *Oration* for the nobles' assembly on the Field of Rákos, which was to make the final choice from among the rival pretenders.[9] In this oration, after enumerating the dynastic and legal arguments in favour of Charles Robert, the bishop used all his eloquence to emphasize that the new king's lineage derived 'from our most saintly kings' ('*ex sanctissimis regibus nostris*'). Apart from Saint Stephen, Saint Ladislaus and Saint Elisabeth, he also mentioned in his long list several blessed princesses from the House of Arpad in the thirteenth century: the Blessed Margaret first of all, followed by her sister Cunegond, who had lived in Poland, and Elisabeth, the granddaughter of Béla IV's half-sister Yolande, who was considered in Aragon to be blessed.[10] This oration was the first document to mention the saints of the Anjou family: King Saint Louis and Saint Louis of Anjou (the latter to be canonized only some years later). Thus the 'sacred charisma' of Charles Robert was being backed from two sides – Charles I was not leaving anything to chance.

His reception at the Synod of Zagreb in 1308 was staged under the emblem and before the shrine of Saint Stephen, who on this occasion was called 'patron deity of the whole Hungarian kingdom' (*'tutelare Numen universi Hungarici Regni'*) in the sermon delivered by the same Augustine of Gazot.[11]

In order to conclude and complete the argument regarding Charles Robert's descent from saintly kings as a legitimation of his claims, let us quote the pontifical legate, Cardinal Gentile da Montefiore, who was the Angevins' most powerful agent in Hungary. In 1309 he made the following appeal to the Hungarian nobility:

> As is only right and by divine providence, Hungary was ruled by Catholic kings; the first of these, the saintly King Stephen, as well as some others, have merited inclusion in the list of saints; they produced legitimate successors, under whose reign this kingdom prospered, became fruitful and enjoyed the blessings of peace, whilst the people flourished in a unity of spirit. But when this reign was usurped by foreign kings, fertility was replaced by sterility, the blessings of peace by the rumble of storms, the unity of spirit by hateful discord. Therefore, we, who have been assigned by the Apostolic See to reform the government of this said kingdom, and wishing to find a salubrious remedy to all this, hereby summon to a general assembly the prelates, the barons and the nobles, so that they may proclaim with one accord the magnificent Prince, the Lord Charles, true descendant of the above-mentioned saintly kings and thereby rightful and legitimate King of Hungary, i.e. their natural sovereign . . .[12]

These arguments, advanced by an Italian pontifical legate at the beginning of the fourteenth century, proved not only the importance of the cult of dynastic saints in relation to the succession of the Angevins to the Arpads, but also the potency of the archaic ideas attached to the sacred, 'charismatic' function of the king (see Bloch 1983: 51–64; Chaney 1970)

The veneration shown by Charles Robert towards his saintly ancestors did not diminish with the passing of times. Apparently, one of his main objectives was to participate in the promotion of the latest cult, that of Margaret. This was a cult that must have been dear to his heart, since he had been familiar with it since his childhood days in Naples.[13]

One of his first actions in ecclesiastic matters was to resume the interrupted proceedings for the canonization of Margaret: in 1306, he sent the Dominican father Andrew to Pope Clement V, with the intention of expediting events.[14] Let us not forget that the procedures for the canonization of Saint Louis of Anjou were then at exactly the same stage. Charles was thus undertaking the same action as his uncle Robert was for the Provence–Neapolitan branch of the family. If it was a matter of rivalry between them, one could say that Robert's endeavours were the more efficient. Yet Charles' lack of success did not discourage him from advancing the cult of Margaret: his second wife, Beatrice of Luxembourg (sister of the King of Bohemia), awarded new privileges to the Dominican convent on Rabbit Island near Buda, where Margaret had spent her life. It was at this time that the island first became known as Margaret Island.[15] During the opening decade of the century, a new tombstone was erected there for the blessed princess, probably sculpted by artists from the Naples workshop of Tino di Camaino.[16] Apart from a host of religious offices and legends connected with Margaret,[17] the Hungarian version of her legend, one of the first literary texts in the vernacular, was probably written at this time. (It has been preserved for posterity in the transcript of a nun who lived in the same convent at the beginning of the sixteenth century).[18]

Numerous indications point to the importance of other family saints. First we must note the dynastic names chosen by Charles Robert for his sons: Ladislaus (1324), Louis (1326) and Stephen (1332). The exceptions are his first-born, bearing his own name Charles (1321) and the penultimate, called Andrew (because of his name day, but also after the last king of the Arpad dynasty).[19] When Charles Robert's wife Beatrice died in 1320, he buried her at Nagyvárad (Oradea), near the tomb of Saint Ladislaus. At the same place, six years later, at the funeral of one of his favoured barons, Sándor Nekcsei, he took the opportunity to emphasize his devotion to his 'saintly predecessor'.[20] In honour of Saint Louis of Anjou, in 1325, Charles Robert decreed the foundation of a Franciscan convent at Lippa which was completed in 1349.[21] In 1331, his third wife Elisabeth, who was of Polish origin (and who was soon to become the central figure in the organization of these cults), was engaged in sending gifts to the tomb of Saint Louis in Marseilles.[22] With regard to Saint Stephen, in 1318 Charles Robert had the saint's Basilica at Székesfehérvár rebuilt and provide it with a lead roof. After the fire of 1328, which – miraculously – spared only the tower where Saint Stephen's relics were kept, Charles Robert had the Basilica rebuilt once again.[23]

All these endeavours were important for Charles Robert as King of Hungary, but they gained added significance in connection with his ambitions in the sphere of dynastic alliances abroad. Being the beneficiary of his great-grandfather's agreements, concluded by the same methods, Charles Robert placed a high value on marriage contracts. His marriages with the princesses of the Luxemburg and the Piaszt houses respectively, were to be followed by his sons' alliance with these same dynasties, in time securing the Polish throne for his son Louis the Great, and, later, the

Hungarian crown for the Luxemburgs.[24] But his most important under-taking was to be the reclamation of the original throne of the Angevins in Naples. In 1328, the death of Charles of Calabria, the surviving son and heir to his uncle Robert, provided the opportunity for Charles Robert. As early as 1331, he launched into the formation of an alliance that would assure the succession for his son Andrew, through marriage to Jeanne, Robert's granddaughter. In 1333–4, he made a journey to Naples to conclude the treaty and the betrothal. This was his opportunity to gather the fruits growing from his Arpadian 'sacred roots': to cover the Hung-arian branch of the Anjous with the glory of their saintly forebears.

The preparation of a book summarizing the dynastic cults of the Angevins, the magnificent *Angevin Legendary*, was very probably linked with this enterprise. According to Ferenc Levárdy's hypothesis, this book of legends, illustrated in the style of Bolognese miniature-painters, – probably by Charles Robert's court painter, a man called Hertul, who studied in Bologna – was based upon the 'Golden Legend' and completed by a compendium of legends relating to Hungarian saints. It was most probably used mainly for the education of Prince Andrew at Naples, but it also served the purpose of enhancing his prestige there.[25] The amount of space given to the dynastic saints – saint Stephen: 16 miniatures; Saint Imre:[26] 8; Saint Ladislaus: 24; Saint Louis of Anjou: 12 – is surpassed only by that representing the Gospel and the lives of the Apostles. A number of other saints were included, on account of their ties with Hungary: Saint Gerard, the martyred bishop from the reign of Saint Stephen; Saint Martin of Tours, venerated in Hungary because of his Transdanubian origin;[27] Saint Stanislas,[28] the patron saint of Poland, this native land of Elisabeth, the queen mother; and Saint George, who, with Saint Ladislaus, was the emblem of the somewhat belated chivalric movement in Hungary. (In 1318, Charles Robert founded in Saint George's name the first Hungarian chivalric order.)[29]

As we can see, the cult of dynastic saints tended to grow into a 'national' collection of cults – a later tendency to which we shall return. But let us first examine the propaganda, based on the portrayal of dynastic saints, which aimed specifically to secure the Neapolitan throne for Andrew. There are few details about the visit of Charles Robert and his entourage to Naples in 1333–4. A great deal more is known, however, about the journey undertaken in 1343–4 by Elisabeth, the queen mother, after the deaths of Charles Robert and of Robert, when Andrew's succession seemed to be in danger.[30] If the *Legendary* was not taken to Naples by Charles Robert in 1333, it must certainly have reached there on this later occasion.

The queen mother, accompanied by a sumptuous entourage, intended to dazzle high society not only in Naples, but also in Rome. On a pilgrimage to the Vatican, she provided the altar and the relics of St Peter with a number of costly presents. Among these gifts was an altarcloth in silk, which showed, in the company of the Apostles Peter and Paul and the Virgin Mary, all the dynastic saints of the Arpads and of the Angevins; the Saints Stephen, Imre, Ladislaus and Elisabeth; the Blessed Margaret and Saint Louis of Anjou.[31] It was probably also Elisabeth who ordered from Simone Martini a portrait of Saint Ladislaus for Filippo di Sangineto, the central figure of the Hungarian party in Naples.[32] These were not her only contributions to the boosting of the cult of Hungarian saints in Italy, but they illustrate sufficiently the extent of her activities.

Apart from the succession, it was funerals that were most closely associated with the dynastic saints. To recap: in Naples, most of these saints were portrayed on tombstones or in memorial chapels. Charles Robert was buried at Székesfehérvár, near the tomb of Saint Stephen. By choosing Székesfehérvár for his burial place, Charles Robert revived an ancient custom of Hungarian kings, a custom that had been discontinued for more than a century, ever since the death of Ladislaus III in 1205. At Charles' funeral rites, the most splendid in Hungarian history, where the ceremonies lasted over a month, Csanád Telegdi, the Archbishop of Esztergom, bid farewell to the late king with these words:

We beseech, with one voice, the Grace of the all-powerful Father for our Lord, King Charles . . . may He deign to place his soul among the ranks of saints and confessors, beside King Stephen and King Ladislaus. Having lived on this Earth covered with glory, may he now rejoice in the company of Angels in the Hereafter.[33]

In all probability, it was at the crowning of Charles Roberts' son Louis that the *Ordo* of Durand was introduced into Hungary; its Hungarian version became established for the rest of the Middle Ages. The ties with Saint Stephen were emphasized by several features; the new king was to be inaugurated beside his tomb, enthroned on his original throne, invested with the mantle assumed to be Saint Stephen's, and – to be sure – crowned with the Holy Crown believed (erroneously) to be Saint Stephen's.[34] Louis completed the ceremonies with a pilgrimage to the tomb of Saint Ladislaus at Nagyvárad.[35] This was a clear expression of his personal preference; in the second half of the century, the cult of Saint Ladislaus tended to eclipse that of the other dynastic saints. He became the central hero during the late flowering of the chivalric culture in Hungary, a flowering that owed much to the young king's knightly adventures and, among other factors, to the punitive wars he waged against Naples, where his brother Andrew had been assassinated in 1347.[36]

The effigy of Saint Ladislaus was to replace that of John the Baptist on the gold florin issued by Louis.[37] In the second half of the fourteenth century Saint Ladislaus appeared everywhere, even on varnished stove tiles and chalice bases.[38] The frescoes of Hungarian churches depict his chivalric adventures in profusion (narrated in the chronicles rather than in his legends[39]) – for example, his combat with the barbaric Cuman, who had ravished the daughter of the Bishop of Nagyvárad, and his heroic deliverance of the maiden. To the paintings from the turn of the thirteenth century (showing an amorous scene with the freed maiden to complete the story), and to the illustration of this same story in the *Angevin Legendary*, some dozen new frescoes were added. On them, Saint Ladislaus bears such a close resemblance to the chivalric ideal that art historians can reconstruct from his iconography, decade by decade, the evolution of the armoury of chivalry in Hungary.[40]

It is therefore not surprising that the saintly and chivalrous king became – in the eyes of contemporaries – a powerful protector of all Hungarians in their military exploits. According to the chronicle of an unknown Franciscan friar, in 1345, during a battle against the Tartars on the eastern borders of Hungary, the king's head disappeared from his shrine at Nagyvárad and was later rediscovered there, covered in perspiration. According to this chronicle, the captured Tartars claimed to have been vanquished by a gigantic Knight, wearing a gold crown and accompanied by a crowned lady, who was bathed in a bright light floating above his head – 'undoubtedly the Blessed Virgin Mary and Saint Ladislaus'.[41] If the soldiers gained questionable advantage, the shrine of Saint Ladislaus at Nagyvárad certainly profited from the growth of this cult: Louis, when repeating his pilgrimage there after he was wounded in 1352, donated a silver crown for the shrine.[42] Two bishops of Nagyvárad, Andrew Báthory and, later, Demeter Futaki, had a new cathedral built there between 1342 and 1366, undoubtedly with assistance from the court.[43] The importance of Saint Ladislaus is clearly illustrated in the Missal of a Dominican convent in Dalmatia, in which King Louis is described as his *famulus* (servant).[44]

In addition to the illustrious cult of Saint Ladislaus, it is noteworthy that during Louis' reign the organization of the courtly representation of the dynastic saints became the responsibility of Elisabeth, the queen mother. She undoubtedly retained the vestiges of the saintly feminine spirit that was so popular with the Piaszt and Arpad dynasties in the thirteenth century. Like Saint Hedwig, Saint Elisabeth, Saint Margaret and a number of blessed princesses in these dynasties, she seemed to regard religious perfection as the duty (and perhaps also the privilege) of women. But with one important difference: she strove to realize this division of labour with the typical tools of fourteenth-century religious life: trying, with donations, foundations and patronage, to extend the cult of each saint connected in some way with the Hungarian royal court.[45]

Elisabeth was undoubtedly responsible for the representation of the dynastic saints during the last decades of Charles Robert's reign and she continued this activity during the reign of her son. I have already mentioned her glittering visit to Naples in 1343–4 and her solemn pilgrimage to Rome, where 'the Queen Elisabeth, radiating virtue, honest morals and constant piety, like a luminous star' was compared to the Queen of Sheba by the Hungarian chronicler John of Küküllö.[46] In 1357 the queen mother set off on a pilgrimage once more; this time she was accompanied by the imperial couple, Charles IV and Anne of Schweidnitz. In their company Elisabeth visited the shrine of Charlemagne at Aachen, where she established a Hungarian chapel; they went on to pay homage to the shrine of Saint Elisabeth at Marburg, stopping on the way in Cologne to honour the Three Wise Men (a 'must' for every royal pilgrimage).[47]

It was probably during this journey that the idea was born of uniting the saintly kings of Hungary – Saint Stephen, Saint Imre and Saint Ladislaus – into a kind of Trinity.[48] As the most celebrated among the dynastic saints, they were already represented together in a number of inconographic paintings mentioned above. In 1343, the Provost Miklós Vásári, an eminent member of Queen Elisabeth's entourage in Italy, commissioned an illustrated codex containing the legend of Saint Stephen, which was decorated by a central band with the enthroned figures of Saint Stephen, Saint Imre and Saint Ladislaus.[49] However, the real increase in representative ceremonies and in donations pertaining to the 'royal saints' (as they started to be called) began in earnest only after the 1357 pilgrimage to Aachen and to Cologne. Ten years later, Louis donated relics of these three kings to the Hungarian chapel, together with numerous gifts of jewellery, among them a splendid silver cloak clasp showing the three royal saints surrounding the Angevin–Hungarian coat-of-arms.[50] A few years later, probably in 1373, a similar gift of relics of the three royal saints was sent to Bamberg, to be associated to the cult of another royal saint, the Emperor Henry II, Saint Stephen's brother-in-law (Folz 1984: 188–9). Another indication of the rise of this new devotion, which was to become a national symbol, was a group of pedestal statues in bronze erected at Nagyvárad, near the cathedral. This was an early work by the Kolozsvári brothers, who later sculpted the magnificent statue in Prague of Saint George slaying the dragon. These statues were honoured as the town's patrons and protectors right up till the time of the Turkish devastation.[51]

Returning to the queen mother's cultic propaganda, it remains to mention that her patronage tended to increase the circle of saints attached to the court. Saint Martin of Tours, already honoured in the *Angevin Legendary*, was now glorified with the building of a new chapel at the royal palace in Buda and a church at Hatvan. In 1349, the queen mother sought authorization from the Vatican to hold pilgrimages and grant pardons at these locations.[52] Saint Martin was also included among the Hungarian saints (the Saints Stephen, Imre, Ladislaus and Elisabeth) who were revered in the cathedral of Pécs.[53] In 1361, after recovering from an illness, Elisabeth had a Benedictine church built at Csanád, which was the centre for the cult of Saint Gerard. She also had a silver-gilt sarcophagus made, to provide a new monument for the martyred bishop.[54]

One could mention also numerous other shrines, items of jewellery, votive paintings and religious foundations donated by Elisabeth. Her artistic and religious patronage – an impressive display of her power – reflected more than just her dominant position at the Hungarian royal court (decisively illustrated by the fact that in 1362 Louis seemed prepared to go to war against Charles IV, because the latter had offended the queen mother). After being a patroness and coordinator of religious representation at the Hungarian court for several decades, in 1370 after the death of her brother, Casimir the Great, King of Poland, when Louis inherited the Polish throne, Elisabeth became Regent in her native land. She held this position for ten years until her death in 1380.

The ultimate political consequence of the singular power held by the queen mother through the administration of the Angevin dynastic cults is clear to see: after the death of Louis in 1382, his kingdoms were inherited by his two surviving daughters. Hedwig (1373–99) became Queen of Poland; Maria (1371–95) Queen of Hungary. Of course, they were too young to be able to hold on to these inherited positions. After a series of vicissitudes, they were forced to cede power to their husbands, chosen for them by the nobles of their respective countries. Hedwig married Vladislaus Jagello in 1386: following family tradition, she chose throughout her marriage to lead a life filled with religion and charity. Maria had a similar fate: for several years she was a pawn of feuding rival factions, each trying to influence the succession by choosing her husband. In 1385 – in accordance with one of the alternatives stipulated by her father – she married Sigismund of Luxemburg, and she disappeared from public life thereafter. Both queens died in childbirth with their first-born. Hedwig was the last to inherit the Angevin charisma of sanctity: attempts to secure her canonization began in 1419.[55] With regard to Maria, of interest to us here is the fact that, through her marriage, the Hungarian Angevins – with their tradition of political–religious representation – allied themselves to the dynasty and the traditions that offered the greatest possible similarity to their own situation and aspirations: the house of Luxemburg. This is the point where we ought to turn to the examination of the situation in Bohemia.

*　　*　　*

In 1306, the Přemysl, the other historic dynasty in Central Europe, became extinct. After the failure of the then-rising Habsburgs to gain the Přemysl throne, Henry, Count of Luxemburg, who became head of the Empire in 1308, succeeded in securing it for his son John. The situation of the Luxemburgs in Bohemia was similar to that of the Angevins in Hungary. First they were forced into a prolonged fight for supremacy in the country; they secured the legitimacy of John's claim through the principle of Bohemian vassalage to the Emperor and reinforced it through the former's marriage to Elisabeth Premysl, sister of Wenceslaus III, last king of the old dynasty. Nevertheless, John of Luxemburg must have felt keenly the difficulties of being a newcomer, of asserting himself as founder of a new dynasty and at the same time adapting himself to local traditions and demands. Undoubtedly, every new dynasty needs time to appreciate the importance of dynastic cults; this may explain the young king's hesitant and ambiguous behaviour in this respect.

When in 1316 he baptised his first son Wenceslaus, thereby associating him with the patron saint of Bohemia,[56] he probably had to surrender his own choice of name (Henry, after his grandfather, Emperor Henry VII), and cede to pressure from his wife and the Czech nobility. Still, he sent the boy, at the tender age of 7, to be educated in Paris at the court of his brother-in-law, Charles IV. Here Wenceslaus was rebaptized Charles, to proclaim his connection with France and the fact that on the paternal side he was descended from Charlemagne. The successive dynastic names chosen by John clearly indicate his indecision: in 1318 he had to give way yet again and call his second son Ottocar Přemysl, according to local tradition; the third was baptized John-Henry in 1322, whilst the fourth, born in 1337 to Beatrice of Bourbon, was also named Wenceslaus – this time not as the result of local pressure, but rather in defiance of it, since the Czech nobility had no interest in this son, who had no Přemysl blood in his veins (Schneider 1977).

All through his reign, John of Luxemburg seemed to remain a stranger, *advena*[57] in his kingdom. Apart from trying to secure the canonization of the Blessed Agnes (a Přemysl candidate for sainthood of the thirteenth century[58]), he did not do a great deal for his saintly ancestors. His son Charles, who returned to Bohemia in 1333 and became a champion of local traditions 'as a new Bohemus' (*ut alter Bohemus*)[59], even in opposition to his own father, went much further. His interest was evident as early as 1328, when he was 22: he wrote a homily to Saint Ludmilla, the grandmother of Saint Wenceslaus.[60] He considered his two given names not only of genealogical significance, but also important for his future ambitions: to secure legitimately both the Czech and the imperial crowns. After being crowned *Rex Romanorum*, he sent a delegation in 1346 to Pope Clement VI, requesting the imperial crown, stressing his descent 'from the roots and the lineage of the most blessed father Wenceslaus, duke and patron of Bohemia' ('*ex radice et stirpe beatissimi Wenczeslai patris, Bohemorum quondam ducis et patronis*'); on the following day, the Pope recognized in his *Collatio* that Charles's virtues stemmed 'not only from his saintly parents but also . . . from his name Charles, for no one had been more devoted and generous to the Church than Charlemagne'.[61]

After his coronation as Bohemian king in 1347 and as Emperor in 1349, Charles IV developed a religious–political representation, almost a state cult, centred on the cult of these two saintly kings. As King of Bohemia, he inclined toward the cult of Saint Wenceslaus, whom, according to Beneš von Weitmühl, he regarded as 'his personal helper and protector'.[62] On 1347 Charles offered the saint his crown which after 1358 was to remain permanently at its new gold shrine, to be removed only on the occasion of coronations. Thus the shrine of Saint Wenceslaus acquired a central role in the coronation ceremony, similar to the cases of Saint Stephen in Hungary and Saint Olaf 'the perpetual king' of Norway (Hoffmann 1975: 88–9). Charles IV showed his devotion to the cult of Saint Wenceslaus in several ways. He established new feast days for 'the knitting of his bones' (27th June) and for 'the consecration of the Saint Wenceslaus Chapel' (10th September). He had this chapel built over the tomb of Saint Wenceslaus between 1358 and 1366 on the model of the Celestial Jerusalem. He attended its dedication in 1367 by Archbishop Jan Očko de Vlašim and made sure that all miracles and healings that took place there were meticulously recorded.[63]

Two features of his devotion merit particular attention. The first was his endeavour to have Saint Wenceslaus elevated to the rank of principal patron of the realm. He tried to achieve this – apart from the afore-mentioned donations – by coining the description '*castrum sancti Wenceslai*' for the Castle of Prague; at the same time the saint appeared on the seal of the newly founded university in Prague.[64] As in Hungary under the Angevins, the patronage of Saint Wenceslaus was gradually extended to embrace a whole group of Bohemian saints: Saint Adalbert, Saint Vitus, Saint Procop and Saint Ludmilla. They can be seen together on a number of paintings and frescoes, but the supremacy of Saint Wenceslaus was never in doubt.

The second original trait in Charles's devotion was the literary aspect: he commissioned the writing of a new legend about Saint Wenceslaus.

Moreover – uniquely among medieval monarchs – he authored a legend himself. If we compare this with traditional hagiographies, we find certain original features, such as praise for the statesman's political prudence and glorification of the virtues of chivalry.[65] This latter aspect in the cult of Saint Wenceslaus took on at this time an intensity comparable to that of Saint Ladislaus in Hungary; it is shown not only by the representations in which he performs miracles of a military nature, but equally by his representations in knightly armour, like the one by Henry Parler in the new Saint Wenceslaus Chapel in Prague.

Let us now examine the imperial aspect of dynastic cults exemplified by the veneration of Saint Charlemagne. This shows the same institutional aspects as the worship of Saint Wenceslaus. After being crowned Emperor in Aachen, Charles IV had a silver-gilt shrine prepared for Charlemagne, adorning it in 1350 with a crown.[66] The ambitious reconstruction of the apse surrounding Charlemagne's tomb was conceived during the reign of Charles IV. Its design emulated the mausoleum of the Emperor Constantine, which was itself modelled on the Holy Sepulchre in Jerusalem.[67] Charles IV attempted to revive the Roman Empire for the last time during the Middle Ages, not only through his patronage of the imperial cult at Aachen, but also by presenting himself as the reincarnation of Charlemagne. The notion had already appeared in certain Sibylline prophecies, in which his ascent to the imperial throne was announced.[68] It is possible that this idea was also cherished by Charles IV: we can see traces of it in the history of Bohemia, written later under his commission by his chaplain, John of Marignola. In this text we can read of his mother, Elisabeth Premysl, the following. From the marriage she concluded with the son of Henry VII, 'like a ray of sunshine in God's Church, the most illustrious Charlemagne, of robust strength and of shining virtue, God's favourite was restored [in the person of Charles IV] on the imperial throne.'[69]

In the course of developing Prague into a worthy capital of the Empire, Charles IV had to introduce the imperial cult here too. The construction of the Karlshof church, built as an exact copy of the Münster at Aachen, served this purpose. However, the foundation in 1354 of the twin provostships for Saint Wenceslaus and for Saint Charlemagne in Ingelsheim, subordinated to Karlshof,[70] proved that the cult of Charlemagne was in no way intended to eclipse the national patron saint; rather, it was envisaged as a joint veneration. The castle of Karlstein, the new centre for state cults (containing not only the imperial and royal insignia, but also the vast collection of relics owned by Charles IV), was given the appellation 'imperial'; yet the paintings depicting Saint Wenceslaus and his grandmother, Saint Ludmilla, outnumbered those of Charlemagne.[71]

At the same time that he imported the cult of Charlemagne to Bohemia, Charles made zealous efforts to export the cult of Saint Wenceslaus – just as the Angevins were doing with their Hungarian dynastic saints. The joint pilgrimage of the Bohemian and the Hungarian ruling families to Aachen, Cologne and Marburg was followed by the founding of the Saint Wenceslaus Chapel in Aachen by Charles IV, where a similar chapel was founded by Louis I for the royal saints of Hungary. Other altars for Saint Wenceslaus were erected in Rome and Nuremberg.[72]

Charles carried the dynastic cult to its logical conclusion in the choice of names for his children. His first two sons were called Wenceslaus, whilst the fifth was baptized Charles (Schneider 1977: 385). His third son, the future king of Hungary, born in 1368, was to receive the name of Saint Sigismund, one of the first medieval royal saints in the western world. Charles IV had Sigismund's relics brought to Prague from Einsiedeln in 1354, and used the ensuing cult of the saint to support his claim to the throne of Burgundy in 1365.[73]

As shown by the example of Saint Sigismund, Charles IV was not content with the major cults; he extended his attention to all the saints he could possibly attach to his realm. Thus his marriage in 1353 with Anne of Schweidnitz gave him dynastic reasons to embrace the cults of Saint Hedwig and Saint Elisabeth. Anne inherited these cults from two sides. On one side she was the granddaughter of Charles Robert and his first wife, Mary of Beuthen, through their daughter Catherine; after the death of her parents she was brought up by the Polish queen mother, Elisabeth, and thus became acquainted with the Arpad traditions. On the other side, her father, Henry II, Duke of Schweidnitz, was descended from the House of the Andechs, another Central European dynasty, which had been trying to gain a saintly reputation for more than a century by claiming these two saints as issues from their house.[74] Anne therefore had every reason to bring these cults to Prague as appanage. The famous *Hedwig Codex*, depicting the two saints in the midst of their Andechs family, and containing the legend and the genealogical tree of Saint Hedwig, was a present from Anne's uncle, the Duke of Liegnitz.[75] The imperial couple honoured Saint Elisabeth not only by a pilgrimage in 1357 to her shrine, endowing it with generous donations,[76] but also by choosing the name Elisabeth for their daughter in 1358. There have been efforts to date for this same year the illustrated legendary on Saint Elisabeth, prepared in the Franciscan convent of Krumau.[77] Saint Elisabeth was also represented among the paintings of dynastic saints at Karlstein.

It seems fitting to conclude the description of the dynastic cults of Charles IV and his endeavours with respect to these cults, by quoting from the funeral oration written at his death in 1378 by John of Jenstein: 'Do not be surprised reverend fathers if I call him Blessed and Saint. . . .' were his words after he had enumerated the seven manifestations of his religious excellence. The second of these was none other than his zeal in protecting the 'sacred affairs' (*negotia sancta*) I have just described.[78]

*   *   *

I have outlined three cases with very similar characteristics: Naples, Hungary and Bohemia. Let us consider the central element in this cult of the royal saints. Are we dealing with a resurgence of *Geblütsheiligkeit*, an archaic conception of consanguineous sanctity, according to which members of certain dynasties are more likely to undertake supernatural tasks as kings (Hauck 1950)? Was this anachronism used by these new dynasties from the West, when they sought to adapt themselves to the less sophisticated spiritual state of Christianity in Central Europe and southern Italy?

In order to answer these questions, we should view the medieval cult of royal saints from a historical perspective. As historical research in recent years has rightly recognized, the cult of royal saints was but one method of lending supernatural support to royal power (Graus 1965; Górski 1969; Folz 1984). Royal or princely sanctity was a new creation of medieval Christianity. Inheriting and then modifying ancient and barbarian traditions, it created a new, distinct type within the framework of the medieval cult of saints, by uniting the resources of religious cults with the power and the objectives of royal dynasties. All the same, when speaking of some sixty medieval saintly kings, queens, princes and princesses, we must remember that these cults evolved over several centuries: each period reflected the special conditions and varied aspirations of the time. We must also take into account geographical differences – the diverse religious and cultural traditions depended on the degree of christianization and the previous beliefs of the country in question.

The dynastic cults promoted by the Angevins and the Luxemburgs represent one of the last phases in this evolution. They inherited the idea of the royal saint and of dynastic sanctity, an idea that had been promoted by the Merovingians and the Anglo-Saxons, then by various Scandinavian, Slavic and Hungarian dynasties and finally by the Holy Roman Empire. They also inherited an enhanced profile in these cults, which at first concentrated on the martyrdom of the king, on the 'suffering monarch' (Vanchez 1981: 186–213) and then sanctified entire dynasties through the sanctity and virtue of *rex iustus* of their founder (Hoffmann 1975). They also made use of these cults in the competition for prestige between ecclesiastic and secular powers; they added colour to royal sanctity with the addition of the chivalric ideal of *miles Christi* and they introduced a feminine aspect to dynastic sanctity in accordance with the thirteenth-century vogue of female sanctity – to mention only a few variants in the development of these cults.[79] Their main factors of inheritance, however, were the original traditions in those countries where they seized the throne, together with the traditions they brought from their country of origin. Leaving aside for the moment the indigenous traditions in southern Italy, we shall examine the integration of Central European dynastic cults and the rise in the cult of the holiest of medieval kings – that of Saint Louis.

The first has been referred to frequently in the preceding discussion. In Hungary, as well as in Bohemia, it was in the second half of the thirteenth century that the cults that had been established during the tenth to twelfth centuries began to develop into a kind of national patronage, in order to sanctify their respective dynasties. In Bohemia, Saint Wenceslaus appeared on the royal seal at this time, replacing the 'peasant' legend of the Premysl handed down from pagan times.[80] In Hungary, there were increasing references to royalty's 'saintly predecessors', the royal court initiated the veneration of the Arpad saints and portrayed them together in a group. In the wake of this ideal of dynastic sanctity, a large number of pious princesses sought to join their saintly ancestors and share in their glory.[81]

Regarding the cult of Saint Louis, there is hardly any need to emphasize its Angevin connections. I have already mentioned the efforts of Charles I to have Louis canonized, and the way that Robert sought to propagate his cult in Italy. Nor did the Hungarian branch moderate its attachment to this saintly predecessor: Charles Robert was able to follow the rise of the cult of Saint Louis in France, because his sister Clemence of Hungary was married to Louis X. The dynastic connections continued later with the Valois: Louis of Orleans was betrothed for a while to Maria, daughter of the Hungarian King, Louis I. For the House of Luxemburg, these ties became even closer during the fourteenth century. As has already been mentioned – apart from numerous dynastic marriages[82] – Charles IV received his education at the court of the French king bearing the same name and was therefore able to witness personally the blossoming cult of Saint Louis.

The example of Saint Louis was primarily a personal one: he was a saintly king, not only in the sense that he was portrayed as such in his posthumous cult, but also because he actually tried to lead a saintly life. In his quest for religious perfection, we can observe a clear strategy: to approximate to the ideal of royal sanctity, which was until then to be found only in legends. At the same time, he wished to incorporate into this ideal new currents of Christianity from his own age, with the help of spiritual experts such as the mendicant orders. Here we have a king who was just and restrained, a true Christian and Knight, whose sanctity was demonstrated not only by his way of life, but also by the traditional attribute of martyrdom in his fight against the Infidel.[83] His ideal of sanctity did not fail to make a deep impression on his successors (Philip the Fair imitated him in his pious acts[84]) – but on the whole it was the Angevins and the Luxemburgs (Robert, Charles Robert, Louis and Charles IV) who strove to follow as closely as possible in his footsteps.

Their emulation included copying some of the rituals of the cult of Louis, which intensified during the reign of Philip the Fair. The bust reliquary containing the head of Saint Louis, prepared in 1306 to be kept at the Sainte Chapelle, became a model for the bust shrines commissioned by the Angevins and the Luxemburgs, which they adorned with their crowns. Charles IV even imitated Saint Louis in inserting pieces from Christ's crown of thorns into the Czech and the imperial crowns.[85] Nor were these rulers unaware of the political advantage their relatives had gained from the cult surrounding the *sancti reges Franciae* (Folz 1984: 145). Philip the Fair was able to prove that royalty strengthened by such a sanctity outshone even the glory of the Papacy.

The Angevins and the Luxemburgs cleverly combined the late flowering of the dynastic cults in Central Europe with a modern representation of royalty, which was nevertheless deeply Christian in spirit and firmly rooted in the cult of Saint Louis. When using the term 'representation', I do not mean only royal processions, pilgrimages, translations of relics, religious foundations or artistic representations, which were becoming more and more luxurious in line with fourteenth-century taste. I am also thinking of the resolution – already observed in connection with Saint Louis – to conform to an ideal and to live one's life in accordance with it, in other words, to 'represent' it. Representation in the fourteenth century meant over-representation: apart from an unprecedented number of religious endowments, the Angevins and the Luxemburgs practised a piety almost as devout as that of Saint Louis – if not always as convincing. In addition, they encouraged the conjecture that the virtues of all their saintly ancestors had been 'reborn' in them. I am deliberately using the word 'rebirth' or renaissance, because all these efforts to seek out, reconstruct and portray the sacred lineage were pointing in the direction of the fancy genealogies of the fifteenth century.[86] Equally, there was no lack of complacency on the part of the Angevins and the Luxemburgs as far as the origins and techniques of their patronage were concerned; indeed, they are depicted on paintings, frescoes and miniatures in the same dimensions and importance as their saintly ancestors. Some of them might even have contemplated promoting a personal saintly cult, as can be seen from the attempts by Charles Robert and Charles IV to have themselves sanctified, which were alluded to in their respective funeral orations.

But alas, the age of royal saints was more or less over by the end of the fourteenth century – at least in the sense of being the support, the patrimony and the symbol of certain reigning dynasties. In fact, the extreme endeavours of the Angevins and the Luxemburgs contributed rather to the desacralization of royal power. In Hungary, only a few years after the death of Louis I, they had the audacity to assassinate Charles II, his relative from Naples who had come to occupy the throne and had been legitimately crowned. Then adding insult to injury, they had the impudence to capture the widow of Louis I and his daughter Maria and to murder the former by strangulation. Sigismund of Luxemburg, son of Charles IV, was no longer so keen on the ancestral saints after his accession to the Hungarian throne.[87] The cult of Saint Ladislaus was meanwhile appropriated by the Hungarian nobility, who in 1403 plotted treason against Sigismund, making their oath upon Ladislaus' relics and (unsuccessfully) supporting the last Angevin pretender to the Hungarian throne, Ladislaus, King of Naples.[88]

The Bohemian example proves that the exaggerated celebration of the cult of saints provoked a contrary religious reaction: instead of supporting it, people turned against it – Beneš of Weitmühl complained as early as 1370 about the lack of popular participation at the feast of Saint Wenceslaus. It was not long before the Hussites refused *en masse* to support the cult of saints.[89]

Saint Wenceslaus, however, fared better during the vicissitudes of the first decades of the fifteenth century. Like the Hungarian and many other royal saints, he was promoted from his position of dynastic saint to become a national symbol in the modern sense of the term.

8

Shamanistic Elements in Central European Witchcraft

Apart from the well-known Finno-Ugrian examples, shamanism is considered to be practically absent from the religious evolution and consequently from the folk beliefs of medieval and modern Europe. I would like to propose a reconsideration of this assumption, relying upon the fairly recent researches of Carlo Ginzburg on the *benandanti* (1966). Ginzburg has come across beliefs centred around persons known as *benandanti* in the documents of the Inquisition relating to the north-east Italian region of Friuli, a region with a remarkable set of archaic beliefs, a kind of melting pot for Italian, German and Slavic folklore, and – as I hope to show – witchcraft and shamanism.

Ginzburg's *benandante* book raised a large number of intriguing questions about popular witchcraft, beneficent sorcery and shamanistic beliefs. Although it generated a considerable echo among historians of witchcraft,[1] it seems to have escaped the notice of specialists in shamanism. Even Mircea Eliade, a most respected specialist in shamanism (1964) was inspired by it only to meditate on the problem of the belief in witches, making no specific comment on the connection these beliefs may have had with shamanism (1975). As a starting point of my own attempt in this direction, let me briefly summarize Ginzburg's findings, which give a unique insight into historical structuring and evolution of folk beliefs in the early modern period.

* * *

We encounter the *benandanti* in a series of Inquisition documents – denunciations, interrogations, reports of their trials – ranging from the year 1575 till the second half of the seventeenth century. They were men and women whose main function was to protect their community and their village from the harmful activities of witches. They did this in two ways. On the one hand, just like diviners, wizards and cunning folk in other regions of Europe (and many other places in the world), they cured the bewitched, identified the witches and, where possible, undertook a counter-attack against the witches' spells. Their other activity, however, puts them in a category all of their own. Four times a year, on Ember Days (the four periods of fertility rites relating to the change of seasons, incorporated into the Church calendar; see Fischer 1914), on Thursday nights, they fell into a trance, and their soul was said to leave their body for several hours to fight with the witches for the crops and the fertility of the animals. These fights took place at different places, on remote plains where the *benandanti*, just like their opponents the witches, arrived *in spirito*, mostly riding a cat, a rabbit or some other animal. At the point of assembly, the *benandanti* and the witches ordered themselves into military battalions. Both groups had their commanders and captains – they even had their own flags: the *benandanti* flag was white silk with a lion, the witches' red or yellow with three black devils. They fought with sticks: the *benandanti* with sticks of fennel, the witches with sticks of sorghum. If the *benandanti* won, there would be a good harvest, if they lost, there would be scarcity. After the battle their souls returned to their bodies, which were said to be completely lifeless during their absence and should not be rolled over, or else the soul could not return to the body and became an errant soul.

According to another set of beliefs from the same region, overlapping but not quite identical with those just described, in the course of his or her soul-journey the *benandante* could take part in the procession of the dead. This enabled him or her to supply information about dead relatives, which again made them popular within their communities.

A person could not become a *benandante*: he or she had to be born one. More precisely: born with a caul. (However, there are some traces of gender specialization: men mostly fought witches whereas women generally saw the dead; but a number of *benandanti* of both sexes carried out both activities.) The parents generally had the caul baptised together with the child, and either preserved it until the child grew up, or, more frequently, made the child carry it around his or her neck or shoulder. (In psychological and sociological terms this was quite a good method of predestining these children to fulfil their special role in their community, of making them absorb the special beliefs about the *benandanti* and acquire the capacity of falling into a trance; in short, of constraining them to their role-taking).[2]

The *benandanti* started exercising their functions when they became adults, at around 20. At this age, at one of the traditional dates (a Thursday during Ember Days), they had an initiatory vision: they were called for their first soul-journey. At this time a man (another *benandante* or an Angel of God) appeared to them, beating a drum, and calling their soul to the assembly of the *benandanti*. There was no way of protesting against or escaping from this function, which (according to the Inquisition documents) a number of *benandanti* assumed only with reluctance. From this time on they had to go out regularly to fight the witches, they had to endure the witches' blows during battle and at any other time when they spoke about them. The *benandanti* saw witches everywhere; they knew who in their village was a witch, but they were not allowed to identify witches except when curing the bewitched. If they spoke about the witches, the latter chastized them with a sorghum stick. The same thing happened if a conjuror of the dead spoke about the dead: he or she got beaten by the spirit of the dead with a sorghum stick. The *benandante* had to endure all this for about twenty years. The only way to stop the regular nightly battles and to cast off his exceptional powers was to lose his caul, but there is no documented case where a *benandante* dared to do this intentionally.

The inquisitors were baffled by this strange, coherent belief system, and especially by the fact that the *benandanti* claimed with authority and dignity that they were fighting for God and Christ – that they were the protectors of their community. The inquisitors naturally tried to fit the dubious belief system of the *benandanti* into the categories of learned demonology: likening their assemblies to the witches' Sabbath, their capacity for travelling *in spirito* to some kind of demonic flight or to the sorcery of rubbing their bodies with unguents (made, according to demonological treatises, mainly out of infants' fat), taking their initiatory vision for pacts with the Devil, etc. However, the *benandanti* obstinately rejected this distortion and were consequently let off at their trials with very mild sentences.

Nevertheless, this intervention of the repressive institutions into popular culture did have its effects upon the folk-beliefs. It transformed them at a speed that historians of religion would scarcely credit. Twenty to thirty years after the discovery of the first *benandanti* (that is from 1610 onwards), we can see the first change: the *benandanti* got caught up in the intensification of the European witch-hunts, taking upon themselves the role of public accusers in their villages (in striking opposition to the *benandanti* of the 1570s who refused to give the Inquisition the names of the witches they claimed to know). This slowly undermined their local prestige. They created tension, they made denunciations (long lists of presumed local witches, which the Saint Office mainly ignored); and because of this activity they were often expelled from the village they lived in. The second phase of the transformation was brought about partly by the accused witches' counter-accusations that the *benandanti* were themselves witches, and partly by the public abjurations of the *benandanti* condemned by the Inquisition, who were constrained to acknowledge and denounce their own presumed demonic alliances. By 1650 (that is, no more than seventy-five years after the first trial of a *benandante*), the whole belief system had become more or less assimilated into witchcraft, in the minds not only of the inquisitors, but of the common people, and even of the *benandanti* themselves. The *benandanti* put on trial in the second half of the seventeenth century gave confessions analogous to those of the witches; they acknowledged their participation at the witches' Sabbath and their use of ointments for their soul-journeys (both charges having been consistently denied in their earlier trials), and they admitted to the demonic origin of their visions. The only enduring element of their original beliefs was that they were still superior to the rest of the witches, for they did not attack children and they did not worship the Devil.

*   *   *

The significance of Ginzburg's analysis of the *benandanti* must be evident to anybody familiar with the historiography of European witchcraft. It reopened the debate about the possible interconnections between witchcraft beliefs and the survival of pagan fertility cults, the theory propagated by Margaret Murray (1921) and her followers (Runeberg 1947; critical and modified restatement by Rose 1962). Ginzburg reformulated Murray's often fantastic and very inadequately documented thesis about the reality of the witches' Sabbath, which was, according to her, a ritual gathering of an ancient fertility cult, organized originally around the worship of Diana and administered by priests in animal disguise (mistaken for the Devil by the Church and later also by the followers of the cult), the witches themselves being the priestesses or followers of this cult spread throughout Europe. In the exceptionally well-documented case of the *benandanti*, we have the chance to see how an existing belief system dealing with the problem of fertility and already constituting a special popular version of witchcraft beliefs gets transformed by and confused with learned notions about witchcraft. On the basis of this example it may be asserted with greater conviction that, even if there is no reason to think that the confessions extorted from witches related to an organized pagan cult surviving from late Antiquity till the sixteenth to seventeenth centuries, there might have been different kinds of sorcerers, diviners and seasonal fertility rites, customs and beliefs relating to evil spirits that did get integrated here and there into the general framework of popular and learned witchcraft beliefs.

Several such beliefs can be enumerated to illuminate the historical explanation of *benandanti* beliefs. Ginzburg carefully examined the historical data on seasonal evil-chasing rites, mythological versions of the battles of Winter and Spring and the popular rites and ceremonies representing this battle, and on beliefs about the souls of the dead wandering around as a 'furious army' during some nights of the year.

Thus, we can see several strands to the possible formation of the *benandante* beliefs. There is one strand, however, that Ginzburg only indicated and, lacking any data, left for others to explore: the 'connection which exists beyond any doubt between benandanti and shamans' (Ginzburg 1966: XIII, 51).

It is this suggestion that I should like to elaborate here, partly by enumerating some close analogies to the *benandanti* beliefs, and partly by posing the question whether it is appropriate to speak about shamanism or elements of shamanism in connection with these beliefs. Before doing so, however, let us recall the main features of the *benandanti* that might be relevant to the present perspective:

They did not receive their magical power by learning or by establishing contact with a superhuman being; rather, they were elected to be protectors of their community by virtue of special circumstances at their birth, i.e. being born with a caul.

They began their magical activity after an initiating vision, which they experienced on reaching adulthood. On this occasion, another *benandante* or an Angel of God appeared to them and called them to the assembly of the *benandanti* to exercise their functions.

This figure appeared to them in sleep, beating a drum.

From this time on they regularly went on soul-journeys, while their body remained motionless at home, as if dead.

However much they would like to protest against their calling, they had no choice but to go.

During these soul-journeys (four times a year) they fought with the witches for the fertility of the soil and animals of their community.

On other occasions during the soul-journeys, they saw the procession of the dead; they could bring back news about the fate of dead relatives.

They had the capacity to detect witches and to cure people bewitched by them.

In the villages where they lived they were held in high esteem and were considered a kind of spiritual leader of their community.

Before posing the question as to how these beliefs relate to shamanism, let us first take into consideration some other related beliefs from Central Europe and the Balkan peninsula.

*   *   *

Searching for Slavic parallels to the *benandanti*, Ginzburg had a strong suspicion that the beliefs surrounding the kresniks (*kerstniks/krsniks*) in neighbouring Slovenia and Istria were closely related to the phenomena he had described (1966: 112). But since he had little reliable information about *kresniks* (Krauss 1908: 41–3) – who took them to be types of sorcerers who fought the witches on Midsummer Night – he could not pursue this comparison much further.

In fact we have much more information about the *kresnik*: Yugoslavian and Hungarian folklorists have collected considerable data about the beliefs connected with this figure, and Maja Bošković-Stulli has attempted a careful reconstruction of the whole belief system (1960; 1975: 205–31). There are not only striking similarities between the *benandanti* and the *kresnik*; viewing them in juxtaposition can also lead to a better understanding of both.

In a description of the folklore of Fiume (Rijeka) we learn that the *kresniks* were human beings who acted as antagonists of the witches (*strigas*). They acquired the power to confront the witches because they were born with a caul (*camisetta*), which they later wore around the shoulder and which should not be lost. During the night the *kresniks* went out to fight the witches in the shape of a dog, a horse or a giant, and the attacked witches fled from them in the form of a white sheet (Kőrösi 1892: 171). Another version of this same belief from the Istrian peninsula had *kresniks* (*krsniks*) opposing *strigos* (witches), again born with a caul, which was sewn together and worn in the armpit. Here we learn that the *kresnik* fell into a sleep before the fight with the witches. Then a big black fly called Parina flew out of his throat and departed for the ninth border to fight the witches. If the *kresnik* won there would be no hail that year. According to other data from Istria, the *kresniks* fought the witches with sticks in the air near a crossroads, or they crossed the sea in an egg-shell to fight in Venice in the air above St Mark's Square. We also know that the sleeping bodies of the *kresniks* should not be turned while they fought the witches, and, if their bodies were turned, they would die (Bošković-Stulli 1960: 277–82).

In other regions of Istria the opponent of the *kresnik* was called the *kudlak* (*ukedlak*). Every clan had one *kresnik* who did good and one *kudlak* who harmed people. These two sorcerers could take the shape of any animal, although they fought each other mostly in the form of goats, bullocks and horses. If the *kudlak* attacked somebody in the night, the *kresnik* would defend the victim (Milcetić 1896:24–5). This same belief was found on the island of Krk, where the lore says that the *kresnik* was born with a caul, which was dried and given to the child. If a *kresnik* and a *kudlak* fought in the shape of an animal, the former was of white or light colours, the latter of black or dark colours. From more scattered information we know that the *kresniks* were called by other *kresniks* to exercise their functions at the ages of 7, 18 or 21 (Bošković-Stulli 1960: 276–8).

There are so many common elements to the beliefs about the *kresniks* and the *benandanti* that it seems possible to consider them as two variants of the same belief system – especially if we take into consideration that even less survives of the *benandante* beliefs in the folkloric tradition of Friuli. The complete identification of the *benandanti* with the witches is echoed in the belief that children born with a caul become witches or sorcerers (Osterman 1940: II, 298–9). A vague memory of their ancient protective function is expressed by the belief in one valley of Friuli, where it is said that at Epiphany the *baladans* are to be seen running around the top of the mountains with torches in their hands to chase away the evil spirits (Ciceri 1981: 157). In some villages of the region they also say that the *benandanti* are *stregoni benefici* who fight the witches (Babudri 1925: 12, 112, 324–5). It would not be possible to deduce from these data the belief system still in full blossom around the sixteenth century. Thus we can presume that in the past the *kresnik* beliefs also represented a more articulated fertility cult. The close relation with the *benandanti* beliefs is strikingly confirmed by the only known seventeenth-century report about the *kresniks* by Giacomo Filippo Tommasini, writing on the popular customs of Istria. Here we are supplied with some of the missing links: he wrote that, in Istria, children born with a caul were believed to become either *cresnichi* or *Vucodlachi*, whose souls went during the night, especially on Ember Days, to the crossroads, where they gathered and fought battles for the fertility of the season to come.[3]

Basically there remain only two important differences between *benandante* and *kresnik* beliefs: the animal shape taken by *kresniks* during their fights and the native of their antagonist, which is more frequently the *vukodlak* (*kudlak, ukedlak*) than the witch (*striga, strigo*). I suspect that these two features represent a more archaic version of the *benandanti/kresnik* belief system than the mythology unearthed by Ginzburg from the Friuli trials. In shamanistic beliefs the souls of the sorcerers very frequently fight in animal shape. This characteristic might have been erased completely from the *benandante* beliefs (and from some *kresnik* beliefs) during the eventual fusion of the archaic fertility cult with the belief system of witchcraft. Perhaps the lack of this capacity of animal transformation made it easier to distinguish the beneficent sorcerer from the witch capable of any kind of metamorphosis.

The more archaic opponent of the *kresnik* also deserves some comment. The *vucodlak* is a well-known mythological figure in southern Slavic popular beliefs: the werewolf. From our perspective it is remarkable that he, too, was capable of soul-journeys, and it was during these that he was transformed into a wolf (Schneeweiss 1935: 29). His supernatural capacities were also related to being born with a caul. Concerning Slavic werewolf beliefs, Roman Jakobson has pointed out that it was precisely the dried caul (worn in the neck, on the body) that enabled the werewolf to change into a wolf. The same motif can be detected in German werewolf beliefs, where they were supposed to use for this purpose a magical belt, made of human skin, mostly infants' skin (Jakobson 1966: 341–7).

Jakobson's investigations of Slavic werewolfs also serve to remind us that the werewolf's role was not necessarily as negative as the average European notion suggests (he tries to explain why the eleventh-century Vseslav of Polock (a successful and victorious Russian prince) was considered to have been a sorcerer and a werewolf by the *Vseslav epic* dedicated to him). It might be that the werewolfs were originally envisaged as sorcerers representing their own communities' interest, and harmful only to outsiders. This suggestion could also be supported by a few examples of seventeenth-century Lithuanian werewolfs, quoted by Carlo Ginzburg because of their extraordinary resemblance to the *benandanti*: fighting for fertility against witches, being organized into *Wahrwolf* societies, making soul-journeys.[4] On the basis of these analogies it is conceivable that the fights of *kresnik* and *vukodlak* did not originally mean the encounter of a positive and a negative force, but simply the clash of sorcerers representing different clans, communities or regions, where each one was fighting for the interests of his own group against the sorcerers of the other groups. A further review of Balkan beliefs could support the suggestion that this Lithuanian example is perhaps the most archaic version of the mythologies we are dealing with here.

Further to the east, in Slovenia, *kresniks* fought with each other. Near Sv Barbara and Sv Anton they were held to be the protectors of the different regions who fought in the clouds for the fertility of their own region; at such times lightning could be seen without thunder (Kelemina 1930: 39). These beliefs demonstrate a closer relation to a different set of Balkan beliefs than to the *benandante/kresnik* belief system. The prototype of these kinds of sorcerers was the *zduhač* (*stuhac, stuha, stuva*), known to the people of Serbia, Bosnia, Hercegovina and Montenegro.

The *zduhač* was a male sorcerer who carried out his malevolent activities against hostile clans and in favour of his own. Every clan, tribe and region had its own *zduhač*, usually a boy born with a caul (which was preserved), but according to some beliefs one could also become a *zduhač* by learning and concluding a pact with the Devil. The *zduhač* was not to tell anybody about his magical capacities or else would lose his power. The *zduhačs* of the different clans fought each other for the fertility of their lands. They fought in the clouds, sometimes in the form of animals, mostly with brooms and milk jars. The one who succeeded in taking away the broom from the other assured good crops for his region, and the one who captured the milk jar of the other assured abundant milk for the cows of his clan. The winner punished the region of the loser with hail. These fights took place when the *zduhač* fell asleep. His soul then went away to fight. Sometimes this fight was performed in groups, for example between the *zduhačs* of the mountains and the *zduhačs* from beyond the Adriatic

Sea (Grgjić-Bjelokosić 1896: 532; Bošković-Stulli 1960: 288).

This same genus of positive sorcerer was to be found throughout the Balkanian peninsula under many different names. The Inquisition reported from Dalmatia in 1661 about 'good spirits who chase away the bad weather' (Ginzburg 1966: 200). Maya Bošković-Stulli gathered data on several other related mythological beings from this region: *lagromant*, *viscani*, *vjedogonja*, *vrimenjak*, *mogut*.[5] However, instead of examining still further analogies such as the Bulgarian *nestinari* (see Arnaudoff 1917: 50), let us comment on these series of beliefs. The least we can assert is the persistence from Friuli to Serbia and Bosnia of an interconnected set of beliefs in certain human beings, who were mostly born with a caul and consequently possessed the magical power to assure fertility for their community, clan, village or region and to protect them from the attacks of evil forces. They were obliged to fight for fertility, sometimes with witches, sometimes with each other. The fight was performed by their souls, which left their seemingly lifeless bodies to confront the enemy, often in the shape of various animals.

One comment is necessary about the role of the caul in these beliefs. It cannot be considered merely as one possible sign of election among others, or an offshoot of the general European belief that birth with a caul brings luck to the child. In a fascinating book, Nicole Belmont (1971: 19–79) gathers an interesting series of data ranging from the Iceland of the Eddas and Sagas, from Ireland and Friesland through France, Italy and Central Europe to Russia, about the visionary, evil-chasing characteristics of people born with a caul. Belmont was able to identify the role of the caul in these beliefs: it was frequently considered to be the seat of the 'external soul', a kind of guardian spirit that could take the form of an animal and appear to the person in sleep. In other versions, it was the caul that enabled the soul to leave the body in sleep and take the form of different animals. Belmont also suspects traces of shamanism in these beliefs (1971: 55–6).

*   *   *

Let us now complete this picture with some relevant data on the Hungarian *táltos*. The *táltos* have already been compared to the *kresnik* and the *zduhač* by Géza Róheim (1925: 23–5) and Vilmos Diószegi (1958: 28–31, 349–52), but on the basis of much less information and from a different perspective. Róheim wanted to disprove, whereas Diószegi restated, the ethnic specificity of the Hungarian *táltos* beliefs, posited as a direct descendant of Siberian shamanism. By pointing to some structural analogies between the Hungarian *táltos* and other Central European beliefs, I should like to pose the question differently. For the present purpose, three elements merit special attention: (1) the *táltos*'s conflict with the witches, (2) the acquisition of magical powers by special circumstances of birth, (3) the motif of fights for agricultural fertility.

(1) The rivalry between the *táltos* and the witches has already been stressed by Géza Róheim (1925: 21–2) and Tekla Dömötör (1982: 157). Bearing in mind the sixteenth- to seventeenth-century *benandante* trials and the Balkan parallels it seems fruitful to make a closer scrutiny of the records of the *táltos* trial, preserved in the documentation of Hungarian witch-trials.[6] The cases of the eight male and fifteen female *táltos* (see Dömötör 1983) are worthy of attention not only because these are the oldest data on actual deeds of sorcerers calling themselves *táltos* in Hungary (the first from 1584, the last from 1766),[7] but also because we learn about them in precisely the context that interests us here; through their relations with witches.

The trials of Hungarian male and female *táltos* resembled those of the *benandanti*: they were accused of being witches, and they defended themselves by arguing that, on the contrary, they healed people harmed by the witches, and they did this 'not by diabolical skills or witchcraft but by virtue of godly science', which is repeated in about half the *táltos* confessions.[8] They also remind us of the *benandanti* by their boasting that 'they would be able to indicate, if they were allowed to do so, all the devils in town'.[9] In 1737, in north-east Hungary, near Munkács, the *táltos* woman Ilona Borsi stressed that 'half the *táltoses* heal, but do no harm to anyone, they recognize the witches and know their deeds' (Lehoczky 1887: 304–6). Another female *táltos*, Anók Fejér, had been healing the victims of the witches with such assiduity that between 1716 and 1732 we read about her in no fewer that seven witch-trials – two of which were conducted specifically against her, and resulted in her expulsion from Debrecen and from Ugocsa county.[10]

The healing ability of the *táltos* was not an acquired attribute; it was related rather to their ecstatic capacity of falling into a trance (*révülés*). In 1720 a female *táltos*, Mrs Antal, told the court that 'she has been lying dead for 9 days and was transported to the other world to God, and she was received there with great splendour and hospitality; and she only came home because God has sent her back to heal; he has even given her a certificate of her science, which was discovered tied to her neck, between her shoulders, when she was resurrected on the ninth day . . .' (Diószegi 1958: 77).

Just as north Italian inquisitors tried to convince the *benandanti*, Hungarian judges also suggested to the *táltos* that their science was of diabolical origin, and that the meetings where they went flying in the air were nothing other than the witches' Sabbath. The female *táltos* of Debrecen, Elisabeth Bartha (née Balási), was even tortured, but she resisted this misrepresentation and thus, like many other *táltoses*, she was able to escape the stake (Komáromy 1910: 354–63). There were, however, *táltoses* who surrendered to the inquisitors' coercion. Such was the case of Kata Oláh (née Baranyai), who was accused in Kamocsa (near Komárom) in 1727. According to the witnesses, her 9–10-year-old daughter boasted of having gone frequently with her mother 'to the end of the world and enjoyed there a great hospitality, then gone to the bottom of the waters and enjoyed a great hospitality there as well'. Mrs Oláh herself also spoke at first about having 'gone to the end of the Skies, on the back of a special cow, and seen there a big fair with a lot of tents'. Under torture she confessed her pact with the Devil, with all the diabolical paraphernalia: Devil's mark, copulation with him once or twice weekly, regular participation in the witches' Sabbath – i.e. anything the judges put into her mouth based on their own learned diabolical mythology. The only point of difference she showed during this confession, which inevitably led to her burning at the stake, was her description of not flying to the Sabbath, but choosing a rather more shamanistic vehicle: 'sailing in a sieve on the river' (Alapi 1914: 17, 26, 34–5).

(2) In similar fashion to other beneficent sorcerers described above, the *táltos* was also predestined for his future role by special circumstances of birth, as the testimonies of the *táltos* trials inform us. Elisabeth Bartha, said that the *táltos* was 'shaped alike by God in the womb of the mother' (Komáromy 1910: 360), and Ilona Borsi also claimed to have received her knowledge from God, 'in the womb of her mother' (Lehoczky 1887: 304). In both cases we are informed that they were born with the principal sign of election of the Hungarian *táltos*, i.e. superhuman capacities was also extended to some other superhuman beings of Hungarian folk-belief: the hail-conjuring, wandering scholar called *garabonciás diák* was born with teeth just like another figure related to the *táltos*, the *tudós* or *látó* (man of knowledge, seer), who was able to see the dead and find lost objects or treasures (Diószegi 1958: 126–8). Róheim had already called attention to this shamanistic feature of *táltos* beliefs, mentioning the analogous case of the Lapp *noid* (1925: 20), and Diószegi completed this hypothesis with other Siberian examples (1958: 134–5). Béla Gunda saw in this belief a survival of totemism in the Hungarian *táltos* tradition, taking into consideration some data according to which at least one parent of the *táltos* was an animal (1968: 41–51). Diószegi, on the other hand, tried to relate the belief about the birth with '*táltos*-teeth' to another possible sign of election of the Hungarian *táltos*, the surplus finger, considered as equivalent to the Siberian beliefs about the surplus bone of the shamans (1958: 136–48).

Let us note here that, in general, special circumstances of birth are by no means the most typical signs of election for the would-be shaman. Among the people of Siberia, the future shaman tended rather to be predestined for his calling by *inheritance*, and, after various pressures by his community to assume his future role, he generally acquired his knowledge during the first, initiatory soul-journey, called the 'saman's illness' (Eliade 1964; Siikala 1978: 330–41). It is probably no accident that birth with teeth as a method of election was to be found on the periphery of the zone of diffusion of shamanistic beliefs: among the Lapps, the Finns, the Hungarians and the Turks. If we add the largely southern Slavic belief of birth with the caul (accepting the hypothesis of their remote relation to shamanism), the picture only becomes more complete.

It could be argued that this way of predetermining the future shaman is already a sign of a decline in the shamanistic beliefs, an index of the loss of the original functions. The sorcerers predestined by this method (instead of by inheritance or election) were already on the way to losing the *public* standing of spiritual leader and magical protector of their communities. Their authority tended to become anonymous – according to some beliefs the extraordinary birth (with teeth or caul) had to be kept secret, for the magical ability could be lost if proclaimed (Bošković-Stulli 1960: 276–7). Thus the relationship of this magical protector with his community became hypothetical: it was not even known how many of them existed. The obvious result of this transformation was that the once priest-like shamans were personified only by wandering sorcerers of uncertain adherence and ambiguous functions; later they continued to exist merely as mythological figures. By the present day, all sorcerer types examined here have reached their ultimate stage of decline; in the seventeenth to eighteenth centuries they seem to have been still at the penultimate stage.

Besides this general typological argument, some of the data about *táltoses* being born with a caul could equally support the impression of closer interconnections between *benandante/kresnik/zduhač* beliefs and the Hungarian *táltos*. One example: at the end of the nineteenth century, a *táltos* girl in the region of Debrecen was said to have been born with teeth and caul. Her mother, however, made the mistake of accidentally burning the coat that had the caul sewn into it; consequently the girl lost her capacity to detect treasure hidden in the ground.[11] These data show that the Slavic beliefs connected with birth with a caul could link up in Hungary the Finno-Ugrian beliefs about birth with teeth. On the other hand, the capacity of transformation into animal shape did not require among the Hungarian *táltos* the additional existence of the caul (as the location of the 'life-soul'). The metamorphosis seems to provide evidence that the *táltos* was definitely closer to the figure of the Siberian shaman than any other being in the region.

(3) Let us now examine the motif of the battles for fertility. The *táltos* did not fight the witches for fertility; they fought among themselves, as the second group of the southern Slavic sorcerers. They generally confronted each other in the shape of bulls of opposing colours (red –blue, light–dark, white–black), sometimes also as stallions, goats, pigs, blue and red fire-balls, fire wheels, metal wheels or birds.[12] Diószegi has tried to prove that these fights took place while the *táltos* was hiding in a trance-like state (*rejtezik, révül*), and that the animals in question were actualy the forms that the soul of the *táltos* took on such occasions (1958: 342–95). As to the reason for these fights, in present-day folk beliefs this is very frequently connected with the question of agricultural fertility. But historical data show rather that this might be a recent addition to the Hungarian *táltos* beliefs.

The *táltos* fights are mentioned in the witch-trials of the seventeenth and eighteenth centuries, but we find no precise information as to why they fought. In 1711, in Debrecen, the female *táltos* Mrs Szaniszlai confessed to 'having fought three times with the German *táltoses* and she has won the battle' (Komáromy 1910: 253). Equally, in 1725, Elisabeth Bartha spoke about *táltoses* 'fighting in the skies for the empire' in ancient times near the Szendelik hill, on the Horto-bágy puszta (Komáromy 1910: 362). In 1721, Kata Barta, from near Komárom, told of going butting in the shape of a bull (Alapi 1914:8). We can read a more colourful description in the 1741 trial of Suska Kőműves in Miskolc still, however, as rivalry for its own sake. She told of male and female *táltos* fighting separately in the skies. She frequently showed neighbours her torn shirt and the blue-green bruises and scars on her body, consequences of these battles. She gave a detailed description of the military organization among the *táltos*: there were 700 in the county, and the light of their flag 'is shining all over the world'. As to their capacity to transform themselves into an animal, according to her it was not necessarily related to the fights: sometimes she took a plate filled with water in her hands, and 'looking into it she turns into a fish' and disappeared for three days. On other occasions, if she wished, she could become a dove or a fox (Bogdál 1960).

From the account of Ilona Borsi (1735) we can conclude that the *táltos* fights (i.e. the experiences during a soul-journey) must have had a kind of initiatory function. She related in her trial that she had been captured at the age of 7 by a female and a male *táltos*. From her home village Pápa they flew on a *táltos*-horse to near Székesfehérvár, to the 'guard-place' of the *táltos*, where they were said to have meetings three times a year – at Pentecost and in the months of Saint James and Saint Michael. Having arrived at the place the two *táltoses* tethered the horses, 'they undressed to become as naked as when they were born', transformed into bulls, rose in the air to butt and fight, and the male *táltos* wounded the female on her left breast. While the terrified young girl looked on, the tethered *táltos*-horses told her 'do not be afraid of what you see in th skies, just sleep, nobody will harm you'. After the whole thing was over, she was apprenticed to a doctor for more than a year. As to the reason for the fights, however, here again we find no explanation: 'the accomplished *táltoses* fight battles, each on behalf of his or her country' (Lehoczky 1887: 304–6).

The earliest known data on *táltoses* fighting for rain derive from the end of the eighteenth century. We are told of battles between the *táltoses* where the winner punished the adversary with hail (Szücs 1951: 404). During the nineteenth century the fertility-protecting role of the *táltoses* presented itself in a national perspective: in the north-western region of Csallóköz they were said to fight foreign *táltoses* every seven years, and the winner's lands would be fertile in the following cycle (Róheim 1925: 14). In the southern village of Szőreg, the Hungarian *táltoses* were reported to fight for rain against the Turkish *táltoses*, both parties riding dragons with swords in their hands.[13] it is only the mass of ethnographic data of the twentieth century that reveals a picture already familiar from Balkan beliefs of *táltoses* fighting above all for the fertility of their own village or region with adversaries from neighbouring villages or regions; they not only decide the issue of fertility by fights but divert drought, hail or animal plague from their own region onto that of the losing adversary.[14]

Vilmos Diószegi surmised that the motif of fighting for good weather came to be incorporated in the *táltos* beliefs from the southern Slavic *grabancias dijak* or its Hungarian equivalent, the *garabonciás diák*. This hypothesis was supported by the fact that the Hungarian *garabonciás* had many attributes of the *táltos*: he was born with teeth, after adulthood he was taken away by other *garabonciás* to be initiated, and he fought in the air in animal forms (Diószegi 1958: 382). It is of course conceivable that there was mutual exchange between the two sets of beliefs. At the same time it is important to note that the *garabonciás* never fought for the fertility of his own region. Although he had power over the weather – being able to conjure storm, thunder and hail – he performed as a lonely, wandering sorcerer belonging to nobody, and he acted mainly out of vengeance because he had not been given the milk or the food he had asked for. Equally, the *garabonciás* was distinguished from the *táltos* by his active

method of acquiring knowledge (in schools), and his magical paraphernalia (books, rings) inherited from medieval ritual magic.[15] The
closest relatives of the *garabonciás* were not the shamanistic beings
discussed in this chapter, but the early medieval figures of the
tempestarii, described in the ninth century by Bishop Agobard in
Lyon, and Bishop Ratherius in Verona (see Boshof 1969; Cohn
1975: 152–3). As Agobard related, not only did they menace with
storm and hail those peasants unwilling to pay them a tribute, but they
also threatened to take away their crops and transport them on their
cloud-ships to sell in 'Mangonia'. Perhaps the *garabonciás* was the
reincarnation of this figure, enriched with some features of medieval
wandering scholars and necromancers.

In the fights of the *táltos* for good weather, the analogy with the
kresnik and the *zduhač* seems to be much closer. As to the problem of
why the motif of fights for fertility became intensified with time, the
answer requires a wider explanation that gives functional reasons for
such historical transformations by taking into account the evolution of
the whole belief system. Before venturing into this, let me mention one
more common feature of the sorcerers examined here, this time from
the two extremes of the chain of interconnections. It is the activity of
seeing the dead practised by the Hungarian *halottlátó*, a type of
cunning folk closely related to the *táltos*.[16] Hungarian historical and
folkloric research has seen clearly the shamanistic character of this
activity, but it has so far attempted to explain the *halottlátó* beliefs by
trying to relate them to medieval visions, other-world journeys,
purgatory descriptions (see Le Goff 1981). Taking into account now
the similar activity of the *benandanti*, we not only get an interesting
new avenue of comparison (exploring popular conceptions of the fate
of the soul after death, the interference of these spirits into the lives of
the living), but we are also once more confirmed in our conviction: all
these sorcerers in Central Europe were somehow genetically connected
to one another, and had an original profile, distinct not only from pan-
European cunning folk, but also from Asian shamanism.

Instead of viewing the Hungarian *táltos* as the only accepted, though not
uncontested (Voigt 1976), specimen of Central European shamanism, it
seems more appropriate to speak of various surviving elements of
shamanism in Central and Southern Europe, transformed and fitted into a
new popular mythology in several distinct ways. Speaking of elements of
shamanism, I have in mind partly the function of these magical experts in
their community and partly some specific aspects of their supernatural
capacities. Let us review these aspects once more.

Even if most of the aforementioned personalities have come to be regarded today as superhuman figures of folk mythology, it seems obvious that they were originally human beings who used the supernatural power they claimed to possess for the benefit of their immediate community (clan, tribe, village, fellow shepherds, surrounding region). They protected their community from evil forces, magical aggression, natural calamities; they tried in turn to inflict these calamities on other groups and regions. Apart from these general functions they also gave magical aid to members of their communities in more minor matters: they offered a chance to communicate with the spirits of the dead, they could tell the future, detect treasure, find lost objects, and heal sick people or putative victims of magical aggression. The most characteristic historical type of this popular community-protecting sorcerer is the Siberian shaman, so it seems legitimate to refer to its features as a kind of *model* when discussing these Central European mythological figures with similar functions.

The main technique for performing this protective function – the sending out of the soul to fight or to acquire information and the falling into a trance in order to do this – is indeed undoubtedly of shamanistic origin. The same can be said about the various animal forms the soul takes on, while leaving a seemingly lifeless body. The use among the Hungarian *táltos* of the shamanistic drum or sieve as an instrument of divination and as a tool facilitating trance induction has frequently been considered as another trace of shamanism (Sebestyén 1900; Diószegi 1958: 171–226; Hoppál 1984b). The appearance of the drum in the *benandanti*'s visions might also be explained in this way. The initiatory vision, the appearance of fellow magicians, superhuman beings or angels to the would-be magician at a certain age in dreams (or, more accurately, when he first falls into trance) the obligatory character of the calling to exercise his functions, his eventual resistance to this calling and the futility of this resistance – all these characteristics bring to mind shamanism. So do some other elements of Hungarian *táltos* beliefs as yet not mentioned here (world-tree, ornaments of feathers and antlers, etc.), which show that among these magicians the Hungarian *táltos* possessed the greatest number of shamanistic traits.

I am fully aware that all this cannot be called shamanism proper, not even in the case of the Hungarian *táltos*; to do so would expand the characteristics of shamanism (see Vajda 1959; Hůltkrantz 1978; Gilberg 1984) in an unacceptable fashion. Nevertheless, all these data can very well be adjusted to the historical process of *disintegration* of shamanistic beliefs. I have already discussed how the predestination of these sorcerers by irregular birth related to the dissipation of the public character of their operation and to the loss of their spiritual leadership of their communities. This can now be underlined by the secret, lonely, night-time character of their trance, in contrast to the public, communal ceremonies of the Siberian shaman (the Hungarian term *rejtezik* means to hide). Even the reports of their soul-journeys and their protective activities were spread by hearsay and not by personal account. In many cases, they were not even allowed to reveal their identity, they had to operate anonymously. According to data of the seventeenth and eighteenth centuries, these magicians represented a version of shamanism disintegrated into various elements without real cohesion; the original functions, attributes and techniques of this shamanism had already become parts of a typologically more recent belief system: witchcraft.

In speaking about witchcraft I do not simply mean the belief that certain malevolent persons possess and use evil powers to harm other people. Since Evans-Pritchard's famous analyses of the Zande witchcraft (1937), witchcraft beliefs have been considered as a complex explanatory system of individual misfortune, with the capacity to express and solve the inner tensions of certain types of communities and societies, to reinforce their basic moral values (see Marwick 1970; Douglas 1970). I should like to refer here to two aspects of this complex belief system. The main concern underlying witchcraft accusations and the legal, individual and magical measures taken against the witches was a presumed magical aggression against the fertility and health of one's person, family, cattle and lands. Secondly, it was not gods, evil spirits or superhuman beings who represented this danger, or even sorcerers or shamans operating on behalf of hostile tribes and peoples – the magical aggression expressed in witchcraft beliefs came from members of one's own immediate community. To quote Philip Mayer (1970), 'the witch is a traitor within the gates', a kinsman a neighbour, who disregarded the elementary laws of loyalty and solidarity.

In one attempt to construct a general sociological account of the different types of magical aggression, witchcraft was characterized as the typical belief system of agricultural societies based on small-scale domestic cultivation (Terrail 1979). Even if this labelling has no more explanatory value than Mircea Eliade's definition of shamanism as the prehistorical religion of Siberian food-collecting tribes (1964: 280), this rough contrast might serve to formulate the problem we have to deal with. Let us posit a hypothetical transition from basically shamanistic beliefs to a belief system dominated by the paradigm of witchcraft, as a consequence of important modifications in the life conditions, economic activities and social structure of certain peoples. If such a transition did take place, it is highly improbable that witchcraft beliefs would have simply substituted for the earlier shamanistic concepts. It seems much more likely that the folk-religion of these peoples would have been characterized by a constantly fluctuating mixture of the two, where

(a) the shaman's figure and many elements of shamanism, instead of disappearing, became reinterpreted in terms of the new dominant system, the witchcraft beliefs;
(b) the shaman's traditional protective function became enriched by new ways of serving his community's interest.

Even if there are no historical data to support this hypothesis in the case of the beliefs examined in this chapter, such a transformation process seems to account very well for some of their traits. It has to be added, naturally, that the real historical circumstances of this transformation were much more complicated than this schematic model: the partial fusion of shamanistic and witchcraft beliefs must have been facilitated by various factors like the hostile treatment of *any* kind of magical activity by Christianity, especially by its sixteenth- and seventeenth-century versions, which intervened with such devastating brutality in the world of popular beliefs.[17]

Taking the first point – the reinterpretation of shamanistic elements in terms of witchcraft – we have several variants to hand. The shamanistic figure can take the role of the positive antagonist of the witches, as in the case of the *benandante*, the *kresnik* and the *táltos*. He or she can also be likened to the witches and enriched by some of the witches' attributes as in the cases of the *vukodlak*, the *zduhač*, some other Balkan sorcerers, and the more recent history of the *benandanti*; nevertheless, even these witch-like figures preserved shamanistic traits, techniques and the feature of serving their immediate communities' interests. The exchange of motifs was necessarily reciprocal in such cases: the witches of these regions might also assume some shamanistic traits.

It might be questioned to what extent the soul-journey of the witches (known all over Europe) was related to the question of shamanism (see Ginzburg 1966: 30–3). The most shamanistic types of these beliefs are beyond doubt those where the soul of the witch was asserted to leave the apparently lifeless body of the witch through the mouth, in the form of a fly, a butterfly, a bug or another kind of small animal, to return there some time later. In Hungarian witch-trials, especially in Transylvania, these descriptions were very frequent.[18] In European folklore the same motif is also well-known, separate from witchcraft beliefs: the early medieval Gunthram legend described a similar soul-journey, where the soul took the form of a lizard – the analysts of this legend also agree on its shamanistic origin (Lixfeld 1972). It is worth noting here that Hungarian witches frequently took on the bull shape of the *táltos* or were especially connected to this animal: some flew up the chimney riding a bull;[19] some entered the room of their victim through the window in the shape of raging bulls;[20] we even hear of midwives butting in the shape of bulls.[21]

The fights and battles among witches show, incidentally, more traces of Serbian *zduhač* beliefs than *táltos* influences. In the eastern part of the Great Hungarain Plain, in Szatmár and Bihar counties, these beliefs probably originated from a large group of Serbian refugees who settled there in the seventeenth century after fleeing from the Turkish aggression. In Örvénd (1716) a Hungarian witch was said to have fought with a Turkish one on the summit of Mount Gellért, near Buda, the most popular location for the witches' Sabbath in Hungary (Schram 1970, I: 80; Dömötör 1939). In two villages in Szatmár county (Bogát in 1735 and Császló in 1745) the witches were reported as fighting with sticks, saying to each other 'I hit you but I don't hurt you', and their blows, indeed, did not inflict pain.[22]

In this region, the battles of the witches were sometimes connected with the issue of agricultural fertility, just as in the case of the shamanistic sorcerers examined in this study. In 1723, in a trial at Nagydiószeg (Bihar county) a witness related the following about the accused Elisabeth Murvai (née Illyes): 'On Saint George's night when the cats were fighting with a terrible mew she said that it was the witches who were distributing the cows of Diószeg among themselves. Mrs Murvai also said that the witches celebrate St George's Day seven times each spring: 1st when the grass comes out of the ground, 2nd on ordinary St George's day, 3rd when the blackthorn is blooming, 4th when the cherry is blooming, 5th when the rye is blooming, 6th when the wheat is blooming, 7th when the winegrape is blooming' (Schram 1970, I: 104–5). Though the witness did not testify to this, it is probable that on each occasion the witches were redistributing goods among themselves. In such cases, the witches could even represent their own community: in 1755 near south-east Hungarian Arad the witches of two villages were reported fighting against each other with sticks (Komáromy 1910: 578). This *zduhač*-like witch figure has survived in that region right up to the present: according to a recent ethnographic account, inhabitants of Szatmár county believe 'that on certain nights the witches fight battles among themselves, and the superstition is that the one who wins will be the effective one during the whole year. In the village Mrs Mándi could bring rain, but only if she previously stole a milkjar' (Bihari 1980: 186, 269). We can match to this series of quarrelsome witches the (geographically fairly close) figure of the Romanian *strigoi*, born with a caul, capable of transformation into any kind of animal, sending out his/her soul on certain nights to the assembly of witches, where they fought each other the whole night, and afterwards embraced each other with tears in their eyes. Such *strigois* became vampires after their death (Eliade 1975: 158–9).

Another motif lent by *táltoses* to Hungarian witches was the magical sieve or drum. Sometimes it was used for casting spells, sometimes for transportation: in 1629, it is reported that a witch accused near the abbey of Pannonhalma 'sat with several other diabolical witch-complices in a sieve, was shipped on it to an island on the Danube, picked there some poplar buds to make various unguents by which they could harm many good Christians'.[23]

It is difficult to establish whether the many reports of the military organization of the Hungarian witches[24] reflect the influence of the *táltos* battalions. Perhaps both phenomena merely show the deep imprint on the mythology of the constant warfare in the country during the sixteenth to eighteenth centuries. The supernatural warrior–sorcerers naturally took on the shape of armies, battalions commanded by officers, proceeding with drums and banners.

The last shamanistic feature of Hungarian witch-beliefs to be mentioned in this series is a special technique of bewitching people and animals: the extraction of bones.[25] Only detailed comparative investigations could establish to what extent this type of abuse was related to the shamanistic practice of dismembering the initiant to count his bones, in order to find out whether he really had a surplus bone (Diószegi 1958: 86–148). One would have to find out whether this mode of abuse existed in European regions with no shamanistic beliefs. The only (limited) comparative possibility that I know of relates Hungary, interestingly enough, once again with northern, Alpine Italy. In the latter region is found a belief, documented several times between the fourteenth and seventeenth centuries, connected to the witches' (or, rather, fairy-like beings') nightly assembly. Here they ate a certain type of beef, then put the bones into the skin and stuffed it with straw, and their leader, the 'Lady of the Game', resurrected the bones, but after such treatment they were good for nothing.[26] There are two versions of this same motif in Hungarian Sabbath descriptions: in 1743, in the western city of Sopron, on a Sabbath, a red cow was eaten by the witches, 'then the bones were again erected and stuffed with straw' (Schram 1970, II: 190); in 1734, in the south-east borough of Hódmezővásárhely, 'a beautiful fat baby . . . was cut to pieces, cooked and eaten, then its bones were again put together and stuffed with straw . . .' (Schram 1970, I: 247).

Now we can turn to the other side of the historical transformation of shamanistic beliefs – to the question of the eventual new functions these shamanistic figures could fulfil. The Hungarian *táltos* data seem to be very instructive here. In particular periods, various *táltos* functions could achieve a special importance. During the time of the great witch-hunts, the *táltoses* became involved in eliminating witches. In the eighteenth century, after the devastated country was reclaimed from the Turks, their main function seems to have been to detect hidden treasure. The *táltoses'* originally irrational propensity for fighting was first rationalized as part of the historical struggle of the Hungarians for their independence, then was increasingly put to the service of the basic concern of the peasants and shepherds, that of agricultural fertility. The fact that all the shaman-like figures of the Balkan regions guaranteed agricultural fertility for their immediate communities must be the result of a similar kind of historical transformation.

In conclusion, it seems to make sense to speak of a manifold integration of shamanistic elements into the witchcraft beliefs of Central Europe and the Balkan peninsula. This does not, of course, mean that all these shamanistic motifs can be isolated and used to construct a pure shamanistic layer in these folk beliefs. Neither can we postulate or reconstruct the kinds of shamanistic beliefs these peoples perhaps had before the emergence of the witchcraft beliefs. These questions can only be answered eventually on the basis of new historical documentation.

*　　*　　*

There is one last brief point to be made. Looking at our problem from the perspective of witchcraft, was there a place in the witchcraft paradigm for these shaman-like personalities, or did their existence lead to some important changes in the witchcraft beliefs of this region?

There was, indeed, a place in the witchcraft beliefs where shamanic figures could and generally did fit in: in the role of the diviner, the cunning folk, the wizard, the professional magician, who engaged in magical counter-aggression against the presumed witches, thus lifting the spell and healing the bewitched. This figure, until recently completely neglected in the historical and folkloric analyses of European witchcraft, is the central hero of Jeanne Favret-Saada's sensational, though contested, account of present witchcraft beliefs in rural France (1977, 1981). Analogous beliefs have also been analysed in present-day Germany (Schöck 1978: 132–53). The nature of the 'power' these witch doctors claimed to possess, the kind of magical actions they undertook in fighting the witches, the ecstatic techniques they used while engaged in eliminating the witches, conjuring or divining, and the fact that election to their profession was often combined with hallucinations – all these features appear to merit the attention of shamanologists or, at least, of historians of religion. Apart from a few remarks by Alan Macfarlane (1970: 115–35), Keith Thomas (1971: 212–51, 548) and Robert Muchembled (1978: 109–16), we know hardly anything about these positive sorcerers, who were frequently mentioned in the documents of the witch-trials and less frequently but still quite often burnt as witches. No historical or folkloric research exists, for example, into the *néző* (seer) or the *tudós* – Hungarian equivalents of the witch doctor – in spite of the great quantity of data about such figures in the edited documents of the trials.[27] It is not by chance that one of the already mentioned female *táltoses*, Mrs Szaniszlai from Debrecen, who claimed to be an opponent of the witches, named herself '*táltos* and *néző*' (Komáromy 1910: 249–50).

Although in the position of the *néző* the *táltoses* could find an appropriate role during their gradual integration into the system of witch-beliefs, there remained a basic difference between witch doctors and shamanistic sorcerers. The former very rarely operated for people of their community; their clients generally came from a great distance away. In their immediate surroundings these doctors were often feared and accused of being witches. They defended themselves in vain by asserting that their power was only good for healing and unwitching; for, according to the paradigm of witchcraft, the one who can unwitch can also bewitch, especially in the immediate surroundings (Muchembled 1978: 110). So if a shaman-like figure took the role of the witch-doctor, as the *benandanti* did, he was trapped by the inevitable logic of being considered as a witch himself by his own community. He was caught in the trap because complex societies had lost the sense of the traditional – absolute and automatic – form of solidarity that was so well-known to archaic communities.

9

Witch-hunting in Hungary: Social or Cultural Tensions?

The theme of witchcraft has attracted a great number of scholars in recent decades. I shall single out just one of the many reasons for this: witchcraft is a topic that cuts across the established disciplinary boundaries and provides us with the possibility of fruitful exchanges between various fields of research, including social, cultural and legal history; the folklore of magical beliefs, practices and mythologies; and anthropological enquiries into social, moral and cultural meanings, functions or dysfunctions. A combination of these different approaches, together with close scrutiny of archival documents, has led to a number of studies and monographs that in turn link this topic with various other concerns of recent historiography, such as community studies, family history, gender approaches, history of the 'reform' of early modern popular culture, historical anthropology, history of *mentalité*.[1] On the other hand, however, the complexity of the problem and the richness of its various forms still defy universal explanations, blur theoretical insights and leave us to hypothesize about why it was that, at given historical moments, large-scale witch persecutions occurred in certain places or regions.

The wide array of theoretical explanatory tools and comparative sets of data stands in puzzling contrast to the ease with which each general proposition can be contradicted. About a decade ago, the anthropologist Rodney Needham characterized these anomalies of current witchcraft research in the following way: 'witches are neighbours, or else they are distant; they are relatives, or else they cannot be relatives; they are marginal, or else they are enemies within; they are lowly misfits, or else they are secure and prosperous just because of their witchcraft; they are so categorized that not everybody can be a witch, or else they are such that anyone can be a witch' (1978: 30). The more we seem to know about the historical and anthropological details of witchcraft, the more numerous become the intriguing riddles and paradoxes we have to face when researching it. While the individual cases, the local and regional panics seem to obey recurrent patterns, the underlying tensions, the passionfilled testimonies and weird phantasies of the persons involved continue to provide lessons about historical, social, cultural, regional differences.

In the following presentation of the sixteenth- to eighteenth-century witch-hunting period in Hungary, I will try to illustrate the unique nature of the Hungarian cases while taking into account the interpretive possibilities and weaknesses of two current sets of explanations about the occurrence of witch persecutions: one that connects it to the social tensions and the other that relates it to the cultural tensions of the period.

*   *   *

Before doing so, however, I shall begin with a brief overall sketch. Apart from a few scattered medieval cases, witch-trials started to multiply in Hungary in the 1560s, and their number rose at a moderate pace throughout the seventeenth century (with two quantitative jumps, in the 1620s and in the 1690s). The real peak of the persecutions came very late in comparison to other countries, between 1710 and 1730 (with more than 200 accused and more than 60 death sentences per decade). Witch-hunting then proceeded fairly actively until stopped from above by the enlightened legislation of Maria Theresa between 1758 and 1766. My calculations are based upon the records of 1,642 persons charged with witchcraft in Hungary between 1520 and 1777, 1,482 of whom were women (89 per cent). The number of known death sentences was 449, and 23 persons died in prison or by lynching, while in 460 cases the accused suffered lesser punishments. Compared with the masses killed, for example, in the South German persecutions (see Midelfort 1972; Behringer 1988), these numbers seem fairly moderate for a country of 3–4 million inhabitants, even if we take into account that in 710 cases the outcome of the trial is unknown, and furthermore that the number of documented trials could be increased by hundreds of additional recorded cases unearthed by recent archival researches and estimations. Witchcraft accusations and trials recurred persistently in Hungarian towns and villages over a lengthy period, but they rarely (in fact only exceptionally) amounted to the type of panic, with mass accusations and group burnings, familiar to some other European countries.[2]

While analysing these data, one should bear in mind that the 250 years in question represent a turbulent period in Hungarian history. Between 1541 and 1686, one-third of the country was under Turkish occupation; the north-western region became part of the Habsburg Empire, and in the east the princes of Transylvania tried to survive by balancing between these two great powers. If we consider the religious and ethnic divisions (Lutherans in the German-inhabited towns of northern Hungary and Transylvania, Calvinists and Unitarians in eastern Hungary and Transylvania, vigorous re-Catholicizing campaigns in the seventeenth to eighteenth centuries, Orthodox and Greek-Catholics among the Serbian and Romanian population, and of course the rule of Islam in the Turkish territories), we can see that the Hungary of this age was torn apart by these conflicts – not only in the metaphorical sense, but also literally.[3]

As for the major course of events, constant warfare against the Turks was coupled with renewed uprisings and wars of independence against the Habsburgs. It is significant that the bulk of the witch-trials occurred after the expulsion of the Turks and especially after the last and greatest anti-Habsburg uprising led by Prince Ferenc Rákóczi, which ended in 1711 with his surrender. This supports the wide-ranging observation that witch-hunting generally became epidemic in intervals of peace after, or between, the various wars of early-modern Europe.[4]

The later peak of witch persecutions in Hungary can, on the other hand, also be attributed to various other factors. The central–southern territories, which were under Turkish rule until 1686, experienced during this time only sporadic witchcraft accusations, rarely supported by the Turkish authorities. In eighteenth-century witch-trials, however, it was these very regions that had an especially high quantitative share.[5]

Another significant proposition could be made by comparing the timing of witch-hunting periods in Europe, where the following model can be observed: recurrent waves of persecution between the fifteenth and early seventeenth centuries in the more developed countries of western and Mediterranean Europe,[6] belated outbreaks in the second half of the seventeenth century in Scandinavia, Austria, north-west Germany, Bohemia and Silesia, and major persecutions in Poland, Hungary and Croatia in the first half of the eighteenth century.[7] This gradual and belated explosion of major witch-hunting waves at the 'periphery' fits into a more general tardiness of social and cultural evolution in these regions, which had been echoing western European models (such as feudalism, urban privileges, chivalry, religious movements) with a similar time lag since the Middle Ages (see Szűcs 1983). But in what way can we regard witch-hunting as an evolutionary model that attracted emulation? And how are we to account for the fact that witchcraft beliefs and the legal mechanisms for persecution had been present in these regions since the early sixteenth century (i.e. the cultural *diffusion* of this model took place very quickly), and yet the mass persecutions broke out only according to the above chronological pattern?

The answer can be sought in two different directions, which, however, become linked at some points. One can attempt to look for the cause of mass persecutions in the increased disciplinary potential of early-modern state power, which emerged later in the regions concerned.[8] This argument finds support in the evidence from Hungary. Habsburg absolutism did indeed intensify its impact upon Hungary from the end of the seventeenth century onwards. The reorganization of the established county jurisdictions (after the reconquest of the country from the Turks in the 1690s and again after 1711, the fall of Rákóczi) had a considerable impact upon renewed persecutions, especially through the importation of the Austrian legal handbook, *Praxis Criminalis* (a compendium of Carpzov's *Practica Rerum Criminalium*), which was packed with demonological concepts and measures for witch-hunting.[9]

Another direction of enquiry would try to correlate the later explosions of witchcraft persecutions with a set of underlying conflicts and tensions, which occurred in these regions with a similar time lag. This brings us to the sociological explanation of witchcraft persecutions.

*   *   *

According to a major paradigm of historical and anthropological writing, witchcraft accusations explained individual or collective misfortune by pinpointing the 'responsible' human agents within the immediate environment, and gave redress to the damaged parties by purging the community of the 'witches' who violated the norms of coexistence (Evans-Pritchard 1937; Marwick 1970). Accusations naturally tended to be embedded in a set of local conflicts; they occurred at 'weak points' of social relations; they expressed 'deep-felt animosities in acceptable guise' (Thomas 1971: 561); they served as a social 'strain-gauge' (Marwick 1964). Consequently, historians could better understand the occurrence of witchcraft accusations by clarifying their social context. Revealing hidden tensions with apparently no other, more direct, outlets or resolutions witchcraft conflicts even offer historians and anthropologists a promise of new insights into obscure but important problems within the affected communities.

This approach, which Alan Macfarlane (1970) called the 'sociology of accusations', provides witchcraft research not only with a new set of explanations, but also with a wide range of previously ignored evidence to be examined a large number of witnesses' depositions in witchcraft trials, voicing various motives for popular accusations and providing ample evidence of the conflicts that gave rise to witch-trials. On the basis of these sources, Macfarlane (1970: 168) and Thomas (1971: 553–67) suggested that the dissolution of traditional communal or neighbourly forms of solidarity in early modern villages, and the rise of a new type of individualistic ethic, could have been among the most typical conflicts leading to witchcraft accusations. This type of investigation has been successfully developed by witchcraft scholars of other regions, who have provided further illustration for this 'neighbourhood conflict' thesis. Subsequent studies also support another observation of Macfarlane's

(1970: 149–51) – that witchcraft conflicts did not necessarily correlate with a socioeconomic crisis, but correlated rather with periods of transformation favouring certain social strata and disadvantaging others.[10]

John Putnam Demos (1982) carried this sociological explanation to its logical conclusion by adding to his analysis of New England witch-trials a crucially important dimension: the identification of the parties involved from other, *independent*, sources (tax rolls, testaments, diaries, other types of trials, civil or ecclesiastical conflicts involving the same people). Using his exceptionally well-preserved documentation, combined with his experience as a social historian, Demos could legitimately speak of the 'social matrix' of witchcraft (1982: 278ff), distinguishing the strained social relations and the typical social situations leading to witchcraft conflicts. By elaborating the biographical and psychological details of the parties involved, and investigating the social structures and religious conflicts of the villages and towns in question, he could at the same time fulfil the need for an investigation of witchcraft conflicts as a process, a kind of social drama within the history of those peoples (Turner 1967).

At the same time, the simplistic versions of the sociological approach generated widespread criticism. The functionalistic trend that sees in witchcraft accusations a pure expression of 'social causes' that lie elsewhere, or a regulating mechanism that serves to resolve those conflicts on the basis of commonly accepted norms – all this has been justifiably rejected by Mary Douglas (1970). Erik Midelfort underlined the *dys*-functional character of early modern European witchcraft accusations, which resist reduction to social causes and fit badly into anthropological categories elaborated for present-day Africa (1972: 179–90). The triumphant 'neighbourhood conflict' thesis was undermined by Macfarlane himself, whose later investigations (1978) pushed back the origins of English individualism into the early middle ages and tried to demolish the myth of historical communities – two elements, among others, upon which his earlier witchcraft interpretation was based. Rodney Needham pointed out that 'it is tautological to say that witchcraft accusations point to weak spots or to difficult relationships, for it is in part the accusations themselves that characterize the spots as weak and the relationships as uneasy'. Although Demos managed to escape this trap by linking these 'weak spots' with the ones detected in independent sources of social history, Needham's 'question would remain whether the weak and difficult spots were so precisely because, for some other reason perhaps, they were conventionally regarded as the loci of witchcraft' (1978: 29). Jeanne Favret-Saada's psychological–ethnographical investigations of present-day French witch-beliefs (1977, 1981) also warned of a sociological–functional reductionism: witchcraft accusations follow the lines of a specific symbolic system where real characteristics merge with stereotypes, real events get continuously reworked in memory to fit into a consistent bewitchment diagnosis of one's misfortune, and the final version of the accusation is a complex therapeutic–narrative–mythological construct to be interpreted with care, rather than a clear testimony of the 'underlying' social conflicts within the community concerned.

It does not follow naturally from all this criticism – much of it justified – that a sociological account of the history of witch-hunting is impossible or useless. Rather, the criticism provides encouragement to seek the complex patterns of the interwoven social, cultural and magical conflicts with fewer preconceptions and with an open attitude towards integrating an even wider sphere of explanatory factors. The most recent complex regional monograph about witch-hunting, that of Wolfgang Behringer dealing with south-eastern Germany (1988), seems to proceed in this way. Without trying to resolve the debate in general (for each witchcraft panic has to be explained within its immediate context), Behringer advances a set of new observations concerning the correlation of natural calamities and subsistence crises with witch-hunting waves, at the same time showing how contemporary demonological reasoning tried to link natural and social disasters with the problem of witchcraft (1988: 96–106).

My aim is similar to Behringer's: without setting out to find a sociological key to Hungarian witchcraft prosecutions, I will investigate (within the limited space of this chapter) certain cases that could illustrate their various social contexts. Two of my five examples concern urban witch-trials, one from the onset of the witch-hunts (the Kolozsvár [Cluj] trials of the late sixteenth century), and one from its eighteenth-century peak (the 1728 panic in Szeged). The aristocratic witchcraft accusations in seventeenth-century Transylvania and the shepherd trials of the western counties in the second half of the seventeenth century present two different social extremes. Finally, the witchcraft cases in the borough of Hódmezővásárhely and its neighbouring villages exemplify the mainstream of Hungarian witchcraft conflicts.

                    *   *   *

The witch-trials of the Transylvanian city of Kolozsvár are of special importance in Hungarian history. They are the first series of trials for which we possess documentation. According to the documents, between 1565 and 1593, nineteen witches were prosecuted here; thirteen were condemned to death by burning (six of these in 1584); the outcome of the rest of the trials is unknown (Komáromy 1910: 3–74). The fact that Kolozsvár became the first centre of this new type of conflict is instructive in several respects. This city of about 8,000 inhabitants – mainly German originally, but in this period becoming increasingly dominated by a Hungarian majority – was the only Transylvanian city to witness spectacular economic growth and prosperity in the sixteenth century, while the other 'Saxon' cities (like Kronstadt [Brasov] or Hermannstadt [Sibiu]) were affected by the general economic decline of Hungarian cities at that time.[11] This rapid expansion was somewhat disturbed by the troubled political climate of Transylvania in the 1580s – which, incidentally, coincided with the 1584 local peak of witchcraft accusations. This correlation, however, cannot be extrapolated too far, since other Hungarian cities with similar or even more alarming economic or political troubles did not experience large-scale witchcraft accusations at that period.[12]

If we try to relate the testimony rendered at these trials to certain more concrete tensions, we find that they do indeed show traces of typical neighbourhood conflicts (stealing the fertility of the neighbour's land or animals), of strained economic relations (accusations against former housekeepers or lodgers, debates about work cooperation). Others can be related to factional struggles: one of the mighty town jurors, Mihály Igyártó, seems to have directed a campaign against his enemies by accusing them of witchcraft – he initiated two witch-trials against women who bore witness against him in another kind of trial (Komáromy 1910: 23–7). Quantitatively, however, the overwhelming motivation of the accusations seems to lie elsewhere: eight of the nineteen 'witches' were healers or midwives, who apparently had no economic or social conflicts with their accusers; three more cases had their origins in jealousy connected to presumed love-magic; in one case a husband accused his wife. In 1565, in the first three trials of the series (Komáromy 1910: 1–13), legal proceedings seem to have been sparked by mutual accusations of three wise women, each of whom attributed people's illnesses to charms inflicted by the other (with the help of the fairy-like *pulchrae mulieres*). Another of the executed witches (1584) presents traits related to the Hungarian version of shamanism falling into trance, making a soul-journey in the shape of a fly and boasting of other special powers (Komáromy 1910: 44–55). Still another fell under suspicion because she possessed a 'devilish book' which enabled her to detect treasure (Komáromy 1910: 24).

The overall impression is of a generalized fear of magical aggression stirring up traditional folk-beliefs, and the reasons for this scare could be religious and cultural rather than social and economic. Kolozsvár was the centre of Transylvanian religious debates in the period. Lutheranism made its appearance here in the 1540s, represented by Reverend Gáspár Heltai, who directed a famous printing press in 1550 and organized a team that aimed at the first complete translation of the Bible into Hungarian. While German inhabitants remained Lutheran, Hungarians tended to become radicalized and to accept the 'Helvetian confession', i.e. Calvinism (like Heltai himself), or even to become Unitarians (like Ferenc Dávid, elected twice as the bishop of Protestant Hungarians, then executed in 1579 because of his increasingly radical views).[13] The Jesuits also made their appearance in the 1570s.

Some of the witchcraft conflicts seem indeed to be related to these religious divisions. The Calvinist juror, Igyártó (a militant promulgator of local statutes against adultery and fornication in the same period and one of the main witch-accusers), was in conflict with the presumed witches precisely on account of their participation in Carnival disorders.[14] Another of the notorious accusers, Peter Grúz (who brought the charges of witchcraft against the two first wise women to be burnt), later became the militant leader of the Catholic party, which proposed to Prince István Báthory in 1575 that he should invite Jesuits into the city of Kolozsvár.[15] Each religious party advocated an increasing hostility towards manifestations of early-modern popular culture (see Burke, 1978: 207–22), the effect of which is shown here by the fact that the accused mostly came under suspicion for having performed traditional fertility rites or healing magic. The criminalization of magical healing (the assertion that it could work only if the 'same devil' that is, the healer himself had previously carried out the bewitching) was pronounced in Kolozsvár in 1584 – the first occurrence in Hungary (Komáromy 1910: 70).

The aristocratic witchcraft accusations of the seventeenth century present a very different picture, in regard both to underlying social patterns and to their cultural background. As for the former, they conform nicely to the general pattern of conflict-motivated fear of magical vengeance, where the victorious party supposed himself (or his wife) to be bewitched, and accused relatives of defeated rivals of practising witchcraft, thus eliminating them in this additional way. Transylvanian Prince Gábor Bethlen (1613–29), after acceding to power following the murder of Gábor Báthory in 1612, initiated a spectacular witch-trial against the deceased's sister, Anna Báthory, and two high-born widows (Kata Török and Kata Iffju), also intimately related to the deceased. They were banished and their considerable estates confiscated. The accusations ranged from fornication (with Bethlen's ill-fated predecessor, Gábor Báthory) to love-magic and using witchcraft to harm the health of Zsuzsanna Károlyi, the wife of Prince Gábor Bethlen. The long drawn-out proceedings, revived several times against Anna Báthory (1614, 1618, 1621) till her final exile and the confiscation of all her properties, were also supported by new legislation concerning the prosecution of witchcraft, enacted by the Transylvanian Diet in 1614.[16]

Similarly, Prince Mihály Apafy (1661–90) staged a major witch-trial between 1679 and 1686, involving twenty-five accused (thirteen noblewomen among them), principally Zsuasanna Vitéz, wife of his defeated rival Pál Béldy. Mrs Béldy, who was arrested after her political agitation and armed uprising in favour of her exiled husband, was alleged to have bewitched Apafy's wife, Anna Bornemisza, causing not only her recurrent illnesses but also the death of several of her new-born children. Although the charges could not be proved against her, Mrs Béldy died in prison, and investigations of the affair remained a feature of Transylvania's troubled political life for about eight years.[17]

It is no accident that witchcraft accusations permeated the conflictual and intrigue-ridden court life of seventeenth-century Transylvanian princes. The recurrent decline and re-emergence of this charming country – prey to Turkish political machinations, uncertain in its relations with Poland, hesitating whether to side eventually with the Habsburgs against the Turks, menaced occasionally by Romanian *voivods*, and torn also by the intrigues of mighty and ambitious aristocrats aspiring to princely dignity – all this served to enhance the contemporary vision that the fate of this land was being influenced by obscure magical forces. It was not by chance that Transylvania was labelled by contemporaries as *Tündérország* (fairy-land) or *Tündérkert* (fairy-garden).[18] Besides, Transylvanians were not the only people to believe in magic operating in the higher spheres of politics; the bewitched fleet of James VI of Scotland is an outstanding example.[19]

From the cultural point of view, two aspects merit attention. One is the stereotype of the aristocratic witch, exclusively female, who did not practise witchcraft herself, but hired professionals (popular wise women, magical specialists) to provide her with effective magical tools to assist her if she wanted to cast spells personally or to harm her enemies in other ways. It is fascinating to see witchcraft notions rearticulated to rely upon this kind of division of labour, appropriate to the new aristocratic life-styles. The actual bewitchment (the dirty work) was done by a team of popular magicians (magic and superstition having become the label of popular culture); they were used as specialized agents within a whole team of servants hired for evil-doing (spies, killers). Although these servants were declared guilty and punished, the responsibility was shared by the cruel lady-witch who embodied the dimension of moral evil. She plotted the whole enterprise and it allegedly served her pleasures, her perversities, or her personal vengeance.

This witch-stereotype tended to be a crystallization point for moral evil in all its dimensions: Anna Báthory, denounced by Prince Bethlen as 'killer devil whore', was accused of incest with her brother and also of killing her own son. Consider also the case of her more famous cousin, Elisabeth Báthory, whose 1609–11 trial (initiated by her two sons-in-law and resulting in life imprisonment and the loss of her estates) depicted her as a sort of female Gilles de Rais and precursor of the marquis de Sade, producing testimony that she had tortured and killed several hundred of her maids. According to the depositions of her servants (not surprisingly) she also experimented with witchcraft.[20] In the year 1637, torturing, beating and killing servants, especially maids, was also the central feature of the witch-trial of another aristocratic lady, Anna Rozina Listius, from north-west Hungary.[21]

Finally, and this is the second culturally relevant aspect, the fashions of learned magic in the late sixteenth and early seventeenth centuries also had their impact upon these aristocratic witchcraft cases. Alongside tales of popular magic, we hear about learned astrology, and also about special amulets. The interrelated nature of the emergent hermetic, occult and magical fashions and witch-hunting attitudes in the sixteenth century has been brilliantly analysed for England by Keith Thomas (1971). This same relation still remains to be examined for the Transylvanian and Polish (Cracovian) courts of the Báthory, the Prague court of Emperor Rudolph II, and the smaller German princely courts, which hosted and provided meeting centres for a large number of famous magical experts who came from all over Europe.[22]

My third example takes us to the very different world of shepherds in the western counties under Habsburg rule. They contributed – under the military–economic protection of the mighty and enterprising lords of the region, the counts Zrínyi, Esterházy or Batthyány – to a traditional cattle trade with Venice and with the southern German cities, which, however, tended to decline in the second half of the century.[23] This, together with various other natural calamities of the seventeenth century, and with the burden of the renewed warfare against the Turks, must have produced serious strains in this pastoral society after 1650. A series of mutual accusations among shepherds between 1651 and 1687, which led to a dozen witch-trials in Körmend (centre of the Batthyányi estate), Lakompak (centre of the Esterházy estate) and the nearby city of Szombathely, could be viewed as the expression of these tensions. The general complaints were that the accused gave a magical unguent to their own animals 'in the name of the devil' (Schram 1970, II: 718), diverted plagues from their own animals onto the flocks of neighbouring shepherds, attacked the animals of rivals by setting wolves upon them, or even assumed the shape of a wolf themselves and acted as werewolves.[24] As for the social side, the trials give an interesting picture of the competitive, individualistic shepherd society of the age, and point towards the above-mentioned theories that explain early modern witchcraft accusations by emerging individualistic tendencies.

An examination of the beliefs disclosed in the depositions, however, warns us to be wary of this explanation. Most of the accusations involved belong to the general Hungarian mythology concerning the 'cunning shepherds' (*tudós pásztor*), whose positive representatives had been considered types of shamanistic sorcerers right up to modern times

(Dömötör 1981: 139–43). On the other hand, the diabolical elements in these trials (devilish associations, covens of male sorcerers, having their own judges, captains, flags, practising strange rituals, having a familiar devil that can be put in a box[25]) seem very alien to Hungarian witchcraft beliefs. The various werewolf concepts first emerged more than a century earlier (1529, 1531) in two cowherd trials in the city of Sopron, which was inhabited principally by a German population.[26] Such beliefs surfaced only sporadically in other Hungarian regions, and then only in the middle of the eighteenth century. They were altogether alien to Hungarian folklore.[27] This might warn us to treat with some caution the foregoing economic and functional explanation and to look for other causes, including foreign influences.

In fact, this campaign was directed not just against shepherds, but also against some other male vagrant sorcerers. All this might be related to the campaign against presumed associations of male sorcerers in neighbouring Styria, such as the *Grindiger Hansel*, trial in 1659 (Valentinitsch 1986) or the singular witch scare in the region of Salzburg between 1675 and 1690, known as *Zauberer Jackl* trials, whose several hundred victims were mostly beggars and marginals, and mostly males (Nagl 1972/3, and 1974). These campaigns resulted in a rather unusual stereotype of the target of witch-hunting in these regions, with more male victims than female (Behringer 1988: 352–5) – and the image of the devilish male sorcerer also recurred persistently in the western border regions of Hungary until the middle of the eighteenth century.[28]

My fourth example is the most significant episode in the history of Hungarian witch-hunting – the scare of the 1720s–1730s in the Szeged region. This involved forty-one accused (and more than 100 denounced persons) between 1728 and 1744 – twenty-one of whom were brought to trial in 1728, fourteen were executed and two died in prison – the brutality of the Szeged panic seems unparalleled in Hungarian history. The only comparable example is the mass trial of eleven witches in the borough of Somorja (Samorin), near the city of Pozsony (Bratislava), in 1691, which resulted in the mass burning of seven of the accused, the beheading of one and the banishment of three others (Horna 1935). Most other panic-type persecutions involved 'only' between five and ten persons; the urban scares so common in Germany and other parts of Europe were almost non-existent in Hungary.[29]

Detailed investigations carried out to find an explanation for the Szeged scare have focused upon several underlying causes: natural calamities in the preceding decades (plague in 1709–13, flood in 1712, serious drought in 1728 – hence the principal accusation against the witches that they sold the rain to the Turks); a precipitate growth of the city population from 3,000 around 1700, to 7,000 around 1719, and 14,000 around

1728 – a result of the arrival of Hungarian, German and Serbian settlers; factional struggles between an 'autonomy' party (mainly Hungarians) and a German party. The German faction's candidate for judgeship, György Podhradszky, was one of the initiators of the persecutions, whose most noteworthy victim was Dániel Rósa, a former Hungarian judge of the city (Rósa, a slightly discredited person because of previous local conflicts, was not a member of the local 'autonomy' party, but was a useful figure to bring it into disrepute).[30]

The pattern of brutal torture, the enforced adoption of demonological stereotypes, and even the rapid extension of witchcraft accusations from lower social circles (midwives and beggars) to socially more elevated targets (like former judges and other municipal functionaries) conforms very much to western European witch scares. It seems that a kind of witch panic similar to those experienced in Germany a century earlier was starting to gather force in the disrupted and rapidly repopulated southern territories of Hungary. Connections with the mass arrival of settlers and with typical crises of precipitate growth of new urban communities could also make it legitimate to compare these persecutions to the New England cases analysed by John Demos (1982). The general intellectual and institutional context, however, was different by the 1720s. The notoriety of these later persecutions and the tempering reaction of the Viennese imperial court constrained the Szeged judges to return to 'regular', more moderate Hungarian standards of witchcraft prosecution.[31]

The catalyzing effect of the Szeged panic can be observed throughout the whole region (simultaneously affected by similar population growth, similar ethnic and social tensions between indigenous and settler populations, and similar natural calamities). Nevertheless, nowhere else did witchcraft accusations give rise to similar panics; they remained rather at the level of heightened manifestations of personal conflicts. Thus – coming to my fifth example – the neighbouring Calvinist borough of Hódmezővásárhely (with 5,000 inhabitants in the 1730s), experienced twenty-four witch-trials between 1729 and 1759, of which six resulted in death sentences.[32] Here the accusations also started with popular healers, easy targets for incrimination. Among the accused there was a considerable percentage of beggars and marginals. One was characterized by her son as follows: 'my mother has spent all she had for drinking. As far as I am concerned she could well be burnt' (Schram 1970, I: 262). There were also many widows, elderly peasant wives, and relatives of convicted witches (daughter, husband). Altogether the whole picture fits the stereotypes. Neighbourly conflicts, cohabitation and unsuccessful healing have their due share among the accusations. It is noteworthy that some members of the local elite, like the schoolmaster, the chanter, a young *studiosus* (Schram 1970, I: 268–71) and the juror and usurer, István Ceglédi,[33] act also as accusers, adding weight to the mass of depositions from the lower social strata.

Another category of accusers deserves a special mention – that of German soldiers residing in the borough and the neighbouring villages, and being compulsorily maintained by the population. Here, as in many other places, they acted as active witch-finders or accusers, using this imported skill to counteract the hostility of the local population.[34] The most spectacular bewitchment stories are to be read in the accusations of a soldier-servant, who made complaints in 1739 against ten inhabitants of the nearby village of Mindszent, four of whom were eventually brought to court (Schram 1970, I: 249–61).

The significance of the Hódmezővásárhely trials – besides offering a rich set of data on the local quarrels underlying witchcraft accusations, and a series of popular, highly exotic witches' Sabbath descriptions, told this time not by tortured witches but reworked in the nightmares of the accusers – lies in the remarkable absence of panic reactions to various calamities. There are no traces in the witchcraft documentation of the two contemporary uprisings of the region, the Péró peasant revolt in 1735 and the Törő-Pető *kuruc* revolt in 1752–3; no traces of religious divisions: Hódmezővásárhely was a slightly insecure Calvinist refuge within its Catholic surroundings; and, more importantly, no trace of the terrible cattle plague of 1736 or the plague of 1738 in which half the population (about 2,500) died. Instead of contributing to tensions that would be relieved by witch hunting, these calamities repeatedly brought the rather sporadic witchcraft accusations to a halt. Those who suffered from these calamities apparently found relief in other types of strain-gauges or conflict-solving mechanisms.

To sum up the results of this schematic enquiry into the social causes of witchcraft prosecutions, one could say that this type of enquiry can be of great help in locating witchcraft accusations in their local historical context, but one should not expect from this a definitive explanation of causes. The sociological approach allows us to formulate more specific questions about the occurrence and the significance of various types of witchcraft conflicts, but it does not provide easy answers.

On the other hand, a sociological examination of accusation narratives could provide various other means of enriching our views about how society was reflected in these magical conflicts. Which were the typical social situations that would be likely to support witchcraft accusations (economic or personal jealousy, refusal of alms or neighbourly favours, quarrels about cooperation or payment, rivalry among healers, midwives)? Where could these accusations or threats be communicated (taverns, spinning houses, markets, family gatherings around sick members)? What sites of social life did the witches allegedly select to break

into and to rejoice in during their nightly Sabbath gatherings?[35] There is a
link between these stereotypes and actual social conditions, but it can only
be unveiled if one takes into account the difference between magic and
reality.

*   *   *

At this point I would like to turn to the other problem to be discussed, that
of cultural tensions. Some of them have already been hinted at during the
preceding examples: religious division; moments of generalized fear of
magical aggression; conflicts related to popular healing and midwifery;
the growing ambivalence towards positive and beneficent magic (healing,
fertility); the confusion of archaic and imported beliefs with the paradigm
of witchcraft; the effect of German witch-beliefs spreading throughout the
country through various channels (Austrian influence in the west,
German town-dwellers in the north and Transylvania, German settlers
throughout the country in the eighteenth century, German soldiers acting
as active witch-finders). Let me add to these factors a few more, and let me
try to regroup them into a coherent synthesis.

When talking about the cultural tensions that led to the early-modern
intensification of witchcraft persecutions, it is customary to refer to a
logical chain of evolution. To enumerate just some characteristic aspects
of this chain: a medieval fusion of several witch-images, folk mythologies
and inquisitorial stereotypes (Cohn 1975); Renaissance flirtations with
neo-Platonic–magical philosophies and practices of ritual magic; confusion in the popular universe of magic resulting from the Reformation
dismissal of ecclesiastical 'white magic' in all its forms (Thomas 1971); the
injection of learned demonological ideologies into popular witchcraft
beliefs, thus making them more explosive and fatal (Ginzburg 1966); an
apocalyptic image of witchcraft as representing God's punishment for the
sins of mankind, by allowing a wider sphere of activity to Satan and his
agents before the end of time (Behringer 1988: 120–5); the early-modern
repression and control of popular culture by making the figure of the
witch its symbol, and the persecution through this symbol of the whole
world-view and praxis of popular culture (Muchembled 1978).

This pan-European cultural evolution cannot be grasped directly
through Hungarian documentation. We do not possess any documents
that could convey details of 'original' medieval witch-beliefs.[36] Although
late-Renaissance magical experts emerged sporadically in Hungary
(especially in Transylvania[37]), and their slight impact on aristocratic
accusations has already been mentioned, the quantitative insignificance of
these trials does not allow us to give much weight to this factor in a general
explanation. As to the fusion of learned and popular demonologies, the
production or translation of demonological handbooks was almost

completely absent in Hungary.[38] A knowledge of the related stereotypes made its entry through popular channels at the end of the sixteenth century (the first diabolical Sabbath confession preserved is from Pozsony in 1602) (Horna 1933). Sabbath descriptions tended to rely upon and to be coloured by a kind of folk demonology.[39] Only in a few exceptional trials (such as the Somorja or the Szeged witch scare) can one detect the direct and detailed influence of scholarly demonological handbooks in altering the beliefs of the tortured witches. Finally, sixteenth- to seventeenth-century views about God's universal and imminent punishment of sinners were not unknown in Hungary, but they served to explain the loss of independence and the miseries of warfare with the Turks and the Habsburgs.

The only explanatory element that seems to retain its relevance to Hungarian witchcraft cases is the early-modern disturbance of the popular universe of magic. As I have stressed in connection with the Kolozsvár trials, reformed preachers who criticized 'papist' superstitious practices had been extremely active throughout the country. In strongly Protestant centres steps were taken against popular festivities and 'immoral' customs similar to those elsewhere in Europe. Witches' Sabbaths frequently provided a diabolized inversion of wedding, carnival and harvest festivities.[40] Many witchcraft cases revealed the growing suspicion of any kind of traditional agricultural magic. The incrimination of popular healers and other types of magical experts (the *táltos* for example) illustrates well how popular ambivalence about magic became more and more self-destructive. Nevertheless, in Hungary it is difficult to speak of a kind of systematic conflict between what is labelled 'popular culture' and an 'elite culture' before the end of the eighteenth century, i.e. well after the close of the period of witch-hunting. Magical notions and practices persisted with remarkable resilience: country nobles shared them with the peasants as part of their somewhat similar way of life; urban culture, although decidedly different (mostly for ethnic reasons), remained rather provincial and isolated.

Where, then, should we look for the cultural tensions of the more than 2,000 Hungarian witch-trials? Instead of a clear answer (which I do not have) let me conclude this presentation with the composite image I have just proposed. The overall picture obtained from Hungarian witchcraft documentation is that of a huge cultural melting pot, collecting and combining magical notions and mythologies of various functions and different regions and peoples. Balkan fairy beliefs contributed to the development of an indigenous imagery of the witches' Sabbath.[41] Shamanistic Hungarian *táltos* women assumed the roles of healers and accusers in witchcraft cases, Serbian settlers infused their *zduhač* mythology into witchcraft beliefs. In the Croatian regions several weather-making *garabonciás diák* made their appearance.[42] Cunning shepherds were transformed into Alpine-type werewolves. In Romanian-inhabited territories, witches were said to have tails and tended to be likened to vampires (Komáromy 1910: 507; Schram 1982, III: 272). Parallel to the peak of witch-hunting in Hungary, the early eighteenth century witnessed the famous vampire scares in Serbia and Transylvania, which found such a resonant echo throughout Europe.[43] The terminologies and varieties of witchcraft and bewitchment are manifold (there are several dozens of them in the Hungarian language alone!), just like the names and the techniques of healers and cunning folk (*néző, látó, tudományos, tudós, orvos,* etc.).

How did all these beliefs and magical specialists fit together? My suggestion is that witchcraft beliefs and endemic witch persecutions provided a wide and loose framework for all of them, offering the possibility for each type of belief to be combined with others or, inversely, to become more and more pronounced in the course of the seventeenth and eighteenth centuries. For contemporary specialists and people trying to master the magical stereotypes in witchcraft accusations, magical counter-actions or attempts, at diagnosis this confusing variety of ambivalent magical beliefs and practices proved to be rather dangerous. Professional rivalry, unsatisfactory healing results or provocative boasting about magical powers, alerted detection or exaggerated suspicion of magical activities by the accused – a large number of Hungarian witchcraft accusations could be ascribed to such purely magical conflicts.

Without denying the possibility that witchcraft accusations could also absorb and express various 'underlying' cultural tensions, I would conclude by emphasizing that the popular universe of magic possessed intrinsic tensions and explosive ambiguities unique unto itself.

One of these ambiguities was beyond doubt the ambivalence of popular magical expertise. In a world of scarce resources and constant danger, there seemed only one way to escape from misfortune – by diverting it onto someone else, presumably the person who had previously done the same to you. This was a solution to the problem of popular theodicy (it located the source of evil in the hidden animosities within one's own surroundings), but at the same time it gave rise to a paradox concerning the nature of magical power and the morals of its users: what is beneficial for one, is harmful witchcraft for another, and vice versa. This is one reason why popular healers were increasingly criminalized, and also why magical conflicts created a special area of tension for those involved, constantly tending toward dramatic confrontation and a possible elimination of one's opponents (by direct interpersonal violence or by the intermediary of the courts, which accepted this kind of litigation), for there was no other solution to this paradox.

These tensions – whatever the nature of the social or cultural background or the specific grievances voiced in the accusations – lend themselves to a type of analysis pioneered by Jeanne Favret-Saada (1977, 1981), in which the interchangeable and subjectively interpreted magical roles (witch, bewitched, diagnostician, witch doctor, healer and, eventually, the public accuser) are the object of analysis. The ambiguities are exploited in these situations, and are also handled by further rationalizing elaborations: witchcraft was only active in the immediate neighbourhood, whereas the same persons could, in theory, exercise their fearful magical powers for healing distant clients; if forced or threatened, the witch was capable of lifting her own spell; if the healing attempt was unsuccessful, perhaps the diagnosis was wrong, or it could even turn out that the person initially asked to heal was actually the real cause of the bewitchment. A further direction of research could be the long-term historical evolution of stereotypes: not only the traditional folkloric descriptions of the witch's person, of the Sabbath, of metamorphoses, or of techniques of supposed sorcery but also the various morphological elements to be found in great abundance in the accusation narratives contained in depositions – the suspected origins of the bewitchment (for the most part conflicts described with a convincing 'reality-effect'); the threats; the social situations, locations and specific times when the parties involved met during their witchcraft conflict; the night-time visions, nightmares and anxieties of the bewitched party; and, finally, the liturgical sequences of counter-magic: diagnosis, divination and attempts at healing.

Although I am not yet able to present a clear and documented demonstration of the presence of these magical tensions in Hungarian witch-trials and their various forms, or whether there had been a meaningful historical change in this field, I can at least promise this for the future. These problems are at the heart of the collective work of our witchcraft research group, which has been striving to build up a database of Hungarian witchcraft documentation, in the hope of providing some answers to this mysterious problem of magical conflicts.

10

The Decline of Witches and the Rise of Vampires under the Eighteenth-Century Habsburg Monarchy

The demise of witch-hunting is generally hailed as the triumph of the modern rational mind over what has been labelled by various ages as 'superstition', 'witch-crazes', 'credulousness', or 'belief in magic'. The question of how a society crosses this watershed between traditional and modern mentality has always been rather a puzzle, and the answers given have depended on the explanations as to why witch-hunting had occurred at all, and what underlying causes might have occasioned its intensification. The other side of the story is, of course, the analysis of the intensification of scepticism, of how 'rational' arguments emerged that gradually dispelled the old system of explanation, and went on to assert themselves in the legal and the religious spheres.

It is hardly necessary to emphasize that it is difficult to construct a general explanation that could account for all the different processes that occasioned this crucial change in mentality and in legal practice. Rather, comparative generalizations should take as their starting point a detailed examination of the concrete circumstances of each region's or country's evolution. This chapter grew out of an attempt to shed some light on the measures adopted by Maria Theresa to outlaw witch-hunting in Hungary in the eighteenth century, by examining the precise circumstances of her initiatives. I intended to relate these initiatives to their intellectual background, to some of the major issues of eighteenth-century intellectual history. However, as so frequently happens, during my enquiries an unexpected problem arose: the discovery of the curious fact that the abolition of Hungarian witch-trials was related to the scandals concerning vampires.

Once the intellectual history had been clarified, I had thus to confront the larger problem of how two different magical accounts of evil were related to each other and how the emergence of one could affect the other. This chapter documents how investigations of intellectual history give rise problems that can be solved only by a kind of historical anthropology, dealing with changing notions and fears related to the human body, and with the gradual transformations of the popular magic universe.

*   *   *

For a proper understanding of the legislation forbidding persecution of witches in Hungary, it is necessary to look briefly at the history of witch-hunting in this region. Although there is little documentary evidence of medieval witch-hunting, and although the first major witch-trials appeared at a relatively late date, in the 1550s, it would be a mistake to underestimate the gravity and the destructive effect of witch persecution in Hungary. The belated emergence of mass trials should not obscure the fact that we are concerned here with phenomena similar to those that occurred in other European countries. The chronology of the trials reveals the impact of greater waves of European witch-hunting: those in the 1550s, initiated mainly by German Protestants, those in the 1580s carried out by both opposing religious parties, and the greatest witch-hunt in European history, the mass burnings during the Thirty Years War.[1] However, in Hungary the peak of witch-hunting came much later, at the beginning of the eighteenth century. Out of about 1,700 witch-trials known to us from the surviving documents, more than two-thirds were held between 1690 and 1760. About half of these trials led to the execution of the accused or their death in prison. We can see from this that the three centuries of witch-hunting in Hungary were far from mild.

Furthermore, witch-hunting under the eighteenth-century Habsburg monarchy can by no means be regarded as a declining superstition in the process of dying out of its own accord. As we have already noted, it was only in the eighteenth century that the persecutions in Hungary first began to mount to the pitch of the witch panic that had raged in Germany, France, England, Spain and Italy a century earlier. The first wave of the Hungarian panic came in the 1720s and 1730s. In addition to the notorious trial at Szeged in 1728, which resulted in the mass burning of 14 witches including a former judge of the city, outbreaks of hysterical chain accusations can be observed in the southern and western regions of Transdanubia, in the environs of the north-eastern city of Miskolc, and elsewhere. In the course of twenty years, more than 450 'witches' were tried throughout the country. After a brief lull around 1740, a second wave of witch-hunting began to gather force around 1755, with the mass trials of Arad, where the confessions extorted by brutal torture and the series of deaths by burning at the stake show the virulence both of witch-craft beliefs and of the traditional legal machinery designed to persecute them.

It is worth noting that this later persecution of witchcraft is charac-teristic not only of Hungary, but in some ways of a whole range of countries on what could be called the 'periphery' of Europe. While witch-hunting was already dying out and forbidden by royal authority in France and was also declining in Germany, in Scandinavia it swelled in the 1660s into a general panic which lasted till the end of the century (Ankarloo 1984). New England had its most spectacular witch-trials in the 1690s (Boyer and Nissenbaum 1974; Demos 1982). And in the eighteenth century the level of persecution was not only high in Hungary, but also in Poland, where the chronology of the indictments shows the same pattern as the Hungarian trials (Baranowski 1952). The general pattern permits us to suppose that, without the recurrent intervention of Maria Theresa, witch-hunting would have continued in Hungary for several decades more, as it did in Poland, where it was forbidden only in 1775.

＊　　　＊　　　＊

Let me briefly outline the royal decrees and laws by which Maria Theresa followed the example of Louis XIV (1682) and Frederick William I (1728), who brought an end in their respective countries to widespread witch-hunting from above. The Empress, it is worth noting, was roused to action not by the persistence or re-emergence of witch-hunting in Hungary, but by the popular panic about a new kind of monstrous being, the vampire, whose frequent appearances in neighbouring Moravia had also aroused considerable interest in Vienna.

In 1755, in Hermersdorf, a village near the Silesian–Moravian border, the corpse of Rosina Polakin, deceased a few months previously, was exhumed by municipal decision, because people were complaining that she was a vampire and had attacked them at night. Her body was found to be in good condition (as befits vampires), without any signs of decom-position, and with blood still present in the veins. According to local custom, the poor family of the deceased was forced to drag the corpse, by means of a hook attached to a rope, through an opening made in the wall of the graveyard, to be beheaded and burnt outside.

After hearing of the Polakin affair, Maria Theresa sent two of her court doctors, Johannes Gasser and Christian Vabst, to Hermersdorf. When she received their report, she asked her principal court doctor, Gerard van Swieten (to whom we shall return later), to advise her as to what should be done. The two doctors and van Swieten counselled her to stamp out such repulsive 'superstitions' by legal measures, so she issued a *Rescriptum* in March 1755 forbidding any traditional measures connected with the so-called *magia postuma*, and a few months later, in a circular letter to the parishes and legal courts of the various counties and cities of Hungary, she was already condemning other 'superstitions' beside the vampire beliefs and indicating that soothsaying, digging for treasure, divination and witch-persecution were also to be prohibited.[2]

This last issue, of course, proved to be the most important and far-reaching. In January 1756 the Empress ordered all material on current witchcraft trials to be submitted to her appeals court for examination by her experts before the execution of the judgements of the local courts (Komáromy 1910: 600). From this moment on, although witch-hunting could not be stopped immediately and although the county courts continued to hand down death sentences, the situation nonetheless became far more favourable for the accused. The experts of the appeals court overturned nearly all the sentences for witchcraft, using the most modern scientific and legal arguments to condemn the unfounded accusations and the 'ignorance of the brutish populace'. In vain did eleven counties protest against this interference in their legal rights, and in vain was the Empress's action opposed by Palatine Lajos Batthyány, who, while condemning the excesses of witch-hunting, had argued that witches existed, referring to Biblical injunctions for their punishment (Komáromy 1910, 639–41). A few years later, a commission was set up in Vienna, which by 1766 had drawn up a new law definitively forbidding any kind of witch-hunting.

The *Imperial and royal law designed to uproot superstition and to promote the rational judgment of crimes involving magic and sorcery*, which became part of the new *Constitutio Criminalis Theresiana* is an interesting early manifestation of so-called enlightened absolutism.[3] Let me quote a few paragraphs that reveal the intellectual foundations of this legislation.

It is well known to what intolerable extremes the craze concerning sorcery and witchcraft has lately extended. Its foundations were laid by the inclination of the stupid and vulgar crowd toward superstition [*Aberglaube*]. Silliness and ignorance, which gave rise to simple-minded amazement and superstitious practices, have finally led to a situation in which gullibility has gained ground everywhere among the people, who have become incapable of distinguishing reality from illusion. Any event which has seemed to them hard to explain (although caused merely by accident, science or speed), has been ascribed to the activity of sorcerers and witches. To these are attributed the causes even for natural events like tempest, animal disease, or human illness. And these fancies about the vicious herd of sorcerers and witches have been transmitted from one generation to the next. The children have been infected from the cradle by terrible fairytales. Thus this craze has spread more and more widely, additionally distorting legal procedures in such matters.

The new law divided cases involving magic into four categories.

(1) witchcraft accusations originating from fantasy, imagination or fraud; (2) cases which derive from depression, madness or other kinds of mental illness; (3) cases when a person, renouncing God and his own salvation, has performed with serious intentions (although without result) the rituals and devices required for a pact with the Devil; (4) if there is infallible proof of some mischief or crime performed by real sorcery or devilish assistance.

According to the new law judges should always enquire whether the incidents mentioned in the accusation could have happened 'as a consequence of natural events': 'they should even consult experienced doctors and people acquainted with the natural sciences.' They should refrain from torturing the accused, searching for the so-called witch-mark or applying the spurious and archaic ordeal by water. As for punishments in accordance with the above-mentioned four categories: fraud was of course condemned, but so was defamation; mental illness was to be treated in hospital; blasphemy, even if harmless in its outcome, was still a major crime to be punished by banishment; and, as for 'real' devilish sorcery, the Queen declared that 'if such an extraordinary event should happen, We reserve to Ourselves the right to decide about its due punishment.' Thus it henceforth became virtually impossible in the Habsburg Empire to send anybody to the stake as a result of witchcraft accusations. In 1768 a series of royal proscriptions ordered the counties to refrain from initiating legal proceedings in cases of accusations of magical activity 'unless they have very clear proofs in the matter' (Komáromy 1910: 715–17).

*   *   *

It would be interesting to discuss how these 'enlightened' measures were received by the wider Hungarian population, how rapidly their 'mentality' changed in this respect. Unfortunately the documentation at our disposal is less plentiful than that available to Robert Mandrou and Alfred Soman, who tried to answer Lucien Febvre's analogous question concerning the end of persecutions in seventeenth-century France (Febvre 1948; Mandrou 1968; Soman 1985). What evidence we do have about eighteenth-century Hungary gives the impression that, after the initial grudging response of the fiercely independent and anti-centralist Hungarian nobility, the mass of the population accepted these measures with relief. Although before the royal proscription on witch-hunting there had not been much polemical writing in Hungary aimed at fighting legal abuses or popular superstitions, in the last decades of the eighteenth century they started to multiply, and at the beginning of the following century writers mentioning the matter demonstrated a total lack of identification with the 'superstitions' of their forefathers.[4]

The fact that the ban on the persecutions came not only from above, but also from an external source, and the absence of previous internal debate on the whole matter make it interesting to enquire into the origins of the terminology we encounter in the new imperial law, which expresses a modern rational outlook and a conscious programme to 'reform popular culture'.[5] Contemporaries ascribed the whole campaign against magic to Gerard van Swieten, the powerful court doctor of Maria Theresa. István Weszprémi (1723–1799), one of the most outstanding doctors in eighteenth-century Hungary, wrote in 1778 with respect to the beliefs in vampires:

> This imaginary illness, due to perverted fantasy, was last analysed marvellously by the immortal van Swieten in his treatise on Vampires, published in Vienna in 1755. By dint of wise advice he managed to convince the queen to chase this illness from the mind of the uneducated and superstitious people, so since that time such absurdities cannot be heard about within the territories of our country.[6]

It is worth taking a closer look at the activities and writings of van Swieten, a remarkable figure who was still venerated by Hungarians at the beginning of the nineteenth century. Through van Swieten we can locate this eighteenth-century campaign against magic within the broader currents of the Enlightenment. Before examining his two treatises on this subject (one on vampires, one on witches), here are a few brief details about his life.

Gerard van Swieten (1700–1772) was born in Leyden, where he studied medicine with one of the most outstanding professors of the time, Herman Boerhave (1668–1738). In 1743 he was invited to become *protomedicus* in the court of Maria Theresa; he accepted with some reluctance and a show of nonconformism (he refused, for example, to wear a wig). Within a few years he became one of the most powerful advisers to the Empress, not just in medical but also in much broader matters. He became the director of the Hofbibliothek, the organizer of the reform of the entire Vienna university, the administrator of hospitals, clinics and midwife education, the adviser on a series of measures that could be characterized as early examples of social welfare policy (asylums for the aged, widows, foundlings, orphans). He became one of the leaders of the Censorship Commission, where he earned fame for exercising a kind of counter-censorship in the name of the new ideas of the Enlightenment: it was not Voltaire and Rousseau whom he put on index, but the literature of the esoteric, demonological and magical.[7]

As we can see, van Swieten was just the person to take charge of the campaign for the elimination of magic beliefs. It is no wonder that (as I have already mentioned) the campaign was initiated on his advice. This advice was formulated in detail in his *Remarques sur le Vampyrisme de Sylésie de l'an 1755, faites à S. M. I. et R.*[8] At first reading, the treatise surprises by its moderate tone: van Swieten starts his work by acknowledging the existence of miracles, of divine omnipotence and even of the power of Satan. He adds, however, that 'since the natural sciences have taken such a great upswing, many things formerly regarded as marvels have turned out to have natural causes . . . The eclipse for example, which produced such terror in olden times, does not frighten any more. We can contemplate calmly the omnipotence of the Creator, who can move these huge objects with such precision in such an infinitely vast space throughout so many centuries'. He refers further to gunpowder, electricity, optical reflection and other optical devices, which would all seem miraculous to the ignorant; jesters and charlatans, he says, had always exploited this ignorance.

He followed the same line of argument against the Moravian vampire beliefs. After describing in detail the story of Rosina Polakin, and some other eighteenth-century vampire cases, he sets out to find the natural causes of the extraordinary phenomena described in these accounts. He advances medical arguments for the existence of bodily fluids resembling blood in the corpse several weeks after death. He puts forward scientific arguments about chemical factors and the lack of air, which could result in the undecayed conservation of corpses for several months, years, even decades after death. He supports his argument by a series of famous cases that for him, show no traces of vampirism. As for the reported nightmares, which might, in fact, have a very powerful impact, he considers them to be the natural consequence of ignorance and lack of education, combined with a kind of indoctrination fostered by fairytales.

He also advances some legal arguments against exhuming corpses on suspicion of vampirism – sacrilegious profanation of the holy ground of the graveyard, violation of the rights of the relatives. He urges the Empress to take speedy measures against all these beliefs, on the plane both of law and of education.

Van Swieten's interest in magical matters did not stop here, but extended to embrace the whole problem of popular magic. While the royal campaign moved on to forbid witch-hunting as well, probably on his initiative, in 1758 he wrote a *Mémoire* on witchcraft (edited by Komáromy 1910: 642–59), which shows very similar traits to the vampire treatise. It also relates to a concrete case – the trial of Magdalene Heruczina (née Lodomer), a Croatian witch sentenced to death but liberated on the orders of Maria Theresa after her case was examined by van Swieten. Here, too, we encounter the formal acknowledgement of the existence of magic and of the workings of Satan, coupled with a scientific explanation of the actual events. Electricity and gunpowder are mentioned here too, and he also describes some 'scientific' experiments, where witches who claimed to have attended the witches' Sabbath were observed meanwhile remaining seated in their rooms, and were apparently only dreaming about their magical adventures.

The main attraction of van Swieten's treatise on witchcraft lies in his detailed enquiry into how the witchcraft accusation was constructed, and into how the distinctive Sabbath confession was obtained. He not only describes the terrible pain the old woman had to suffer under torture, but also how the judges put questions into her mouth, how the investigators took every item of hearsay as the truth, etc. His conduct in this case, where he personally supervised the medical treatment and the hospitalization of the poor woman, is a nice example of the unity of theory and practice in the time of the Enlightenment.

*   *   *

Van Swieten's ideas, which had such a revolutionary effect upon the entire body of legislation dealing with magic, were imported into Austria from other countries. It is evident that van Swieten's sceptical and rationalist approach must have evolved primarily out of his native Dutch culture. Indeed, if we examine the history of scepticism about witchcraft beliefs, and of the way in which criticism of such beliefs developed, Holland was one of the countries in the vanguard. It was in Holland that witch-hunting claimed the fewest victims (about thirty executions in total), and it was there, too, that this aberration of early-modern civilization was most rapidly corrected: the last known execution took place in 1603 (Faber 1984). It was probably this enlightened mentality which accounted for the surprisingly large number of critics of Dutch origin who attacked witchcraft beliefs.

After a few inept treatises on the subject in the fifteenth century (Ziegeler 1973), the first serious attack on witch-hunting and the belief in the witches' Sabbath was elaborated by Johan Wier (1515–1588), a disciple of Cornelius Agrippa von Nettesheim, an Erasmian doctor who started his career at the court of Francis I, and later became the protégé of William V, Duke of Cleves. In his treatise *De Praestigiis Daemonum* (first published in 1563 and condemned and burnt several times in the following decades), Wier recognized the existence of magical powers and also of witchcraft and sorcery (thus following the tradition of Renaissance neo-Platonism), but on the other hand he denied the reality of witches' capacity to fly to the Sabbath, which he described as scientific nonsense. As for the large number of confessions on the subject, he ascribed them partly to devilish illusion, which cheated the accused themselves, and, partly to the effects of torture (Baxter 1977a). Although it was no lesser authority than Jean Bodin himself who undertook the task of refuting Wier's doubts in his *Démonomanie des sorciers* (Baxter 1977b; Anglo 1976), a few decades later another Dutchman, Cornelis Loos, repeated essentially the same assertions as Wier. In his treatise written in 1592, Loos asserted that descriptions of the witches' Sabbath were simply tales of imaginary flights, that the *incubi* and *succubi* had no real existence, and that torture was not a way of extracting the truth, but 'a new kind of alchemy, by which one can transform human blood into gold and silver'. Since the printer promptly denounced Loos, he was compelled to withdraw his statements, leaving only a self-critical refutation in the work edited by one of the major demonologists of the age, the Jesuit theologian Del Rio (Trevor-Roper 1969: 82).

Among the polemicists of the seventeenth century, it was once again a Dutchman, a priest named Balthasar Bekker (1643–1698), who, fascinated by Cartesian ideas, went furthest in criticizing the belief in witches. His treatise, *The Enchanted World* (*De Betoverte Weereld*, 1690) was the first to take decisive steps towards breaking the spell: he denied the effect and the existence of any kind of supernatural magical power. He based his arguments partly on rationality, partly on scientific reasoning. The 'magic', according to him, had reality only as fraud, and the 'devilish' acquired existence only in human wickedness and malignity (Trevor-Roper 1969: 102–3).

Did van Swieten know of these works? It is highly likely that he did – although he does not refer to them in his treatises – for they were among the works in the Viennese Hofbibliothek, which he directed for more than a decade. His commitment to this Dutch type of rationalist disbelief in magic was able to find support and example not only in the writings of these three outstanding critics, but also in the teachings of his master, Herman Boerhave, whose works frequently fulminated against fraudulent charlatans presenting themselves as sorcerers and deceiving the ignorant.[9]

Having examined one of the intellectual sources of the Austro-Hungarian campaign against superstition, let me now briefly present another, much closer to Vienna in geographical and cultural terms. In the north of Italy the representatives of the Italian Enlightenment held their first important public discussion around this time, in the 1740s and 1750s, and on exactly the same subject: the workings of magic and witchcraft. Using the historical, rationalist, psychological and scientific arsenal of the new era, they tried to deal a *coup de grâce* to these 'superstitions' that persisted so scandalously in that century of Reason (see Rapp 1874: 71–108; Venturi 1969: 355–89; Bonomo 1971: 417–46; Parinetto 1974). It was Lodovico Antonio Muratori who launched the debate in an ingenious book called *The Forces of Human Fantasy*, which aroused public opinion on these issues. According to Muratori it was precisely the disgraceful persistence of witch-hunting in Hungary and in Germany, and the absurd witchcraft confessions to be heard there even in those modern times, that dictated a discussion of the question. As for his own opinion, he called these accounts 'the most obscene dreams, the products of a corrupt fantasy, and of the silly gossip of people incapable of distinguishing the false from the real'.[10]

It was with Muratori's encouragement that the Roveretan scholar Girolamo Tartarotti started to write a book entitled *Congresso notturno delle lammie*, which he finished in 1749. His book was a highly erudite inventory and history of belief in witchcraft from late Antiquity to his own era. Remaining within the hermetic–neo-Platonist tradition, which still held some sway in Italy, Tartarotti accepted the reality of so-called natural magic, but he firmly denied the existence of the witches' Sabbath and refuted it with scientific arguments. He also gave an account of how the stereotype of the witch had emerged in the history of ideas, and how the different authors of treatises had borrowed their descriptions from one another (Tartarotti 1749). Tartarotti's book led to passionate controversies in which some of his compatriots, such as Scipione Maffei and Gian Rinaldo Carli, attacked him from an even more radical point of view in several pamphlets, written between 1749 and 1754, denying the possibility of magic in general.[11]

Was van Swieten aware of this debate among the enlightened scholars grouped around the Academia degli Agiati in Rovereto? Here we have more than conjecture and the fact that these works were, of course, also in the Hofbibliothek. We know that the Italian thinkers were familiar with and appreciated van Swieten's work. A friend of Tartarotti's, Giuseppe Valeriano Vannetti, edited an annotated translation of van Swieten's treatise on vampires, which thus became incorporated into the Italian debate about magic.[12] And that these discussions were watched from Vienna with an attentive eye, is shown by the fact that in 1762 the Empress Maria Theresa tried (in vain) to use her personal influence to get a memorial erected at the grave of the deceased Tartarotti in the church of San Marco in Rovereto (Rapp 1874: 94–101).

In 1767, the same year that witch-trials were conclusively forbidden in the domain of the Habsburg monarchy, a vast synthesis on this theme was published in Vienna by Konstantin Franz von Cauz, a firm friend of most of the Italian leaders of enlightened thought. In this book, *De cultibus magicis*, we find a recap of the whole intellectual background to the Habsburg campaign against superstition: he praises the Queen, who could 'set an example to other sovereigns' in 'chasing this barbarian superstitious ignorance from the brains of the people'; he honours van Swieten for initiating the package of measures and contributing to their promotion with his treatises; and he bases his arguments mainly on the Dutch and Italian polemicists I have referred to above.[13]

✳   ✳   ✳

We could end the description here of the intellectual background to Maria Theresa's enlightened legislation and that to van Swieten's treatises. But there is a way to proceed further with the present enquiry, as I have already indicated at the beginning of this chapter: to posit a problem on the basis of our new evidence that the sequence of legislation against magical practices arose from the scandals caused by the newly emerging belief in vampires, and, in consequence of this new type of scandal, moved on to forbid witch-hunting altogether.

Before trying to work through this problem, let me sketch the historical background of European beliefs in vampires. Let us leave open the question as to whether Montague Summers was right, in *The Vampire, his Kith and Kin* (1928), in developing a universal category that included every variety of phenomena such as the returning dead, bloodsucking witches or cannibalistic killers from Antiquity to the Indians. I prefer a more specific definition that focuses mainly on the historically unified concept of the vampire that emerged in early-modern Central and Balkan Europe. According to the accounts of folklorists, the vampire synthesizes various traits from five different sets of magical beliefs: the revenants, the *Alp*-like nightly pressing spirits, the bloodsucking *stryx* of Antiquity, those witches from Slavic and Balkan territories who were said to persist in harmful activities after their deaths, and finally the werewolf, a person capable of adopting the form of a wolf in order to attack and devour humans.[14]

After a few obscure medieval references, it was in the seventeenth century that the accounts of these monstrous beings started to multiply. The first clear vampire cases were reported from Silesia in 1591,[15] from Bohemia in 1618,[16] and there are some stories of *upierzyca* from Poland (near Cracovia) in 1624.[17] We can see here a remarkable geographical unity, which culminated in the second half of the seventeenth century with the Balkan (Greek, Bulgarian, Romanian and Serbian) stories of *moroi* and *broucholachi*.[18] Typically the stories describe cases of dead people, quite frequently deceased in irregular circumstances such as suicide, or dying unbaptised or excommunicated, or being deviant or abnormal in some other way (Lawson 1911: 375), who return from the grave in human or in animal shape. They cause trouble or infestation, and kill men and beasts, until their undecayed bodies, still veined with blood, are exhumed and pierced by a pole, or beheaded, or have the heart extracted and burnt. Unfortunately, a more detailed analysis of these early cases is not possible, since the stories have been handed down by chronicles and other reports based upon hearsay, do not identify precisely the alleged vampire and say nothing about the 'victims' or the accusers.

Although vampire beliefs were basically of Slavic and Greek origin, eighteenth-century European public opinion nevertheless connected them mainly to Hungary, because nearly all the famous vampire cases of the eighteenth century occurred in the peripheral territories of the Hungarian kingdom. I shall review these cases briefly, not only because some of them are unknown to the vast literature about vampires, but also because of their relevance to the specific topic of this chapter. In 1706, the first widely read book on vampires was published, entitled *De magia postuma* (it was popularized by Calmet 1751: 33–6). Written by Karl Ferdinand Scherz, the book describes vampire cases on the Moravian–Hungarian border. In 1707, the Lutheran synod of Rózsahegy (Ružomberok) devoted time to a special discussion of the spreading custom of exhuming, beheading and burning corpses (Magyari-Kossa 1930, IV: 88). In 1709, Samuel Köleséri, a Hungarian doctor, narrating the events of the plague in Transylvania, gave a shocked account of the number of corpses dug up and pierced by a pole or beheaded because they were considered responsible for spreading the plague (Magyari-Kossa 1930, IV: 29–30).

One of the strangest events was recorded in 1718 in the town of Lubló on the Hungarian–Polish border. A certain merchant called Kaszparek, who stole the fortune of his Polish customer and died shortly afterwards, returned from the grave to be with his wife and to generate fear in other people. The panic led to a series of municipal investigations and hearings of witnesses testimonies. Despite the resistance of Kaszparek's wife, there were several attempts to destroy the corpse, all of which were reported as unsuccessful, until eventually the entire body was burnt. The case became so noteworthy that not only did chroniclers (among them Mathias Bél, the outstanding scientist of the age) describe it in great detail, but it also became the theme of a novel by the famous nineteenth-century Hungarian writer, Kálmán Mikszáth (who, regrettably, transformed the figure of Kaszparek first from a vampire into a ghost, then from a ghost into a charlatan).[19]

In the 1720s the vampire epidemic was further magnified by reports from Késmárk in north Hungary and Brassó and Déva in Transylvania.[20] The most famous instances occurred, however, in Serbia. For example, the case in 1730 of the *hajdú* Arnold Paul (a kind of peasant soldier) became the most widely known account of vampires, described in most European journals of the time and included ever since in every manual on vampires. This soldier, who came from Medvegia, a village near Belgrade, had always complained of being tormented by a Turkish vampire. Despite his attempts to cure himself (for example, by eating earth from the graves of presumed vampires), he died prematurely through an accident and became a vampire himself. According to the fable-like extremely confused account of this case, forty days after his death Paul was exhumed, found to have blood in his veins and was heard to emit a terrifying shriek when pierced by a pole. In the same period, from this same region, which must indeed have witnessed an intensive vampire epidemic, there were several testimonies to other, similar cases. The accounts of the persons involved are very imprecise and stereotyped, but remain as authentic testimonies to the spread of the belief. There even survived several brief medical reports by doctors of the Austrian imperial army who were present at exhumations carried out at the demand of local people.[21]

This series of cases signalled the start of the great debate of the 1730s about vampires. A long list of more or less scientific works discussed these phenomena, and in the 1740s continued to draw upon more recent vampire cases from Transylvania, Serbia and Moravia.[22] It therefore comes as no surprise that the contemporary authority in the field, the Benedictine abbot Dom Augustin Calmet, acknowledged this geographical specificity in his *Treatise on the apparitions, bad spirits and vampires of Hungary and Moravia* (1751). In consequence, the Hungarian word *vámpir* (itself derived from the Polish *upyr*) became the internationally recognized name for these monstrous beings.

However, it is not the folkloric or ethnic characterization of this belief that interests me here, but rather the question of how these few dozen stories about vampires attracted considerably greater attention in the Europe of the time than the burnings of several hundred alleged witches during this same period in Hungary, Poland, Austria and Germany. This shift of popular and intellectual interest to vampires, this 'vampire scandal', is worthy of attention, for it signals some of the essential contemporary preoccupations concerning magic. Although the witchcraft debate and the problem of witches were far from being completely resolved, in Western Europe this had begun to pale because witch persecution had long been in decline there. In these circumstances the more exotic East European bloodsuckers were bound to excite much greater popular interest.

The vampires provided doctors with a new and exciting riddle to be explained by the application of their newly elaborated system of scientific reasoning. P. Gabriel Rzaczynski was already puzzling over the question in describing the Polish accounts of vampires in his *Historia naturalis curiosa regni Poloniae* (1721).[23] In polemical writings about vampires one meets similar kinds of historical examples and accounts by physicians (on the incorruptibility of corpses, on the characteristics of blood) to those found in van Swieten's treatise.[24] The most detailed medical analysis of the period on vampires was prepared by a Hungarian doctor called George

Tallar, who over several decades studied these phenomena among the Serbians and the Romanians. He not only observed the exhumation of corpses suspected of being vampires, but also examined people who complained of a certain illness accompanied by fever, digestive problems, pallor and sickness – which they generally attributed to having been bitten or touched by vampires. They tried to heal themselves by smearing their bodies with the blood of corpses exhumed from cemeteries, and by other magical devices. George Tallar had a different explanation of this illness: he attributed it to the extreme diets of the Orthodox church, which reached their peak in winter time, and resulted in digestive problems. He tried to heal these people accordingly, and – if we can believe his account – with considerable success.[25]

As for the religious polemicists, vampire beliefs represented a serious challenge, for they were forced to recognize in them the blasphemous reversal of some crucial Christian dogmas and cults. The vampire belief touched upon Christian ideas about resurrection. The vampire, like the Christian saint, was also a 'very special dead' (a term borrowed from Peter Brown speaking of Christian saints – Brown 1981), whose corpse resisted decay, whose grave radiated with a special light, whose fingernails and hair kept growing – like those of several medieval saints, e.g. Saint Oswald, Saint Edmund and Saint Olaf (see Hoffmann 1975: 80) – thus demonstrating the persistence of vital energy beyond death. The apparitions of the vampires and the miracles connected with them were, in a way, negative reflections of the attributes of the saints. And as for the most haunting capacity of the vampire, the bloodsucking – not only can one account for it in terms of the history of sacrificial blood (see Agazzi 1977: 11–31) but one could also see it as a reversal of its Christianized version, the holy communion, which was depicted by late-medieval and early-modern mystics as a highly tangible bodily and material absorption of Christ's flesh and (more significantly) blood (Bynum 1982: 152; 1987: 176).

So here we are with this wicked, blasphemous belief, which had to be criticized and refuted in order to protect the holy model on which it was based. Calmet's chief intention in his book was to uphold the original Christian dogmas on resurrection, miracles and even the existence of Satan, as special signs of divine omnipotence (it was probably from this source that analogous passages of Swieten's treatises derived). At the same time, Calmet described all accounts of vampires and the witches' Sabbath as the consequences of 'illusion, superstition and prejudice', which could be explained either as natural phenomena or as fantasies on the part of the people concerned (Calmet 1751, I: 148; II: 219–22; see Goulemot 1980: 1232–3).

A similar view was expressed by Giuseppe Davanzati, bishop of Trani in southern Italy, who wrote his *Dissertation about vampires* in 1739 on the basis of first-hand information given to him by Schrattenbach, Bishop of the Moravian town Olmütz (Venturi 1969: 383–5). His explanation was partly geographical, partly social. According to him, the belief was gaining ground in Moravia and Hungary rather than in, say, Spain or France, because the inhabitants of these latter countries were less gullible. Moreover, it was current among 'the brutish, uneducated lower classes' and not among cultivated noblemen and scientists, because it was more difficult to deceive the latter. For this reason the educated should indeed consider it their duty to rid the ignorant of their 'superstitions'.

The extent to which this ecclesiastical fight against superstition served to maintain some basic Christian beliefs in magic is perhaps best illustrated by the fact that Pope Benedict XIV felt it necessary to refer to the 'vanity of the vampire beliefs' in his 1752 treatise on the canonization of saints.[26] On the other hand, it was precisely this anomalous position adopted by the Catholic polemicists that gave Voltaire the opportunity, in writing about the absurdity of beliefs in vampires, to discuss in similarly sarcastic mode the Christian belief in miracles and in resurrection dogmas. Presenting the vampire stories in a mock-heroic style loaded with irony in his *Questions sur l'Encyclopédie* (1772), he went on to ask: 'hearing all this, how could we cast doubt any longer on the stories about resurrected dead which our legends are so full of, and on the miracles described by Bollandus or by the sincere and very respectable Dom Ruinald?'[27]

Alongside the medical view, the attempts of the Church to rescue basic dogmas by distancing itself from popular superstitions, and the sarcastic and rationalist critiques expounded by Enlightenment thinkers, we should make note of a fourth current that played an active part in the debates about vampires. It is tempting to call this tendency the occult revival of the eighteenth century, which developed as a kind of counter-current to the rationalist, Cartesian mainstream of philosophical thought of the age. In the early eighteenth century a spate of literature attempted to explore the occult, mystical, spiritualist and psychic explanations for the 'forces of human fantasy'. It was not by chance that Muratori dedicated his first philosophical enquiry (mentioned above) to this subject, and in a much less dogmatic, dryly rationalist tone than Voltaire would have adopted. We should also bear in mind that the second half of the eighteenth century saw the emergence and triumphant success of Mesmerism, the 'magnetic', 'hypnotizing' method of healing (see Darnton 1968; Leventhal 1976; Goulemot 1980; Gallini 1983).

From this angle it seems quite obvious that the real sensation value of vampire stories was achieved in the 1730s by means of the occult interpretations advanced to explain them. In a series of learned treatises,

Michael Ranft reasoned about the notion of *vis vegetans*, the idea that vital bodily energy was still present in corpses, which had been speculated about as far back as Plato and Democrite. Ranft also had something to say about the 'sympathy' and 'antipathy' by which the dead could influence the fate of their relatives.[28] Johann Christoph Harenberg tried to connect the vampire stories to the types of visions that can be induced by taking opium, datura or other hallucinogenic drugs. Other authors used the notions of Paracelsus (distinguishing *corpus, anima* and *spiritus*) and explained the vampire apparitions by some 'astral' influence on the *spiritus*.[29] A more rational, but still pyschological, explanation of vampires was offered by the Marquis Boyer d'Argens in his *Lettres juives* in 1737, in which he reflected on phantoms that appear in nightmares and literally scare people to death (quoted by Calmet 1751, II: 47). Recall that similar arguments were also present in the treatises of van Swieten, who recognized that a generalized fear of imaginary beings can be destructive and even fatal.

We can see from this that the mythology of vampires fascinated the people of the age in a variety of ways, and provided them with new possibilities for articulating some important problems, for exercising their curiosity and for expressing their fantasies. Once firmly established on the supernatural horizon of eighteenth-century Europe, the vampire continued to serve similar purposes and went on to make his appearance in literature, where he (or she) acquired a new dimension: that of sexuality. The vampire's bite was gradually transformed into a deadly kiss: bloodsucking and the transformation of the victim into a vampire evoked age-old questions and persistent mysteries related to the history of sexuality.

Leaving aside more ancient examples, it is possible to detect the prehistory of the sexual vampire in the erotic fantasies of the previous century. The symbolic, skeletal (but apparently male) figure of Death made his appearance as the Middle Ages waned: he was increasingly frequently contrasted with the most extreme expression of secular beauty, that of the young woman. By the beginning of the sixteenth century the confrontation implicit in this contrast had developed into a morbid sexual picture. In the paintings of Hans Baldung Grien, Death embraces and seduces attractive naked ladies; he bites their throats very much in the fashion of the later literary vampires (Koerner 1985: 79ff). In the sixteenth and seventeenth centuries, the detailed accounts of the witches' Sabbath and of the Devil's sexual union with witches carried similar overtones. Finally, the linking of sexual symbolism with the new vampire mythology occurred at precisely the same historical moment that a different but equally extreme fantasy of deadly sexuality was being expressed and elaborated by the Marquis de Sade.

Indeed, the first association with sexuality occurred as a feature of a vampire story we have already discussed: that of Kaszparek, the early eighteenth-century vampire of the north Hungarian town Lubló, who kept on returning from the grave to pay secret nightly visits to his widow. The decisive link, however, was forged by an obscure German poet, Heinrich August Ossendorfer, who published a poem entitled *Der Vampir* in the review *Der Naturforscher* (nos 47–48, 1748), which appeared in Leipzig, the centre of the debates about vampires. Here a young lover deplores the fact that his beloved is too obedient to her mother's strictures, in the same way that people believe in God or in 'the deadly vampire'. He decides to have his revenge by taking a 'vampire draught' near Mount Tokaj while the lady is asleep: he plans to suck the blood of her beautiful cheeks: 'Alsdann wirst do erschrecken/ Wenn ich dich werde küssen/ Und als ein Vampir küssen' – and when the terrified lady lies pale as death in the lover's arms, he will ask her vengefully whose precepts are better – his or those of her beloved mother . . . (Ronay 1972: 38; Agazzi 1977: 153).

This reshaping of vampire mythology will come as no surprise to psychologists and cultural historians, who are familiar with the deep attraction between *Eros* and *Thanatos* expressed in many human cultures (see Eisler 1951; Bataille 1957: 103–59). The passage from the eighteenth to the nineteenth century brought further elaborations of this aspect of vampire mythology. Goethe's *Die Braut von Corinth* (1797), Coleridge's *Christabel* (1800) and Kleist's *Penthesilea* (1808) associated vampires with cruel Amazons or mistresses returning from the grave to haunt their former lovers – thus creating a feminine vampire figure. An Englishman of Italian origin, Polidori, a close friend of Byron and Mary Shelley, was equally fascinated by morbid fantasies. He opted for a male vampire in his novel *The Vampire: a Tale by Lord Byron* (1816) and his choice was to prevail (see Agazzi 1977: 158–65; Ronay 1972: 47–50). Although female vampires continued to make their appearance in nineteenth-century literature – and, of course, the contagious character of vampirism transformed many women into vampires in these novels and short stories – the sex of the vampire remained essentially male. As Christopher Craft (1984) demonstrated with reference to the 'classic' of the genre, Bram Stoker's *Dracula*, the biting, penetrating sexuality of the vampire had of necessity to be conceived as male, preserving its male aspect even when transmitted to females.

*   *   *

We can now see fairly clearly the reasons for the popularity of vampires in the first half of the eighteenth century. But, apart from obscuring the popularity of the witch theme in public debate, how did all this contribute to the end of witch-hunting? In the first place, one could say that vampire beliefs provided an alternative explanatory system for persistent problems in the field of magic, so the contradictions of the previous explanations could be discussed more openly. This is the argument Keith Thomas advanced to explain the role of Renaissance neo Platonism in the rise of doubt in witch-belief in sixteenth-century England (Thomas 1971: 578–9). Unfortunately, this parallel is too remote to help us here – there are too many discrepancies: at that time the efforts to stop persecution were unsuccessful and the learned magical beliefs of the Renaissance caused no real scandals in their time, nor could they obscure in any way the popular tradition of belief in witches.

However, speaking of parallels raises the possibility of a more fruitful analogy: let us compare my account of the eighteenth century with what happened in France at the end of the seventeenth century, where, according to Robert Mandrou, witch persecutions were brought to an end partly as a result of public scandals inspired by famous cases of diabolical possession. This new type of magical phenomenon was exemplified by the spectacular and widely known cases of the Ursuline nuns of Loudun (1633) and Louviers (1643) who claimed to be possessed by the Devil, who had approached them through their confessors (Mandrou 1968).

Of course I am not suggesting that there is any close resemblance between seventeenth-century French cases of diabolical possession and eighteenth-century Central European vampire scandals. There is obviously a difference between the two processes of 'decriminalizing' witchcraft. As Alfred Soman has shown, the growing doubts about witch-craft accusations and the stricter jurisdictional scrutiny in witchcraft cases started in France well before the possession cases, which acted only as catalysts to the existing public debate on the question (1977; 1985). In the eighteenth-century Habsburg Empire, on the other hand, it was the vampire scandals that forced the initiation of the entire campaign to abolish persecution. Yet I think a meaningful analogy can be drawn in two respects: at the level of the internal logic of the historical evolution of the popular magical universe, and at the level of the effect that the emerging new beliefs had upon those held previously. More generally: at both levels these scandals presented the effects of harmful magical power in new and exciting terms for the people of that era. They thus contributed to the restructuring of witchcraft beliefs and to the reform of plurisecular judicial persecution in that domain. On the one hand, the seventeenth-century nunnery, diabolically possessed by a priest to the extent of trans-forming it into the sinister setting for perverted orgies; on the other hand, the monstrous bloodsuckers crawling out from their graves on the periphery of Europe – two extremes that first brought into play every existing belief in supernatural evils and terrors, and then, in the second phase, somehow provided illumination for contemporary thinkers trying to come to terms with these phenomena. It must have indicated how they could step out of the magic circle of witch-hunting.

In seventeenth-century France the theatrical appetite of Jesuitic spirituality was obviously left unsatisfied by the conception of evil inherent in previous witchcraft accusations, which involved a secret crime and a hazy identification of the criminal with him or her Satanic affiliations. The obscene spasms of the possessed nuns and the terrifyingly cruel rituals of exorcism placed Satan in centre stage much more efficiently. The traditional experts on sacred knowledge, the priests, were also quite logically destined to be the principal objects of suspicion and accusation (is it possible to imagine a more provocative and shrewd idea of the Devil than to pervert an entire monastery of nuns by means of their confessors?). However, the contradictions exposed by this extreme actualization of magical beliefs rapidly led to a kind of demystifying explosion. The accused, like Urbain Grandier of Loudun, defended themselves by the logical argument that one should not trust the voice of Satan speaking through the possessed nuns, for here again he is out to deceive and destroy the innocent (Mandrou 1968: 233).

Since this inner contradiction could no longer be resolved within the paradigms of witchcraft beliefs, the decisive role in the argument was very soon given over to the medical experts, with their dissertations on the psychic consequences of 'melancholy' and the mental effects of bodily *humeurs*. On the other hand, increasing numbers of people came to see the whole thing as pure deception and fraud, which view, though far from accounting for the complex psychological process of diabolical possession,[30] had the beneficent effect of putting a speedy end to witch-hunting.

As for eighteenth-century vampire beliefs, I have already attempted to explore their attraction for the people of that time. Here, too, the comparison with witchcraft could add a useful dimension. Vampire beliefs involved much more spectacular fantasies than traditional witchcraft accusations, by producing tangible proof not by means of the 'theatre of the Devil' but by the discovery of corpses showing unusual signs of life. At the same time, bloodsucking was a quasi-medical concept that appeared to explain magical aggression in terms more acceptable to the eighteenth-century mentality than the witches' invisible and unexplained power to cast spells. Another possible parallel between possession and vampire cases is that they both represented a more spiritualized conception of the workings of evil magic. Here I am thinking not only of demons, spirits and ghosts, but of the fact that, whereas witchcraft accusations were aimed at finding living scapegoats within the community – the witch was the 'traitor within the gates' (Mayer 1970) – whereas they tried to account for misfortune by relating it to past human conflicts and present evil behaviour, the theory of diabolical possession shifted the focus of attention onto Satan and the devils, who used human beings only as passive media. Finally, vampire beliefs were shifted onto dead men returning from their graves, and increasingly explained the spreading of this evil as pure contagion, which naturally exculpated the living victims attacked by or related to vampires.

The vampire scandals also presented a more general paradigm for transcending the persisting belief in harmful magic. As we can see from contemporary opinion, this paradigm suggested the notion of civilizing the ignorant and superstitious East European savage (who was considered far from 'noble'). According to the intellectuals of that era, this mission of the Enlightenment, this civilizing process, could only come from 'above' in the social sense and from the 'west' in the geographical sense. This type of thinking was present not only in the royal decrees of Maria Theresa, but also in the descriptions by Hungarian doctors, who, like George Tallar, took pleasure in lamenting the ignorance of Serbian and Romanian peasants and the evil effects of the 'superstitious' Orthodox religion.[31] It was this ideology that initiated the campaign against magical beliefs. And it was very soon generalized not only to the abolition of witch-hunting, but also to fighting any beliefs, practices and representatives of traditional popular culture. In the 1780s in the Habsburg monarchy a wave of pamphlets appeared attacking and stigmatizing popular superstitions. By the beginning of the nineteenth century the time was ripe for Hungarian followers of Herder to rediscover the once-shared but now-forgotten values of popular culture.

There is a final observation to be made on the consequences of eighteenth-century vampire scandals. The most radical counter-reaction, that of Voltaire and some other French thinkers, offered another method for doing away with vampire beliefs: they attempted to shift public attention from mythical vampires to 'bloodsuckers' in the real social sense of the term (the metaphor 'bloodsucker' was coined by Mirabeau in the 1770s).

> One does not hear about vampires in London nowadays – [wrote Voltaire]. I can however see merchants, speculators, tax-collectors, who have sucked the blood of the people in broad daylight, but who were definitely not dead, although they had been corrupted quite enough. These real bloodsuckers do not live in cemeteries but in very pleasant palaces.[32]

This sociological redefinition of bloodsucking quickly found support in Hungary, where Samuel Tessedik, an enlightened eighteenth-century thinker, labelled the rich peasants and the tax-collectors as the 'vampires' of the poor.[33] This new notion was to be recycled by nineteenth-century writers like Bram Stoker, who selected the sinister historical figure of Vlad the Empaler to bestow his name, *Dracula*, on our most familiar 'celluloid' vampire, whom Stoker portrayed as a lord, a sexual maniac and a blood-sucker at one and the same time.[34]

The immediate impact of Voltaire's idea was, however, quite different. Whilst in earlier centuries it was imaginary magical conflicts that served to resolve or release real social and cultural tensions, now it was social and cultural conflicts that began to assume a somewhat magical dimension. The magical mystery of vampirism was dissipated by reinvoking the scapegoat mechanism of witch persecution. And within a few decades it was no longer the blood of the exhumed corpses, but that of the 'social bloodsuckers' that was going to flow.[35]

A vivid illustration of this new twist in the eighteenth-century obsession with blood and bloodsuckers is provided by the following lines from the 1794 Hungarian version of the 'Marseillaise' (translated by the Jacobin sympathizer and poet Ferenc Verseghy):

> The bloodsucking tyrant race
> Points his arms against your breasts
> And dips his ugly hands into your blood
> If he cannot make you his serf
> Take up arms, champions
>   . . .
> Attack these thirsters for blood
> Cut them into pieces!

Bibliographic Abbreviations

The following abbreviations have been used in bibliographic references:

AESC	*Annales (Économies, Sociétés, Civilisations)*, Paris
CC	Corpus Christianorum
CSEL	Corpus Scriptorum Ecclesiasticorum Latinorum
E	*Ethnographia*, Budapest
FRB	Fontes Rerum Bohemicarum
ITK	*Irodalomtörténeti Közlemények*, Budapest
MGH SS	Monumenta Germaniae Historica, Series Scriptorum
MPH	Monumenta Poloniae Historica, vol. IV, 1884, Lwów
MRV	Monumenta Romana Episcopatus Vesprimiensis, vol. I 1103–1276 (ed. Fraknói), 1896, Budapest
MVH	Monumenta Vaticana Historiam regni Hungariae illustrantia
PG	Patrologiae cursus completus. Series Graeca (ed. Migne)
PL	Patrologiae cursus completus. Series Latina (ed. Migne)
RHF	Recueil des Historiens de la Gaule et de la France (ed. Boucquet)
SC	Sources Chrétiennes
SCH	*Studies in Church History*, Oxford
SRH	Scriptores Rerum Hungaricarum (ed. Szentpétery), 1938, Budapest
Sz	*Századok*, Budapest

Notes

CHAPTER 2   THE CARNIVAL SPIRIT

1.   Two recent intellectual biographies: Tzvetan Todorov, *Mikhail Bakhtine. Le Principe dialogique* (Seuil, Paris, 1981; English transl. by Wlad Godzich, Univ. of Minnesota Press, 1985); Katerina Clark and Michael Holquist, *Mikhail Bakhtin* (Harvard Univ. Press, Cambridge MA, 1984); see Clive Thomson, 'Bakhtin-Baxtin-Bakhtine-Bachtin-Bakutin. Sull' evoluzione della critica bachtiniana', *L'immagine riflessa*, 7 (1984), pp. 37–56.; Joseph Frank, 'The voices of Mikhail Bakhtin', *The New York Review of Books*, 33 23 October (1986), pp. 56–60. In writing my study, I drew upon biographical and philological information in the following publications by Bakhtin's Hungarian translator, editor and expert, Csaba Könczöl: 'Mihail Bahtyin – a viták kereszttüzében' [M. B. in the centre of debates], *Literatura*. 2. 3/4) (1975), pp. 49–67; M. Bahtyin, *A szó esztétikája. Tanulmányok* [The aesthetics of the word. Studies], ed. by Cs. Könczöl (Gondolat, Budapest, 1976), pp. 381–93.; M. Bahtyin, *A beszéd és a valóság. Filozófiai és beszédelméleti írások* [Speech and reality. Writings on philosophy and speech-theory], ed. by Cs. Könczöl (Gondolat, Budapest, 1986), pp. 548–57; Könczöl was also the translator of Bakhtin's Rabelais book, *François Rabelais müvészete, a középkor és a reneszánsz népi kultúrája* (Európa, Budapest, 1982), the appearance of which gave me the impetus to write this study.
2.   Todorov, *Bakhtine*, pp. 16–24; Clark and Holquist, *Bakhtin, passim*; Könczöl (ed.), *A beszéd*, pp. 548–51.
3.   On the circumstances of this refusal, drawing from accounts by Bakhtin's disciples, see Könczöl, 'Mihail Bahtyin', p. 60.
4.   Michael Holquist has pointed out in his 'Prologue' to the second American edition of the Rabelais book – Mikhail Bakhtin, *Rabelais and His World*, transl. by Hélene Iswolsky (Indiana Univ. Press, Bloomington, 1984), p. xviii – that this 'safety-valve' theory must have been well known to Bakhtin from the current political praxis of his age, precisely in the years preceding the

conception of the Rabelais book. His protector, Anatoly Lunacharsky, set up a government commission in 1933 to study satiric genres; he intended to write a book on 'the social role of laughter', and in a completed published extract from it, in 1935, he stresses the historical importance of carnival. The carnival-type feasts, according to him, help to express passions of the common people that might otherwise be directed towards revolution.

5.   The page numbers in parentheses without author designation are references to the above-mentioned 1984 American edition. The text of 1444, on the Feast of Fools, appeared originally in the *Chartularium Universitatis Parisiensis*, ed. H. Denifle (Paris, 1897), vol. 4, p. 656, no. 2595; a recent analysis of the subject by Jacques Heers is *Fêtes des fous et carnavals* (Fayard, Paris, 1983). The details of medieval carnival and the pertinence of Bakhtin's analysis from this angle are not examined in this study. A good treatment of this subject, comparing Bakhtin's approach to Emmanuel Le Roy Ladurie's *Carnival in Romans* (New York, 1979), is made in the as yet unpublished paper by Peter Flaherty (York University, Canada): 'Reading carnival: towards a semiotics of history'. For a general overview see Umberto Eco, V. Ivanov and Monica Rector, *Carnival*, ed. Thomas A. Sebeok (Mouton, Berlin/New York/Amsterdam, 1984).

6.   On Bakhtin's relations to Buber's philosophy – Todorov, *Bakhtine*, pp. 52, 151; Clark and Holquist, *Bakhtin* p. 27; Frank, 'The voices', p. 56 (the quotation is from here, its source: M. Kagaskaya, 'Shutovskoi Khorovod', *Sintaksis*, 12 (1984), p. 141).

7.   This relation was detected and described in detail by Clark and Holquist, *Bakhtin*, pp. 80 ff.

8.   I have tried to develop this argument in Chapter 3 below.

9.   It is beyond my scope to give even a generally informative bibliography of these studies. I mention here only some of my favourite readings in this field, such as the writings of Georges Bataille, grouped for example in *L'érotisme* (10/18, Paris, 1957); the anthropological 'classics' like Bronislaw Malinowski's *Sex and Repression in Savage Society* (Routledge & Kegan Paul, London, 1927); *The Sexual Life of Savages in North-Western Melanesia: An Ethnographic Account of Courtship, Marriage and Family Life among the Natives of the Trobriand Islands*; E. E. Evans Pritchard's 'Some collective expressions of obscenity in Africa', in *The Position of Women in Primitive Societies and Other Essays in Social Anthropology* (Faber & Faber, London, 1965); Victor Turner's 'Paradoxes of twinship in Ndembu ritual', in Turner (1977), pp. 44–93; and finally, among the historical approaches, *The History of Sexuality* by Michel Foucault (1981).

10.   Bakhtin could not yet use here the conclusions of the two most significant researchers on this subject, but his sources and findings do converge with theirs – Rudolf Wittkower, 'Marvels of the East. A study in the history of monsters', *Journal of the Warburg and Courtauld Institutes*, 5 (1942), pp. 159–97; Jurgis Baltrusaitis, *Le Moyen Age fantastique, antiquités et exotismes dans l'art gothique* (Paris, 1955); idem. *Réveils et prodiges, le gothique fantastique* (Paris, 1960).

11.   Norbert Elias, *Über den Prozess der Zivilisation. Soziogenetische und*

psychogenetische Untersuchungen (Basle, 1939; Bern–Munich, 1969; English translation: Elias 1978). On the reception of this study, see Peter Gleichmann and Johan Goudsblom, *Materialien zu Norbert Elias' Zivilisationstheorie* (Suhrkamp, Frankfurt, 1979, 2nd edn); Rod Aya, 'Norbert Elias and the civilising process', *Theory and Society*, 5 (1978), pp. 219–28; Roger Chartier, 'Norbert Elias, interprète de l'histoire occidentale', *Le Débat*, 5 (1980), pp. 138–43.

12. V. N. Voloshinov (M. Bakhtin), *Freudianism: A Marxist Critique* (Academic Press, New York).

13. Wilhelm Reich, *Geschlechtsreife, Enthaltsamkeit, Ehemoral* (Wien, 1930); idem., *Die Sexualität im Kulturkampf. Zur sozialistischen Umstrukturierung des Menschen* (Sexpol Verlag, Copenhagen, 1936).

14. A. J. Gurevich, 'Smeh v narodnoi kulture srednievekovya' [Laughter in medieval popular culture], *Voprisi Literatur*, 6 (1966), pp. 207–11.

15. M. Bakhtine (V. N. Voloschinov), *Le Marxisme et la philosophie du langage. Essai d'application de la méthode sociologique en linguistique* (Minuit, Paris, 1977), pp. 38–40, 99, 137.

16. Bakhtin's stimulus in relation to the change in the pattern of studies on popular culture is underlined by Carlo Ginzburg, *Il formaggio e i vermi. Il cosmo di un mugniaio del '500* (Einaudi, Turin, 1976), pp. xiv–xv; his influence can be felt in the various studies of Natalie Zemon Davis, who first mentions his compatibility with the theses of Victor Turner in *Society and Culture in Early Modern France* (Stanford Univ. Press, Stanford, 1975), p. 300; the sixteenth–seventeenth-century tendency, emphasized by Bakhtin, to suppress or reform popular culture, is further elaborated in the studies of Thomas (1971), Burke (1978), Robert Muchembled, *Culture populaire et culture des élites dans la France moderne (XVᵉ–XVIIIᵉ-siècles)* (Flammarion, Paris, 1978), Bob Scribner, 'Reformation, carnival and the world turned upside down', *Social History*, 3 (1978), pp. 303–29; in the 1980s the number of studies in this branch of research became so abundant that only a separate study could evaluate them. For some aspects of Bakhtin's influence in Britain see Peter Burke, 'Bakhtin for historians', *Social History*, 13 (1988), pp. 85–90.

17. Jean Larmat, *Le Moyen Age dans le Gargantua de Rabelais* (Belles Lettres, Paris, 1973).

18. M. A. Screech, *The Rabelaisian Marriage. Aspects of Rabelais' Religion, Ethics and Comic Philosophy* (Arnold, London, 1958); idem., *Rabelais* (Duckworth, London: 1979); in connection with Rabelais' religious background mention should be made of Lucien Febvre, *Le Problème de l'incroyance au XVᵉ siecle, la religion de Rabelais* (Paris, 1942); Alan J. Krailsheimer, *Rabelais and the Franciscans* (Clarendon, Oxford, 1963).

19. This aspect is even more accentuated by the recent study of Richard M. Berrong, *Rabelais and Bakhtin. Popular Culture in Gargantua and Pantagruel* (Univ. of Nebraska Press, Lincoln/London, 1986), which appeared after the completion of my study. On the other hand, Berrong finds a way to solve this contradiction by pointing out that the same process of distancing from popular culture observed by Bakhtin among the representatives of the 'elite' can also be documented in Rabelais' work; he gradually turned away from the coarser and

more vulgar style of the *Pantagruel* when writing *Gargantua*, or the Third Book. Since he became at exactly that time a member of distinguished humanistic and court circles, this change can be interpreted as a reflection of his social and cultural ascendancy; in a wider framework one can also add that the general loss of favour of popular culture in the sixteenth century even had an impact on its chief Renaissance exponent: even Rabelais became an active participant in this exclusion.

CHAPTER 3   RELIGIOUS MOVEMENTS AND CHRISTIAN CULTURE

1. Raoul Manselli, 'Il Medioevo come "Christianitas": una scoperta romantica', and 'La "Christianitas" medioevale di fronte all 'eresia', in *Concetto, storia, miti e immagini del Medio Evo*, ed. Vittore Branca (Sansoni, Venice, 1973), pp. 51–134.
2. This study originates from my essay entitled 'Kereszténység és ideológia. Mozgáslehetőségek egy zárt ideológiai rendszerben' [Christianity and ideology. Possibilities of movement within a closed ideological system], *Világosság*, 20 (1979), pp. 352–60, 416–24. I enlarged the essay into a dissertation in 1983, and intended possibly to develop it into a book on medieval religious movements – but it has remained unfinished; the two essays translated here (Chapters 3 and 4) are among its completed chapters. At certain points I have updated the bibliography, without however altering much of the text itself, which reflects an attempt to rethink the historical problems of medieval Christianity in anthropological terms, and is rooted in the late 1970s. Since then there have appeared not only important philological–historical studies, but also an excellent anthropological approach to medieval heresy (though very different from mine), by Talal Asad, 'Medieval heresy: An anthropological view', *Social History*, 11 (1986).
3. Heresy is, of course, no qualification in itself: throughout the ages the notion has reflected the various ideological exclusions operated by the Church. As to the medieval meanings of the term, see H. Grundmann, 'Oportet et haereses esse. Das Problem der Ketzerei im Spiegel der mittelalterlichen Bibelexegese', *Archiv für Kulturgeschichte*, 45 (1963), pp. 129–64.
4. For a general treatment of dualist heresies in Christianity, see S. Pétrement, *Le Dualisme chez Platon, les Gnostiques et les Manichéens* (Paris, 1947); Steven Runciman, *The Medieval Manichee. A Study of the Christian Dualist Heresy* (Cambridge Univ. Press, Cambridge, 1947); Dmitri Obolensky, *The Bogomils. A Study in Balkan Neo-Manicheism* (Cambridge Univ. Press, Cambridge, 1948); Milan Loos, *Dualist Heresy in the Middle Ages* (Academia, Prague, 1974).
5. A. von Harnack, *Marcion. Ein Evangelium vom fremden Gott* (Leipzig, 1924), pp. 89–90.
6. The early-medieval re-evaluation of wealth is described by Karl Bosl, 'Potens und Pauper. Begriffsgeschichtliche Studien zur gesellschaftlichen Differenzierung im frühen Mittelalter und zum Pauperism des Hochmittelalters', in

Festschrift für O. Brunner (Göttingen, 1963); G. Miccoli, 'Dal pellegrinaggio alla conquista: povertà e ricchezza nelle prime crociate', in *Povertà e ricchezza nella spiritualità dei secoli XI e XII* (Todi, 1969).

7. Frederick H. Russell, *The Just War in the Middle Ages* (Cambridge, 1975).

8. See John Bugge, *Virginitas: An Essay in the History of a Medieval Ideal* (The Hague, 1975); Peter Brown, 'The notion of virginity in the early Church', in *Christian Spirituality. Origins to the Twelfth Century*, eds Bernard McGuinn and John Meyendorff (New York, 1985); Georges Duby, *Medieval Marriage. Two Models from Twelfth-Century France*, transl. E. Forster (Johns Hopkins Univ. Press, Baltimore, 1978); idem., *Le Chevalier, la femme et le prêtre. Le Mariage dans la France médiévale* (Hachette, Paris, 1981).

9. The broad universality and the extremely widespread use of Victor Turner's categories have rendered them a bit suspect to anthropologists and non-anthropologists in the second half of the 1980s. Although I have to accept the critical warning of Clifford Geertz in *Local Knowledge. Further Essays in Interpretive Anthropology* (Basic Books, New York, 1983, pp. 27–8) that it could make 'vividly disparate matters look drably homogeneous', I still feel that Turner's theory has good explicatory qualities for Christianity – his Catholic world-view is not a disadvantage from this point of view.

10. On children's Crusades see Pierre Toubert, 'Croisades d'enfants et mouvements de pauvreté au XIIIᵉ siècle', *Recherches sur les pauvres et la pauvreté*, Université Paris-Sorbonne, No. 4, (1965–66); late-medieval prophesy by children, so frequently mentioned for example in the chronicle of Salimbene de Adam, ed. G. Scaglia (Laterza, Bari, 1966), remains a question to be examined. For the Renaissance continuation of this phenomenon see Richard C. Trexler, 'Ritual in Florence: adolescence and salvation in the Renaissance', in *The Pursuit of Holiness in Late Medieval and Renaissance Religion*, eds Charles Trinkaus and Heiko A. Oberman (Leyden, 1974), pp. 200–64.

11. This problem is elucidated by Vauchez (1981), pp. 439–46; more recently, see Bynum (1987), pp. 13–30.

12. The evolution of the peasant saviour's imagery can be traced from William Langland's *Piers the Ploughman* to the German Peasant War. On the latter, see R. W. Scribner, 'Images of the peasant, 1514–1525', *Journal of Peasant Studies*, 3 (1975), pp. 27–48.

13. The notion of 'liminality', well known from the analyses of Victor Turner and his followers, refers to the anti-structural or *communitas* principles mentioned above, defined here in the terminology coined by Arnold van Gennep (1909). Liminality is characteristic of the central phase of the rites of passage, in which the participant, already separated from the previous status but not yet integrated into the new one, is constrained to spend some time on the margins, the *limen* of social existence, and confront the effects of this 'liminal' status. See Victor Turner, 'Betwixt and between: The liminal period in *rites de passage*', in idem., *The Forest of Symbols. Aspects of Ndembu Ritual* (Cornell Univ. Press, Ithaca/London, 1967), pp. 93–111.

14. *Sancti Bernardi . . . epistolae*, Ep. 472 (*Evervini Steinfeldensis praepositi ad*

S. Bernardum), PL 182, col. 677; the quotation is in Walter L. Wakefield and Austin P. Evans (eds), *The Heresies of the High Middle Ages. Selected Sources translated and annotated* (Columbia Univ. Press, New York/London, 1969), p. 129.

15. *Sancti Bernardi Sermones in Cantica*, Sermo 65, PL 183, cols 1089–93. See Raoul Manselli, 'Evervino di Steinfeld e San Bernardo di Clairvaux', in *Studi sulle eresie del secolo XII, idem* (Rome, 1975), pp. 141–56.

16. The category 'religious movement' was used to encompass various medieval heterodox and orthodox religious groups and their aims by Gioacchino Volpe, *Movimenti religiosi e sette ereticali nella società medievale italiana, Secoli XI–XIV* (Florence, 1922) and Grundmann (1935). The many studies on the history of medieval religious studies are listed in several bibliographies. To quote two of these Zsuzsanna Kulcsár, *Eretnekmozgalmak a XI–XIV. században (Bibliográfia)* (Tankönyvkiadó, Budapest, 1964); H. Grundmann, 'Bibliographie des études récentes (après 1900) sur les hérésies médiévales', in *Hérésies et sociétés dans l'Europe préindustrielle, 11e–18e siècles*, ed. J. Le Goff (Mouton, Paris/La Haye, 1968), pp. 407–74. On the history of Catharist heresy let me quote here just the seminal study of Arno Borst (1953). Three recent studies on the whole period: Lambert (1977); R. I. Moore, *The Origins of European Dissent* (New York, 1977), Bolton (1983).

17. On the apostolic lifestyle see E. W. McDonnell 'The Vita Apostolica: diversity or dissent', *Church History* (1955), pp. 15–31. On hermits see Léopold Génicot, 'L'Érémitisme du XIe siècle dans son contenu économique et social', in *L'Eremitismo in occidente nei secoli XI e XII*, Miscellanea del Centro di Studi Medioevali, IV (Milan, 1965), pp. 45–69.

18. Ovidio Capitani, 'San Pier Damiani e l'instituto eremitico', in *L'Eremitismo in occidente*, op. cit. (n 17), pp. 122–63; Lester K. Little, 'The personal development of Peter Damian', in *Order and Innovation in the Middle Ages. Essays in Honor of J. R. Strayer* (Princeton, 1976), pp. 317–43; Marie-Claude Derouet-Besson, ' "Inter duos scopulos". Hypothèses sur la place de la sexualité dans les modèles de la représentation du monde su XIe siècle', *AESC*, 36 (1981), pp. 930–4.

19. 'Mundum relinquere, carnem a concupiscentis frenare, de laboribus manuum suarum victum parere, nulli laesionem quaerere, charitatem cunctis, quos zelus hujus nostri propositi teneat, exhibere . . .', in *Acta synodi atrebatensis*, PL 142, col. 1272. This description was critically examined by Jeffrey Burton Russell, *Dissent and Reform in the Middle Ages* (Los Angeles, 1965), pp. 22–7. As to the heretical teachings enumerated in the document, Russell's point can be accepted: it is possible that some of them were not professed by the heretics themselves, but became incorporated into the polemical speech of Gérard de Cambrai for the sake of completing the argument. There is no way, however, of knowing about this, and it does not alter the fact that the difficulties mentioned must have seemed problematic at that times to have needed a special apologia. So it seems legitimate for me to take this splendid document as a starting point for the illustration of the typical arguments of the religious movements. A recent interpretation of it: Giuseppe

Cracco, 'Le eresie del Mille: un fenomeno di rigetto delle strutture feodali?' in *Structures féodales et féodalisme dans l'Occident méditerranéen, X^e–XIIIe siècles* (École Française, Rome, 1980), pp. 345–60.

20. The ritualized Christianity of the Carolingian age is characterized by Étienne Delaruelle, 'La pietà popolare nel secolo XI', in *La Piété populaire* (Bottega d'Erasmo, Torino, 1975), pp. 3–27; A. Vauchez, *La Spiritualité du Moyen Age Occidental (VIIIe–XIIe siècles)* (PUF, Paris, 1975); on Cluny see Helmut Richter (ed.), *Cluny. Beiträge zu Gestalt und Wirkung der Cluniazenser Reform* (Wege der Forschung 241, Darmstadt, 1975); Giles Constable, *Cluniac Studies* (Variroum Reprints, London, 1986).

21. É. Delaruelle, 'Le Crucifix dans la piété populaire et dans l'art du VIe au XIe siècles', in *La Piété*, op. cit. (n 20), pp. 27–42.

22. Raoul Glaber, *Les Cinq Livres de ses histoires*, ed. Maurice Prou (A. J. Picard, Paris, 1886), p. 49.

23. R. Manselli, 'Pierre de Bruis', in *Studi*, op. cit. (n 15), p. 83; for a detailed account of his teachings, see Petri Venerabilis, *Contra Petrobrusianos hereticos*, ed. J. Fearns (Turnholt, 1968). I have used the older edition in PL 189. On the crucifix, see PL 189, cols 773–4.

24. ' . . . dicentes in templo Dei nihil esse, quod sit alique cultu religionis dignum magis quam proprii domicilii cubiculum, nihilque in eo sanctum praeter coementa et lapides artificum opere digestos . . .' *Acta syn. atreb.*, op. cit. (n 19), col. 1284; similar critiques of churchbuilding by Peter of Bruis: Petri Venerabilis, *Contra*, op. cit. (n 23), PL 189, cols 719–20; on Catharist hostility towards church edifices, see Christine Thouzellier (ed.), *Une Somme anti-cathare. Le Liber contra manicheos de Durand de Huesca* (Louvain, 1964), p. 91; Borst (1953), p. 219, n. 22; the arguments of the Waldenses against churchbuilding are exemplified by the descriptions of the Anonymous of Passau: Alexander Patschovsky and Kurt-Viktor Selge (eds), *Quellen zur Geschichte der Waldenser* (Gerd Mohn, Gütersloh, 1973), pp. 94–5.

25. Analysed in great detail by John W. Baldwin, *Masters, princes and merchants. The social view of Peter the Chanter and his circle* (Princeton, 1970), vol. I, pp. 66–8, vol. II, p. 48; the same ideas appear in a more concise form in Petrus Cantor, *Verbum abbreviatum*, PL 205, cols 205–59.

26. Interesting points on this question by Pierre Francastel, 'Art et hérhésie', in *Hérésies et sociétés*, ed. Le Goff, op. cit. (n 16), pp. 31–46; heretics reported in 1135 destroying images of saints: *Gesta Nicholai episcopi cameracensis*, MGH SS, XIV, p. 244; Catharist arguments against images of saints: Borst (1953), p. 219, n. 22.; similar stand of Waldenses, e.g. Patschovsky and Selge, *Quellen*, op. cit. (n 24), p. 96.

27. For the iconoclastic tendencies of the Cistercians, see J. A. Lefèvre, 'Le Vrai Récit des origines de Citeaux est-il l'Exordium Parvum?', *Le Moyen Age*, 61 (1955), pp. 79–120 and 329–61, esp. p. 119; Saint Bernard's chief opus on this subject: *Apologia ad Guillelmum*, PL 182, cols. 897–918; see Georges Duby, *Saint Bernard. L'art cistercien* (Arts et métiers, Paris, 1976).

28. 'Dixit idem Petrus quod omnes illi qui ululabant in ecclesia cantando voce non intelligibili decipiebant populum simplicem . . .', Célestin Douais,

Documents pour servir à l'histoire de l'inquisition dans le Languedoc (Paris, 1900), vol. II, p. 97.

29. Quotation from the Anonymous of Passau: 'in verbis, non in melodia vis est; cantum ecclesie subsannant', Patschovsky and Selge, *Quellen*, op. cit. (n 24), p. 96.

30. Stephani de Borbone, *Tractatus de diversis materiis praedicabilibus*, ed. Albert Lecoy de la Marche, *Anecdotes historiques, légendes et apologues tirés du recueil inédit d'Étienne de Bourbon, dominicain du XIIIe siècle* (Société de l'histoire de la France, Publications CLXXXV, Paris, 1877), p. 295.

31. Huguette Taviani, 'Le Mariage dans l'hérésie de l'an mil', *AESC*, 32 (1977), pp. 1074–89; Derouet-Besson, ' "Inter duos scopulos" ', op. cit. (n 18), pp. 924–9; Catharist arguments against marriage collected by Edina Bozóky, (ed. comm.), *Le Livre secret des cathares. Interrogatio Iohannis. Apocryphe d'origine bogomile* (Paris, 1980), pp. 166–8; see Borst (1953), pp. 180–2.; on Waldenses, see Patschovsky and Selge, *Quellen*, op. cit. (n 24), p. 88; some heretics, however, did not seem to object to marriage as such, more to its ecclesiastical sanction: 'nuptias cum benedictione non debere fieri sed accipiat quisque qualitercumque voluerit' – as seems to be professed by the 1022 Orleans heretics (see Taviani, p. 1076); in 1115, Henry, the scandalous itinerant preacher, staged in a collective marriage ceremony in Le Mans for the prostitutes he had converted: *Gesta Pontificum Cenomanensium*, RHF XII, p. 548.

33. The exclusive authority of the Bible was stressed by the popular movements as well as by the more learned religious reformers. The latter are represented first by the itinerant preachers of the early twelfth century, and two generations later by the Piacenzan lawyer. Hugo Speroni – see Ilarino da Milano, *L'eresia di Ugo Speroni nella confutazione del Maestro Vacario. Testo inedito del secolo XII con studio storico e dottrinale* (Studi e testi 115, Città del Vaticano, 1945), pp. 66 and 522; on the standpoint of the Catharist, see Christine Thouzellier, 'L'Emploi de la Bible par les Cathares (XIIIe s.)', in *The Bible and Medieval Culture* (Mediaevalia Lov niensia, Ser. I, VII, Leuven, 1979), pp. 141–56; on the Waldenses, see L. I. Newman, *Jewish Influence on Christian Reform Movements* (New York, 1966), pp. 219–28.

34. Two examples: end of the twelfth century – Geoffroi d'Auxerre, *Super Apocalipsim*, excerpts in Giovanni Gonnet (ed.), *Enchiridion Fontium Valdensium (recueil critique des sources concernant les Vaudois au moyen âge)* (Torre Pellice, 1958), I, p. 48; thirteenth century (Anonymous of Passau) – Patschovsky and Selge, *Quellen*, op. cit. (n 24), p. 80.

35. The cultural mechanisms and historical conflicts of written and oral culture have been frequently discussed over the past few decades. The most theoretical synthesis in this respect remains Jack Goody, *The Domestication of the Savage Mind* (Cambridge Univ. Press, Cambridge/London/New York/Melbourne, 1977).

36. Thus Catharist women startled her audience in Reims in 1176 – Radulphus de Coggeshall, *Chronicon anglicarum*, RHF XVIII, p. 93; Ecbert, Abbot of Schönau, one of the first polemical writers against Catharism, stressed their

expert knowledge of the Bible in 1163 – Ecbertus Schonaugiensis, *Sermones XIII contra Catharos*, PL 195, cols 11–102, esp. cols 13–14; Peter Waldo 'evangelia . . . corde retinuerat', according to Stephen of Bourbon – Lecoy de la Marche, *Anecdotes*, op. cit. (n 30), p. 291; it is also he who reported of early thirteenth-century Waldenses that they 'repeterent infra corde' several parts of the Gospel of Matthew and Luke – ibid., p. 309. These examples could be multiplied.

37. Especially the four-level explanation of the Scripture, which can be traced back to Saint Jerome – Ep. 120, PL 25, col. 1005; see E. von Dobschütz, 'Vom vierfachen Schriftsinn. Die Geschichte einer Theorie', in *Harnack-Ehrung* (Leipzig, 1921), pp. 1–15.

38. It can be found already among the Arras heretics, *Acta syn. atreb.*, op. cit. (n 19), col. 1274; among the Waldenses, Patschovsky and Selge, *Quellen*, op. cit. (n 24), p. 104.

39. '*osculum pacis*', among the Cathars, Borst (1953), p. 199.

40. '*fractio panis*', among the Cathars, ibid., p. 210.; see R. Manselli, *L'eresia del male* (Naples, 1963), p. 232; among the Waldenses, Patschovsky and Selge, *Quellen*, op. cit. (n 24), pp. 63 and 105.

41. This was done by Manasses, a blacksmith, follower of Tanchelm in the early twelfth-century Netherlands. The complaint of the Utrecht canons is published in the work edited by P. Frederick, *Corpus documentorum inquisitionis haeretice pravitatis Neerlandice* (Ghent, 1889), I, p. 17.

42. The relationship between medieval religious movements and marginality was noticed first by Antonio de Stefano, *Riformatori ed eretici nel medioevo* (Palermo, 1938), pp. 115–17. The same problem was recently analysed by Jean-Claude Schmitt, *Mort d'une hérésie. L'église face aux béguines et aux béghards du Rhin supérieur du XIVe au XVe siècle* (Mouton, Paris/La Haye, 1978), pp. 35 ff.

43. For the itinerant preachers, the best overall account remains Johann von Walther, *Die ersten Wanderprediger Frankreichs* (Leipzig, 1903–1906); see also Dalarun (1985).

44. *Gest. pont. cenom.*, op. cit. (n 31), p. 548: 'victus ejus a publico in promptu dissimilis, hospitium in aedibus Burgensium, mansio in porticu, coena, cubile in coenaculo . . .'

45. *Sancti Bernardi Epistolae*, No. 195, PL 182, col. 363: '. . . ita vagus et profugus super terram, quod iam non licet inter suos, non cessat apud alienos . . .'

46. Itinerant preachers as ideologists contrasted with more introverted eleventh-century heretical groups – Giorgio Cracco, 'Gli eretici nella "societas christiana" dei secoli XI e XII', in *La cristianità dei secoli XI e XII in Occidente: Coscienza e strutture di una società* (Milan, 1983), pp. 339–73. The data for those mentioned in the enumeration: Peter the Hermit – Hagenmeyer (1879), p. 114; Robert d'Arbrissel – Walther, *Die ersten*, op. cit. (n 43), vol. I, p. 188; Henry – *Gest. pont. cenom.*, op. cit. (n 31), p. 549; Peter of Bruis – Petri Venerabilis, *Contra*, op. cit. (n 23), passim.; Tanchelm – Frederick, *Corpus*, op. cit. (n 41), vol. I, p. 15.

47. On Saint Bernard's personality and his relation to the religious movements

of his age, see Duby, *Saint Bernard*, op. cit. (n 27); the importance of this passage was emphasized by Caroline Walker Bynum (1982), pp. 127–8. The quotation comes from *Sancti Bernardi Epistolae*, No. 87, PL 182, col. 217: Efficimur opprobium abundantibus, et despectio superbis. Nam revera quid aliud saecularibus quam ludere videmus, cum, quod ipsi appetunt in hoc saeculo, nos per contrarium fugimus; et quod ipsi fugiunt, nos appetimus? More scilicet joculatorum et saltatorum, qui capite misso deorsum, pedibusque sursum erectis, praeter humanum usum stant manibus vel incedunt, et sic in se omnium oculos definqunt . . . Hoc ludo et nos interim ludamus, ut illudamur, confundamur, humiliemur, donec veniat qui potentes deponit, et exaltat humiles . . .'

48.   On Catharist dualism, besides the cited works of Runciman and Loos (op. cit, n 4) and Borst (1953), see *Livre des deux principes*, ed. comm. Christine Thouzellier, SC 198 (Cerf, Paris, 1973); Jean Duvernoy, *Le Catharisme: la religion des cathares* (Privat, Toulouse, 1976).

49.   The 1157 Synod of Reims gives a similar image of the Cathars (named as *textores*): 'per abjectissimos textores qui saepe de loco fugiunt in locum nominaque commutarunt . . .', J. D. Mansi, *Sacrorum conciliorum nova et amplissima collectio*, vol. XXI, col. 843. See Grundmann, (1935), p. 31.

50.   Let me quote only a small selection of the vast literature on Saint Francis – the first classical synthesis: Paul Sabatier, *Vie de Saint François d'Assise* (Paris, 1894) and two recent ones: Lambert (1961) – one of the basic examples used by Victor Turner when applying his theory to medieval Christianity; and Kajetan Esser, *Anfänge und Zielsetzungen des Ordens der Minderbrüder* (Leiden, 1966).

51.   On Bogomil apocryphal writings see Jordan Ivanov (ed.), *Livres et légendes bogomiles (Aux sources du Catharisme)* (Maisonneuve et Larose, Paris, 1976); Catharist apocryphal writings are reviewed by Duvernoy, *Le Catharisme*, op. cit. (n 48), pp. 33–5; the two main texts are: Bozóky, *Interrogatio Iohannis*, op. cit. (n 31), and Thouzellier, *Livre des deux principes*, op. cit. (n 48).

52.   There are several such comprehensive presentations of medieval Christianity – William Southern, *Western Society and the Church in the Middle Ages* (Penguin, Harmondsworth, 1970); Jacques Le Goff, *La Civilisation de l'Occident médiéval* (Arthaud, Paris, 1972); Georges Duby, *Le Temps des cathédrales. L'Art et la société 980–1420* (Gallimard, Paris, 1976).

53.   After a series of conference volumes of the early 1970s such as Delaruelle, *La Piété*, op. cit. (n 20), Vauchez, *La Spiritualité*, op. cit. (n 20), or R. Manselli, *La Religion populaire au Moyen Age. Problème de méthode et d'histoire. Conférence Albert le Grand, 1973* (Montréal, 1973), the methodological problems of popular religion were elaborated by Jean-Claude Schmitt, ' "Religion populaire" et culture folklorique', *AESC*, 31 (1976), pp. 941–53; see also *Religioni delle classe popolari*, ed. Carlo Ginzburg, *Quaderni Storici*, 41 (1979).

54.   The reference is to Max Weber, *Wirtschaft und Gesellschaft* (Berlin/Cologne, 1964), p. 332; on relics see Nicole Hermann-Mascard, *Les Reliques des saints. Formation coutumière d'un droit* (Paris, 1975); Geary (1978); idem., 'Humiliation of saints', in *Saints and their Cults. Studies in*

Religious Sociology, Folklore and History, ed. Stephen Wilson (Cambridge Univ. Press, Cambridge/London, 1983), pp. 123–40. The problem of to what extent the cult of saints could be related to popular culture has been convincingly reformulated in the above-quoted work by Peter Brown (1981).

55.   All this does not mean, of course, that popular religion represented only the principles of 'structure'. In Chapter 2 I have already amply discussed the 'anti-structure' and *communitas* aspects of popular culture.

56.   Among the many syntheses of medieval philosophical and scientific achievements and the cultural strivings of the medieval university intellectuals, let me refer only to Étienne Gilson, *La Philosophie au moyen âge* (Payot, Paris, 1944); Le Goff (1957); Alexander Murray, *Reason and Society in the Middle Ages* (Clarendon, Oxford, 1978); R. L. Benson and Giles Constable (eds), *Renaissance and Renewal in the Twelfth century* (Harvard Univ. Press, Cambridge, MA, 1982); Brian Stock, *The Implications of Literacy, Written Language and Models of Interpretation in the Eleventh and Twelfth centuries* (Princeton Univ. Press, Princeton, NJ, 1983).

57.   On the problems encountered by the School of Chartres and Abélard see note 63 below.

58.   Quoted by Le Goff (1957), pp. 23–4.

59.   For the religious policies of Gregory VII, see Raffaello Morghen, *Medioevo christiano* (Laterza, Bari, 1974); how celibacy helped the Church to strive for a new kind of Christian matrimonial ideal for the laity *and* simultaneously against the heretical ascetic criticism is well described by Duby, *Le Chevalier*, op. cit. (n 8), pp. 117.

60.   Petri Abelardi, *Introductio ad Theologiam*, II, 4, PL 178, cols 1056–7.

61.   John F. Benton, (ed.), *Self and Society in Medieval France. The Memoirs of Abbot Guibert of Nogent* (Univ. of Toronto Press, Toronto/Buffalo/London, 1984), p. 214.

62.   R. Manselli, 'Aspetti e significato dell'intolleranza popolare nei secoli XI–XII', in idem., *Studi*, op. cit. (n 15), pp. 19–38.

63.   See Le Goff (1957), pp. 47–50; Guilleaume de Saint-Thierry, *Disputatio adversus Petrum Abaelardum*, PL 180, cols 248–82; *Pierre Abélard – Pierre le Vénérable. Les Courants philosophiques, littéraires et artistiques en Occident au milieu du XIIᵉ siècle*, Actes du colloque de Cluny, 2–9 July 1972 (CNRS, Paris, 1975).

64.   G. de Saint-Thierry, *Lettre aux frères du Mont-Dieu (Lettre d'or)*, ed. Jean Déchanet, SC 223 (Cerf, Paris, 1975).

65.   'Quid hoc audio de te? Nutritus et eruditus in scola Spiritui Sancti cui ad docendum nulla mora est, et ea relicta saecularem scolam adisti . . .', MGH SS XII, 678; see Milis (1979), p. 47.

66.   'Experto crede: aliquid plus invenies in silvis quam in libris. Ligna et lapides docebunt te quod a magistris audire non possis . . .', *Sancti Bernardi Epistolae*, No. 106, PL 182, col. 242; in his letter to Aelred of Rievaulx he wrote: 'Sub umbris arborum senseris quale nunquam didicisses in scolis . . .', see E. Gilson, ' "Sub umbris arborum . . . " ', *Medieval Studies*, 14 (1952), pp. 149–51; see also Anselme Dimier, 'Les premiers cistreciens étaient-ils ennemis des études?' in *Los monjes y los estudios* (Abadia de Poblet, 1963), pp. 119–47.

67. Le Goff (1957), pp. 73–83.

68. The religious policies of Innocent III concerning religious movements are analysed in Grundmann (1935), pp. 38–50; Thouzellier (1966), pp. 133–213; and Brenda Bolton, 'Tradition and temerity: Papal attitudes to deviants 1159–1216', in *Schism, Heresy and Religious Protest*, ed. Derek Baker (Cambridge, 1972), pp. 79–92; the decidedly anti-heretical activity of the Humiliati was praised by James of Vitry in 1216 – *Lettres de Jacques de Vitry*, ed. R. B. C. Huygens (Leiden, 1960), pp. 72–3; the anti-Catharist polemical activity of Durand de Huesca was expressed in two pamphlets – the *Liber antihaeresis*, published in Selge (1967), vol. II; and the *Liber contra manicheos*, in Thouzellier, op. cit. (n 24).

69. The circumstances of the founding of the Dominican order are described by Grundmann (1935), pp. 102–5; M. H. Vicaire, *Saint Dominique. La Vie apostolique* (Paris, 1965). As for the personal role of the Pope, see *Innocentii III pp. Epistolae*, 7, 76, PL 215, cols 358 skk.

70. P. Glorieux, 'Prélats français contre religieux mendiants – Autour de la bulle "Ad fructus uberes" (1281–90)', *Revue d'Histoire de l'Église de France*, 11 (1925).

71. As to their fight against wordly luxury, I analyse this problem in Chapter 4. Their fight against superstition, Stephen of Bourbon's action against the 'holy greyhound' and its wider context are analysed by Jean-Claude Schmitt (1979).

The widening influence of the mendicant orders among thirteenth-century laity is described by H. Hefele, *Die Bettelorden und das religiöse Volksleben Ober- und Mittelitaliens im XIII. Jahrhundert* (Leipzig/Berlin, 1910); André Vauchez, 'Une Campagne de pacification en Lombardie autour de 1233. L'Action politique des ordres mendiants d'après la réforme des statuts communaux et les accords de paix', *École Française de Rome. Mélanges d'archéologie et d'histoire*, 78 (1966), pp. 503–49.

CHAPTER 4   FASHIONABLE BEARDS AND HERETIC RAGS

I owe special thanks to R. Howard Bloch for helping me to find the English translations of several of the cited texts.

1. The *Mantel mautaillé* [The ill-fitting coat] is published in *Recueil général et complet des fabliaux*, ed. A. de Courde de Montaiglon (Librairie des Biblio-philes, Paris, 1872–90), III, 8. It is lucidly analysed and related to the semiotic function of dress in Howard Bloch, *The Scandal of the fabliaux* (Univ. of Chicago Press, Chicago/London, 1986), pp. 23–58.

2. Among the vast sociological and anthropological literature that reveals the interrelatedness of social structure and bodily or vestimentary signs, the best starting points are still in the seminal studies of Georg Simmel, 'Fashion', *International Quarterly*, 10 (1904), pp. 130–55, and Edward Sapir, 'Fashion', in *Encyclopedia of Social Sciences* (Macmillan, New York, 1931), pp. 139–44. Of later sources let me quote only two influential analyses and a useful selection of studies: Roland Barthes, 'Histoire et sociologie du vêtement, quelques

observations méthodologiques', *AESC*, 12 (1957), pp. 430–41; Marshall
Sahlins, 'Notes on the American clothing system', in idem., *Culture and Practical Reason* (The Univ. of Chicago Press, Chicago/London 1976), pp. 179–95;
Mary Ellen Roach and Joanne Bubolz Eichler (eds), *Dress, Adornment and the
Social Order* (Wiley, New York/London/Sidney, 1965).

3. See the more detailed discussion of this in Chapters 2 and 3 in this volume.

4. R. Hercher, *Epistolographi Graeci*, Scriptorum Graecorum Bibliotheca, 16
(Firmin Didot, Paris, 1873), Nos 2 and 46, pp. 235, 257. Although these letters
are very probably forgeries from the second or third centuries AD, they must
have been written by a representative of the Cynic movement, so they can be
taken as illustrative of its spirit.

5. Lucian, *The Passing of Peregrinus*, in *Lucian with an English Translation*, ed.
A. M. Harmon (Harvard Univ. Press/Heinemann, Cambridge, MA/London,
1913), vol. V, pp. 1–52. quot.: p. 17.

6. J. C. M. Van Winden (ed.), *An Early Christian Philosopher. Justin Martyr's
Dialogue with Trypho* (Brill, Leiden, 1971), I, 1; Tertullianus, *De pallio*, VI, 4,
ed. V. Bulhart, CSEL 76 (Vindobonae, 1957), p. 125; the quotation used as
motto is also from here, VI, 1, p. 124; English translation in A. Roberts and J.
Donaldson (eds), *The Ante-Nicene Fathers* (Buffalo, 1885), p. 12.

7. Lucian, *The Cynic*, in Harmon, *Lucian*, op. cit. (n 5), vol. VIII, pp. 381,
405, 409 (note that Lucian's authorship of this dialogue is doubted by some
scholars); his other dialogues mentioning Cynics: *Demonax*, in ibid., vol. I,
pp. 141–74; *Dialogues of the Dead*, in ibid., vol. VII, pp. 1–177. See Jakob
Bernays, *Lucian und die Kyniker* (Berlin, 1879).

8. Thomas: 23; Robert M. Grant and David Noel Freedman, *The Secret Sayings
of Jesus with an English translation of the Gospel of Thomas* (Doubleday, New
York, 1960), p. 143.

9. At the beginning of Chapter 3 in this volume.

10. Philipp Oppenheim, *Das Mönchskleid im Christlichen Altertum* (Freiburg
im Breisgau, 1931). On the deliberate emulation of prophetical and apostolical
models, see e.g. Johannes Chrysostomus, *In Evangelium Matthaei homilia*, 68
PG 58, col. 644 – in Latin: 'Vestis autem viris digna est: neque enim perinde
vestiuntur atque ii qui tunicas trahunt per vicos, enervati et effeminati: sed ut
beati illi angeli, Elias, Elisaeus, Joannes, apostoli vestiuntur, alii ex pilis
caprinis, alii ex pilis camelorum . . .'

11. The mass of data about them in *Vitae Patrum – Verba seniorum* (PL 73)
and Theodoret, *Historia Religiosa* (PG 82) is gathered by Oppenheim, *Das
Mönchskleid*, pp. 22 ff.

12. This view is represented by his most beloved disciple, Paula, who led a
female monastery in Bethlehem after her conversion. See J. Hilberg (ed.),
Hieronimus Eusebius, Sanctus. Epistulae, CSEL 55 (Vindobonae/Lipsiae,
1912), Letter 108, 20, p. 336.

13. *Vitae patrum*, op. cit. (n 11), V, 15, 6, PL 73, col. 953: 'Dicebant autem de
eo qui supra, quia sicut dum in palatio esset, nemo melioribus vestibus eo
utebatur; ita et dum in conversatione moraretur, nemo eo vilius tegebatur . . .'.

14. Pachomius, Precept 49, in Amand Boon, *Pachomiana latina* (Louvain,
1932), p. 26. A detailed analysis of this problem can be found in Giles

Constable, 'The ceremonies and symbolism of entering religious life and taking the monastic habit, from the fourth to the twelfth century', in *Segni e riti nella chiesa altomedievale occidentale* (Spoleto, 1987), pp. 771–834.

15. Cassianus, *De institutione coenobiorum*, ed. Petschenig, CSEL 17, IV, 5, pp. 50–1. See Constable, 'The ceremonies', p. 809 (I quote his translation).

16. Cassianus, *De institutione*, I, 2, p. 21, '. . . postremo sic ab huius mundi separentur ornatu, ut cultui servorum dei in omnibus communia perseverent'

17. On monastic habit, see P. Oppenheim, *Symbolik und religiöse Wertung des Mönchskleides im christlichen Altertum, vornehmlich nach Zeugnissen christlicher Schriftsteller der Ostkirche* (Münster, 1932).

18. Johannes Chrysostomus, *In Evangelium Matthaei homilia*, 69 PG 58, col. 645. The quotation is translated from Latin.

19. There is not space to give a detailed analysis of this evolution here. In the past few years a wider scholarly interest in this question has been observed, partly due to the investigations of Michel Foucault, *The Care of the Self* and *The Use of Pleasures*, both translated by R. Hurley (Pantheon, New York, 1985). See also Aline Rousselle, *Porneia. De la maîtrise du corps à la privation sensorielle* (PUF, Paris, 1983). The whole problem is reformulated in the recent book by Peter Brown, *The Body and Society. Men, Women and Sexual Renunciation in Early Christianity* (Columbia University Press, New York, 1988).

20. Tertullianus, *De virginibus velandis*, XVII, 4, in CSEL 76, ed. V. Bulhart, p. 102; English translation: Roberts and Donaldson, *Ante-Nicene*, op. cit. (n 6), p. 37.

21. Tertullianus, *De cultu feminarum*, IV, 1–2, XIII, 7, ed. M. Turcan, *La Toilette des femmes* SC 173 (Cerf, Paris, 1971); English translation: Roberts and Donaldson, *Ante-Nicene*, op. cit. (n 6), p. 25.

22. Arthur Vööbus, *The Didascalia Apostolorum in Syriac* (Louvain, 1979), pp. 13 and 24.

23. Clemens Alexandrinus, *Protrepticus und Paedagogus*, ed. O. Stählin (Leipzig, 1905), pp. 237–44; Hieronimus, *Epistulae*, 22, *Ad Eustochium*, CSEL 54; Cyprianus, *De habitu virginum*, CSEL 3, pp. 190–200; Johannes Chrysostomus, *Homilia*, 69 PG 59, col. 520; idem., *De virginitate*, ed. H. Musurillo, SC 125 (Cerf, Paris, 1966); idem., *Lettres à Olympias*, SC 13 (Cerf, Paris, 1947), pp. 125–33.

24. Letter 22, *Ad Eustochium*, 28; Hieronimus, *Epistulae*, CSEL 54, p. 185, English translation in Philip Schaff and Henry Wace (eds), *A Select Library of Nicene and Post-Nicene Fathers* (Grand Rapids, 1887), VI, p. 34 see Oppenheim, *Das Mönchskleid*, op. cit. (n 10), p. 72. A similar argument by Epiphanius against Messalians, *Adversus haereses*, II, 2, PG 42, col. 765.

25. Lucian, *The dead come to life or the Fisherman*, in Harmon, *Lucian*, op. cit. (n 5), vol. III, p. 67.

26. Salvianus, *Adversus Avaritiam Timothei ad Ecclesiam*, IV, 5, 24, ed. Pauly, CSEL 8, p. 380; see Oppenheim, *Das Mönchskleid*, op. cit. (n 10), p. 111.

27. *Capitula aquisgranensia*, 20, *Consuetudines monasticae* (Montecassino, 1907), vol. III, p. 121.

28. Ennodius: 'Quod agunt in aliis dominis diademata hoc in rege meo operata

est, Deo fabricante, natura', MGH, Auct. Ant. VII, p. 214; on Liudprand: 'multos nobiles de Romanis more Langobardorum totondit atque vestivit', L. Duchesne (ed.), *Liber pontificalis*, I, p. 420.

29.	René König, *Sociologie de la mode* (Payot, Paris, 1969), p. 111.

30.	Einhardi, *Vita Karoli Magni*, ed. O. Holder-Egger, MGH Scriptores Rerum Germanicarum ad usum scolarum (6th edn, Hanover 1911), III, 23; Einhard and Notker the Stammerer, *Two Lives of Charlemagne*, translation Lewis Thorpe (Penguin, Harmondsworth, 1969), pp. 77–8.

31.	Monachus Sangallensis, *De Karolo Magno*, I, 34, MGH SS, II, pp. 726–63; Einhard and Notker, *Two Lives*, pp. 132–3.

32.	Liutprandi Cremonensis, *Relatio de legatione Constantinopolitana*, PL 136, col. 925: 'Graecorum rex crinitus, tunicatus, manicatus, teristratus, mendax, dolosus, immisericors, vulpinus, superbus, falso humilis, parcis, cupidus, allio cepe et porris vescens, balnea bibens; Francorum rex contra pulchre tonsus, muliebri vestitu diversus, pileatus, verex, nil doli habens, satis ubi competit misericors . . .'; Ratherius Veronensis, *Praeloquia*, PL 136, cols 294–5; *Vita Sancti Brunonis archiepiscopi Coloniensis auctore Ruotgero*, in *Lebensbeschreibungen einiger Bischöfe des 10–12. Jahrhunderts*, ed. H. Kallfelz (Darmstadt, 1973), p. 222: 'Molles et delicatas vestes, in quibus nutritus et ad hominem usque perductus est, etiam in domibus regum multoties declinavit; inter purpuratos ministros et milites suos auroque nitidos vilem ipse tunicam et rusticana ovium pelles induxit'; see C. Stephen Jaeger, *The Origins of Courtliness. Civilizing Trends and the Formation of Courtly Ideals 939–1210* (Univ. of Pennsylvania Press, Philadelphia, 1985), pp. 154–5.

33.	Raoul Glaber, *Les cinq Livres de ses histoires*, ed. Maurice Prou (Picard, Paris, 1886), p. 89; I quote the translation of Jaeger, *The Origins*, p. 178: On these waves of medieval male fashions see the excellent study by Henri Platelle, 'Le Problème du scandale: les nouvelles modes masculines aux XIe et XIIe siècles', *Revue belge de philologie et d'histoire*, 53 (1975), pp. 1071–96.

34.	Wilhelm von Giesebrecht, *Geschichte der deutschen Kaiserzeit* (Duncker & Humbolt, Leipzig, 1885), p. 718; transl. from Jaeger, *The Origins*, p. 179.

35.	'Laicus namque cum sis et, juxta morem laicorum barba minime rasa incedere deberes, tu e contra, divinae legis contemptor, quasi clericus barbam tuam rasisti', Othloni Ratisboniensis, *De cursu spirituali*, PL 146, cols 241–4; see Platelle, 'Le Problème', p. 1085.

36.	William of Malmesbury, *Gesta Regum Anglorum*, Liber III, PL 179, col. 1225: '. . . serio addiderunt, pene omnes in exercitu illo presbiteros videri, quod totam faciem cum utroque labio rasam haberent . . .'

37.	Adalbéron de Laon, *Poème au roi Robert*, ed. Claude Carozzi (Belles Lettres, Paris, 1979), pp. 8–10 (lines 90–140).

38.	Eadmer, *Historia novorum*, PL 159, col. 376; *Eadmer's History of Recent Events in England (Historia Novorum in Anglia)*, transl. Geoffrey Bosanquet (London, 1964), pp. 47–9; see Frank Barlow, *William Rufus* (Univ. of California Press, Berkeley/Los Angeles, 1983), pp. 192–3.

39.	Malmesbury, *Gesta*, op. cit. (n 36), cols 1278–9: 'Tunc fluxus crinium tunc luxus vestium, tunc usus calceorum cum arcuatia aculeis inventus: mollitie corporis certare cum foeminis, gressum frangere, gestu soluto et latero nudo incedere, adolescentium specimen erat'; see Barlow, *William*, p. 104; Jaeger, *The Origins*, op. cit. (n 32), pp. 180–1.

40. Ordericus Vitalis, *Historia Ecclesiastica*, VIII, PL 188, col. 587; Marjorie Chibnall (ed., tranl.), *The Ecclesiastical History of Ordericus Vitalis* (Clarendon, Oxford, 1969), vol. IV, pp. 188–9.

41. Ordericus, *Historia*, col. 586; Chibnall, *The Ecclesiastical*, vol. IV, p. 187: 'ita ut operiret pedes, et eorum celaret tubera quae vulgo vocantur uniones'.

42. Herimanni, *Liber de restauratione Sancti Martini Tornacensis*, MGH SS XIV, pp. 275–7; see Platelle, 'Le Problème', op. cit. (n 33), p. 1081.

43. Eadmer, *Historia*, op. cit. (n 38), col. 376.

44. Ordericus, *Historia*, op. cit. (n 40), col. 808; Chibnall, *The Ecclesiatical*, vol. VI (London, 1978), pp. 64–7.

45. Ordericus, *Historia*, col. 607: 'ut nullus homo comam nutriat, sed sit tonsus, sicut decet Christianum'.

46. At the 1103 London synod it was accepted as a norm that the hair should be cut so that the eyes and ears became visible – see Platelle, 'Le Problème', op. cit. (n 33), p. 1079.

47. Lamberti Ardensis, *Historia Ghisnensium Comitum*, RHF 13, p. 427.

48. Ordericus, *Historia*, op. cit. (n 40), col. 613: 'Militares viri mores paternos in vestitu et capillorum tonsura derelinquerunt, quos paulo post burgenses et rustici et pene totum vulgus imitati sunt . . .'

49. These tendencies of the Gregorian reform are described in A. Vauchez, *La Spiritualité du Moyen Age occidental (VIIIe–XIIe siècles)* (PUF, Paris, 1975), pp. 67 ff; G. Duby, 'Guerre et société dans l'Europe féodale. Ordonnancement de la paix. La Morale des guerriers', in *Concetto, storia, miti e immagini del Medio Evo*, ed. Vittore Branca (Sansoni, Florence, 1973), pp. 449–82.

50. See notes 38–46 above; in 1106, in the presence of Count Robert II of Flanders, a similar demand was put to the *milites* by Godefroid, Bishop of Amiens: *Vita Godefridi episcopi Ambianensis*, Acta Sanctorum, Nov. III, p. 926; see Platelle, 'Le Problème', op. cit. (n 33), p. 1081.

51. Ordericus, *Historia*, op. cit. (n 40), col. 807; Chibnall, *The Ecclesiastical*, pp. 65–7.

52. *Liber ad milites Templi de laude novae militiae*, eds J. Leclecq and H. M. Rochais, in *Sancti Bernardi opera*, 3 (1963), pp. 217, 220; let us quote the characterization of the Christian knight: 'nunquam compti, raro loti, magis autem neglecto crine hispidi, pulvere foedi, lorica et caumate fusci . . .', see Josef Fleckenstein, 'Die Rechtfertigung der geistlichen Ritterorden nach der Schrift "De laude novae militiae" Bernhards von Clairvaux', in *Die Geistlichen Ritterorden Europas*, eds J. Fleckenstein and M. Hellmann, Vorträge und Forschungen 26 (Thorbeke, Sigmaringen, 1980), pp. 9–22.

53. Ordericus, *Historia*, op. cit. (n 40), col. 807; Chibnall, *The Ecclesiastical* p. 65.

54. Quotations from Lucian, *The Cynic*, op. cit. (n 7), p. 403. The longest and wittiest treatment of the Cynic beard is the *Misopogon* of Emperor Julian the Apostate, written in 353: *The Works of Emperor Julian* ed. Wilmer C. Wright (London/New York, 1913), pp. 420–511.

55. H. P. L'Orange, 'Plotinos–Paul' (1958), reprinted in *Likeness and Icon*

(Odense, 1973), pp. 32–42. See Giles Constable, 'Beards in history', in *Apologiae duae, Gozechini epistola ad Walcherum, Burchardi, ut videtur, abbatis Bellevallis Apologia de barbis*, ed. R. B. C. Huygens, CC Cont. Med. LXII (Turnholti, 1985), p. 65.

56. The quotation is from the thirteenth-century *Legenda Aurea* by James of Voragine, drawing on Antique sources. That the Apostles were bearded is doubted by J. M. D. Derrett, 'Religious hair', *Man*, N. S. 8 (1973), p. 102.

57. Vööbus, *Didascalia*, op. cit. (n 22), pp. 13–14; the various positions taken by Christianity on this issue are well reviewed by two ancient monographs: A. Fangé, *Mémoires pour servir à l'histoire de la barbe de l'homme* (Liege, 1774); Barnabae Vaerini, *De Vario Veterum et Recentiorum Barbae cultu et ritu* (Venice, 1778).

58. Tertullianus, *De cultu feminarum*, op. cit. (n 21), V, 3; Roberts and Donaldson, *Ante-Nicene*, op. cit. (n 6), vol. IV, pp. 20–1.

59. This debate has been examined by Philip Hofmeister, 'Der Streit um des Priesters Bart', *Zeitschrift für Kirchengeschichte*, 62 (1943–4), pp. 72–94, especially pp. 78–85; see Constable, 'Beards', op. cit. (n 55), p. 103–14.

60. Columban, *Regula coenobialis*, 4, in *Sancti Columbani opera*, ed. G. S. M. Walker, Scriptores Latini Hiberniae, 2 (Dublin, 1957), pp. 148; see Constable, 'Beards', op. cit. (n 55), p. 115.

61. Isidorus de Sevilla, *De ecclesiasticis officiis*, Lib. II, PL 83, col. 302 (with reference to Jerome); Hrabanus Maurus, *De institutione clericorum*, III, 29, PL 107, col. 341.

62. Gregorius Magnus, *Moralia in Job*, II, 52, PL 75, cols 595–6; similar symbolic interpretations in Constable, 'Beards', op. cit., (n 55), pp. 71–2.

63. Isidorus, *De ecclesiasticis officiis*, op. cit. (n 61), cols 779–80.

64. Honorius Augustodunensis, *Gemma Animae*, cap. 93. 'De tonsura clericorum', PL 172, cols 602–3; the religious context of sacrificing one's hair is outlined by Adolph Franz, *Die Kirchliche Benediktionen im Mittelalter* (Freiburg im Breisgau, 1909), vol. II, pp. 245–52; see Constable, 'Beards', op. cit. (n 55), p. 58.

65. Many such examples in Constable, 'Beards', op. cit. (n 55), pp. 115–16.

66. Benediction of the beard in Franz, *Die Kirchliche*, op. cit. (n 64), vol. II, pp. 254–6; Fangé, *Mémoires*, op. cit. (n 57), pp. 299–300; Hofmeister, 'Der Streit', op. cit. (n 59), p. 79; *Smaragdi abbatis expositio in regulam S. Benedicti*, ed. A. Spannagel, *Corpus consuetudinum monasticarum*, VIII, p. 298.

67. Ordericus, *Historia*, op. cit. (n 40), col. 807; Chibnall, *The Ecclesiastical*, vol. V, pp. 64–7.

68. Hugo de Sancto Victore, *Sermo*, 49, PL 177, col. 1038: 'Omnia quae praeputia sunt, abscindenda sunt, projicienda sunt, sive exterioris, sive interioris hominis sunt. Sit autem perfecta nostra circumcisio . . .'

69. Johannis Beleth, *Summa de ecclesiasticis officiis*, ed. M. Douteil, CC Cont. Med. XLI A. 215, quoted by Constable, 'Beards', op. cit. (n 55), p. 72.

70. Burchardus de Bellevaux, *Apologia de Barbis*, ed. E. Ph. Goldschmidt (Cambridge, 1935); I must thank Prof. Michel Mollat, who suggested that I should study this interesting treatise when I presented a first version of this

paper in 1976 at his seminar on 'L'Histoire de la pauvreté'; the most recent edition is by R. B. C. Huygens, *Apologiae due*, op. cit. (n 55) and the page numbers refer to this.

71. Burchardus, *Apologia*, p. 166.
72. Ibid., pp. 161–2.
73. Ibid., pp. 169–70.
74. *Vita venerabilis viri Stephani Muretanis a Stephano de Libiaco seu alio coaevo redacta*, in *Scriptores ordinis grandimontensis*, ed. Joannes Becquet, CC Cont. Med. VIII (Turnholti, 1968), p. 114; see ibid., pp. 239, 431, 519.
75. Eastern parallels to the self-torturing devices of eleventh–twelfth-century hermits are analysed by J. T. Milik, *Swiety Swierad – Saint Andrew Zoerardus* (Hosianum, Rome, 1966), pp. 70–84.
76. Alexander Gieysztor, 'La Légende de saint Alexis en Occident: idéal de pauvreté', in *Études sur l'histoire de la pauvreté (Moyen Age–XVIᵉ siècle)*, ed. Michel Mollat (Sorbonne, Paris, 1976), pp. 125–40; Gaston Paris (ed.), *La Vie de saint Alexis, poème du XIᵉ siècle* (Honoré Campion, Paris, 1974).
77. Paris, *La Vie*, verses 85–100, 248–50, 406, 431, 451–5.
78. Guibert de Nogent, *Gesta Dei per Francos*, PL 156, col. 705; other sources relating to him are quoted by Hagenmeyer (1879), pp. 114–15; it seems characteristic that the major miracle at the 1242 *translatio* of his remains was the unusually well-preserved condition of his *beard*; ibid., p. 297.
79. *Epistolae Marbodi Redonensis episcopi*, PL 171, col. 1183; for Robert d'Arbrissel see note 43 of Chapter 3 (page 000).
80. The text of the debate between William and Henry is edited by Raoul Manselli, 'Il monaco Enrico e la sua eresia', *Bolletino dell'Istituto storico italiano per il mdio evo e Archivio Muratoriano*, 65 (1953), pp. 44–63, the quotation is from p. 47; English translation in *The Birth of Popular Heresy*, ed. R. I. Moore (Arnold, London, 1975), pp. 46–59.
81. *Gesta pontificum cenomanensium*, RHF XII, p. 547; English translation in *Heresies of the High Middle Ages, Selected Sources translated and annotated*, eds Walter L. Wakefield and Austin P. Evans (Columbia Univ. Press, New York/London, 1969), p. 108.
82. Johannes Salisburiensis, *Historia pontificalis*, MGH SS XX, p. 537.
83. Otto von Freising, *Gesta Friderici imperatoris*, I, 28, MGH Scriptores Rerum Germanicarum (Hannover, 1912). p. 47.
84. *Epistolae Marbodi*, op. cit. (n 79), col. 1183; similar views were expressed by Petrus Cantor, *De mala singularitate*, PL 205, col. 204.
85. Gaufridus Grossus, *Vita Bernardi Tironiensis*, PL 172, col. 1410: 'rudes atque bestiales homines, in illis partibus habitantes, quia ante non noverant, abhorrebant, nec monachos eos, sed Saracenos, per subterraneas cavernas ad explorandas cives suos advenisse existimabant . . .', others, such as a knight, however, 'ex ipso humilitate et paupertatis habitu, bonae conscientiae viros ac mundi contemptores existimavit', ibid., col. 1407.
86. *Gest. pont. cenom.*, op. cit. (n 81), p. 548.
87. Ibid., p. 549.
88. On Eon de Stella: William of Newburgh, *Historia rerum anglicarum*, RHF XIII, pp. 97–8; see Moore, *The Birth*, op. cit. (n 80), pp. 63–6; on Tanchelm:

Vita Norberti, PL 170, col. 1312: 'cum pretiosu apparatu, in vestibus deaureatis, triplici funiculo crinibus intortis, et auriphrygii ligamine triplicatis incedebat . . .', see also note 41 of Chapter 3 (page 000).

89.   Sancti Bernardi, *Apologia ad Guillelmum*, PL 182, cols 912–13; see J. Mahn, *L'ordre cistercien et son gouvernement des origines au milieu du XIIIe siècle (1098–1265)* (Paris, 1951, 2nd edn), pp. 34, 45–6; on the debate between Cistercians and Cluny monks on this issue, there is a lengthy description in Ordericus Vitalis – Chibnall, *The Ecclesiastical*, op. cit. (n 40), vol. IV, pp. 311–27; see also R. B. C. Huygens (ed.), *Le Moine Idung et ses deux ouvrages: 'Argumentum super quator questionibus' et 'Dialogus duorum monachorum'* (Spoleto, 1980); on beards among Gilbertines, see Janet Mayo, *The History of Ecclesiastical Dress* (Holmes & Meier, New York, 1984), p. 154; on Norbert of Xanten, founding father of the Premonstratensians, *Vita Norberti*, op. cit. (n 88), cols 1272–4.

90.   Caesarius Heisterbacensis, *Dialogus Miraculorum*, ed. J. Strange (Cologne, 1851) vol. I, p. 296; 'Duos hoines, non mente sed habitu simplices, non oves sed lupi rapaces, Bizuntium venerunt, summam simulantem religiositatem. Erant autem pallidi et macilenti, nudis pedibus incedentes, et quotidie ieiunantes . . . tali hypocrisi totius populi in se provocassent affectum . . .'

91.   *Sancti Bernardi, Sermones in Cantica*, Sermo 65, PL 183, col. 1092: 'clerici et sacerdotes, populis ecclesiisque relictis, intonsi et barbati apud eos inter textores et textrices plerumque inventi sunt . . .', see Caesarius, *Dialogus*, op. cit. (n 90), I, p. 150; A. Hilka (ed.), *Die Wundergeschichten des Caesarius von Heisterbach* (Bonn, 1933–7), I, p. 150: 'quidam heresiarchus, homo maturus etate, barba habens prolixam . . .', and after the triumphant refutation of his teachings by the priest, according to the story, the crowd is dragging him by his beard on the ground: 'tam diu eam capillis et barbas trahebant, donec exalaret spiritum . . .'

92.   Christine Thouzellier (ed.), *Une Somme anti-cathare. Le Liber contra manicheos de Durand de Huesca* (Louvain, 1964), p. 70: 'capillis mulierum quasi ornate . . .'; F. Pfeiffer and J. Strobl, *Berthold von Regensburg. Vollständige Ausgabe seiner Predigten* (Vienna, 1862–1880), I, pp. 403 ff: 'Gingen sie gar in geistlichen Gewande, tragent nur die Ketzer swert und meszer, langes har, langes gewant . . .'

93.   *Acta concilii Lumbariensis*, RHF XIV, p. 433.

94.   A. Lecoy de la Marche, *Anecdotes historiques, légendes et apologues tirés du recueil inédit d'Étienne de Bourbon, dominicain du XIIIe siècle* (Société de l'histoire de la France, Paris, 1877), pp. 79, 213–14.

95.   Walter Map, *De nugis curialium*, the passage on waldenses in G. Gonnet, *Enchiridion fontium valdensium* (Torre Pellice, 1958), pp. 122–3: ' . . . hii certa nusquam habent domicila, bini et bini circuerunt nudipedes, laneis induti, nihil habentes, omnia sibi communia tanquam apostoli, nudi nudum Christum sequentes . . .'; Lecoy de La Marche, *Anecdotes*, pp. 75–7; A. Patschovsky and K. V. Selge (eds), *Quellen zur Geschichte der Waldenser* (Gerd Mohn, Gütersloh, 1973), p. 74.

96.   Patschovsky and Selge, *Quellen*, p. 75.

97. Selge (1967), pp. 139, 159, 184, 304; Ebrard de Béthune, *Antiheresis Liber*, in Gonnet, *Enchiridion*, op. cit. (n 95), pp. 144 ff.

98. Bernard Gui, *Manuel de l'inquisiteur*, ed. G. Mollat (Belles Lettres, Paris, 1926), I, 38: '. . . Insabbatati autem dicti sunt quia olim a principio sui valdenses perfecti speciale signum in modum quasi scuti in parte superiori sotularium deferebant, in quo signo ab aliis suis complicibus et credentibus differabant . . .', partial English transl. of the book in Wakefield and Evans, *Heresies*, op. cit. (n 81), pp. 375–445; Petrus Vallium Sarnaii Monachus, *Historia Albigensis*, ed. P. Guébin and E. Lyon (Paris, 1926–39), I, 19: '. . . dummodo haberet sandalia . . . posse conficere corpus Christi . . .'; Patschovsky and Selge, *Quellen*, p. 66.

99. Petrus Vallium Sarnaii, *Historia*, ibid., p. 66.

100. Gottfied Koch, *Frauenfrage und Ketzertum im Mittelalter* (Akademie, Berlin, 1962), p. 189; Lecoy de la Marche, *Anecdotes*, op. cit. (n 94), p. 289.

101. *Chronicon Universale Anonymi Laudunensi*, MGH SS XXVI, p. 449: 'Tincta indumenta non vestientes, simplici sunt conteni . . .'; J. F. Hinnebusch (ed.), *The Historia Occidentalis of Jacques de Vitry*, Spicilegium Friburgense 17 (Freibourg, 1972), p. 144.

102. *Innocentii III PP. Regestorum Lib. XII*, PL 216, cols 75–6; G. G. Meersseeman, *Dossier de l'ordre de la pénitence au XIIIe siècle* (Freibourg, 1961), pp. 283–9; O. Holder-Egger and B. von Simson, *Die Chronik des Propstes Burchard von Ursberg*, MGH Scriptores Rerum Germanicarum in usum scolarum (Hanover/Leipzig, 1916), p. 107.

103. Paul Sabatier (ed.), *Speculum perfectionis seu S. Francisci Assisiensis Legenda Antiquissima auctore frate.Leone* (Paris, 1898), pp. 55–6.

104. Lecoy de la Marche, *Anecdotes*, op. cit. (n 94), p. 78; Guilelmus de Podio Laurensi, *Chronica*, ed. J. Beyssier (Paris, 1904), p. 127.

105. *Innocentii III. PP. Epistolae*, 7 and 76, PL 215, cols 358, 1024–5.

106. Lecoy de la Marche, *Anecdotes*, op. cit. (n 94), pp. 228–42, quotation from p. 235; see Caesarius Heisterbacensis, *Dialogus*, op. cit. (n 90), p. 287; Berthold von Regensburg, *Predigten*, op. cit. (n 92), vol. I, pp. 483, 526, vol. II, pp. 68, 83, 141; for sermons against vanity in female dress, see Salimbene de Adam, *Cronica*, ed. G. Scaglia (Bari, 1966), pp. 411–12.

107. Meersseeman, *Dossier*, op. cit. (n 102), pp. 4–95, 114.

108. For a detailed history of these signs, see Ulysse Robert, *Les Signes d'infamie au moyen âge. Juifs, Sarrasins, hérétiques, lépreux, cagots et filles publiques* (Honoré Campion, Paris, 1891); also see D. O. Hughes, 'Distinguishing signs: ear-rings, Jews and Franciscan rhetoric in the Italian Renaissance city', *Past and Present*, 112 (1986), pp. 3–60.

109. Guilielmo Peraldo, *Summae Virtutum ac vitiorum* (Venetiis, 1584), vol. II, pp. 176–89. 'Superbie speciebus exterioris'; see A. Dondaine, 'Guillaume Peyraut, vie et oeuvres', *Archivum Fratrum Praedicatorum*, 18 (1948), pp. 162–236, esp. pp. 184–97.

110. These popular movements are described in Salimbene, *Cronica*, op. cit. (n 106), pp. 99–101.

111. Ibid., pp. 366–417.

112. Ibid., p. 246. Salimbene ascribes a sumptuary law in Lombardy, in the time of Pope Nicholas III, to the initiative of the Dominician Frate Latino: '. . . turbavit mulieres haberent vestimenta curta usque ad terram et tantum plus, quanta est unius palme mensura. Trahebant enim prius caudas vestimentorum per terram longas per brachium et dimidium . . . omnes mulieres, tam iuvencule sive domicelle, quam maritate et vidue et matrone, in capitibus vela portarent . . .'

113. A thirteenth-century Toulouse sumptuary law is described in R. Nelli, *La Vie quotidienne des cathares en Languedoc au XIIIe siècle* (Hachette, Paris, 1969), pp. 79–81, 183; the quoted *Sirventès del tot vey remaner valor* in J. Coulet, *Le Troubadour Guilhem Montangahgol* (Toulouse, 1898), pp. 87–9.

114. Rutebeuf: 'Li abis ne fait pas ermite' (*De Frère Denise*); these examples are analysed by Bloch, *The Scandal*, op. cit. (n 1), pp. 34–6, 44.

115. Hans Walther, *Proverbia sententiaeque Latinitatis Medii Aevi* (Göttingen, 1967), vol. V. Two nice examples: No. 33268 c (697): 'Vestra notat vestis, quales intrinsecus estis/Ante Deum testis mens est, non aspera vestis'; No. 30563 (167): 'Sub specie tincta macie, sub simplice veste/Sunt hodie fraus, invidie, mentes inhoneste'; similar views are to be found in Burchardus, *Apologia*, op. cit. (n 70), p. 195: 'In barba non iacet sapientia'.

CHAPTER 5   FROM SACRAL KINGSHIP TO SELF-REPRESENTATION

1. E. Madzsar (ed.), *Annales Posonienses*, SRH, I, p. 126. '1083. In carcere missus et dominus rex Stephanus et Henricus filius eius et Gerardus episcopus revelantur et Salomon rex fugit.'

2. *Alcuinus Aethelredum regem Northanhumbrorum*, MGH, *Epistolae*, IV, Ep. 18.51; see Hauck (1950), p. 227.

3. For a general overview see Graus (1975), pp. 159–81 ('St Wenzel, der heilige Patron des landes Böhmen'); Heinrich Jilek, 'Die Wenzels und Ludmilla-Legenden des 10. und 11. Jahrhunderts', *Zeitschrift für Ostforschung*, 24 (1975), pp. 79–148; the quotation: 'quid facimus quia [qui] princeps debeat esse, perversus est a clericis et est monachus', is from the eleventh-century *Crescente fide* legend, FRB I, 185.

4. *Pamjat i pochvala knjazju ruskomu Vologimeru*; for editions, translations and analysis see Gerhard Podskalsky, *Christentum und theologische Literatur in der Kiever Rus (988–1237)* (Munich, 1982), pp. 117 ff.

5. For a general overview and sources see Ludolf Müller, *Die altrussische Hagiographische Erzählungen und liturgischen Dichtungen über die heiligen Boris und Gleb* (Munich, 1967); the date of the real emergence of the cults is postponed from the 1030s to the 1070s by Andrzej Poppe, 'La Naissance du culte de Boris et Gleb', *Cahiers de civilisation médiévale*, 24 (1981), pp. 29–54. For an analysis of princely name-giving, ibid. p. 43. For the incident of the fingernails, see Martin Dimnik, 'Oleg Svyatoslavich and his patronage of the cult of Ss. Boris and Gleb', *Medieval Studies*, 50 (1988).

6. For their cult, see J. T. Milik, *Swiety Swierad. Saint Andrew Zoerardus*

(Rome, 1966); Richard Prazak, 'A Legenda Sanctorum Zoerardi et Benedicti történelmi és kultúrális összefüggései' [Historical and cultural context of the Legenda Ss. Zoerardi et Benedicti], *ITK*, 84 (1980), pp. 393–408.

7. János Karácsonyi, *Szent Gellért* (Budapest, 1925); László Szegfű, 'La missione politica ed ideologica di San Gerardo in Ungheria', in Vittore Branca (ed.) *Venezia ed Ungheria nel Rinascimento* (Sansoni, Florence, 1973), pp. 23–36; I have dedicated a study to the spatial aspect of this cult: 'Il monte di San Gerardo e l'isola di Santa Margherita. I spazi di santità nel Buda medioevale', in Sophia Boesch Gajano and Lucetta Scaraffia, *Luoghi sacri e spazi della santità*, forthcoming.

8. Editions of Stephen's legends by Emma Bartoniek, *Legendae Sancti Stephani regis maior et minor, atque legenda ab Hartvico conscripta*, SRH, II, pp. 363–440. In German translation with commentary: Thomas von Bogyay, János M. Bak, Gabriel Silagi (eds), *Die heiligen Könige* (Styria, Graz/Vienna/Cologne, 1976), pp. 26–71.

9. Ilona Király, *Szent Márton magyar király legendája. A magyar bencések Árpád-kori francia kapcsolatai* [The legend of Saint Martin, king of Hungary. French connections with Hungarian Benedictines in the age of the Árpád] (Budapest, 1929).

10. Karl Bosl, 'Adalbert von Prag – Heiliger einer europäischer Zeitwende', in *Ein Leben, drei Epochen. Festschrift H. Schütz* (Munich, 1971) pp. 107–21; F. Graus, *Die Nationenbildung der Westslawen im Mittelalter* (Thorbeke, Sigmaringen, 1980), pp. 66–7.

11. On Hungarian pre-Christian ideas about sacral kingship, see Géza Róheim, 'A kazár nagyfejedelem és a turulmonda' [The Khasar grand prince and the legend of the Turul bird], *E*, 28 (1917), pp. 58–98; György Györffy, 'Kurszán és Kurszán vára', in idem. *Tanulmányok a magyar állam eredetéröl* [Studies on the origins of the Hungarian state] (Akadémiai, Budapest, 1959), pp. 129–60; Dezső Dümmerth, *Álmos, az áldozat* [Álmos, the victim] (Budapest, 1982); sacral legitimation attempts by the predecessors of Ladislaus are described by D. Dümmerth, *Az Árpádok nyomában* [On the track of the Arpadians] (Budapest, 1977), pp. 210, 226, 236, 259, 264.

12. This *Gesta*, incorporated into later chronicles, is edited by A. Domanovszky, *Chronici Hungarici compositio saeculi XIV*, SRH, I, pp. 217–506; see József Gerics, 'Textbezüge zwischen den ungarischen Chroniken und die Sankt-Ladislaus Legende', *Acta Historica Academiae Scientiarum Hungaricae*, 19 (1973), pp. 274–303.

13. *Chronici*, ibid., p. 388. Coronation by an angel is more common in the Byzantine culture, mentioned e.g. by Constantine VII Porphyrogenitus in his *De administrando imperio*, ed. Gy. Moravcsik (Budapest, 1950), pp. 66–7, c. 13; see Péter Váczy, 'The angelic crown', *Hungarian Studies*, 1 (1985), pp. 1–18. Crowning by Christ is equally present in Byzantium – ivory plaque showing Constantine VII crowned by Christ in G. Ostrogorsky, *History of the Byzantine State* (Blackwell, Oxford, 1980, 3rd ed) p. 279 – but more frequent in the West. In the *Liuthar Gospels* we are told of the coronation of Otto III by the hand of God – see Percy Ernst Schramm, *Die deutschen Kaiser und Könige in Bildern ihrer Zeit. 751–1190* (Prestel, Munich, 1983), No. 107; in the

Sacramentary of Henry II, he is crowned by Christ, ibid. No. 124; the same theme is connected to Saint Wenceslaus in the eleventh-century legend of Gumpold – see F. Graus, 'La Sanctification du souverain dans l'Europe centrale des Xe et XIe siècles', in *Hagiographie, cultures et sociétés* (Études Augustiniennes, Paris, 1981), pp. 567–8.

14. *Chronici*, op. cit. (n 12), p. 401.

15. Ibid., pp. 394–5: 'Vere non servus sed angelus Dei erat . . . nec sunt cornua sed ale . . . pedes vero fixit, quia ibi locum demonstravit, ut ecclesiam Beate Virgini . . . hic edificari faceremus.' The motif of the miraculous stag is very ancient, appearing (among other sources) in the migration legend of the Hungarians – see Carl Pschmadt, *Die Sage von der verfolgten Hinde* (Abel, Greifswald, 1911). It is depicted in the legends of various holy rulers, e.g. the Merovingian Dagobert I and Dagobert II – see Graus (1965), pp. 400, 404–5. In Hungary it also occurs in the legends of Saint *Henry* – see Tekla Dömötör, 'Árpádházi Imre herceg és a csodaszarvas-monda' [Prince *Henry* of the Árpád and the legend of the miraculous stag], *Filológiai Közlöny* (1958), pp. 317–23; Sarolta Tóth, *Magyar és lengyel Imre-legendák* [Hungarian and Polish legends of *Henry*] (Acta Historica 11, Szeged, 1962), pp. 56 ff.

16. Josephus Balogh (ed.), *Libellus de institutione morum*, SRH, II, pp. 611–27; see Jenő Szűcs, 'König Stephans "Institutionen" – König Stephans Staat', in idem., *Nation und Geschichte. Studien* (Corvina, Budapest, 1981), pp. 245–62.

17. János Bollók, 'Szent Imre alakja középkori krónikáinkban' [The figure of Saint *Henry* in our medieval chronicles], in Erik Fügedi (ed.), *Művelődéstörténeti tanulmányok a magyar középkorról* [Studies in the cultural history of the Hungarian Middle Ages] (Gondolat, Budapest, 1986), pp. 61–75.

18. This is the first hagiographical document written in Hungary, edited by E. Madzsar, *Legenda Sanctorum Zoerardi et Benedicti*, SRH, II, pp. 347–61.

19. For contemporary features of hermit spirituality, see the works quoted in notes 17–18 of Chapter 3 (page 000).

20. Sándor Fest, *The Hungarian Origin of St Margaret of Scotland* (Debrecen, 1940); József Herzog, 'Skóciai Szent Margit származásának kérdése' [The problem of the origin of St Margaret of Scotland], *Turul*, 53 (1939), pp. 1–42, and 54 (1940), pp. 36–46; Derek Baker, 'A nursery of saints. St Margaret of Scotland reconsidered', in Baker (1978), pp. 119–42.

21. *Chronici*, op. cit. (n 12), pp. 381–6; Graus (1975), pp. 165–9, idem., *Nationenbildung*, op. cit. (n 10), pp. 58–60.

22. For the dynastic relations of the Arpadians see Mór Wertner, *Az Árpádok családi története* [Family history of the Arpadians] (Nagybecskerek, 1892), pp. 22 ff; on Ladislaus' presence in Kiev, *Chronici*, op. cit. (n 12), p. 380.

23. The various legends have been edited by E. Bartoniek, op. cit. (n 8).

24. On such traditions see József Deér, *Az Árpádok vérségi joga* [The inherited consanguine rights of the Arpadians] (Budapest, 1937); on the Hunnish origins, see J. Szűcs, *Theoretical Elements in Master Simon of Kéza's Gesta Hungarorum (1282–1285 a.d.)* (Akadémiai, Budapest, 1975).

25. Bartoniek, *Legendae*, op. cit. (n 8), p. 433. Hungarian historiographers

have long debated the veracity of this assertion – see Györffy (1977a), pp. 386–9.

26. E. Bartoniek, (ed.), *Legenda Sancti Emerici ducis*, SRH, II, pp. 441–60; see L. Erdélyi, *Szent Imre legendárja* (Budapest, 1930). Concerning Saint Henry, the emperor, see Klauser (1957). On Saint Alexis, see note 76 of Chapter 4 (page 000).

27. This motif is emphasized by the petition asking for his canonization; see Marianne Schwartz, 'Heiligsprechungen im 12. Jahrhundert und die Beweggründe ihrer Uhrheber', *Archiv für Kulturgeschichte*, 39 (1957), pp. 49, 55.

28. Both edited by M. C. Gertz, *Vitae Sanctorum Danorum* (Copenhagen, 1908–12): *Passio Sancti Canuti regis et martyris*, pp. 62–71; *Ailnothi Gesta Swenomagni et filicrum eius et Passio gloriosissimi Canuti regis et martyris*, pp. 77–136.

29. See Hoffmann (1975), pp. 107–9; the treatise of the Norman Anonymous, *De consecratione pontificum et regum*, is edited in MGH, Libelli de Lite, III, pp. 664 ff; for its interpretation, see Kantorowicz (1957), pp. 46–54.

30. Hoffmann (1975), pp. 132–96, idem., *Königserhebung und Thronfolgeordnung in Danemark bis zum Ausgang des Mittelalters* (Berlin/New York, 1976), pp. 172–4.

31. Graus, 'La Sanctification', op. cit. (n 13), pp. 568–71, points out that the emergence of the many rival branches of the dynasty in the eleventh century can be explained by the fact that these canonization attempts did not succeed.

32. MGH, Ep. sel. ad usum scholarum, 2, p. 558.

33. *Sancti Bernardi Epistolae*, No. 244, in PL 182, col. 440.

34. Podskalsky, *Christentum*, op. cit. (n 4), p. 143; on more holy princes in Russia, W. Philip, 'Heiligkeit und Herrschaft in der Vita Aleksandr Nevskijs, *Forschungen zur Osteuropäischen Geschichte*, 18 (1973), pp. 67 ff; Martin Dimnik, *Mikhail, Prince of Chernigov and Grand Prince of Kiev 1224–1246* (Pontifical Institute, Toronto, 1981).

35. F. Kämpfer, 'Nationalheilige in der Geschichte der Serben', *Forschungen zur Osteuropäischen Geschichte*, 20 (1973), pp. 7–22.

36. E. Bartoniek, *Legenda Sancti Ladislai regis*, SRH, II, pp. 507–27; Bogyay, Bak and Silagi, *Die heiligen*, op. cit. (n 8), pp. 148–65.

37. The Ladislaus frescoes are analysed by Zsuzsa Lukács, 'A Szent László legenda a középkori magyar falképfestészetben' [The Saint Ladislaus legend in medieval Hungarian fresco-painting], in László Mezey (ed.), *Athleta Patriae. Tanulmányok Szent László történetéhez* [Studies concerning the history of Saint Ladislaus] (Szent István Társulat, Budapest, 1980), pp. 161–204.

38. György Sántha, *A harcos szentek bizánci legendái* [Byzantine legends of military saints; on chivalric culture in Manuel's court see Charles Diehl, *Figures Byzantines* (Paris, 1925), II, pp. 19–22 for Béta III's residence there, see Gyula Moravcsik, 'Les Relations entre la Hongrie et Byzance à l'époque des croisades', in idem., *Studia Byzantina* (Akadémiai, Budapest, 1967), pp. 314–19.

39. On his cult in the fourteenth century, see the references in Chapter 7 below.

40. Comment further on this development in Chapter 6 below.

41. See Vauchez (1981), pp. 402–9 and 427–48 idem., ' "Beata stirps" sainteté

et lignage en Occident aux XIIIe et XIVe siècles', in G. Duby and J. Le Goff (eds), *Famille et parenté dans l'Occident médiéval* (École Française, Rome, 1977), pp. 397–406 see Kämpfer, 'Nationalheilige', op. cit. (n 35).

42. This argument is developed in Chapter 7 below.

43. Shils (1975), pp. 127–34. In making this interpretation I am relying upon a suggestion made by Peter Brown.

CHAPTER 6   LEGENDS AS LIFE-STRATEGIES FOR ASPIRANT SAINTS

1.   This anecdote is described by Johan Huizinga, *The Waning of the Middle Ages* (London, 1924), ch. 1, who also provides a full analysis of the following examples. On historical ideals from a more theoretical point of view, see 'Historical ideals of life', in idem., *Men and Ideas. History, the Middle Ages, the Renaissance*, transl. by J. S. Holmes and H. van Marle (Eyre & Spottiswoode, London, 1960), pp. 77–96. On late – medieval secular feasts involving spectacular impersonations, see Sidney Anglo, *Spectacle, Pageantry, and Early Tudor Policy* (Clarendon, Oxford, 1969).

2.   For general remarks about, the religious aspirations of the age, see the literature quoted in the notes to Chapter 3, esp. notes 16, 17, 50, 52.

3.   This ideal was first voiced by the Calabrian Cistercian abbot Joachim of Fiore at the end of the twelfth century. For information about Joachim see Bernhardt Töpfer, *Das kommende Reich des Friedens* (Akademie, Berlin, 1964); Reeves (1969); Herbert Grundmann, *Ausgewählte Aufsätze, 2: Joachim von Fiore* (Hiersemann, Stuttgart, 1977). Joachim's theories were later developed by the 'spiritualist' Franciscans throughout the thirteenth century. See Lambert (1977), pp. 182–207.

4.   On the influence of mendicant orders on the laity, see Heinrich Hefele, *Die Bettelorden und das religiöse Volksleben Ober- und Mittelitaliens im XIII. Jahrhundert* (Leipzig/Berlin, 1910); and *Faire croire. Modalités de la diffusion et de la réception des messages religieux du XIIe au XVe siècle* (École Française, Rome, 1981).

5.   On Margaret's life the most important studies and monographies in Hungarian are: Elemér Mályusz, 'Árpád-házi Boldog Margit. (A magyar egyházi műveltség problémája.)' [Blessed Margaret of the Arpad. The problem of Hungarian ecclesiastical culture], in *Károlyi Emlékkönyv* (Budapest, 1933), pp. 341–84; Elemér Lovas, *Árpádházi Boldog Margit* (Szent István Társulat, Budapest, 1940; Ilona Király, *Árpádházi Szent Margit és a sziget* [Saint Margaret of the Arpad and the island] (Szent István Társulat, Budapest, 1979); there is a short piece about her in Vauchez (1981), pp. 402–10; on the mendicant orders in Hungary in this period, see Erik Fügedi, 'La Formation des villes et les ordres mendiants en Hongrie', *AESC* 25 (1970), pp. 966–87; on the situation of Hungary in the second half of the thirteenth century, see Jenő Szűcs, *Az utólsó Árpádok* [The last of the Arpadians], forthcoming.

6.   The legend was preserved in a codex of the Venetian Dominicans (actually in Bologna), the material for which was gathered in the late fourteenth century by Tommaso Caffarini to support his attempt to get Saint Catherine of Siena

canonized. See Hyacinthe Laurent, 'Un légendrier dominicain peu connu', *Analecta Bollandiana*, 58 (1940), pp. 28–47, Tommaso Caffarini, *Libellus de supplemento. Legende prolixe virginis beate Catherine de Senis*, eds I. Cavallini and I. Foralosso (Edizioni Cateriniane, Rome, 1974), pp. 173–4. The legend was rediscovered and edited by Kornél Bőle, *Árpádházi Margit szenttéavatási ügye és a legidősebb latin Margit-legenda* [The canonization case of Margaret of Arpad and the oldest Latin Margaret legend] (Budapest, 1937), reprinted in Albinus F. Gombos, *Catalogus Fontium Historiae Hungaricae* (Budapest, 1938), vol. III, pp. 2007–29 the attribution to Marcellus was established by E. Lovas, 'Árpádházi B. Margit első életrajzának írója – Marcellus' [The author of the first biography of Blessed Margaret of the Arpad – Marcellus], in *A pannonhalmi Szt. Gellért főiskola évkönyve* (1940–1), pp. 21–85. Though some doubts about it persist – see György Györffy, 'Budapest története az Árpádkorban' [History of Budapest in the age of the Arpads], in *Budapest története* (Corvina, Budapest, 1973), vol. I, p. 342 – it is accepted by the majority of scholars. The first investigations into Margaret's sanctity were started in July 1271 and were still in train in September 1275. The proceedings of the hearings were not preserved, but much of them has been incorporated into the Marcellus legend.

7. The documentation (petitions, papal bull ordering the investigation and the proceedings of the witnesses' hearings) were edited by Vilmos Fraknói in MRV I.

8. The most important of those (the 'Neapolitan' legend, Guarinus, Ranzanus) are reprinted in Gombos, *Catalogus*, op. cit. (n 6), vol. III, pp. 2468–551. As to the filiation and the philological order of fourteenth to fifteenth-century Margaret legends, see László Mezey, *Irodalmi anyanyelvűségünk az Árpád-kor végén* [The beginnings of vernacular literature at the end of the Arpad age (Akadémiai, Budapest, 1955).

9. This change in religious perspectives on women has generated a vast literature in the past few decades. Pioneering studies in the field have been those of Grundmann (1935) pp. 170–354; Gottfried Koch, *Frauenfrage und Ketzertum im Mittelalter. Die Frauenbewegung im Rahmen des Katharismus und des Waldensertums und ihre soziale Wurzeln (12–14 Jahrhundert)* (Akademie, Berlin, 1962). The state of the research is summed up in Baker (1978); Kaspar Elm, 'Die Stellung der Frau in Ordenwesen, Semireligiosentum und Häresie zur Zeit der Elisabeth', in *Sankt Elisabeth. Fürstin Dienerin Heilige* (Thorbeke, Sigmaringen, 1981), pp. 7–29; Peter Dronke, *Women Writers of the Middle Ages. A Critical Study of Texts from Perpetua (+203) to Marguerite Porete (+1310)* (Cambridge Univ. Press, Cambridge, 1984); Bynum (1987), pp. 13–30. The early thirteenth-century change in the evaluation of women's affinity for sanctity is characterized by Vauchez (1981), pp. 427–46;; Michael Goodich, *Vita perfecta: The Ideal of Sainthood in the Thirteenth Century* (Hiersemann, Stuttgart, 1982), pp. 173–85.

10. James of Vitry, *Historia orientalis et occidentalis*, ed. F. Moschus (Douai, 1597), pp. 305 ff. The English translation is that of Goodich, *Vita*, ibid., p. 173. For more on Vitry and the Beguines see Brenda Bolton, '*Vitae Matrum*: a further aspect of the *Frauenfrage*', in Baker (1978), pp. 253–74.

11.   On Saint Elisabeth, the current state of study is summed up in *Sankt Elisabeth*, op. cit. (n 9); Ilona Jónás, *Árpád-házi Szent Erzsébet* (Akadémiai, Budapest, 1986).

12.   The legends of Saint Hedwig (*Vita sanctae Hedwigis ducissae Silesiae*) and of the Blessed Anne (*Vita Annae ducissae Silesiae*) are edited by Aleksander Semkowicz in MPH, IV, pp. 501–655, 656–61; those of Salomea (*Vita sanctae Salomeae reginae Halicensis*) and Cunegond (*Vita et Miracula sanctae Kyngae ducissa Cracoviensis*) by Wojciech Ketrzynski, MPH, IV, pp. 770–96, 662–744; the legends of Hedwig are also available in German translation by Konrad and Franz Metzger, *Das Leben der heiligen Hedwig* (Patmos, Düsseldorf, 1967), 2nd edn; for her life and deeds see the thorough monograph by Joseph Gottschalk, *St Hedwig. Herzogin von Schlesien* (Böhlau, Cologne/Graz, 1964). The legend of the Blessed Agnes of Bohemia is edited by Jan Kapistrán Vyskocil, *Legenda blahoslavené Anezky a ctyri lity sv. Kláry. Kriticky rozbor* (Universum, Prague, 1932), discussed by idem., *Blahoslavená Anezka Ceská. Kulturní obraz svetice XIII. stoleti* (Universum, Prague, 1933) and György Balanyi, 'Csehországi Boldog Ágnes 1205–1282', *Regnum*, 1 (1938–9), pp. 137–68. The obvious parallelism of these cults has already occurred to Ortrud Reber, *Die Gestaltung des Kultes weiblicher Heiliger im Spätmittelalter. Die Verehrung der Heiligen Elisabeth, Klara, Hedwig und Brigitta* (Hersbruck, 1963); Johanna von Herzogenberg, 'Agnes von Böhmen, Elisabeth von Thüringen, Hedwig von Schlesien. Versuch eines Triptychons', in *800 Jahre Franz von Assisi* (Krems, 1982), pp. 150–6; the Polish historian Halina Manikovska has written a dissertation comparing these legends, under the direction of Bronisaw Geremek – its theses are published in B. Geremek (ed.), *Kultura elitarna i kultura popularna v Polsce poznego Srednióvjecza* (Ossolineum, 1978). As for the Blessed Elisabeth of Töss, the last of the figures representing the above model, her *Vita* is published by Ferdinand Vetter, *Das Leben der Schwestern zu Töss beschrieben von Elsbet Stagel samt der Vorrede von Johannes Meyer und dem Leben der Prinzessin Elisabet von Ungarn*, Deutsche Texte des Mittelalters, VI (Berlin, 1906), pp. 99–122. See Mária Puskely, *Árpádházi Boldog Erzsébet és a 14. századi misztika* [Blessed Elisabeth of the Arpad and the mysticism of the fourteenth century] (Rome, 1980).

13.   On the basis of the witnesses' hearings, the inhabitants of Margaret's convent were described and identified by E. Lovas, 'B. Margit történetének részletes forráskritikája' [A detailed criticism of the historical sources on the Blessed Margaret], *A pannonhalmi főapátsági főiskola évkönyve* (1915–16), pp. 16–18. The royal princesses in question were her cousin Margaret, daughter of Princess Anne, her niece Elisabeth, daughter of Stephen V (see the genealogical table in Figure 6.1), and Margaret of Macsó, a more distant relative within the royal family. The most prominent aristocratic nuns were the widow and the daughter of Palatine Majs and the widow and several relatives of Mathew Csák, Duke of Transylvania, one of the most powerful barons of the country, whose descendants became serious rivals for royal power a few decades later.

14.   For royal saints and their sanctifying effect on their dynasties see the bibliographical references in the notes to Chapter 5 above.

15.   This shift in perspective was noted by André Vauchez, 'Beata Stirps: sainteté et lignage en Occident aux XIIIe et XIVe siècles', in *Famille et parenté dans l'Occident médiéval*, eds G. Duby and J. Le Goff (École Française, Rome, 1977), pp. 397–406. For Hedwig's saintly descendants see Gottschalk, *St Hedwig*, op. cit. (n 12). The fullest discussion of this topic is in Reber *Die Gestaltung*, op. cit. (n 12), pp. 116–52; on the Blessed Gertrud, ibid., p. 148.

16.   The *Tractatus sive speculum genealoye Sancte Hedwigis quondam ducisse Slesie* is published in MPH, IV, pp. 642–56.

17.   See Reber, *Die Gestaltung* op. cit. (n 12), pp. 72–82, 102; Gottschalk, *St Hedwig*, op. cit. (n 12), pp. 271–95.

18.   Stephen V was in Cracow on 27th–30th of August 1270 to conclude an alliance against Ottacar II with Boleslaus V, Duke of Cracow and Sandomir, husband of Cunegond. For the beginnings of the cult of Salomea and the active role of Cunegond in it, see Cunegond's *Vita* in MPH, pp. 710–11.

19.   The petition was not preserved; it is mentioned in the papal bull issued by Pope Innocent V in 1276 ordering the second investigation – MRV, p. 160.

20.   'Elyzabeth die ist und sie was ein botte, den ich gesant habe ze den unseligen vrowen, die in den burgen sassen, mit der unkuscheit also sere durflossen und mit dem homuote also sere uberzogen und mit der italkeit also stete umbevangen. das si nach rehte in das abgrunde solten sin gegangen. Irme bilde ist manig vrowe gevolget, dermasse si wolten und mohten', quoted from Reber *Die Gestaltung*, op. cit. (n 12), p. 113, where a series of the exemplary features of Elisabeth's life is elaborated. For Mechtild, see Bynum, (1982) pp. 177–8, 228–47.

21.   On the influence of Elisabeth's example on the vow of Margaret's parents, Király, *Árpádházi*, op. cit. (n 5), pp. 44–5; on the consecration, MRV, p. 172; on the miraculous vision of Alexander Kalászi, MRV, p. 379.

22.   Bőle, *Árpádházi*, op. cit. (n 6), p. 22.

23.   The earliest version of Elisabeth's threat is found in the *Dicta IV ancillarum*: 'si aliam viam evandendi non haberem, secrete proprium nasum meum truncarem, et sic nullus curaret me, tam deformiter mutilatam', Albert Huyskens (ed.), *Der sogenannte Libellus de dictis quatuor ancillarum St Elisabeth confectus* (Munich, 1911), p. 38. This episode found its way into most of Elisabeth legends, among them the *Legenda Aurea* of Jacobus a Voragine; similar utterances by Margaret, reported by the witnesses: 'Ego faciam me talem, quod ego ero deformata, et scindam mihi nasum et labia', MRV, p. 191; see ibid., pp. 172, 176, 214, 233, 247, 259, 264.

24.   'ad imitacionem beate Elyzabeth consobrine sue, hospitale sollempne pro infirmis . . . construxit', Vyskocil, *Legenda*, op. cit. (n 12), p. 106.

25.   Anne's devotion is mentioned in her legend, MPH IV, p. 659; for the crown offered by her for Elisabeth's grave, see Reber *Die Gestaltung*, op. cit. (n 12), p. 96; Cunegond's dream: MPH IV, p. 730; the Blessed Elisabeth of Töss: Puskely, *Árpádházi*, op. cit. (n 12), p. 67–71.

26.   Although the expression 'celestial court' is not used in the sources, it is not a complete invention. In the life of Agnes of Bohemia we find the following: 'Nam ipsius exemplo plures illustres persone . . . ceperunt monasteria construere, innumere nobiles uirgines et uidue ad religionem comfluere et in carne preter

carnem uiuentes celicam uitam actitare'. Vyskocil, *Legenda*, op. cit. (n 12), p. 107. The Blessed Anne 'monasterium pauperum dominarum in propria curia construxit', MPH IV, p. 659. In the fourteenth century, Henry Suso, eminent representative of Dominican mysticism and a spiritual father favoured by several communities of nuns (among them the monastery of Töss, where the Blessed Elisabeth lived), was describing saints as 'viros gloriosos celestis aule milites . . .', J. Strange (ed.), *Horologium sapientiae* (Cologne, 1861), p. 117. On the monasteries and hospitals themselves: Hedwig (Trebnitz, 1202) – Gottschalk, *St Hedwig* op. cit. (n 12), pp. 119–31; Elisabeth (Marburg, 1228) – Werner Moritz, 'Das Hospital der heiligen Elisabeth in seinem Verhältnis zum Hospitalwesen des frühen 13. Jahrhunderts', in *Sankt Elisabeth*, op. cit. (n 9), pp. 101–16; Agnes (Prague Clarissan convent, 1234) – Balanyi, 'Csehországi', op. cit. (n 12), p. 147; Margaret (Rabbit Island, 1252) – Király, *Árpádházi*, op. cit. (n 5), Cunegond (Szandecz, 1279) – *Vita*, MPH, IV, pp. 669–71.

27. 'vestes habitus sui si de panno notabiliter precioso supra alias coevas fuissent, erubescebat portare et si quando cogebatur ob reverentiam parentum, scaloribus coquine ablutionibus ollarum et ceterorum vasorum pulveribusque scopatorum denigrare festinabat et vestem, quam induebat novam, vix unquam mutabat, donec vetustate esset laniata', Bőle, *Árpádházi*, op. cit. (n 6), p. 18.

28. *Vita*, MPH, IV, pp. 518, 520, 529, 531–4.

29. 'duos scofonos cum clavis ferris parvis intus a latibus', MRV, p. 199.

30. 'spreto regni fastigio et omni gloria mundana contempta, cum septem nobilissimis regni sui virginibus ut columba innocua de diluvio nequam seculi ad archam sacrae religionis convolavit. Cumque in monasterio crinibus tonsis vestes regias deposuisset . . . pauperi se habitu conformaret . . . Non iam vestitu deaureato ut regina profulsit: non amiciebatur mollibus ut olym existens in domo regia . . .', Vyskocil, *Legenda*, op. cit. (n 12), pp. 106–7, 111.

31. Concerning Elisabeth, see Huyskens, *Libellus*, op. cit. (n 23), pp. 18, 21; Margaret: MRV, pp. 168, 247, 261; Anne: MPH, IV, p. 657.

32. MRV, pp. 167, 185, 201, 213, 260.

33. MPH, IV, p. 235.

34. This question has been lucidly analysed and contrasted with anthropological theories of symbolic reversal, such as Turner (1977), by C. W. Bynum (1984), pp. 105–25, and (1987), pp. 260–96.

35. A. Huyskens, *Quellenstudien zur Geschichte der heiligen Elisabeth Landgräfin von Thüringen* (Marburg, 1908), p. 136; for her 'strange and unusual' behaviour, which shocked her husband, see Huyskens, *Libellus*, op. cit. (n 23), p. 21; on her making a point of ranking with the poor in processions, ibid., p. 25.

36. 'quo precellebat omnes nobilitate eo amplius preire humilitate satagebat', Bőle, *Árpádházi*, op. cit. (n 6), p. 20.

37. 'Deus, vellem quod ego essem una ancilla pauperis potius, quam filia regis, quia magis possem servire Deo', MRV, p. 261.

38. 'Vidi, quod purgabat necesaria conventus, et usque ad genua stabat in mlatna', MRV, p. 201; 'recepit plenas budellas ipsas, sicut de porco tracte

fuerant, et evacuavit eas, et lavit et paravit, et super vestes suas sparsa fuit illa putredo, que erat in istis budellis . . .', ibid., p. 268.

39. 'ut gemmula carbunculi in ornamento auri, sic et generositas huius preclare virginis humilitatis decore preradians ipsam deo amabilem ac ceteris imitabilem reddidit', Vyskocil, *Legenda*, op. cit. (n 12), p. 108.

40. On rain: MRV, pp. 174, 179–80, 221; on sun: MRV, pp. 210, 215; on floods: MRV, pp. 183, 186, 191–2, 196, 223, 242–3, 280–1.

41. On Elisabeth's charity, see André Vauchez, 'Charité et pauvreté chez sainte Elisabeth de Thuringe, d'après les actes des procès de canonisation', in *Études sur l'histoire de la pauvreté*, ed. Michel Mollat (Sorbonne, Paris, 1974), pp. 163–75, Huyskens, *Libellus*, op. cit. (n 23), pp. 27, 44; for Agnes redistributing presents received from her brother Wenceslaus, see Vyskocil, *Legenda*, op. cit. (n 12) p. 109; for Margaret redistributing presents from the royal family, see Bőle, *Árpádházi*, op. cit. (n 6), p. 22.

42. For the peace treaty, see Gyula Pauler, *A magyar nemzet története az Árpádházi királyok alatt* [History of the Hungarian nation under the reign of the Arpadian kings] (Budapest, 1899), vol. II, p. 261; the document is edited in Georgius Wenzel, *Okmányi kalászat a magyar történet legrégibb idejétöl 1561-ig* [Documents of Hungarian history from the oldest times up to 1561] (Pest, 1856), vol. III, p. 136; mediatory letters of Cunegond, ibid., vol. III, pp. 262–3.

43. Hedwig's political activity, including diplomatic moves and personal embassy to liberate her husband from captivity, is summed up by Gottschalk, *St Hedwig*, op. cit. (n 12), pp. 167–80; Agnes's influence in political matters lasted till her brother Wenceslaus was on the throne. After 1253, her nephew Ottacar II had to forbid her to interfere in matters of Bohemian church policy – see Balanyi, 'Csehországi', op. cit. (n 12), p. 162.

44. Jerome's famous *libellus*-like letters (Nos 22, 38, 49, 54, 77, 79, 108, 117, 128) are edited by J. Hilberg, *Hieronimus Eusebius, Sanctus. Epistulae*, CSEL 54–56 (Vindobonae-Lipsiae, 1910–12), analysed by David S. Wiesen, *St Jerome as a Satirist* (Cornell Univ. Press, Ithaca/London, 1964), pp. 113–65; for Johannes Chrysostomus, see his *Lettres à Olympias*, SC 13 (Paris, 1947).

45. Betty Radice (ed., tr.), *The Letters of Abelard and Héloïse* (Penguin, Harmondsworth, 1974), pp. 212–13; T. P. McLaughlin, 'Abelard's rule for religious women', *Medieval Studies*, 17 (1955), pp. 241–91.

46. 'Si hominem mortalem tantum timeo, quantum dominus omnipotens est timendus qui est dominus et iudex omnium', and other examples, Huyskens, *Libellus*, op. cit. (n 23), pp. 69–71. For her relationship with Conrad, see Matthias Werner, 'Die heilige Elisabeth und Konrad von Marburg', in *Sankt Elisabeth*, op. cit. (n 9), pp. 45–69.

47. Vitry's work concerning the Beguines has already been mentioned; for Conrad's *Summa vite* about Elisabeth, see Huyskens, *Quellenstudien*, op. cit. (n 35), pp. 155–60; for Marcellus' relationship with Margaret, see Lovas, 'Árpádházi', op. cit. (n 6); the author of Hedwig's *Legenda maior* is unknown: for the hypotheses concerning this, see Gottschalk, *St Hedwig*, op. cit. (n 12), pp. 14–17.

48. On the wider context of this re-evaluation, see Marie-Thérèse d'Alverny, 'Comment les théologiens et les philosophes voient la femme', in *La Femme dans les civilisations des Xe–XIIIe siècles* (CÉSCM, Poitiers, 1977), pp. 15–39.

49. The problem of religious men's image of religious women has been thoroughly examined and put into critical perspective by Bynum (1987), pp. 28–30, 282–5.

50. Saint Bernard's warnings (Sermo 65) are analysed in Bynum (1982), pp. 145 ff; for some scandalous cases illustrating that these admonitions were not unfounded, see Giles Constable, 'Aelred of Rievaulx and the nun of Watton: an episode in the early history of the Gilbertine order', in Baker (1978), pp. 205–26.

51. The whole story is described in her *Vita*, MPH, IV, pp. 713–14.

52. For more on urban roles of mendicant orders, see Hefele, *Die Bettelorden*, op. cit. (n 4); for the universities, see the references in Chapter 3 above; on Saint Louis and the mendicant orders, see Colette Beaune, *Naissance de la nation France* (Gallimard, Paris, 1985), pp. 126–64; Béla IV's confessors and their influence are described in Fügedi, 1970.

53. Bőle, *Árpádházi*, op. cit. (n 6), p. 20; Saint Thomas à Becket was popular in Hungary for various reasons – see György Györffy, 'Thomas à Becket and Hungary', *Hungarian Studies in English*, 4 (1969), pp. 45–52.

54. Bőle, *Árpádházi*, op. cit. (n 6), pp. 21–2.

55. How much he tried to attain this exemplary behaviour is emphasized by J. Le Goff, 'Saint Louis, a-t-il existé?' *L'Histoire*, 40 (1981), pp. 90–9.

56. On this evolution, see Sofia Boesch-Gajano, 'Dai leggendari medioevali agli "Acta Sanctorum". Forme di trasmissione e nuove funzioni dell'agiografia', *Rivista di storia a letteratura religiosa*, 21 (1985), pp. 219–44.

57. I analyse these fourteenth-century cults in the next chapter.

CHAPTER 7   THE CULT OF DYNASTIC SAINTS IN CENTRAL EUROPE

1. G. Fejér, *Codex diplomaticus Hungariae ecclesiasticus et civilis* (Buda, 1829–44), 4/1, p. 510: 'Dominus Stephanus . . . natus est de genere sanctorum et maximorum regum . . .'

2. On these saints and their historical analyses, see Chapter 5 and 6 above.

3. P. Riant, 'Déposition de Charles d'Anjou pour la canonisation de S. Louis', in *Notices et documents publiés par la Société de l'Histoire de la France, à l'occasion de son 50e anniversaire* (Paris, 1889), pp. 155–80: '. . . sancta illa anima soluta est, unde sancta radix sanctos ramos protulit . . .'. See Vauchez (1981), p. 214.

4. Before this marriage treaty, Charles had asked to marry Béla IV's daughter, Margaret, who had refused to leave her convent.

5. F. de Meyronnes, 'Sermon sur S. Louis de Toulouse', in *Analecta Ordinis Minorum Capucinorum*, 13 (1897), p. 311: 'Nam mater sua Maria Ungarie fuit de stirpe sanctorum Stephani, Ladislai et Emerici Ungarorum regum . . . novissime nulla mulier de alio sanguine regio fuit canonizata nisi sancta

Elizabeth de cuius stirpe mater beati Ludovici fuit'; see A. Vauchez, ' "Beata stirps": sainteté et lignage en Occident aux XIIIe et XIVe siècles', in *Famille et parenté dans l'Occident médiéval*, eds G. Duby and J. Le Goff (École Française, Rome, 1977), p. 403.

6. A. Riegl, 'Ein angiovinisches Gebetbuch in der Wiener Hofbibliothek', *Mitteilungen des Institutes für österreichische Geschichtsforschung*, 8 (1887), pp. 431–54; 'Istoria beati Ludovici clare memoire domini regi Robertis', ibid., p. 446.

7. On this inherent sainthood, see the references for Chapters 5 and 6 above. See J. Deér, *Az Árpádok vérségi joga* [The consanguineous rights of the Arpads] (Budapest, 1937).

8. A. Domanovszky (ed.), *Chronici Hungarici compositio saeculi XIV*, in SRH, I, p. 481.

9. *Oratio S. Augustini Gazotti. Dicta in Campo Rakos pro Carolo*, in B. A. Kerchelich, *Historiarum cathedralis Ecclesiae Zagrabiensis* (Zagreb, n.d. [1776]), I, pp. 11–114. After mentioning the 'Sanctissimus Rex Ladislaus', the 'Sanctissimus Apostolus Ungariae Stephanus', and the fact that through his grandmother Charles Robert descended 'ex Bela propaginis sacrae masculae Ungaricae', he added the following enumeration of the holy forebears: '. . . Sed Caroli juribus illud quoque, quod ipsius stemma, Coelo teste, ex sanctissimis regibus nostris profluere comprobatur. Ut enim Bela Quartus ipsius Proavus Elizabetham sororem, Germaniae, aliam Elizabetham ex alia sorore neptem, Hispaniae, Margaretham filiam, Dalmatiae (tanquam concivem meam, Tragurii nempe editam) Cunegundam, aliam filiam, Poloniae, sanctitatis gloriae syderibus insertas, produxisse laetatur; ita ex Maria Nepote Mater Caroli nostri, Lodovicum Sanctissimum Tolosae Praesulem, primo Italiae, in qua vitales hausit auras, Demum Galliae ex qua ad aeternitatis evolavit praemia, Caroli nostri fratrem, stirpem agnoscit suam Perinde sicuti Coelo, Terraeque acceptissimus, Francorum Regum praestantissimus Ludovicus Nonus, qui ab adolescentia sua ad ultimum usque spiritum, nunquam sibi, sed Christo militavit regem nostrum Carolum, per fratrem Carolum pronepotem suam . . .'

10. As I have documented in Chapter 6, the above list of blessed Arpadian princesses is far from complete.

11. The bishop's *Sermo* is published in Kerchelich, *Historiarum*, op. cit. (n 9), I, p. 109.

12. *Acta legationis Cardinalis Gentilis*, in MVH, I/2, p. 269: 'Sane, per divinam providentiam, regno Hungarie reges catholici prefuerunt, quorum primus, sanctus rex Stephanus, et alii nonnulli sanctorum cathalogo meruerunt ascribi; relinquentes ex se legitimos successores, sub quorum felici regimine regnum ipsum fertilitate floruit, obtinuit pacis dulcedinem, et inter ipsius incolas viguit unitas animarum. Ex quo non [sic] regnum ipsum reges exteri usurpabunt, fertilitati sterilitas, pacis dulcedini tempestati fremitus, et concordibus animis dissensio detestanda successit. Nos itaque ad eiusdem regni status reformationem per sedem apostolicam destinati, cupientes super his omnibus salubre remedium adhibere, prelatorum, baronum et nobilium convocavimus generale concilium, in quo prelati et barones iidem communiter magnificum

principem dominum Carolum, ex primorum sanctorum regum vera progenie propagatum, recognoverunt verum et legitimum regem Hungarie ac eorum dominum naturalem . . .'

13. As for the unofficial cult of Margaret in Naples, demonstrated not only by artistic representations but also by legends and false attributions of certain writings to her authorship, see Nándor Knauz, 'A nápolyi Margitlegenda', in *Magyar Sion* (1867–8); Jenő Kastner, *Együgyű lelkek tüköre* [Mirror of simple souls] (Budapest, 1929), pp. 22–5; Florio Bánfi, 'Specchio delle anime semplici dalla B. Margarita d'Ungaria scripto', *Memorie Domenicane* (1940), pp. 3–10, 133–40; Tibor Klaniczay, 'Attività letteraria dei Francescani e dei Domanicani nell 'Ungheria Angioina', in *Gli Angioini di Napoli e di Ungheria. Atti del Colloquio italo-ungherese* (Rome, 1974), pp. 27–40.

14. V. Fraknói, 'Prolegomena', in MRV, I, p. LXII.

15. G. Wenzel, *Codex diplomaticus Arpadianus continuatus* (Pest, 1860; Budapest, 1889), I, p. 507; on the name of the island, ibid.; see Ilona Király, *Árpádházi Szent Margit és a sziget* [Saint Margaret of the Arpad dynasty and the island] (Szent István Társulat, Budapest, 1979), pp. 15–16.

16. Jolán Balogh, 'Tino di Camaino Magyarországi kapcsolatai', *Művészettörténeti Értesitő*, 2 (1953), pp. 107–9; Pál Lővei, 'The sepulchral monument of Saint Margaret of the Arpad dynasty', *Acta Historiae Artium*, 27 (1980), pp. 175–222.

17. Király, *Árpádházi*, op. cit. (n 15), pp. 183–8.

18. László Mezey, *Irodalmi anyanyelvűségünk kezdetei az Árpád-kor végén* (Budapest, 1955).

19. The connection between the dynastic name-giving by Charles Robert and the cult of dynastic saints was underlined by Ferenc Levárdy, 'Il Leggendario ungherese degli Angiò conservato nella Biblioteca Vaticana, nel Morgan Library e nell'Ermitage', *Acta Historiae Artium*, 10 (1963), pp. 75–138.

20. Antal Pór, *Lipóczi és Nekcsei Demeter és Sándor, Sz*, 24 (1890), p. 26; see Domanovszky, *Chronici*, op. cit. (n 8), SRH, I, p. 490.

21. ibid., p. 491; see Dezső Dercsényi, *Nagy Lajos és kora* [Louis the Great and his age] (Budapest, n.d. [1940]), p. 11.

22. Wenzel, *Codex*, op. cit. (n 15), I/2, p. 10; Eva Sniezýnska-Stotot, 'Studies on Queen Elisabeth's artistic patronage', in *Critica d'Arte*, (1979), pp. 166–8 idem., 'Tanulmányok, Lokietek, Erzsébet királyné műpártolása köréből. (Ötvöstárgyak)' [Studies on Queen Elisabeth's artistic patronage (works of orphrey)], *Művészettörténeti Értesitő*, 30 (1981), p. 233.

23. Domanovszky, *Chronici*, op. cit. (n 8), SRH, I, p. 490; see D. Dercsényi, *A székesfehérvári királyi bazilika* [The royal basilica of Székesfehérvár] (Budapest, 1943), pp. 50–2.

24. In 1327 his elder son Ladislaus was betrothed to Anne, daughter of John of Luxemburg (two years later, Ladislaus died); in 1338 a treaty was concluded with Charles, Viscount of Moravia (later Charles IV), declaring that he would support Louis and his sons in their eventual accession to the Polish throne; at the same time Louis and Margaret, daughter of Charles, were betrothed (they married in 1345, she died in 1348); in 1339 another treaty was concluded

between Charles Robert and Casimir the Great concerning the Angevin inheritance of the Polish throne.

25. F. Levárdy, 'Il Leggendario', op. cit. (n 19); see his 'Preface' to the edition of the Legendary, in *Magyar Anjou Legendárium* (Budapest, 1973).

26. After several centuries of rather limited intensity, the cult of Henry, son of Saint Stephen, started to emerge with the Angevins, where the number of cults became an important factor.

27. I, Király, *Szent Márton magyar király legendája* [The legend of Saint Martin, king of Hungary] (Budapest, 1929).

28. For the cult of Saint Stanislas, patron saint of Poland, see František Graus, *Die Nationenbildung der Westslawen im Mittelalter* (Thorbeke, Sigmaringen, 1980), pp. 66–7.

29. László Erdélyi, 'Bajtársi egyesületek a magyar lovagkorban', [Military associations in the Hungarian age of chivalry], in *Klebesberg-Emlékkönyv* (Budapest, 1925), pp. 249–58.

30. The trip was described by the Franciscan chronicler, Joh . of Küküllő, and later incorporated by John of Thurocz into his *Chronica Hungarorum*, eds E. Galántai and J. Kristó (Akadémiai, Budapest, 1985), pp. 162–5.

31. E. Sniezýnska-Stotot, 'Tanulmányok Erzsébet királyné mecénási tevékenységéröl (Liturgikus textiliák és paramentumok)' [Studies on Queen Elisabeth's artistic patronage – liturgical textiles and paraments], *Ars Hungarica*, 7 (1979), p. 27; the altarcloth was described in the inventory of 1361, see E. Muntz and A. L. Frottingham, 'Il tesoro della Basilica di S. Pietro in Vaticano dal XII al XV secolo', *Archivio della R. Società di Storia patria*, 6 (1883), p. 14.

32. Ernő Marosi, 'St. Ladislaus als Nationalpatrone', (manuscript).

33. John of Thurocz, *Chronica*, op. cit. (n 30), p. 159: 'Imploranda ergo est unanimi consensu clementia dei omnipotentis pro eodem domino rege Karolo, ut cum anima ipsius clementer dispenset eidem indulgendo et in numerum ipsius animam ac cetum sanctorum confessorum omnium ac regum Stephani et Ladislai dignetur collocare, et prout quod in presenti seculo regali triumpho vixerit, ita etiam in futuro seculo cum angelis valeat exultare'.

34. Erik Fügedi, 'Coronation in medieval Hungary', in idem., *Kings, Bishops, Nobles and Burghers in Medieval Hungary* (Variorum Reprints, London, 1986), I, pp. 182–3.

35. Dercsényi, *Nagy Lajos*, op. cit. (n 21), pp. 54–5.

36. A. Cutolo, *La questione ungherese à Napoli nel secolo XIV* (Budapest, 1929). Louis' campaigns are described in the chronicle of John of Küküllő, op. cit. (n 30); on Hungarian chivalric culture, see Ágnes Kurcz, *A magyarországi lovagi kultúra (13–14. század)* [Hungarian chivalric culture, 13–14th century] (Akadémiai, Budapest, 1988).

37. E. Marosi, M. Tóth and L. Varga (eds), *Müvészet I. Lajos király udvarában, 1342–1382. Katalógus* [Art in the court of King Louis I] (Budapest, 1982), pp. 153–4.

38. See the examples in Marosi *et al.*, ibid., and Dercsényi, *Nagy Lajos*, op. cit. (n 21), p. 162; see also László Gerevich, 'Tendenze artistiche nell'Ungheria

angioina', in *Gli Angioini di Napoli*, op. cit. (n 13), pp. 121–58.

39. Zsuzsa Lukács, 'A Szent László legenda a középkori magyar falképfestészetben', in *Athleta Patriae. Tanulmányok Szent László történetéhez*, ed. L. Mezey (Budapest, 1980), pp. 161–204.

40. Marosi, *St Ladislaus*, op. cit. (n 32).

41. The chronicle was published by Flórián Mátyás (M. Florianus), *Historiae Hungaricae Fontes Domestici* (Quinque-Ecclesiae, 1884), III. The passage describing the miracle is on p. 152: 'Dicitur quoque, quod quamdiu bellum inter christianos et ipsos tartaros duravit, caput sancti regis Ladislai in ecclesia Waradiensi non inveniebatur. Mira certe res. Cum igitur subcustos eiusdem ecclesie causa requirendi ipsum caput sacristiam ingressus fuisset, reperit ipsum caput in suo loco iacer ita insudatum, ac si vinus de maximo labore vel calore estus aliunde reversus fuisset . . . Ad probacionem vero predicti miraculi, quidam ex predictis tartaris captivis valde decrepitus aiebat, quod non ipsi siculi et hungari percussissent eos, sed ille Ladislaus, quem ipsi in adiutorium, suum semper vocant. Dicebantque et aly socy, sui, quod cum ipsi siculi contra eos processissent, antecebat eos quidam magnus miles, sedens super arduum equum, habensque in captie eius coronam auream, et in manu sua dolabrum suum, qui omnes nos cum validissimis ictibus et percussionibus consummebat. Super caput enim huius militis in aere quedam speciosissima domina mirabili fulgure apparuit, in cuius capite corona aurea, decore nimio ac claritate adornata videbatur. Unde manifestum est, predictos siculos pro fide Jesu Christi certantes, ipsam beatam virginem Mariam et beatum regem Ladislaum contra ipsos paganos . . . adiuvasse.' On the subject of military miracles see Graus (1977).

42. Mátyás, *Historiae Hungaricae*, op. cit. (n 41), p. 166; Éva Kovács, 'Magyarországi Anjou koronák' [Hungarian Anjou crowns], *Ars Hungarica*, 4 (1976), pp. 10–11.

43. Jolán Balogh, *Varadinum* (Akadémiai, Budapest, 1982), pp. 15–19; Gerevich, 'Tendenze artistiche', op. cit. (n 38), p. 153.

44. Kurcz, *A magyarországi lovagi*, op. cit. (n 36), p. 261; Emma Bartoniek, *Codices latini medii aevi* (Budapest, 1940), No. 334.

45. On Saint Hedwig see Joseph Gottschalk, *St. Hedwig. Herzogin von Schlesien* (Böhlau, Cologne/Graz, 1964); on Queen Elisabeth see the studies of E. Sniezýnska-Stotot referred to in notes 22 and 31 above.

46. John of Thurocz, *Chronica*, op. cit. (n 30), p. 163: 'Audientes autem terrigene reginam Elisabeth virtutibus morum honestate et devotione continua ut sydus prefulgidum radiare . . .'

47. A. Pór, *Erzsébet királyné Aacheni zarándoklása 1357-ben*, Sz, 3, (1901), pp. 1–14; E. Thoemmes, *Die Wallfahrten der Ungarn an der Rhein* (Aachen, 1937), pp. 27 ff; P. Wöster, 'Überlegungen zur Pilgerfahrt Karls IV nach Marburg 1357', in *700 Jahre Elisabethkirche in Marburg. 1283–1983*, ed. Herwig Gödeke (Marburg, 1983), pp. 27–34.

48. Marosi, *St Ladislaus*, op. cit. (n 32), describes the iconographic evolution of this triad.

49. L. Gerevich, 'Vásári Miklós kódexei', *Művészettörténeti Értesítő*, 6 (1957), pp. 133–7.

50. Fejér, *Codex diplomaticus*, op. cit. (n 1), IX/4, pp. 91–2; Marosi *et al.*, *Müvészet*, op. cit. (n 37), pp. 105–8.

51. Balogh, *Varadinum*, op. cit. (n 43), pp. 20–1.

52. L. B. Kumorovitz, 'A budai várkápolna és a Szent Zsigmond-prépostság történetéhez' [On the history of the royal chapel and the Saint Sigismond provostry in Buda], *Tanulmányok Budapest Múltjából*, 15 (1963), p. 119; A. Bossányi, *Regesta Supplicationum* (Budapest, 1916–18), II, pp. 201–2.

53. ibid., pp. 295–6.

54. Emericus Madzsar (ed.), *Legenda S. Gerhardi*, SRH, II, p. 506; Arnold Ipolyi, *Magyar ereklyék* [Hungarian relics], *Archeológiai Közlemények*, 3 (1863), p. 125; the sarcophagus got lost in later times, but a similar one, modelled on this one in 1377 and offered for Saint Simeon of Zara by Elisabeth, wife of Louis, still exists.

55. A. Meszlényi, *Magyar szentek, szentéletű magyarok* (Munich, 1976), pp. 26–7.

56. On his cult see F. Graus, 'St Wenzel, der heilige Patron des landes Böhmen', in Graus (1975), pp. 159–81; Giulia Barone, 'Les Épitomés dominicains de la vie de saint Wenceslas', in *Faire croire. Modalités de la diffusion et de la réception des messages religieux du XIIᵉ au XVᵉ siècle (Table Ronde, Rome 1979)* (École Française, Rome, 1981), pp. 167–87.

57. The term was mentioned by Charles IV in his autobiography – E. Hillenbrand (ed.), *Vita Caroli Quarti. Die Autobiographie Karls IV* (Stuttgart, 1979), p. 122.

58. György Balanyi, 'Csehországi Boldog Ágnes', *Regnum*, 3 (1938–9), pp. 167–8.

59. Hillenbrand, *Vita Caroli*, op. cit. (n 57), p. 117; on his conflicts with his father, ibid., pp. 121–3; see R. Schneider, 'Karls IV. Auffassung vom Herrscheramt', *Historische Zeitschrift*, 2 (1973), pp. 123–50.

60. Edited by K. Wodke in *Zeitschrift der Verein Mährens und Schlesiens*, I, 4 (1897), pp. 41–76.

61. The address of the delegation, headed by the Archbishop of Prague, is edited in MGH, Constitutiones, 8, pp. 138–41; for the *Collatio* of Clement VI, ibid., pp. 143–63; loc. cit., p. 146; see R. Folz, *Le Souvenir et la Légende de Charlemagne dans l'Empire germanique médiéval* (Paris, 1950), pp. 123–4.

62. F. Machilek, 'Privatfrömmigkeit und Staatsfrömmigkeit', in *Kaiser Karl IV. Staatsmann und Mäzen*, ed. Ferdinand Seibt (Munich, 1978), p. 90; see FRB, IV, p. 527: 'protectorem et adiutorem precipuum'.

63. Machilek, 'Privatfrömmigkeit', ibid., pp. 90–1.

64. ibid.; see Graus (1975), pp. 173–4.

65. A. Blaschka (ed.), 'Die St Wenzelslegende Kaiser Karls IV.', in *Quellen und Forschungen aus dem Gebiet der Geschichte*, 14, (Prague, 1934); idem., *Kaiser Karls IV. Jugendleben und St Wenzelslegende* (Weimar, 1956).

66. Machilek, 'Privatfrömmigkeit', op. cit. (n 62), p. 92; H. P. Hilger, 'Der Weg nach Aachen', in Seibt, *Kaiser Karl IV*, op. cit. (n 62), pp. 350–1.

67. Hilger, 'Der Weg', ibid., pp. 352–3.

68. Folz, *Le Souvenir*, op. cit. (n 61), pp. 425–6.

69. The *Chronica Bohemorum* of Marignola is edited by J. Emler in FRB, III,

pp. 492–604, loc. cit., p. 525; see Folz, *Le Souvenir*, op. cit. (n 61), pp. 440–1.

70.   ibid., pp. 444–5.

71.   Joseph Neuwirth, *Mittelalterliche Wandgemälde und Tafelbilder der Burg Karlstein* (Prague, 1896); idem., *Der Bildercyclus des Luxemburger Stammbaumes aus Karlstein* (Prague, 1897); V. Dvořaková and D. Menclová, *Karlstejn* (Prague, 1965).

72.   Machilek, Privatfrömmigkeit', op. cit. (n 62), p 91.

73.   Schneider, 'Karls IV. Auffassung', op. cit. (n 59), pp. 130–1; Machilek, 'Privatfrömmigkeit,' op. cit. (n 62), p. 99.

74.   For the house of the Andechs, see Gottschalk, *St Hedwig.* op. cit. (n 45), which includes a detailed genealogy illustrating their sainthood.

75.   W. Braunfels (ed.), *Der Hedwigs Codex* (Berlin, 1972).

76.   Wöster, 'Überlegungen', op. cit. (n 47).

77.   G. Schmidt (ed.), *Krumauer Bildercodex* (Graz, 1967).

78.   edited in FRB, 3, p. 429; see Hauck (1950), p. 213; Folz, *Le Souvenir*, op. cit. (n 61), p. 431; Schneider, 'Karl IV. Auffassung', op. cit. (n 59), pp. 146–7.

79.   All these aspects are discussed in greater detail and with references in Chapters 5 and 6 above.

80.   On the intensification of the cult of Saint Wenceslaus see Barone, 'Les Épitomés', op. cit. (n 56), p. 179; Graus, (1975), p. 166; on the legend of the Přemysl, see F. Graus, 'Kirchliche und heidnische (magische) Komponenten der Stellung der Přemyslidensage und St Wenzels-Ideologie', in *Siedlung und Verfassung Böhmens in der Frühzeit*, eds F. Graus and H. Ludat (Wiesbaden, 1967), pp. 148–61.

81.   See Deér, *Az Árpádok*, op. cit. (n 7).

82.   As well as the marriage of John to Beatrice of Bourbon, and that of his sister Marie of Luxemburg to Charles IV, King of France, I should mention the first marriage of Emperor Charles IV to Blanche de Valois (1323) and that of his sister Gutta to John II (1332).

83.   On Saint Louis see Folz, (1984), pp. 107–13; Vauchez (1981), pp. 416–17; Colette Beaune, *Naissance de la nation France* (Gallimard, Paris, 1985), pp. 126–64.

84.   E. M. Hallam, 'Philip the Fair and the cult of saint Louis', in *Religion and National Identity*, (*SCH* 18), ed. S. Mews, pp. 201–14.

85.   Beaune, *Naissance*, op. cit. (n 83), p. 114.

86.   Apart from the various genealogies mentioned throughout this chapter, let me add here that Marignola traced Charles IV's genealogy not only back to Charlemagne, but right back to Noah; see note 69.

87.   He had introduced the veneration of his patron saint, Sigismond, to Buda and he naturally supported the veneration of Saint Ladislaus, though with considerably less zeal than Louis.

88.   On this king see A. Cutolo, *Re Ladislao d'Angiò-Durazzo* (Milan, 1936).

89.   FRB, IV, p. 542; see Graus (1975), pp. 175–6.

CHAPTER 8   SHAMANISTIC ELEMENTS IN CENTRAL EUROPEAN
WITCHCRAFT

1. On this evaluation see E. William Monter, 'The historiography of European witchcraft: progress and prospects', *The Journal of Interdisciplinary History*, 2 (1971–2), pp. 435–51. Peter Burke, 'Good witches', *New York Review of Books*, 32 (1985), 28 February, pp. 32–4. The results of Ginzburg's findings have been largely incorporated into Jeffrey Burton Russell, *Witchcraft in the Middle Ages* (Cornell Univ. Press, Ithaca/New York, 1972); also, though with unwarranted critical overtones, in Cohn (1975). Significant new research concerning the archaic roots of European witch-beliefs has been inspired by Ginzburg's work: Hans Peter Duerr, *Traumzeit. Über die Grenze zwischen Wildnis und Zivilisation* (Syndicat, Frankfurt/Main, 1978); Gustav Henningsen, ' "Die Frauen von Ausserhalb": Der Zusammenhang von Feenkult, Hexenwahn und Armut um 16. und 17. Jahrhundert auf Sizilien', in *Die Mitte der Welt: Aufsätze zu Mircea Eliade*, ed. H. P. Duerr (Frankfurt, 1984), pp. 164–82; Éva Pócs, *Fairies and Witches at the boundary of South Eastern Europe*, forthcoming in FFC Communications. (These works were not yet available at the time I wrote this chapter.)

2. There are good analyses of similar phenomena related to shamans: L. Honko, 'Role-taking of the shaman', *Temenos*, 4 (1969), pp. 26–55; Siikala (1978).

3. The text of G. F. Tommasini's *Costumanze nell'Istria* is in the Biblitheca Marciana, in Venice. It has been published in *Commentari Storici-Geografici della Provincia dell'Istria di mons. Archeografo Triestino*, vol. IV (Trieste 1837). The passage referring to *kresniks* is on p. 519; it is quoted also by Bošković-Stulli (1960), p. 277: 'Tengono ancora e non si puo cavar della fantasia, che siano alcuni uomini, i quali nati sotto certe costellazioni, e quelli specialmente che nascono vestiti in una certa membrana (questi chiamano cresnidi [*cresnichi*] e quegli altri uncodlachi [*vucodlachi*] vadino di notte sulle strade incrociate con lo spirito ed anco per le case a far paura o qualche danno e che si sogliono congregar insieme in alcune piu famose crociere, particolarmente nel tempo delle quatro tempora ed ivi combatter gli uni con gli altri per l'abbondanza o carestia di ciascuna specie di entrate.'

4. Ginzburg (1966), pp. 47–51, describes the extremely interesting judicial records on the Lithuanian *Wahrwolf* Thiess, who claimed to have participated with the society of werewolves in positive sorcery for agricultural fertility, falling into a trance when he transformed into wolf's shape, and travelling to the other world to fight the witches, the enemies of fertility. Ginzburg relied on the publication of H. von Bruiningk, 'Der Werwolf in Livland und das letzte im Wendeschen Landgericht und Dörptschen Hofgericht i. J. 1692 deshalb stattgehabte Strafverfahren', *Mitteilungen aus der livländischen Geschichte*, 22 (1924–8).

5. The *lagromant* or *nagromant* of Dubrovnik was born with a tail, protected his village from hail and fought other villages' *lagromants* in the form of a wild boar; the *viscani (viscak)* of Poljice fought for good weather for their villages in the shape of bulls or wild boars of different colours; the *vjedogonja* of Montenegro were born with a caul, and fought with opponents from overseas,

for example from Naples – this happened while they were asleep and it was actually their soul that went out to fight; after their deaths these *vjedogonja* became vampires; the *vrimenjaki* of South Croatia were born with a caul, flew in the air and protected their village. See Bošković-Stulli (1960), pp. 285–8. The *moguts* of north Croatian Turopolje also belonged to this series: these protectors of the villages were born after a prolonged pregnancy or from a dead mother; they could speak immediately after birth; they fought each other for the crops of their villages in the shape of a wild boar; and they had good relations with the dragon (*pozoj*). See D. Chloupek, 'Mogut', *Zbornik za narodni zivot i obicaje juznih slavena*, 37 (1953), pp. 241–50.

6. For more information about this, see Chapter 9 below.

7. Komáromy (1910), pp. 44–5, on Kolozsvár/Cluj, 1584; István Sugár, *Bűbájosok, ördöngösök, boszorkányok Heves és Külső Szolnok megyében* [Charmers, possessed and witches in Heves and Külső Szolnok county] (MTA Könyvtár, Budapest, 1987), pp. 210–11, on Eger, 1766. The 23 cases do not all mention the designation *táltos*, but specific features such as falling into a trance (*révülés*) can qualify certain healers or other cunning folk as belonging to this species. I give a list here of the cases not mentioned separately in the following analysis: Komáromy (1910), p. 91, on Debrecen, 1626; Schram (1970), I, pp. 459–60, on Kecskemét, 1691; Károly Csákabonyi, *Békés megyei boszorkányperek a XVIII. században* [Witch-trials in Békés county in the 18th century] (Gyula, 1961), p. 34, on Gyula 1720; ibid. pp. 27–29, on Szentandrás, 1721; Schram (1970), II, pp. 506–7, on Dunapataj, 1743; Sugár, *Bűbájosok*, pp. 173–9, on Jászberény, 1748.

8. The quotation is from the trial of Mrs Czuppon, Szombathely, 1640 – Tibor Antal Horváth, *Boszorkányok és boszorkányperek Szombathelyen* (Szombathely, 1937), pp. 23–4.

9. The quotation is from the trial of Mrs Szaniszlai, Debrecen, 1711 – Komáromy (1910), p. 250; similar statements appear in Horváth, *Boszorkányok*, p. 23 (Mrs Czuppon, 1640); István Szentkirályi, 'Garabonciás-per Pécsett' [Trial of weather-man in Pécs], *Pécs-Baranyamegyei Múzeum Egyesület Értesítője*, 9 (1917), pp. 1–7 (M. Szvetics, 1752).

10. Komáromy (1910), pp. 272, 349–85, 420, 443, 457; Schram (1970), II, p. 333.

11. Margit Luby, 'Táltosokról és lidércekről' [On *táltoses* and *alps*], E 39 (1938), p. 118. Similar data on relatives of the *táltos* appear in the Transdanubian Csákánydoroszló. The *garabonciás diák* is reported to be born with teeth and caul – see Diószegi (1958), p. 126. Also on this figure, in 1752 in Pécs – Szentkirályi, 'Garabonciás-per', op. cit. (n 9), pp. 1–2. In the eastern part of Hungary, in Szalonta the *látó* was the seventh child of the seventh child born with a caul on Palm Sunday – see Zsigmond Szendrei, 'Ember- és természetfeletti lények a szalontai néphitben' [Superhuman and supernatural beings in the folk beliefs of Szalonta], *E*, 25 (1914), p. 317; also on the *látó* in Sármellék – Bihari (1980), p. 192.

12. Lajos Kálmány, 'Összeférhetetlen Tátosainkról' [On our quarrelsome *tátoses*], *E*, 28 (1917), pp. 260–6; János Kodolányi, 'A táltos a magyar néphagyományban' [The *táltos* in Hungarian folk tradition], *E*, 56 (1945),

pp. 31–7; Diószegi (1958), pp. 342–95; Bihari (1980), pp. 104–5.

13. Kálmány, 'Összeférhetetlen', ibid., p. 264. The presence of dragons here is probably a sign of Croatian influences, perhaps stemming from the figure of the *mogut* – see note 5.

14. Further data on these beliefs are in Margit Luby, 'Babonás történetek I–IV' [Superstitious stories], *E*, 38 (1927), p. 206. A series of good examples are to be found in the article by Sándor Szűcs (1951), and idem., 'A samanizmus emléke a nagykunsági népi orvoslásban' [Traces of shamanism in the popular medicine of the Nagykunság], *Alföld*, 26 (1975), no. 6, pp. 45–54.

15. On the *garabonciás*, see V. Jagić, 'Die südslavischen Volkssagen von den Grabancias dijak und ihre Erklärung', *Archiv für slavische Philologie*, 2 (1877); Domokos Holló, 'A garabonciás diák alakja a magyar néphagyományban' [The shape of the *garabonciás* in Hungarian popular tradition], *E*, 45 (1934), pp. 19–34, 110–26; Tibor Kardos, *Középkori kultúra, középkori költészet* [Medieval culture, medieval poetry] (Budapest, 1941), pp. 136–8; Dezső Paizs, *A magyar ősvallás nyelvi emlékeiből* [Linguistic remnants of the ancient Hungarian religion] (Akadémiai, Budapest 1975), pp. 143–63.

16. Vilmos Diószegi has a still unpublished monograph, written in 1952, on the *halottlátó*. For a general overview, see Gábor Barna, 'Totenseher im ungarischen Volksglauben', in *Ethnographica et Folkloristica Carpathica*, ed. Zoltán Ujvári (Debrecen, 1981), pp. 177–89.

17. I write more about this process in Chapter 9 below.

18. Some typical cases: 1584 in Kolozsvár/Cluj – Komáromy (1910), p. 49; 1670 and 1685 in Segesvár/Sigisoara – Friedrich Müller, *Beiträge sur Geschichte des Hexenglaubens in Siebenbürgen* (Braunschweig, 1854), p. 58; Szászkeresztur/Deutschkreutz in 1699 – Carl Göllner, *Hexenprozesse in Siebenbürgen* (Cluj/Napoca, 1971), p. 144; an explicit mention of the witch leaving her body at home appears in Gábor Kazinczy, 'Megyaszói boszorkányok 1731-ben' [Witches of Megyaszó in 1731, *Witches of Megyaszó in 1731*], *Hazánk*, 3 (1885), pp. 374–5.

19. Heinrich Müller, 'Zur Geschichte des Repser Stuhls', *Archiv des Vereins für siebenbürgische Landeskunde*, N. F., 37 (1910), p. 144.

20. Two typical cases: Ugocsa in 1707 – Komáromy (1910), p. 212; Békés in 1755 – Schram (1982), p. 135.

21. A case in Békés in 1755 – Schram (1982), p. 136; see Dömötör (1981), p. 130.

22. Schram (1970), II, p. 352; the quotation is from Antal Szirmay, *Szathmár megye fekvése, történetei és polgári esmérete* [History and geography of Szatmár county] (Buda, 1809), p. 82.

23. László Erdélyi and Pongrác Sörös, *Pannonhalmi Rendtörténet* [History of the abbey of Pannonhalma] (Budapest, 1906), vol. IV, p. 237. Similar data from the 1728 Szeged trials appear in János Reizner, *Szeged története* (Szeged, 1900), vol. IV, p. 409; Schram (1970), I, p. 299.

24. The data on military organizations of Hungarian witches are assembled and analysed by Tamás Körner, 'Boszorkányszervezetek Magyarországon' [Witch-organizations in Hungary], *E* 80 (1969), pp. 196–211.

25. We find a long list of such cases in Schram (1982), p. 385. Let me add an

interesting one from early eighteenth-century Transylvania, where a soldier falsely diagnosed nine 'holes' in the arm of the victim as originating from bewitchment by bone-extraction (Göllner, *Hexenprozesse*, op. cit. (n 18), p. 143).

26. The medieval and early-modern data are analysed by Maurizio Bertolotti, 'Le ossa e la pelle dei buoi. Un mito popolare tra agiografia e stregoneria', *Quaderni Storici*, 41 (1979), pp. 470–99. It was Carlo Ginzburg who suggested to me that I analyse this shamanistic connection.

27. Some of the data: Komáromy (1910), pp. 29, 38, 64, 69, 72, 74, 102, 149, 154–7, 211, 319; Schram (1970), I, pp. 45–6, 112, 387, 412, 501, 543–8; the sole analysis of these Hungarian folk-healers is Tekla Dömötör, 'The cunning folk in English and Hungarian witch trials', in *Folklore Studies in the Twentieth Century* (Proceedings of the Centenary Conference of the Folklore Society), ed. V. T. Newall (Woodbridge/Totowa, 1981), pp. 183–7.

CHAPTER 9   WITCH-HUNTING IN HUNGARY

Let me express here my special thanks to Alfred Soman for commenting on the first version of this paper, and helping me to improve it from both the theoretical and the stylistic point of view.

1. Ginzburg (1966); Mandrou (1968), Macfarlane (1970), Thomas (1971), Kieckhefer (1976), Muchembled (1978), Demos (1982), David Warren Sabean, 'The sacred bond of unity: Community through the eyes of a thirteen-year-old witch (1683)', in idem., *Power in the Blood. Popular culture and village discourse in early modern Germany* (Cambridge Univ. Press, Cambridge, 1984), pp. 94–112.

2. This rough statistical evaluation is taken from a longer analysis in my study, 'Witch-trials in Hungary (1520–1777): The accusations and the popular universe of magic', in *Early Modern European Witchcraft: Centres and Peripheries*, eds Bengt Ankarloo and Gustav Henningsen (Oxford Univ. Press, Oxford, 1989), pp. 219–55. A group of historians and folklorists at the Hungarian Academy of Sciences is currently constructing a database on witch-trials, which will refine these calculations and allow a more precise evaluation.

3. For a general outline of Hungarian history in this period, see László Makkai *et al.*, *A History of Hungary* (Akadémiai, Budapest, 1983), pp. 119–94.

4. Comparative data on the inverse relationship between military operations and witch-trials are in Jean Delumeau, *La Peur en Occident* (Fayard, Paris, 1978), p. 358; similar observations in E. William Monter, *Witchcraft in France and Switzerland. The Borderlands during the Reformation* (Cornell Univ. Press, Ithaca/London, 1976), p. 81; Marie-Silvie Dupont-Bouchat, Willem Frijhoff and Robert Muchembled, *Prophètes et sorciers dans les Pays-Bas XVIᵉ–XVIIIᵉ siècles* (Hachette, Paris, 1978), p. 35; Behringer (1988), p. 321.

5. This problem has been statistically examined (using a sample of 1,432 trials)

by András Iklódi, 'A magyarországi boszorkányüldözés történeti alakulása' [The historical development of witch-hunting in Hungary], *E*, p. 297. He found that, whereas we know of only 44 trials in these territories while they were under Turkish domination (1541–1690), between 1690 and 1770 there were 467 trials. This ten-fold growth can be contrasted with the doubling elsewhere in the number of trials for the same period.

6. Joining the old syntheses of Wilhelm Gottlieb Soldan, *Geschichte der Hexenprozesse* (Stuttgart/Tübingen, 1843) and Joseph Hansen *Zauberwahn, Inquisition und Hexenprozesse im Mittelalter und die Eutstehung der grossen Hexenverfolgung* (Munich/Leipzig, 1900) and the criticized (but still not superseded) overview by Trevor-Roper (1969), are a recent range of new regional monographs: Macfarlane (1970); Midelfort (1972); Monter, *Witchcraft*, op. cit. (n 4); Dupont-Bouchat, Frijhoff and Muchembled, *Prophètes*, op. cit. (n 4); Christina Larner, *Enemies of God: the Witch-Hunt in Scotland* (London, 1981); Henningsen (1980); Marijke Gijstwijt-Hofstra and Willem Frijhoff (eds), *Nederland betoverd. Toverij en Hekserij van de veertiende tot in de twintigste eeuw* (De Bataafsche Leeuw, Amsterdam, 1987); Behringer (1988).

7. Bengt Ankarloo, *Trolldomsprocesserna i Sverige* (Lund, 1971; repr.: Ankarloo 1984); Christian Degn, Hartmut Lehmann and Dagmar Unverhau, *Hexenprozesse. Deutsche und skandinavische Beiträge* (Wachholz, Neumünster, 1983); the same problem receives ample treatment in Ankarloo and Henningsen, *Early Modern Witchcraft*, op. cit. (n 2); Gerhard Schormann, *Hexenprozesse in Nordwestdeutschland* (Hildesheim, 1977); Heide Dienst, 'Magische Vorstellungen und Hexenverfolgungen in den österreichischen Landern' in *Wellen der Vervolgung in der österreichischen Geschichte*, ed. Erich Zöllner (ÖBV, Vienna, 1986), pp. 70–94; Helfried Valentinitsch (ed.), *Hexen und Zauberer. Die grosse Verfolgung – ein europäisches Phänomen in der Steiermark* (Leykam, Graz/Vienna, 1987); Bedrich Sinderar, 'Konec "honu na čarodějnice" v teresiánské době u nás' [End of witch-hunting in the Theresan period, *Sborník Prací Filosofické Fakulty Brněnské University*, Series historica, 19 (1970), pp. 89–107; Josef Koči, *Čarodějnické procesy; z dějin inkvizice a čarodějnickych procesu v ceských zemich v 16–18 stoleti* [Witch-trials; Inquisition data on witch-trials from the Bohemian territories in the 16th to 18th centuries], (Prague, 1973); Wladyslaw Korcz, *Wspólniczki diabla czyli o procesach czarownic na Śląsku w XVII wieku* [Allies of the devil, witch-trials in Silesia in the 17th century] (Śląski Institut Naukowy, Katowice, 1985); Vladimir Bayer, *Ugovor s davlom. Procesi protiv čarobnjaka u Evropi a napose u Hrvatskoj* [Pact with the devil. Witch-trials in Europe and Croatia], 3rd edn (Zagreb, 1982); Baranowski (1952); Janusz Tazbir, 'Hexenprozesse in Polen', *Archiv für Reformationsgeschichte*, 71 (1980), pp. 280–307.

8. On this point, the reader will recall the theses of Foucault on the disciplinary institutions of early-modern times (1973, 1979), and those of Elias (1978). Robert Muchembled relies upon these theories (1978: 223–339). The effect of modern justice and administration is seen in a more positive light by Soman (1985). The problem of the disciplinary power of the early-modern state is also considered by Behringer (1988). For a comparative analysis of the emergence of

early-modern state institutions, see Perry Anderson, *Lineages of the Absolutist State* (Verso, London, 1974); see also Szűcs (1983).

9. The importance of this legal handbook in the rise of the persecutions is stressed by Iklódi, 'A magyarországi boszorkányüldözés', op. cit. (n 5).

10. Boyer and Nissenbaum (1974); Jens Christian V. Johansen, 'Denmark: the sociology of accusations', in Ankarloo and Henningsen, *Early Modern*, op. cit. (n 2).

11. On the history of Transylvania see László Makkai, *Histoire de Transylvanie* (Budapest/Paris, 1946); László Makkai and András Mócsy (eds), *Erdély története. A kezdetektől 1606–ig* [History of Transylvania from the beginnings to 1606] (Akadémiai, Budapest, 1986), esp. pp. 471–4; on Kolozsvár, see Elek Jakab, *Kolozsvár története* [The history of Kolozsvár] (Budapest, 1888); Samuil Goldenberg, 'Kolozsvár kereskedelme a XVI. században' [The trade of Kolozsvár in the 16th century], in *Kelemen Lajos Emlékkönyv* (Kolozsvár, 1957), pp. 293–310; see Carl Göllner, *Hexenprozesse in Siebenbürgen* (Cluj-Napoca, 1971).

12. In Transylvanian 'Saxon' cities, like Hermannstadt (Sibiu) and Kronstadt (Brasov), minor witchcraft prosecutions started only in the seventeenth century.

13. Antal Pirnát, *Die Ideologie der siebenbürger Antitrinitarier in der 1570-er Jahren* (Akadémiai, Budapest, 1961); Róbert Dán and Antal Pirnát (eds), *Antitrinitarianism in the Second Half of the 16th Century* (Akadémiai/Brill, Budapest/Leiden, 1982).

14. The background to this affair is based upon the unpublished archival research of the Kolozsvár historian András Kiss.

15. Jakab, *Kolozsvár*, op. cit. (n 11), vol. II, p. 201.

16. János Szendrei, 'Török Katalin pere. (A bűbájosság történetéhez a XVII-ik században.)' [The trial of Katalin Török. Data on the history of witchcraft in the 17th century], *Történelmi Tár* (1891), pp. 317–34; András Komáromy, 'A "bűbájos" Báthory Anna' [Anna Báthory, the 'enchantress'], *Sz*, 28 (1894), pp. 298–314; the witchcraft act of 1614 is covered in Sándor Szilágyi (ed.), *Erdélyi országgyűlési emlékek* (Budapest, 1876–98), vol. VI, p. 413; see László Nagy, *Erdélyi boszorkányperek* [Transylvanian witch-trials] (Kossuth, Budapest, 1988).

17. János Herner, *Rontás és igézés. Politikai boszorkányper Erdélyben 1668–1688* [Sorcery and enchantment. Political witch-trials in Transylvania 1686–1688] (Interart, Budapest, 1988).

18. Nagy, *Erdélyi*, op. cit. (n 16), pp. 96–7.

19. Stuart Clark, 'King James's *Demonologie*', in Anglo (1977), pp. 156–61.

20. The affair of Elisabeth Báthory, long the subject of unreliable studies, has recently been investigated by László Nagy, *A rosszhírű Báthoryak* [The notorious Báthorys] (Budapest, 1984); another detailed study based on the recently discovered documents from her trial is Katalin Péter, *A csejtei várúrnő: Báthory Erzsébet* [The Lady of the Csejte castle: Elisabeth Báthory] (Helikon, Budapest, 1985).

21. Andor Komáromy, 'Listius Anna Rozina bűnpöréhez' [The trial of A. R. Listius], *Történelmi Tár* (1897), pp. 626–52.

22. See R. J. W. Evans, *Rudolph II and his World. A study in intellectual history*

1576–1612 (Clarendon, Oxford, 1973; on the relation of the Bavarian princes to Trithemius, and its connection with witchcraft matters, see Behringer (1988), p. 80.

23. Vera Zimányi, 'L'attività commerciale dei conti Zrinyi nel secolo XVII: i loro rapporti con Venezia', in *Venezia e Ungheria nel contesto del barocco europeo*, ed. Vittore Branca (Olschki, Florence, 1979), pp. 409–20; István György Tóth, 'A körmendi uradalom társadalma a XVII. században' [The society of the Körmend estate in the 17th century], *Agrártörténeti Szemle* (1983), pp. 327–91.

24. On the series of trials in question: 1651 in Lakompak – Ferenc Eckhart, *A földesúri büntetőbíráskodás a XVI–XVII. században* [Feudal criminal jurisdiction in the 16th to 17th centuries] (Budapest, 1954), p. 133; 1653 in Körmend (a trial involving 3 cowherds and incriminating many more by means of their confessions) Schram (1970) II, pp. 715–21; 1654 in Körmend – Schram (1970), II, pp. 722–4; 1665 in Lakompak Eckhart, *A földesúri*, p. 134; 1676 in Körmend – Schram (1970) II, pp. 725–6; 1687 in Szombathely – Tibor Antal Horváth, *Boszorkányok és boszorkányperek Szombathelyen* (Szombathely, 1937), p. 32.

25. Not only do some of the above-mentioned shepherd trials present such traits (see Schram, 1970, II, pp. 718–19, 725–6, but so do some additional trials of male sorcerers from the region: 1632 in Sopron (*tudós Hántzl*) – Schram (1970) II, p. 71; 1640 in Lipót – István R. Kiss, 'Történelmi adatok a boszorkányság és ördöngösség történetéhez' [Historical data on witchcraft and devil-worship], *E*, 16 (1905), pp. 212–16; 1642 in Lózs – Schram (1970) II, p. 9; 1679 in Körmend – ibid., p. 524.

26. János Házy, *Sopron szabad kir. város története* [History of Sopron, free royal city] (Sopron, 1929), I/7, pp. 363–6, 339–40, 428–31.

27. Ferenc Gönczi, 'A csordás farkas' [The werewolf], *E*, 16 (1905), pp. 93–6; female witches attacking in wolf's form in the 'Great Plain' region, 1734 – Schram (1970), II, p. 430; 1735 – Komáromy (1910), pp. 475–6, 478; 1756 – Schram (1982), III, pp. 145–6; 1754 – a strange werewolf case from the central–northern Nógrád county Gábor Török, 'Történeti adatok a küldött farkas mondájához' [Historical data on werewolf legends], *Néprajzi Közlemények*, 4/1–2 (1959), pp. 278–88.

28. 1730 – Schram (1970), II, p. 45; 1742 – ibid., pp. 145–6; 1743 – ibid., pp. 183–92, 201, 615; 1758 – Komáromy (1910), pp. 669–92.

29. There is no evidence of any witch-trials in the Turkish-occupied Buda or Pest (or after their seventeenth-century reconquest); Sopron, the largest city in the western region, had some scattered witch-trials in the sixteenth century (a total of 10 people were incriminated), see Schram (1970), II, pp. 7–8, and later also remained moderate. Pozsony (Bratislava), the capital of the Habsburg-dominated western region, experienced scares in its neighbourhood in 1574 (see Komáromy, 1910, p. 22); two witches charged with pacts with the devil were burnt there in 1602 (see Horna, 1933), but there were no subsequent traces of prosecutions; there was not a single documented witch-trial in Kassa (Košice), the biggest city in the north of Hungary; only one Hungarian city could match sixteenth-century Kolozsvár and eighteenth-century Szeged in witch-hunting:

Debrecen, the headquarters of Hungarian Calvinism. Debrecen had a series of trials starting in 1575 and ending in 1735, in which 64 people were accused, of whom 26 were executed (documents in Komáromy, 1910, *passim*.). These persecutions have been analysed by Ildikó Kristóf, 'Witches, healers, adultresses in 17th–18th-century Debrecen', paper presented at the 1988 Budapest conference on Central European witchcraft.

30. The documents of the trials are published in János Reizner, *Szeged története* [The history of Szeged] (Szeged, 1900), vol. IV, pp. 373–536; on the history of the city, see József Farkas (ed.), *Szeged története* [History of Szeged] (Szeged, 1985); a student of mine, Ildikó B. Varga, has prepared a dissertation on the subject: 'A szegedi boszorkányperek 1728–1744' [Witch-trials in Szeged 1728–1744], the results of which I have used in this chapter.

31. The imperial letters of Charles VI are published in Reizner, *Szeged*, ibid., IV, pp. 455–6, 458–61.

32. The trials are published, together with those from neighbouring villages, in Schram (1970), I, pp. 225–348.

33. On Ceglédi, mentioned in the trials, see Schram (1970), I, pp. 229, 247, 299; see also Samu Szeremley, *Hódmezővásárhely története* [The history of Hódmezővásárhely] (Hódmezővásárhely, 1907), vol. III, p. 317; Ernő Tárkány Szűcs, *Vásárhelyi statútumok* [Statutes from Vásárhely] (Budapest, 1961), pp. 137, 311.

34. On the role of German soldiers as witchcraft accusers, see my 'Witch-trials' study in Ankarloo and Henningsen, op. cit. (n 2), note 15.

35. These stereotypes of the accusation narratives are among the central targets of our computer-based program, mentioned above in note 2.

36. The few surviving data on medieval Hungarian witch-beliefs are cited in my 'Witch-trials' study, op. cit. (n 2).

37. On the visits of experts of learned magic (like John Dee in 1564 and 1583–9) to Hungary and Transylvania, see Endre György Szőnyi, *Magyar aranycsinálók* [Hungarian alchemists] (Magvető, Budapest, 1980), pp. 44–5.

38. The few demonological treatises written in Hungary (three altogether) are referred to in my 'Witch-trials' study, op. cit. (n 2), notes 33–37. Note that this is in striking contrast to the copious Polish demonological literature; see Baranowski (1952).

39. The process by which the witches' Sabbath evolved from popular witchcraft folklore is analysed in my 'Witch-trials' study, op. cit. (n 2), notes 98–101.

40. This suggestion, stressed by Robert Muchembled, 'L'Autre Côté du miroir: mythes sataniques et réalités culturelles aux XVe et XVIIIe siècles', *AESC*, 40 (1985), pp. 288–306, is supported by various data of my 'Witch-trials' study, op. cit. (n 2).

41. The mythological substratum of popular demonologies has been explored by Éva Pócs in various studies, for example, her paper 'Popular foundations of the devil's pact and sabbath in South Eastern Europe', presented at the 1988 Budapest conference on witchcraft.

42. See Chapter 8 above.

43. These phenomena are analysed in detail in the next chapter.

CHAPTER 10   THE DECLINE OF WITCHES AND RISE OF VAMPIRES
UNDER THE EIGHTEENTH-CENTURY HABSBURG MONARCHY

1. The following data and this short account are based on the detailed investigations described in my study 'Witch-trials in Hungary (1520–1777): The accusations and the popular universe of magic', in *Early Modern European Witchcraft: Centres and Peripheries*, eds Bengt Ankarloo and Gustav Henningsen (Oxford Univ. Press, Oxford, 1989), pp. 219–55; see also the previous chapters in this volume.

2. The reports of the doctors and various royal proscriptions are published in Franziscus Xaverius Linzbauer, *Codex sanitario-medicinalis Hungariae* (Buda, 1852–6), vol. I, pp. 722–5; and in Konstantin Franz von Cauz, *De cultibus magicis eorumque perpetuo ecclesiam et rempublicam habitu libri duo, cum adjacente quibusdam eo pertinentibus ad jurisprudentiae legumlatione illustrationem* (Vindobonae, 1767), pp. 196, 367.

3. The text of the law is published in Linzbauer, *Codex*, ibid., vol. II, pp. 776–85.

4. See István Sándor, *Sokféle* [Miscellanea] (Vienna, 1808), p. 103; Antal Szirmay, *Szathmár vármegye fekvése, történetei és polgári esmérete* [Situation, exploration and histories of Szathmár county] (Buda, 1809), p. 77.

5. The expression is borrowed from Peter Burke's monograph on popular culture (1978), which is cited several times in the previous chapters in this volume. It would be interesting to contrast the processes he describes with an analysis of the writings by Hungarian priests, village teachers and intellectuals ridiculing popular 'superstitions', all written in the decades following the official ban on witch-hunting. However, all this would require a separate study.

6. István Weszprémi, *Magyarország és Erdély orvosainak rövid életrajza. Második száz* repr. [Short biography of the doctors of Hungary and Transylvania. Second hundred] (Budapest, 1962), pp. 110–11.

7. On van Swieten, see Erna Lesky and Adam Wandruszka (eds), *Gerard van Swieten und seine Zeit* (Böhlau, Cologne/Vienna/Graz, 1973), especially the studies of E. Lesky, 'Gerard van Swieten. Auftrag und Erfüllung', ibid., pp. 11–62 and Éva H. Balázs, 'Van Swietens Ideen und die Ungarische Gesellschaft', ibid., pp. 150–62; see also Frank T. Brechka, *Gerard van Swieten and his World 1700–1772* (The Hague, 1970); on his activities in the Hofbibliothek, see Walter G. Wieser, 'Die Hofbibliothek in der Epoche der beiden van Swieten', in *Die Hofbibliothek, 1638–1922*, ed. Josef Stummvoll (Vienna, 1968), pp. 235–6.

8. This treatise has so far received only brief mentions in the historiography on van Swieten: see Erna Lesky, 'Heilkunde und Gesundheitswesen', in *Maria Theresia und ihre Zeit*, ed. Walther Koschatzky (Vienna, 1979), pp. 192–6. The original French version, preserved in the Hofbibliothek, was never published. In 1756 it was published in German translation, which was reprinted by Andreas A. Mayer, in his *Abhandlung des Daseyns der Gespenster* (Augsburg, 1768), and Linzbauer, *Codex*, op. cit. (n 2), vol. I, pp. 725–37. I have used this latter edition for the above quotations.

9. Herman Boerhave wrote about these problems in his *Elementa chemiae*

(Venice, 1737), vol. I, thesis 2, cited by Linzbauer, *Codex*, op. cit. (n 2), vol. I, p. 729.

10. Lodovico Antonio Muratori, *Della forza della fantasia umana* (Giambattista Pasquali, Venice, 1745). I have used an edition of 1760, by the same editor. See there especially pp. 102–13.

11. Scipione Maffei wrote three excellent treatises on the matter: *L'arte magica dileguata . . .* (Verona, 1749); *L'arte magica distrutta . . .* (Trento, 1750); and *Arte magica annichilata . . .* (Verona, 1754). Carli's letters on the same debates and Maffei's treatises are analysed by Parinetto (1974), pp. 155–225.

12. Giuseppe Valeriano Vannetti (ed.), *Considerazione intorno alla pretesa magia postuma, presentata al Supremo Direttorio di Vienna dal signor barone Gerardo van Swieten archiatro della cesarea maesta e prefetto della loro bibliotheca, dal francese nell 'italiano recata con annotazioni del traduttore* (Rovereto, 1756); see Venturi (1969), pp. 379–82.

13. Cauz, *De cultibus*, op. cit. (n 2), Prologue and pp. 193–6.

14. Among the mass of publications on vampires, 1,300 of which are listed in the bibliography of Martin V. Riccardo, *Vampires unearthed: the complete multi-media vampire and Dracula bibliography* (Garland Press, New York, 1983), let me name a few that have been useful for a general overview: Stephen Hock, *Die Vampyrsagen und ihre Verwertung in der deutschen Literatur* (Berlin, 1900); as well as Summers (1928), his *The Vampire in Europe* (E. P. Dutton, New York, 1929); Leonard Wolf, *A Dream of Dracula. In Search of the Living Dead* (New York, 1972); Bernhardt J. Hurwood, *The Vampire Papers* (Pinacle Books, New York, 1976). Unfortunately I could not get access to a copy of D. Sturm and K. Völker (eds), *Vom Erscheinen der Vampire. Dokumente und Berichte* (DTV, Munich, 1973).

15. The story is described in Henry More, *An Antidote against Atheism, or an Appeal to the Natural Faculties of the Mind of Man whether there be not a God* (1653), cited by Summers, *The Vampire*, op. cit. (n 14), p. 133; it is about a shoemaker in Wroclaw (Breslau) who was reported to have haunted and harmed people after having committed suicide, and was exhumed and burnt by municipal decision.

16. Described by Martin Zeiler in his *Trauergeschichten* (1625), reporting vampire cases from the locality of Eibenschütz; see Hock, *Die Vampyrsagen*, op. cit. (n 14), pp. 30–2.

17. Gabriel Rzaczynski, *Historia naturalis curiosa regni Poloniae, magniducatus Litvaniae, annexarumque provinciarum* (Sandomiriae, 1721), p. 365.

18. Such stories are described by Lawson (1911), pp. 373–87, and Agazzi (1977), pp. 72–97. There were interesting vampire investigations by the Osman Turkish authorities near the city of Edirne in 1702, which were related to the beliefs of the Greek population – see Markus Köhbach, 'Ein Fall von Vampirismus bei den Osmanen', *Balkan Studies*, 20 (1979), pp. 83–90. I am grateful to Peter Brown for this reference. He also called my attention to an extremely interesting seventeenth-century description of vampirism in the Caucasus (among the Circassians and Georgians) by Evliya Celebi, *Seyahatname* (Devlet Matbasi, Istanbul, 1928), vol. 7, pp. 733–7. This description not only raises the problem of a widespread region of Balkan–East

European folklore (already hinted at in Chapter 8), but its night battles also reveal closer connections with the shamanistic type of popular mythology. The most detailed contemporary account of Greek vampirism was given by the Marquis de Tournefort in his *Voyage au Levant* (La Haye, 1705), cited among others by van Swieten in his treatise.

19. The proceedings of the municipal investigation were not published, but were reported on in detail by Bertalan Matirko, 'Egy szepességi népmondáról' [About a legend in the Szepesség], *E*, 1 (1890), pp. 261–72; Kálmán Mikszáth's novel is entitled *Kísértet Lublón* [A Ghost in Lubló].

20. The medical expertise of Georg Buchholz displayed in the Késmárk case is cited by Weszprémi, *Magyarország*, op. cit. (n 6), vol. II, pp. 108–10; the Transylvanian cases are reported in *Quellen zur Geschichte der Stadt Brassó* (Brassó/Kronstadt, 1903) vol. IV, p. 409.

21. The famous cases and the various European reports of them are reprinted in Calmet (1751), vol. II, pp. 37–46, 64–8, 216–19; the Arnold Paul story is analysed by Tekla Dömötör, 'De strigis que non sunt', in *Miscellanea Peters* (Antwerpen, 1975), pp. 207–13; Béla Köpeczi, 'Les Vampires de Hongrie – un scandale des Lumières', *Artes populares*, 7 (1981), pp. 87–105; some of the expert opinions are published in Lajos Thallóczy, 'Beiträge zur Vampyr-Glauben der Serben', *Ethnologische Mitteilungen aus Ungarn* (1887), pp. 162–4; Dieter Harmening, *Der Anfang von Dracula: zur Geschichte von Geschichten* (Würzburg, 1983).

22. These vampire debates, which will be the basis of some of my subsequent analyses, are best described by Hock, *Die Vampyrsagen*, op. cit. (n 14). The later vampire cases (mostly very brief reports) are the following: Transylvania: Ujpalánk, 1738 – Magyari-Kossa (1930), IV, p. 86; Brassó (Kronstadt), 1743 – *Quellen*, op. cit. (n 20), p. 146; Brassó, 1756 – Magyari-Kossa (1930) IV, pp. 149–50.

23. Rzaczynski, *Historia*, op. cit. (n 17), pp. 364–8, a chapter entitled 'De cruentibus cadaverum'.

24. See a list of these examples in Hock, *Die Vampyrsagen*, op. cit. (n 14), pp. 51–2.

25. Georg Tallar, *Visum repertum anatomico-chirurgicum von den sogenannten Vampier, oder Moroi in der Wallachei, Siebenbürgen und Banat, welche eine eigens dahin abgeordnete Untersuchungskommission der löbl. K. K. Administration in Jahre 1756 erstattet hat* (Vienna/Leipzig, 1784).

26. 'De vanitate vampyrorum', in Benedictus XIV, *De servorum Dei beatificatione et Beatorum canonizatione* (Rome, 1752), II, Diss. 5.

27. Voltaire, 'Questions sur l'Encyclopédie', (1772), in *Oeuvres complètes de Voltaire*, ed. Molland (Paris, 1879), vol. XII, pp. 547 ff.

28. Michael Ranft, *Traktat von dem Kauen und Schmatzen der Todten in Grabern, Worin die wahre Beschaffenheit derer Hungarischen Vampirs und Blut-Sauger gezeigt* (Leipzig, 1734).

29. Johann Christoph Harenberg, *Vernünftliche und Christliche Gedanken über die Vampirs oder blut-saugenden Todten* (Wolfenbüttel, 1733); further works are analysed in Hock, *Die Vampyrsagen*, op. cit. (n 14), p. 47.

30. For recent and detailed analyses of these, see Michel de Certeau, *La*

Possession de Loudun (Gallimard, Paris, 1980); D. P. Walker, *Unclean Spirits Possession and Exorcism in France and England in the late 16th and Early 17th Centuries* (Scolar, London, 1981); Stephen Greenblatt, 'Loudun and London', *Critical Inquiry*, 12 (1985), pp. 327–46.

31. Tallar, *Visum repertum*, op. cit. (n 25), pp. 9–12; the same argument by van Swieten is in Linzbauer, *Codex*, op. cit. (n 2), vol. I, p. 732.

32. Voltaire, *Oeuvres*, op. cit. (n 27), vol. XII, p. 550.

33. Sámuel Tessedik, *A parasztember Magyarországon* (1884) [The peasant in Hungary], ed. J. Zsigmond (Budapest, 1979), p. 144.

34. On his historical figure see Harmening, *Der Anfang*, and the rather uncritical account by Raymond T. McNally and Radu Florescu, *In Search of Dracula* (Graphic Society, New York, 1972).

35. This bloody extermination of the 'social' bloodsucker has caused a further transformation of the metaphor: after the years of revolutionary Terror, the radical Jacobins earned the epithet of 'blood-drinker' (*buveurs de sang*). See Dominique Godineau, 'Buveurs de sang/Sang/Sanguinaire', in *Dictionnaire des usages socio-politiques (1770–1815)* (Klincksieck, Paris, 1986), pp. 39–53. I am grateful to Lise Andries for drawing my attention to this article.

References and Bibliography

Agazzi, Renato (1977) *Il mito del vampiro in Europa*, Bologna: Antonio Lalli

Alapi, Gyula (1914) *Bűbájosok és boszorkányok Komárom vármegyében* [Charmers and witches in Komárom county], Komárom

Alföldi, Andreas (1970) *Die monarchische Repräsentation im römischen Kaiserreiche*, Darmstadt: WBG

Anglo, Sidney (1976) 'Melancholia and witchcraft: the debate between Wier, Bodin and Scot', in *Folie et déraison à la Renaissance*, Brussells, pp. 209–22.

——(1977) (ed.) *The Damned Art, Essays in the Literature of Witchcraft*, London: Routledge & Kegan Paul

Ankarloo, Bengt (1984) *Trolldoms processerna i Sverige*, Stockholm: A.-B. Nordiska Bokhandelin

Ariès, Philippe (1960) *L'Enfant et la vie familiale sous l'ancien régime*, Paris: Plon

Arnaudoff, M. (1917) *Die bulgarischen Festbräuche*, Leipzig

Babudri, F. (1925) *Fonti vive dei Veneto-Giuliani*, Milan

Baker, Derek (ed.) (1978) *Medieval Women*, Studies in Church History, Subsidia Oxford: Blackwell

Bakhtin, Mikhail (1984) *Rabelais and his World* (transl. by Helene Iswolsky, 2nd edn), Bloomington: Indiana University Press

Baranowski, Bohdan (1952) *Procesy czarownicz w Polsce w XVII i XVIII wieku* [Witch-trials in Poland in the 17–18th centuries], Łódz

Barlow, F. (1980) 'The king's evil', *English Historical Review*, 95: 1–27

Bataille, Georges (1957) *L'Érotisme*, Paris: Minuit

Baxter, Christopher (1977a) 'Johan Weyer's *De Praestigiis Daemonum*: unsystematic psychopathology', in Anglo (1977), pp. 53–75

——(1977b) 'Jean Bodin's *De la Démonomanie des Sorciers*. The logic of persecution', in Anglo (1977), pp. 76–105

Behringer, Wolfgang (1988) *Hexenverfolgung in Bayern. Volksmagie, Glaubenseifer und Staatsräson in der frühen Neuzeit*, Munich: Oldenbourg

Belmont, Nicole (1971) *Les Signes de la naissance. Étude des représentations symboliques associés aux naissances singulières*, Paris: Plon

Benton, John F. (1982) 'Consciousness of self and perceptions of individuality', in Robert L. Benson and Giles Constable, *Renaissance and Renewal in the Twelfth Century*, Cambridge, Mass.: Harvard University Press, pp. 263–95

Berger, Peter L. (ed.) (1981) *The Other Side of God. Polarity in World Religions*, New York: Doubleday

Berger, Peter L. and Luckmann, Thomas (1966) *The Social Construction of Reality*, New York: Doubleday

Bertaux, D. (ed.) (1981) *Biography and Society. The Life History Approach in Social Sciences*, Beverly Hills, CA

Bertaux, E. (1900) 'Les Saints Louis dans l'art italien', *Revue des deux mondes*, 158: 610–44

Bihari, A. (1980) *A Catalogue of Hungarian Folk Belief Legends*, Budapest: MTA

Blake, Ernest O. and Morris, Colin (1985) 'A hermit goes to war: Peter and the origins of the First Crusade', in W. J. Sheils (ed.), *Monks, Hermits and the Ascetic Tradition*, Oxford: Blackwell

Bloch, Marc (1983) *Les Rois thaumaturges. Étude sur le caractère surnaturel attribué à la puissance royale particulièrement en France et en Angleterre*, 2nd edn, Paris: Gallimard

Blom, G. A. (1981) 'St Olaf in norvegischer Geschichte. Königsheiliger in vielen Gestalten', in *S. Olav, seine Zeit und sein Kult* (Acta Visbiensia VI), ed. Gunnar Svahnström, Uddevalla

Bogdál, Ferenc (1960) 'Egy miskolci "Tátos" 1741-ben' [A *tátos* of Miskolc in 1741], *Néprajzi Közlemények* 3: 308–11

Bolton, Brenda (1971) 'Innocent III's treatment of the *Humiliati*', SCH 8: 73–82

——(1983) *The Medieval Reformation*, London: Arnold

Bonomo, Giuseppe (1971) *Caccia alle streghe. La credenza nelle streghe dal sec. XII al XIX con particolare riferimento all'Italia*. Palermo: Palumbo

Borst, Arno (1953) *Die Katharer* (Schriften der MGH 12), Stuttgart: Anton Hierseman

Boshof, Egon (1969) *Erzbischof Agobard von Lyon*, Cologne

Bošković-Stulli, Maya (1960) 'Kresnik – Krsnik, ein Wesen aus der kroatischen und slovenischen Volksüberlieferung', *Fabula* 3: 275–98

——(1975) *Usmena Knjizevnost kao umjenost Rijeci*, Zagreb

Bourdieu, Pierre (1971) 'Genèse et structure du champ religieux', *Revue Française de Sociologie*, 12: 295–334

Boyer, Paul and Nissenbaum, Stephen (1974) *Salem Possessed*, Cambridge, Mass.: Harvard University Press

Bredekamp, Horst (1975) *Kunst als Medium sozialer Konflikte. Bilderkämpfe von der Spätantike bis zur Hussitenrevolution*, Marburg/Lahn: Suhrkamp

Brooke, Rosalind B. and Christopher N. L. (1978) 'St Clare', in Baker (1978), pp. 275–88

Brown, Peter (1970) 'Sorcery, demons and the rise of Christianity from late Antiquity into the Middle Ages', in Douglas (1970), pp. 14–46

——(1981) *The Cult of Saints. Its Rise and Function in Latin Christianity*, Chicago: University of Chicago Press

——(1983) 'The saint as exemplar in late Antiquity', *Representations*, 1: 1–26

Buber, Martin (1958) *I and Thou* (transl. by R. G. Smith), Edinburgh: Clark

Burke, Peter (1978) *Popular Culture in Early Modern Europe*, London: Temple Smith

Bynum, Caroline Walker (1982) *Jesus as Mother. Studies in the Spirituality of the High Middle Ages*, Berkeley/Los Angeles: University of California Press

——(1984) 'Women's stories, women's symbols: A critique of Victor Turner's theory of liminality', in Robert L. Moore and Frank E. Reynolds (eds), *Anthropology and the Study of Religion*, Chicago: Center for the Scientific Study of Religion, pp. 105–23

——(1987) *Holy Feast and Holy Fast. The Religious Significance of Food to Medieval Women*, Berkeley/Los Angeles: University of California Press

Caillois, Roger (1938) *L'Homme et le sacré*, Paris

Calmet, Augustin (1751) *Traité sur les apparitions des esprits et sur les vampires ou revenants de Hongrie, de Moravie etc.*, Paris

Capitani, Ovidio (ed.) (1977) *Medioevo ereticale*, Bologna: Il Mulino

Capp, Bernard (1979) *Astrology and the Popular Press. English Almanacs 1500–1800*, London/Boston: Faber & Faber

Carozzi, Claude (1981) 'Le Roi et la liturgie chez Helgaud de Fleury', in *Hagiographie, cultures et sociétés*, Paris: Études Augustiniennes, pp. 417–32

Chaney, W. A. (1970) *The Cult of Kingship in Anglo-Saxon England. The Transition from Paganism to Christianity*, Manchester

Ciceri, A. (1981) 'Tradizioni popolari', in *Friûl-Friuli*, Udine, pp. 141–68

Cocchiara, Giuseppe (1956) *Il paese di Cuccagna*, Turin: Boringhieri

Cohn, Norman (1975) *Europe's Inner Demons. An Enquiry Inspired by the Great Witch-Hunt*, New York: Basic Books

Constable, Giles (1985) 'The diversity of religious life and acceptance of social pluralism in the twelfth century', in Derek Beales and Geoffrey Best (eds), *History, Society and the Churches. Essays in Honour of Owen Chadwick*, Cambridge/London: Cambridge University Press

Cracco, Giorgio (1977) 'Pataria: "opus" e "nomen" (tra verità e autorità)', in Capitani (1977), pp. 153–84

Craft, Christopher (1984) ' "Kiss me with those red lips". Gender and inversion in Bram Stoker's Dracula', *Representations*, 8: 207–13

Dalarun, Jacques (1985) *L'Impossible Sainteté. La Vie retrouvé de Robert d'Arbrissel (v1045–1116) fondateur de Fontevrault*, Paris: Cerf

Darnton, Robert (1968) *Mesmerism and the End of the Enlightenment in France*, Cambridge, Mass.: Harvard University Press

Davis, Natalie Zemon (1975) *Society and Culture in Early Modern France*, Stanford: Stanford University Press

Demos, John (1982) *Entertaining Satan. Witchcraft and the Culture of Early New England*, New York

Diószegi, Vilmos (1958) *A sámánhit emlékei a magyar népi műveltségben* [Remnants of shamanism in Hungarian popular culture], Budapest: Akadémiai

Dömötör, Sándor (1939) 'Szent Gellért hegye és a boszorkányok' [The Mount

Saint Gerard and the witches], *Tanulmányok Budapest múltjából*, 7: 92–111

Dömötör, Tekla (1982) *Hungarian Folk Beliefs*, Budapest: Corvina; Bloomington: Indiana University Press

——(1983) The problem of the Hungarian female *táltos*, in Hoppál (1984a) pp. 423–9

Douglas, Mary (ed.) (1970) *Witchcraft Confessions and Accusations*, London: Tavistock

Duby, Georges (1978) *Les Trois Ordres ou l'imaginaire du féodalisme*, Paris: Gallimard. (English translation: *The Three Orders: Feudal Society Imagined*, Chicago: Chicago University Press, 1978)

Durkheim, Émile (1926) *The Elementary Forms of Religious Life* (transl. by J. W. Swain), London: Allen & Unwin

Eisenbart, Liselotte, C. (1962) *Kleiderordnungen der deutschen Städte zwischen 1350 und 1700*, Göttingen: Musterschmidt

Eisler, Robert (1951) *Man into Wolf. An anthropological interpretation of sadism, masochism and lycanthropy*, London

Eliade, Mircea (1957) *Das Heilige und das Profane. Vom Wesen des Religiösen*, Hamburg: Rowohlt

——(1964) *Shamanism: Archaic Technique of Extasy*, New York: Pantheon

——(1975) 'Some observations on European witchcraft', *History of Religions*, 14: 149–72

Elias, Norbert (1978) *The Civilizing Process. The History of Manners, State Formation and Civilization* (transl. by Edmund Jephcott), Oxford: Blackwell

Evans-Pritchard, Edward E. (1937) *Witchcraft, Oracles and Magic among the Azande*, Oxford

Faber, Sjoerd (1984) 'Witchcraft and criminal justice in Netherlands – Dutch moderation?' Paper presented at the 1984 conference of the Olin foundation in Stockholm

Favret-Saada, Jeanne (1977) *Les Mots, la mort, les sorts. La Sorcellerie dans le Bocage*, Paris: Gallimard. (English translation: *Deadly Words. Witchcraft in the Bocage*, Cambridge, 1980)

——(1981) *Corps pour corps. Enquête sur la sorcellerie dans le Bocage*, Paris: Gallimard

Febvre, Lucien (1948) 'Sorcellerie, sottise ou révolution mentale?' *AESC*, 3: 9–15

Fischer, L. (1914) *Die Kirchlichen Quatember. Ihre Entstehung, Entwicklung und Bedeutung*, Munich

Folz, Robert (1963) 'Tradition hagiographique et culte de saint Dagobert, roi des Francs', *Le Moyen Age*, 69: 17–35

——(1964) 'La chancellerie de Frédéric Ier et la canonisation de Charlemagne', *Le Moyen Age*, 70: 13–31

——(1984) *Les Saints rois du moyen âge en Occident (VIᵉ–XIIIᵉ siècles)*, Brussells: Société des Bollandistes

Foucault, Michel (1973) *Madness and Civilization. A History of Insanity in the Age of Reason* (transl. by Richard Howard), New York: Vintage Books

——(1979) *Discipline and Punish. The Birth of the Prison* (transl. by Alan Sheridan), New York: Vintage Books

——(1981) *The History of Sexuality. Vol. I. An Introduction* (transl. by R. Hurley), Harmondsworth: Penguin

Frugoni, Arsenio (1954) *Arnaldo di Brescia nelle fonti del secolo XII*, Rome

Gaier, Claude (1966) Le Rôle militaire des reliques et de l'étendard de Saint Lambert dans la principauté de Liège', *Le Moyen Age*, 72: 235–50

Gallini, Clara (1983) *La somnambula meravigliosa. Magnetismo e ipnotismo nell'Ottocento italiano*, Milan: Feltrinelli

Geary, Patrick J. (1978) *Furta Sacra. Thefts of Relics in the Central Middle Ages*, Princeton, NJ: Princeton University Press

Geertz, Clifford (1983) 'Centers, kings and charisma: Reflections on the symbolics of power', in idem., *Local Knowledge. Further Essays in Interpretive Anthropology*, New York: Basic Books

Gennep, Arnold van (1909) *The Rites of Passage* (transl. by M. Z. Vizedom and G. L. Caffee), London: Routledge & Kegan Paul

Geremek, Bronislaw (1976) *Les Marginaux Parisiens aux XIVᵉ au XVIᵉ siècles*, Paris: Flammarion

——(1987) *La Potence ou la pitié. L'Histoire des marginaux du XIIIᵉ au XVIIIᵉ siècles*, Paris: Gallimard

Gilberg, R. (1984) 'How to recognize a shaman among other religious specialists?' in Hoppál (1984a), pp. 21–7

Ginzburg, Carlo (1966) *I Benandanti. Stregoneria e culti agrari tra Cinquecento e Seicento*, Turin, Einaudi. (English translation by J. Tedeschi: *The Night Battles: Witchcraft and Agrarian Cults in the 16th and 17th Centuries*, London: Routledge & Kegan Paul, 1983)

Gluckmann, Max (1954) *Rituals of Rebellion in South-East Africa*, Manchester: Manchester University Press

Goglin, Jean-Louis (1976) *Les Misérables dans l'Occident médiéval*, Paris: Seuil

Gonnet, Jean and Molnár, Amedeo (1974) *Les Vaudois au Moyen Age*, Turin: Claudiana

Górski, Karol (1969) 'Le Roi saint. Un Problème d'idéologie féodale', *AESC*, 24: 370–6

Goulemot, Jean-Marie (1980) 'Démons, merveilles et philosophie à l'âge classique', *AESC*, 35: 1233–50

Graus, František (1965) *Volk, Herrscher, Heiliger im Reich der Merowinger. Studien zur Hagiographie der Merowingerzeit*, Prague: Nakladatelství Ceskoslovenské akademie ved

——(1975) *Lebendige Vergangenheit*, Cologne/Vienne: Böhlau

——(1977) 'Die Heilige als Schlachtenhelfer. Zur Nationalisierung einer Wundererzählung in der mittelalterlichen Chronistik', in K. V. Jäschke and R. Wenskus (eds), *Festschrift für H. Beumann, zum 65. Geburtstag*, Sigmaringen: Thorbeke

Grgjić-Bjelokosić, L. (1896) 'Narodno sujevjerje', *Glasnik zemaljskog muzeja u Bosni i Herzegovini*, 8: 530–4

——(1899) 'Volksglaube und Volksbräuche in der Herzegowina', *Wissenschaftliche Mitteilungen aus Bosnien und Herzegowina*, 6

Grundmann, Herbert (1935) *Religiöse Bewegungen im Mittelalter*, Berlin (2nd ed, 1970, Darmstadt: WBG)

Gunda, Béla (1968) 'Survivals of totemism in the Hungarian táltos tradition', in *Popular Beliefs and Folklore Tradition in Siberia*, ed. Vilmos Diószegi, Budapest: Akadémiai, pp. 41–51

Gurevich, Aron J. (1985) *Categories of Medieval Culture* (transl. by W. Campbell), London: Routledge & Kegan Paul

Györffy, György (1977a) *István király és műve* [King Stephen and his deeds], Budapest: Gondolat

——(1977b) 'A lovagszent uralkodása' [The reign of the knight saint], *Történelmi Szemle*, 20: 533–64

Hagenmeyer, H. (1879) *Peter der Eremite. Ein kritischer Beitrag zur Geschichte der ersten Kreuzzuges*, Leipzig

Hallpike, C. R. (1969) 'Social hair', *Man* N. S., 4: 256–64

Harmening, Dieter (1979) *Superstitio. Überlieferungs- und theoriegeschichtliche Untersuchungen zur kirchlich-theologischen Aberglaubensliteratur des Mittelalters*, Berlin: Schmidt

Hauck, Karl (1950) 'Geblütsheiligkeit', in *Liber Floridus. Festschrift für Paul Lehmann*, St Ottilien

Helgaud, de Fleury (1965) *Vie de Robert le Pieux*, ed. R.-H. Bautier and G. Labory, Paris

Henningsen, Gustav (1980) *The Witches' Advocate. Basque Witchcraft and the Spanish Inquisition*, Reno: University of Nevada Press

Hill, Christopher (1972) *The World Turned upside down. Radical Ideas during the English Reformation*, Harmondsworth: Penguin

Hoecke, Willy van and Welkenhuysen, Andrian (1981) *Love and Marriage in the Twelfth Century* (Mediaevalia Lovaniensia, Ser. I, VIII), Leuwen

Hoffmann, Erich (1975) *Die Heiligen Könige bei den Angelsachsen und den skandinavischen Völkern. Königsheiliger und Königshaus*, Neumünster: Wachholz

Hofmann, H. (1975) *Die Heiligen drei Könige. Zur Heiligenverehrung im kirchlichen, gesellschaftlichen und politischen Leben des Mittelalters*, Bonn

Hoppál, Mihály (ed.) (1984a) *Shamanism in Eurasia*, Göttingen: Herodot

——(1984b) 'Traces of shamanism in Hungarian folk beliefs', in Hoppál (1984a), pp. 130–50

Horna, Richard (1933) *Zwei Hexenprozesse in Pressburg zu Beginn des XVII. Jahrhunderts*, Bratislava

——(1935) *Ein Monstre-Hexenprozess in Samorin gegen Ende des XVII. Jahrhunderts*, Bratislava

Horsley, Richard (1979) 'Who were the witches? The social roles of the accused in the European witch trials', *Journal of Interdisciplinary History*, 9: 689–715

Hoyoux, Jean (1948) 'Reges criniti. Chevelures, tonsures et scalps chez les Mérovingiens', *Revue belge de philologie et d'histoire*, 26: 479–508

Hůltkrantz, A. (1978) 'Ecological and phenomenological aspects of shamanism', in *Shamanism in Siberia*, ed. Vilmos Diószegi and Mihály Hoppál, Budapest: Akadémiai, pp. 27–58.

Ingham, N. W. (1984) 'The martyred prince and the question of Slavic cultural continuity in the early Middle Ages', in *Medieval Russian Culture* (California Slavic Studies XII), ed. H. Birnbaum and M. S. Flier, Los Angeles

Jakobson, Roman (1966) 'The Vseslav Epos', in idem., *Selected Writings*, vol. IV, *Slavic Epic Studies*, Paris/The Hague: Mouton, pp. 27–58

Kantorowicz, E. H. (1957) *The King's Two Bodies: a Study in Medieval Political Theology*, Princeton
Kelemina, J. (1930) *Bajke in pripovedke slavanskega ljudstva, z mitoloskim uvodom*, Celje
Kemp, E. W. (1948) *Canonization and Authority in the Western Church*, Oxford
Kieckhefer, Richard (1976) *European Witch Trials. Their Foundation in Popular and Learned Culture, 1300–1500*, Berkeley/Los Angeles: University of California Press
Klauser, Renate (1957) *Der Heinrichs- und Kunigundenkult im mittelalterlichen Bistum Bamberg*, Bamberg
Kleinschmidt, D. (1909) 'St Ludwig von Toulouse in der Kunst', *Archivum Franciscanum Historicum*, 2: 197–215
Koerner, Joseph Leo (1985) 'The mortification of the image: death as hermeneutic in Hans Baldung Grien', *Representations*, 10: 52–102
Komáromy, Andor (1910) *Magyarországi boszorkányperek oklevéltára* [Sourcebook of Hungarian witch-trials], Budapest: Magyar Tud. Akadémia
Kőrösi, Sándor (1892) 'Fiume néprajza' [Ethnography of Fiume], *E*, 3: 141–74
Krauss, F. S. (1908) *Slavische Volksforschungen*, Leipzig
Kroeber, A. L. and Richardson, Jane (1940) 'Three centuries of women's dress fashions: a quantitative analysis', *Anthropological Records*, 5: 111–53

Labande, Edmond-René (1958) 'Recherches sur les pélerine dans l'Europe des 11e et 13e siècles', *Cahiers de civilisation médiévale*, 1: 159–69, 339–47
Lambert, Malcolm D. (1961) *Franciscan Poverty*, London: Allenson
——(1977) *Medieval Heresy. Popular Movements from Bogomil to Hus*, London: Arnold
Laurent, M. H. (1954) *Le Culte de S. Louis d'Anjou a Marseille au XIVe siècle*, Rome
Lawson, John Cuthbert (1911) *Ancient Greek Religion and Modern Greek Folklore*, Cambridge: Cambridge University Press
Leach, Edmund R. (1958) 'Magical hair', *Journal of the Royal Anthropological Institute of Great Britain and Ireland*, 88: 147–64
Le Goff, Jacques (1957) *Les Intellectuels au moyen âge*, paris: Minuit
——(1960) 'Au Moyen Age: Temps de l'Église et temps du marchand', *AESC*, 15: 417–33 (repr. in Le Goff, 1977, pp. 46–66)
——(1977) *Pour un autre Moyen Age, temps, travail et culture en Occident: 18 essais*, Paris: Gallimard. (English translation; *Time, Work and Culture in the*

Middle Ages, Chicago: University of Chicago Press, 1980)

——(1981) *La Naissance du Purgatoire*, Paris: Gallimard. (English translation: *The Birth of Purgatory*, Chicago: University of Chicago Press, 1984)

Le Goff, Jacques and Vincent, Bernard (eds) (1979) *Les Marginaux et les exclus dans l'histoire*, Paris: Union Générale d'Éditions

Lehoczky, Tivadar (1887) 'Beregmegyei boszorkányperek', *Hazánk*, 7: 296–306

Lerner, R. E. (1972) *The Heresy of the Free Spirit in the Later Middle Ages*, Berkeley/Los Angeles: University of California Press

Le Roy Ladurie, Emmanuel (1978) *Montaillou, The Promised Land of Error* (transl. by Barbara Bray), New York: George Braziller

Leventhal, Herbert (1976) *In the Shadow of Enlightenment. Occultism and Renaissance Science in Eighteenth-Century America*, New York: NYU Press

Lévi-Strauss, Claude (1966) *The Savage Mind*, Chicago: University of Chicago Press

——(1964–1971) *Mythologiques I–IV (Le Cru et le cuit; Du miel aux cendres; L'Origine des manières de table; L'Homme nu)*, Paris: Plon

Leyser, K. J. (1979) *Rule and Conflict in an Early Medieval Society. Ottonian Saxony*, Bloomington/London: University of Indiana Press

Lixfeld, Hannjost (1972) 'Die Guntramsage (AT 1645 A). Volkserzahlungen und Alter Ego in Tiergestalt und ihre schamanistische Herkunft', *Fabula*, 13: 60–107

McDonnell, E. W. (1955) 'The Vita Apostolica: diversity or dissent', *Church History*, 15–31

Macfarlane, Alan (1970) *Witchcraft in Tudor and Stuart England. A Regional and Comparative Study*, New York/Evanston

——(1978) *The Origins of English Individualism. The Family, Property and Social Transition*, Oxford

McNeill, J. T. and Gamer, H. M. (1938) *Medieval Handbooks of Penance. A translation of the principal 'libri poenitentiales' and selections from related documents*, New York (repr. 1965)

Magyari-Kossa, Gyula (1930) *Magyar orvosi emlékek* [Documents of Hungarian medical history], vol. IV, Budapest

Mandrou, Robert (1968) *Magistrats et sorciers en France au XVIIe siècle*, Paris

Mannheim, Karl (1936) *Ideology and Utopia. An Introduction to the Sociology of Knowledge* (transl. by L. Wirth and E. Shils), New York: Harcourt, Brace & World

Mannteufel, Tadeusz (1970) *Naissance d'une hérésie, les adeptes de la pauvreté volontaire au moyen âge*, Paris/La Haye: Mouton

Manselli, Raoul (1975) *Studi sulle eresie del secolo XII*, Rome: Instituto Storico Italiano

Marwick, Max (1964) 'Witchcraft as a social strain-gauge', *Australian Journal of Science*, 26: 263–8

——(1970) (ed.) *Witchcraft and Sorcery. Selected Readings*, Penguin: Harmondsworth

Mayer, Philip (1970) 'Witches', in Marwick (1970), pp. 45–64

Miccoli, Giovanni (1977) 'Per la storia della pataria milanese', in Capitani (1977), pp. 89–152

Middleton, John (ed.) (1967) *Magic, Witchcraft and Curing*, Austin/London: University of Texas Press

Midelfort, H. C. E. (1972) *Witch Hunting in Southwestern Germany, 1562–1684. The Social and Intellectual Foundations*, Stanford

Milcetić, I. (1896) 'Vjera u csobita bica', *Zbornik za narodni zivot i obicaje juznih slavena*, 1: 24–5

Milis, Ludo (1979) 'Ermites et chanoines réguliers au XIIe siècle', *Cahiers de civilisation médiévale;*, 22: 39–80

Mollat, Michel (ed.) (1974) *Études sur l'histoire de la pauvreté (Moyen Age–XVIe siècle)*, Paris: Publications de la Sorbonne

——(1978) *Les Pauvres au moyen âge. Étude sociale*, Paris: Hachette

Morris, Colin (1972) *The Discovery of the Individual: 1050–1200*, New York

Muchembled, Robert (1978) *Culture populaire et culture des élites dans la France moderne (XVe–XVIIIe siècles)*, Paris: Flammarion

Müller, Ludolf (1962) *Des Metropoliten Ilarion Lobrede auf Vladimir den Heiligen und Glaubensbekenntnis*, Wiesbaden

Murray, Margaret (1921) *The Witch-Cult of Western Europe*, Oxford

Nagl, H. (1972/3, 1974) 'Der Zauberer-Jackl Prozess. Hexenprozesse im Erzstift Salzburg (1675–1690)', *Mitteilungen der Gesellschaft für Salzburger Landeskunde*, 112/113: 385–541, 114: 79–243

Needham, Rodney (1978) 'Synthetic images', in idem., *Primordial Characters*, Charlottesville: University Press of Virginia

Nelson, Janet (1971) 'National synods, kingship as office, and royal anointing: an early medieval syndrome', in *Councils and Assemblies*, ed. G. J. Cuming and D. Baker, *SCH* 7, Cambridge, pp. 41–59

——(1972) 'Society, theodicy and the origins of heresy: towards a reassessment of the medieval evidence', in *Schism, Heresy and Religious Protest*, ed. Derek Baker, *SCH* 8, Cambridge, pp. 65–77

——(1973) 'Royal saints and early medieval kingship', in *Sanctity and Secularity: the Church and the World*, ed. D. Baker, *SCH* 10, Oxford: Blackwell, pp. 39–44

——(1978) 'Queens as Jezebels: the careers of Brunhild and Bathild in Merovingian history', in Baker (1978), pp. 31–8

Nyberg, Tore (1981) 'St Knud and St Knud's church', in *Hagiography and Medieval Literature. A Symposium*, Odense, pp. 100–10

Osterman, V. (1940) *La vita in Friuli* (2nd edn by G. Vidossi), Udine

Ostrogorsky, Georg (1929) *Studien zur Geschichte des byzantinischen Bilderstreites*, Breslau (2nd ed., Amsterdam, 1964)

Panofsky, Erwin (1939) *Studies in Iconology, Icon*, New York/ Evanston: Harper & Row

Parinetto, Luciano (1974) *Magia e ragione. Una polemica sulle streghe in Italia intorno al 1750*, Florence

Pfaff, Carl (1963) *Kaiser Heinrich II. Sein Nachleben und sein Kult im mittelalterlichen Basel*, Basle/Stuttgart

Price, S. R. F. (1984) *Rituals of Power. The Roman Imperial Cult in Asia Minor*, Cambridge: Cambridge University Press

Radding, Charles M. (1979) 'Superstition to science: nature, fortune and the passing of the medieval ordeal', *The American Historical Review*, 84: 945–69

Rapp, Ludwig (1874) *Die Hexenprozesse und ihre Gegner aus Tirol*, Innsbruck

Reeves, Marjorie (1969) *The Influence of Prophecy in the Later Middle Ages: A Study in Joachimism*, Oxford: Clarendon

Riis, Thomas (1977) *Les Institutions politiques centrales du Danemark 1100–1332*, Odense

Robinson, Dwight E. (1976) 'Fashions in shaving and trimming of the beard: The men of the *Illustrated London News* 1842–1972', *American Journal of Sociology*, 81: 1133–41

Róheim, Géza (1925) *Magyar néphit és népszokások*, Budapest: Officina

Ronay, Gabriel (1972) *The Truth about Dracula*, New York

Rose, Eliot (1962) *A Rasor for a Goat*, Toronto

Rosenwein, Barbara (1971) 'Feudal war and monastic peace: Cluniac liturgy as ritual agression', *Viator*, 2: 129–57

Runeberg, A. (1947) *Witches, Demons and Fertility Magic*, Helsingfors

Sacral (1959) *The Sacral Kingship* (Contributions to the central theme of the VIIIth international congress for the history of religions, Rome, April, 1955) Leiden: Brill

Schmid, Karl and Wollasch, J. (1967) 'Die Gemeinschaft der Lebenden und Verstorbenen in Zeugnissen des Mittelalters', *Frühmittelalterliche Studien*, 1: 294–401

Schmitt, Jean-Claude (1978) 'L'Histoire des marginaux', in *La Nouvelle Histoire*, ed. Jacques Le Goff, Roger Chartier and Jacques Revel, Paris, pp. 344–69

——(1976) ' "Religion populaire" et culture folklorique', *AESC* 31: 911–53

——(1979) *Le Saint lévrier. Guinefort, guérisseur d'enfants depuis le XIIIe siècle*, Paris: Flammarion

Schneeweiss, E. (1935) *Grundriss des Volksglaubens und Volksbrauches der Serbokroaten*, Celje

Schneider, Reinhard (1977) 'Karolus, qui et Wenzeslaus', in *Festschrift für Helmut Beumann*, ed. Kurt-Ulrich Jäschke and Reinhard Wenskus, Sigmaringen: Thorbeke

Schöck, Inge (1978) *Hexenglaube in der Gegenwart. Empirische Untersuchungen in Südwestdeutschland*, Tübingen

Scholz, Bernhardt W. (1961) 'The canonization of Edward the Confessor', *Speculum*, 36: 38–60

Schram, Ferenc (1970) *Magyarországi boszorkányperek. 1529–1768* [Hungarian witch-trials], vols I–II, Budapest: Akadémiai

——(1982) vol. III, Budapest: Akadémiai

Schramm, Percy Ernst (1954–6) *Herrschaftszeichen und Staatssymbolik* (MGH Schriften 13/I–III), Stuttgart: Hierseman

Sebestyén, Gyula (1900) 'A magyar varázsdob', *E*, 11: 433–46

Seibt, Ferdinand (1972) *Utopica. Modelle totaler Sozialplanung*, Düsseldorf: Schwann

Selge, Kurt-Viktor (1967) *Die ersten Waldenser*, Berlin

Shils, Edward (1975) *Center and Periphery: Essays in Macrosociology*, Chicago

Siikala, Anna-Lena (1978) *The Rite Technique of the Siberian Shaman*, Folklore Fellows Communications 220, Helsinki

Soman, Alfred (1977) 'Les Procès de sorcellerie au Parlement de Paris (1565–1640)', *AESC*, 32: 790–814

——(1985) 'La Décriminalisation de la sorcellerie en France', *Histoire, Économie et Société*, 4: 179–203

Spätling, L. (1947) *De Apostolicis, Pseudoapostolicis, Apostolinis*, Munich

Summers, Montague (1928) *The Vampire: his Kith and Kin*, London: Routledge & Kegan Paul

Szűcs, Jenő (1983) 'The three historical regions of Europe', *Acta Historica Academiae Scieciarum Hungaricae*, 29: 131–84

Szűcs, Sándor (1951) 'Időért viaskodó táltosok' [*Taltoses* fighting for weather], *E*, 62: 403–9

Tartarotti, Girolamo (1749) *Del congresso notturno delle lammie*, Rovereto

Taylor, Lily Ross (1931) *The Divinity of the Roman Emperor*, Middletown, Connecticut

Terrail, Jean-Pierre (1979) 'La Pratique sorcière. Éléments pour une sociologie de l'agression magique', *Archives des sciences sociales des religions*, 24: 21–42

Thomas, Keith (1971) *Religion and the Decline of Magic. Studies in popular beliefs in sixteenth and seventeenth century England*, London: Routledge & Kegan Paul

Thouzellier, Christine (1966) *Catharisme et Valdéisme en Languedoc à la fin du XIIᵉ et au début du XIIIᵉ siècle*, Paris: PUF

Toynbee, M. (1927) *S. Louis of Toulouse and the Process of Canonisation in the Fourteenth Century*, Manchester

Trevor-Roper, Hugh (1969) *The European Witch-Craze of the 16th and 17th Centuries*, Harmondsworth: Penguin

Turner, Victor (1967) 'Witchcraft and sorcery: 'taxonomy versus dynamics', in idem., *The Forest of Symbols. Aspects of Ndembu Ritual*, Ithaca/London: Cornell University Press

——(1974) *Dramas, Fields and Metaphors. Symbolic Action in Human Society;*, Ithaca/London: Cornell University Press

——(1977) *The Ritual Process. Structure and Anti-Structure*, 2nd edn, The L. H. Morgan Lectures 1966, Ithaca/London: Cornell University Press

Turner, Victor and Edith (1978) *Image and Pilgrimage in Christian Culture. Anthropological Perspectives*, New York: Columbia University Press

Ullmann, Walter (1963) *The Growth of Papal Government in the Middle Ages*, Cambridge

——(1966) *The Individual and Society in the Middle Ages*, Baltimore

Vajda, L. (1959) 'Zur phaseologischen Stellung des Schamanismus', *Ural-Altaische Jahrbücher*, 31, Wiesbaden

Valentinitsch, Helfried (1986) 'Bettlervervolgung und Zaubereiprozesse in der Steiermark. Der Prozess gegen die "Grindigen Hansel" in Rottenmann 1659', *Mitteilungen des Steiermarkischen Landesarchivs*, 35/36: 105–29

Vauchez, André (1981) *La Sainteté en Occident aux dernièrs siècles du Moyen âge. D'après les procès de canonisation et les documents hagiographiques*, Rome: École Française

Venturi, Franco (1969) *Settecento riformatore. Da Muratori a Beccaria*, Turin: Einaudi

Violante, Cinzio (1972) 'I laici nel movimento patarino', in idem., *Studi sulla christianità medioevale*, Milan: Vita e pensiero, pp. 145–247

Vogel, Cyril (1969) *Le Pécheur et la pénitence au Moyen Age*, Paris: Cerf

Voigt, Vilmos (1976) 'Der Schamanismus als ethnologisches Forschungs-problem', in *Glaube und Inhalt*, Budapest, pp. 75–120

Vries, Jan de (1956) 'Das Königtum bei den Germanen', *Saeculum*, 8: 289–309

Warner, Marina (1976) *Alone of All Her Sex: The Myth and the Cult of Virgin Mary*, New York: Knopf

Weber, Max (1964) *Social and Economic Organization*, ed. Talcott Parsons, New York: Free Press

Werner, Ernst (1959) 'Die Nachrichten über die böhmischen "Adamiten" in religionsgeschichtlicher Sicht', in *Circumzellionen und Adamiten. Zwei Formen mittelalterlicher Haresie*, Berlin: Akademie

Young, A. B. (1937) *Recurring Cycles of Fashion, 1760–1937*, New York

Zanoni, Luigi (1921) *Gli umiliati nei loro rapporti con l'eresia, l'industria della lana ed i communi nei secoli XII e XIII*, Milan

Ziegeler, Wolfgang (1973) *Möglichkeiten der Kritik am Hexen- und Zauberwesen im ausgehenden Mittelalter. Zeitgenössische Stimmen und ihre soziale Zugehörigkeit*, Cologne/Vienna

Index

Note: Saints are listed under individual names.

Index by Meg Davies